PREFACE

1. Scope

This publication is designed for use at the tactical and operational levels. This manual provides multiservice tactics, techniques, and procedures (MTTP) for chemical, biological, radiological, and nuclear (CBRN) decontamination. It defines the roles of military units and staffs involved in the preparation, planning, and execution of decontamination operations. It addresses the requirements for the different techniques used in decontamination. This manual focuses on the need for all United States (US) forces to be prepared to fight and win in a CBRN environment. It addresses the support the Department of Defense (DOD) may have to provide to support homeland security (HLS). The planning and coordination for CBRN decontamination takes place with the realization that the potential CBRN environment could be one in which there is deliberate or accidental employment of CBRN weapons, or deliberate or accidental attacks or contamination with toxic industrial material (TIM) (see *Joint Doctrine for Operations in Nuclear, Biological, and Chemical [NBC] Environments*).

2. Purpose

This publication provides a reference for CBRN decontamination; bridges the gap between service and joint doctrine; and contains tactics, techniques, and procedures (TTP) for planning and executing operations in a CBRN environment. This manual addresses concepts, principles, and TTP to include planning, operational considerations, and training and support functions. It serves as the foundation for the development of multiservice manuals and refinement of existing training support packages (TSPs), mission training plans (MTPs), training center and unit exercises, and service school curricula. It drives the examination of organizations and materiel developments applicable to CBRN decontamination.

3. Application

The audience for this publication is combatant commands, joint task forces (JTFs), functional and service component units, and staffs in foreign and domestic locations that could be challenged by operations in a CBRN environment.

4. Implementation Plan

Participating service command offices of primary responsibility (OPRs) will review this publication; validate the information; reference and incorporate it in service and command manuals, regulations, and curricula as follows:

Army. The United States Army (USA) will incorporate this publication in USA training and doctrinal publications as directed by the Commander, United States Army Training and Doctrine Command (TRADOC). Distribution is according to the USA publication distribution system.

Marine Corps. The United States Marine Corps (USMC) will incorporate the procedures in this publication in USMC training and doctrinal publications as directed by the Commanding General (CG), Marine Corps Combat Development Command (MCCDC). Distribution is according to the USMC publication distribution system.

Navy. The United States Navy (USN) will incorporate the procedures in this publication in training and doctrinal publications as directed by the Commander, Navy Warfare Development Command (NWDC). Distribution is according to the DOD 4000.25-1-M.

Air Force. The United States Air Force (USAF) will validate and incorporate appropriate procedures according to applicable governing directives. It will develop and implement this and other NBC MTTP through a series of USAF manuals providing service-specific TTP. Distribution is according to the USAF publication distribution system.

Coast Guard. The United States Coast Guard (USCG) will validate and refer to appropriate procedures when applicable. No material contained herein should conflict with USCG regulations or other directives from higher authority or supersede or replace any order or directive issued by higher authority.

5. User Information

a. The United States Army Chemical School (USACMLS) developed this publication with the participation of the approving service commands.

b. This publication reflects current service and joint doctrine, command and control (C2) organizations, facilities, personnel, responsibilities, and procedures.

c. Recommended changes are encouraged for improving this publication. Key any comments to the specific page and paragraph, and provide a rationale for each recommendation. Send comments and recommendations directly to—

Army

Commandant
US Army Chemical School
ATTN: ATSN-TD
464 MANSCEN Loop, Suite 2617
Fort Leonard Wood, MO 65473-8926
COMM (573) 596-0131, extension 3-7364
Web Site: https://www.us.army.mil/

Marine Corps

Commanding General
US Marine Corps Combat Development Command
ATTN: C42 (Director)
3300 Russell Road
Quantico, VA 22134-5001
DSN 278-6234; COMM (703) 784-6234
Web Site: https://www.doctrine.usmc.mil/

Navy

Commander
Navy Warfare Development Command
ATTN: N5
686 Cushing Road
Newport, RI 02841-1207
DSN 948-4201; COMM (401) 841-4201
Web Site: https://www.nko.navy.mil/

Air Force

Headquarters Air Force Doctrine Center
ATTN: DJ
155 North Twining Street
Maxwell AFB, AL 36112-6112
DSN 493-7442; COMM (334) 953-7442
Web Site: https://www.doctrine.af.mil/

6. Other

The following commonly accepted symbols are used throughout this manual to represent different chemical and biological agents: Vx, VX, GA, GB, GD, HD, HN, TGD, THD, V, and G (see *Potential Military Chemical/Biological Agents and Compounds* for further descriptions of these agents).

Unless this publication states otherwise, masculine nouns and pronouns do not refer exclusively to men.

THIS PAGE IS INTENTIONALLY LEFT BLANK.

*FM 3-11.5
MCWP 3-37.3
NTTP 3-11.26
AFTTP(I) 3-2.60

FM 3-11.5	US Army Training and Doctrine Command Fort Monroe, Virginia
MCWP 3-37.3	Marine Corps Combat Development Command Quantico, Virginia
NTTP 3-11.26	Navy Warfare Development Command Newport, Rhode Island
AFTTP(I) 3-2.60	Headquarters Air Force Doctrine Center Maxwell Air Force Base, Alabama

4 April 2006

MULTISERVICE TACTICS, TECHNIQUES, AND PROCEDURES FOR CHEMICAL, BIOLOGICAL, RADIOLOGICAL, AND NUCLEAR DECONTAMINATION

TABLE OF CONTENTS

Page

EXECUTIVE SUMMARY xv

CHAPTER I   DECONTAMINATION: CONCEPTS, PRINCIPLES, AND LEVELS
  Background I-1
  Hazard I-3
  Concepts—Combat Operations I-3
  Concepts—Homeland Security I-8
  Service Capabilities I-10
  Training and Exercises I-10

DISTRIBUTION RESTRICTION: Approved for public release; distribution is unlimited.

_____
*This manual supersedes FM 3-5 and MCWP 3-37.3, 28 July 2000.

CHAPTER II	DECONTAMINATION OPERATIONS: PLAN, PREPARE, AND EXECUTE
	Background.. II-1
	Decontamination Planning... II-1
	Wartime Planning Considerations... II-3
	Homeland Security Planning Considerations II-6
	Preattack Decontamination Operations II-7
	Execution II-10
	Postdecontamination Operations.. II-11
CHAPTER III	IMMEDIATE DECONTAMINATION
	Background... III-1
	Skin Decontamination III-1
	Personal Wipe Down III-1
	Operator Wipe Down III-2
	Spot Decontamination III-3
CHAPTER IV	OPERATIONAL DECONTAMINATION
	Background... IV-1
	Planning IV-1
	Phases IV-2
CHAPTER V	THOROUGH DECONTAMINATION
	Background... V-1
	Planning V-2
	Preparation V-3
	Execution V-3
	Predecontamination Staging Area V-6
	Vehicle Crews V-6
	Detailed Equipment Decontamination and Detailed Troop Decontamination Areas V-7
	Thorough Decontamination Under Unusual Conditions V-30
	Colocation of Patient Decontamination With Troop Decontamination V-30
CHAPTER VI	CLEARANCE DECONTAMINATION
	Background... VI-1
	Postconflict Intelligence Preparation of the Battlespace............. VI-2
	Force Protection VI-3
	Decontamination VI-3
	Containment of Residual Hazards VI-3
	Recovery and Control of Enemy Chemical, Biological, Radiological, and Nuclear Capabilities....................................... VI-3
	Force Health Protection VI-4
	Coordination With Multinational Forces or Nonmilitary Entities VI-4
	Contaminated Materials Retrogradation VI-4
CHAPTER VII	FIXED-SITE, PORT, AND AIRFIELD DECONTAMINATION
	Background.. VII-1
	Assessing Capability VII-2

	Organizing for Decontamination	VII-2
	Buildings and Mission-Essential Operating Areas and Surfaces	VII-2
	Personnel Processing Procedures (Chemical)	VII-3
	Personnel Processing Procedures (Radiological)	VII-12
CHAPTER VIII	**AIRCRAFT AND AIRCREW DECONTAMINATION**	
	Background	VIII-1
	General Planning	VIII-1
	Aircraft Decontamination Levels and Procedures	VIII-3
	Civil Reserve Air Fleet and Contract Airlift Operations	VIII-21
	Aircraft Munitions Decontamination	VIII-21
	Air Cargo Movement Decontamination	VIII-23
CHAPTER IX	**SHIPBOARD/MARITIME DECONTAMINATION**	
	Background	IX-1
	Shipboard Chemical, Biological, and Radiological Decontamination	IX-1
	Recovery Chemical, Biological, Radiological, and Nuclear Decontamination	IX-5
CHAPTER X	**PATIENT EVACUATION AND DECONTAMINATION**	
	Background	X-1
	Patient Decontamination	X-3
	Army Patient Decontamination Procedures	X-5
	Marine Corps Patient Decontamination Procedures	X-6
	Navy Patient Decontamination Procedures	X-7
	Air Force Patient Decontamination Procedures	X-7
CHAPTER XI	**DECONTAMINATION IN SUPPORT OF HOMELAND SECURITY**	
	Background	XI-1
	Federal Assistance	XI-1
	Response to a Homeland Security Incident—Decontamination Considerations	XI-2
	Department of Defense Decontamination Capabilities	XI-9
CHAPTER XII	**LOGISTICS**	
	Background	XII-1
	Consumption Rates and Replenishment	XII-1
	Maintenance Considerations	XII-7
APPENDIX A	**CONVERSIONS AND MEASUREMENTS**	
APPENDIX B	**TECHNICAL ASPECTS OF CHEMICAL, BIOLOGICAL, RADIOLOGICAL, AND NUCLEAR, AND TOXIC INDUSTRIAL MATERIAL DECONTAMINATION**	
	Background	B-1
	Nuclear and Radiological Weapons	B-1
	Biological Warfare Agents	B-3
	Chemical Agents	B-7
	Toxic Industrial Material	B-9
	Technical Reach-Back	B-10

APPENDIX C	**DECONTAMINANTS**	
	Background	C-1
	Types of Decontaminants	C-1
	Decontamination Solution Preparation	C-9
	Storage and Shelf Life	C-10
	Decontaminants	C-10
APPENDIX D	**DECONTAMINATION OF SPECIFIC SURFACES AND MATERIALS**	
APPENDIX E	**SPECIAL DECONTAMINATION CONSIDERATIONS**	
	Background	E-1
	Vulnerable/Sensitive Equipment	E-1
	Chemical, Biological, Radiological, and Nuclear Munitions Disposal	E-4
	Sample Transfer, Evacuation, and Processing	E-5
	Depleted-Uranium Decontamination	E-5
	Decontamination of Specific Radioisotopes	E-7
	Contaminated-Remains Decontamination	E-9
	Animals	E-10
APPENDIX F	**EFFECTS OF THE ENVIRONMENT ON DECONTAMINATION**	
	Background	F-1
	Cold Weather	F-1
	Hot Weather (Desert and Jungle)	F-3
	Urban Areas	F-5
	Mountains	F-5
APPENDIX G	**DECONTAMINATION UNITS AND ASSETS**	
	Background	G-1
	Army	G-1
	Marine Corps	G-4
	Air Force	G-7
	Navy	G-10
	Other Units	G-11
APPENDIX H	**DECONTAMINATION KITS, APPARATUSES, AND EQUIPMENT**	
	Background	H-1
	Decontamination Devices for Personnel	H-4
	Decontamination Devices for Equipment	H-5
	Power-Driven Decontamination Systems	H-7
	Fixed-Site Decontamination System Tactics, Techniques, and Procedures	H-10
APPENDIX I	**TERRAIN DECONTAMINATION**	
	Background	I-1
	Terrain Decontamination Methods	I-1
	Types of Surfaces	I-4
APPENDIX J	**THOROUGH DECONTAMINATION STATION CHARTS FOR SUPERVISORS AND ATTENDANTS**	

APPENDIX K	CONTAMINATED-WASTE COLLECTION AND DISPOSAL	
	Background	K-1
	Responsibility	K-1
	Contaminated-Waste Holding Area	K-1
	Unit Waste Accumulation Points	K-1
	Equipment and Material	K-2
	Procedures for the Collection of Contaminated Waste	K-3
	Transportation Procedures	K-5
	Waste Collection Point	K-6
	Disposal Procedures	K-6
	Open Storage	K-7
	Burying	K-7
	Open Burning	K-7
	Marking Requirements	K-9

REFERENCES	References-1
GLOSSARY	Glossary-1
INDEX	Index-1

FIGURES

I-1	How Decontamination Affects Combat Effectiveness	I-7
IV-1	Two-Lane Wash Down	IV-4
IV-2	Dispersed Operational-Decontamination Setup	IV-5
IV-3	Rolling the Cuff in the Trouser	IV-12
IV-4	Wiping From the Head to the Bottom of the Hood	IV-13
IV-5	Rolling the Hood to the Center of the Head	IV-14
IV-6	Unsnapping the Trousers from the Jacket	IV-15
IV-7	Pulling the Jacket Down and Away	IV-15
IV-8	Loosening the Overboots	IV-15
IV-9	Stepping on the Black Lining of the Jacket	IV-16
IV-10	Removing the Gloves	IV-16
IV-11	Putting on the New BDO	IV-17
IV-12	Putting on M9 Detector Paper	IV-18
IV-13	Securing Individual Gear	IV-18
IV-14	Removing the Garment and Turning it Inside Out	IV-21
IV-15	Removing Your Leg and Foot From the Garment	IV-21
IV-16	Reapplying the M9 Detector Paper	IV-22
IV-17	Tying the Microphone Cord to the Hose of the Mask	IV-24

IV-18	Removing the Outer Garment	IV-26
V-1	Thorough Decontamination Site	V-5
V-2	DTD Layout	V-8
V-3	Decontaminating Individual Equipment	V-10
V-4	Shuffle Pit Decontamination	V-12
V-5	Removing the Overgarment Jacket	V-13
V-6	Station 4 Layout	V-14
V-7	Liquid Contamination Control Line	V-15
V-8	Checking for Contamination	V-17
VI-1	Decontamination Support	V-I
VII-1	Sample Decontamination Site Layout	VII-7
VII-2	Example of a Ground Crew CCA Layout	VII-9
VII-3	Example of an Aircrew CCA Layout	VII-10
VIII-1	Aircraft Operational Decontamination Site Layout	VIII-10
VIII-2	Helicopter Operational Decontamination Site Layout	VIII-10
VIII-3	Sample Layout for a DAD Station	VIII-17
VIII-4	Sensitive Areas for the UH-60/E60, CH-47, and AH-64	VIII-18
VIII-5	Sensitive Areas for the OH-58 and UH-1	VIII-19
H-1	M291 Skin Decontamination Kit	H-5
H-2	M295 IEDK	H-6
H-3	M100 SDS	H-7
H-4	M17 LDS	H-8
H-5	MPDS	H-9
H-6	FSDS Placed in a Civilian Vehicle	H-10
H-7	Two FSDS Conducting Terrain Decontamination	H-13
H-8	FSDS Overlap Operation	H-14
H-9	Decontamination Control Point	H-14
H-10	Resupply COAs (Options 1 and 2)	H-15
H-11	Large-Area Missions	H-16
H-12	Hose Reel Operation (Two-Person)	H-17
I-1	Decontamination by Exploding	I-3
J-1	Sample Station 1 Checklist	J-2
J-2	Sample Station 2 (BDO) Checklist	J-3
J-3	Sample Station 2 (JSLIST) Checklist	J-4
J-4	Sample Station 3 (BDO) Checklist	J-5
J-5	Sample Station 3 (JSLIST) Checklist	J-6

J-6	Sample Station 4 Checklist	J-7
J-7	Sample Station 5 Checklist	J-8
J-8	Sample Station 6 Checklist	J-9
J-9	Sample Station 7 Checklist	J-10
J-10	Sample Station 8 Checklist	J-11
K-1	Glove Decontamination	K-4
K-2	Markings	K-4

TABLES

I-1	Decontamination Levels and Techniques	I-5
1-2	Special Medical Considerations	I-5
II-1	Work/Rest Cycles and Water Replacement Guidelines	II-5
II-2	Preattack Decontamination Actions	II-10
IV-1	Advantages and Disadvantages of Operational Decontamination Techniques	IV-2
IV-2	Operational Decontamination Phases	IV-2
IV-3	Vehicle Wash-Down Process	IV-6
IV-4	Steps for the Buddy Team Method of MOPP Gear Exchange With the JSLIST Chemical-Protective Ensemble	IV-7
IV-5	Steps for the BDO MOPP Gear Exchange	IV-11
IV-6	Steps for the CVCUS and CPU (Buddy Team Method) MOPP Gear Exchange	IV-19
IV-7	Steps for the Triple Buddy Method of MOPP Gear Exchange With the M40A1 and M42	IV-23
IV-8	Steps for the CVCUS and CPU (Triple Buddy Method) MOPP Gear Exchange With the M40A1, M42, and M43 (Aviation and Armor)	IV-28
IV-9	Steps for the JSLIST, Individual (Emergency Method) MOPP Gear Exchange	IV-32
IV-10	Steps for the Individual (Emergency Method) BDO MOPP Gear Exchange	IV-36
IV-11	Steps for the CVCUS and CPU, Individual (Emergency Method) MOPP Gear Exchange	IV-39
V-1	Planning Factors for the Rinse Station	V-3
V-2	Thorough Decontamination Support Matrix (Land Forces)	V-4
V-3	DTD Personnel and Equipment Recapitulation	V-8
V-4	Effectiveness of Types of Wash	V-20
V-5	Common Interferences for the CAM	V-22

V-6	Personnel and Equipment Requirements for the Optimum DED Layout of an M12A1 PDDA-Equipped Unit	V-23
V-7	Personnel and Equipment Requirements for the Alternate DED Layout of an M12A1 PDDA-Equipped Unit	V-25
V-8	Recommended Work/Rest Cycles for DED	V-26
V-9	Personnel and Equipment Requirements for the Optimum DED Layout of an M17 LDS-Equipped Unit	V-27
V-10	Personnel and Equipment Requirements for the Alternate DED Layout of an M17 LDS-Equipped Unit	V-28
VIII-1	Aircraft Spot Decontamination	VIII-4
VIII-2	Sample Aircraft Sizes and Recommended Pad Containment Areas	VIII-11
VIII-3	Personnel Requirements for DAD	VIII-16
VIII-4	Cargo Movement Mission Criticality Level	VIII-23
VIII-5	Cargo Movement Hazard Category	VIII-23
VIII-6	Cargo Decontamination Actions (Negligible)	VIII-24
XII-1	Estimated Water Consumption	XII-2
XII-2	Decontamination Resources Available at Each Organizational Level (Army)	XII-3
XII-3	Equipment and Supplies Needed for Decontamination Operations (Army)	XII-4
XII-4	Medical Equipment Set Chemical-Agent Patient Decontamination	XII-7
A-1	Measurements and Weights of Decontaminant Containers	A-1
A-2	Table of Commonly Used Prefixes	A-1
A-3	Conversion Factors	A-2
B-1	Nuclear-Weapon Detonation Downwind Radioactive Fallout Hazard Estimate	B-2
B-2	Survival of Selected Bacterial and Rickettsial Agents in Some Environments	B-4
B-3	Protective Capability of Common Barrier Material (in Minutes)	B-8
B-4	Categories of TIM	B-10
B-5	Technical Reach-Back POCs	B-10
C-1	Guidelines for the Use of Soil as a Decontaminant	C-4
C-2	Preparation of Decontamination Solution Using HTH (6-Ounce Bottles)	C-5

C-3	Preparation of Decontamination Solution Using HTH (Granular)	C-5
C-4	Preparation of 0.5 Percent Available Chlorine Solutions	C-5
C-5	Operational Limitations of DF 200	C-9
C-6	Standard Decontaminants Available in the Supply System	C-11
C-7	Miscellaneous (Nonstandard) Decontaminants	C-13
C-8	Natural Decontaminants	C-21
D-1	Decontamination Procedures for Specific Surfaces and Materials	D-1
F-1	Freezing Points and Melting Points of Selected Chemical Agents	F-2
G-1	USAF UTCs	G-9
G-2	CE and Medical CBRN Decontamination Capabilities	G-10
G-3	USA Reserve Component Platoon Equipment for Casualty Decontamination	G-12
H-1	Decontamination Equipment and Materials	H-1
H-2	Detection Equipment and Materials	H-2
H-3	Typical Mission Parameters (1,000 gallons of DF 200)	H-11
K-1	Weather Conditions	K-8

EXECUTIVE SUMMARY

Multiservice Tactics, Techniques, and Procedures for Chemical, Biological, Radiological, and Nuclear Decontamination

Chapter I
Decontamination: Concepts, Principles, and Levels

Chapter I addresses the threats, purposes, and principles behind CBRN decontamination.

Chapter II
Decontamination Operations: Plan, Prepare, and Execute

Chapter II addresses the planning of decontamination operations for wartime and for civil support (CS). It also addresses the reconnaissance and preparation of decontamination sites.

Chapter III
Immediate Decontamination

Chapter III addresses the steps used for immediate decontamination. This chapter also discusses the techniques and procedures for using the most common decontamination kits and equipment available in the US inventory.

Chapter IV
Operational Decontamination

Chapter IV addresses the planning, preparing, executing, and implementing techniques for operational decontamination. It covers vehicle wash down and mission-oriented protective posture (MOPP) gear exchange.

Chapter V
Thorough Decontamination

Chapter V addresses planning, preparing, and executing the techniques for thorough decontamination. It covers predecontamination requirements, decontamination techniques, detailed troop decontamination (DTD), detailed equipment decontamination (DED), postdecontamination operations, site closure, and resupply.

Chapter VI
Clearance Decontamination

Chapter VI addresses decontamination of equipment and personnel to levels that allow unrestricted transportation, maintenance, employment, and disposal.

Chapter VII

Fixed-Site, Port, and Airfield Decontamination

Chapter VII addresses planning, preparing, executing, and implementing the techniques for fixed-site, port, and airfield decontamination.

Chapter VIII

Aircraft and Aircrew Decontamination

Chapter VIII addresses aircraft, aircraft cargo, and aircrew decontamination. Detailed aircraft decontamination (DAD) procedures are provided in this chapter.

Chapter IX

Shipboard/Maritime Decontamination

Chapter IX addresses the considerations pertaining to shipboard and maritime decontamination.

Chapter X

Patient Evacuation and Decontamination

Chapter X addresses patient evacuation procedures; the decontamination procedures for litter or ambulatory patients for chemical, biological, and radiological (CBR) contamination; and decontaminant preparation.

Chapter XI

Decontamination in Support of Homeland Security

Chapter XI addresses decontamination support for HLS.

Chapter XII

Logistics

Chapter XII identifies the logistical considerations for the various decontamination techniques.

PROGRAM PARTICIPANTS

The following commands and agencies participated in the development of this publication:

Joint

Defense Threat Reduction Agency, 8725 John J. Kingman Road, MCS 6201, Fort Belvoir, VA 22060-6201

Army

United States Army Chemical School, 464 MANSCEN Loop, Suite 2617, Fort Leonard Wood, MO 65473

United States Army Medical Department Center and School, 1400 E. Grayson Street, Fort Sam Houston, TX 78234

United States Army Edgewood Chemical and Biological Center, Aberdeen Proving Ground, MD 21040

Marine Corps

United States Marine Corps Combat Development Command, 3300 Russell Road, Suite 318A, Quantico, VA 22134-5021

Navy

United States Navy Warfare Development Command, 686 Cushing Road, Sims Hall, Newport, RI 02841

United States Navy Surface Warfare Development Group, 2200 Amphibious Drive, Norfolk, VA 23521

Air Force

Headquarters Air Force Doctrine Center, ATTN: DJ, 155 North Twining Street, Maxwell AFB, AL 36112-6112

United States Air Force Civil Engineer Support Agency, 139 Barnes Drive, Suite 1, Tyndall AFB, FL 32403

Chapter I
DECONTAMINATION: CONCEPTS, PRINCIPLES, AND LEVELS

1. Background

The hazards associated with CBRN attacks and events often force US forces into protective equipment, thereby degrading their ability to perform individual and collective tasks and reducing combat power. Such hazards may be created by the deliberate use of CBRN weapons or a release from industrial sources. Additionally, they may be created by accidental release, natural disasters, or collateral damage release from industrial sources (TIM). These hazards may require decontamination of personnel, equipment, facilities, or terrain.

    a. Forms of Contamination. CBRN agent contamination is the deposition on or absorption of CBRN agents by personnel, materiel, structures, and terrain. US forces may encounter CBRN agent contamination through direct attack, movement through contaminated areas, the unwitting use of contaminated facilities, or the movement of agent clouds. Forms of contamination may be—

        (1) Vapor. Vapors can be generated by generators or bursting munitions. Vapor in an open or outdoor area will generally disperse rapidly.

        (2) Liquid. CB agents can be disseminated as liquids. Liquid droplets can range from thick and sticky to the consistency of water. Liquids can also be disseminated as an aerosol.

        (3) Aerosol. An aerosol is a liquid or solid composed of finely divided particles suspended in a gaseous medium. Examples of common aerosols are mist, fog, and smoke. They behave much like vapors.

        (4) Solids. Solid forms of contamination include radioactive particles, biological spores, and dusty agents. A dusty agent is a solid agent that can be disseminated as an aerosol.

    b. Hazard Transmission. When CBRN contamination cannot be avoided, resources may require decontamination. Contaminated hazards can be transmitted as follows:

        (1) Transfer. Anything that contacts a surface covered with liquids or solids contamination will tend to pick up that contamination and move it from one surface to another.

        (2) Spread. Touching a surface covered with liquid or solid contamination can spread contamination on that same surface.

        (3) Desorption. Liquid contamination absorbs into porous material. Once absorbed, it begins to desorb or give off low levels of vapor that pass into the air.

        (4) Vapor and Aerosol. Vapors and aerosols can be carried through the air and will disperse rapidly.

c. Decontamination. CBRN agent contamination should be avoided when possible. When this is not possible, personnel and equipment must be decontaminated to reduce or eliminate the risk to personnel and to make equipment serviceable. Decontamination procedures will not degrade the performance of personnel or equipment and will not harm the environment. The levels of decontamination are immediate, operational, thorough, and clearance.

(1) Immediate Decontamination. Immediate decontamination minimizes casualties and limits the spread or transfer of contamination.

(2) Operational Decontamination. Operational decontamination sustains operations by reducing the contact hazard, limiting the spread of contamination, and eliminating or reducing the duration that MOPP equipment must be used.

(3) Thorough Decontamination. Thorough decontamination reduces contamination to the lowest detectable level by the use of tactical-level capabilities. The intent of thorough decontamination is to reduce or eliminate the level of MOPP. This is accomplished by units (with or without external support) when operations and resources permit.

(4) Clearance Decontamination. Clearance decontamination provides decontamination to a level that allows unrestricted transportation, maintenance, employment, and disposal.

d. Methods of Decontamination. Decontamination is accomplished by neutralization, physical removal, and weathering.

(1) Neutralization. Neutralization is the most widely used method of decontamination, particularly for chemical warfare (CW) agents. Neutralization is the reaction of the contaminating agent with other chemicals to render the agent less toxic or nontoxic. When mixed with a reactive decontaminant, the agent is converted into other substances (i.e., reaction products). The reactive decontaminant may be a commonly available material (e.g., household bleach) or a specifically designed decontaminating agent (see Appendix A for measurements and weights of containers that could be used).

(2) Physical Removal. Physical removal is the relocation of the contamination from one mission-critical surface to another less important location. Physical removal generally leaves the contamination in toxic form. It often involves the subsequent neutralization of the contamination. For example, if soap and water are used to remove the agent, the runoff may be drained into a pit containing bleaching powder. However, depending on mission requirements, physical removal can be an effective technique without subsequent neutralization.

(3) Weathering. Weathering involves such processes as evaporation and irradiation to remove or destroy the contaminant. The contaminated item is exposed to natural elements (e.g., sun, wind, heat, precipitation) to dilute or destroy the contaminant to the point of reduced or negligible hazard. This may be as simple as letting a vehicle sit in the hot desert sun to bake off the contaminant. Natural weathering is the simplest and most often preferred method of decontamination, particularly for terrain and non-mission-essential buildings and roads.

2. Hazard

The potential for the increased use of CBRN weapons and the increased risk of TIM hazards from commercial, industrial and medical facilities has increased the urgency for developing more effective detection, protection, and decontamination procedures and equipment (see Appendix B for more information on the technical aspects of CBRN decontamination). Opposing forces may acquire or produce CBRN agents or seize TIM from commercial facilities. During the conflict in the former Yugoslavia, Muslim forces deliberately positioned canisters of chlorine from the Tuzla industrial chemical plant to deter Serb artillery attacks.

a. CW Agents and Delivery Means. Typically classified by their effects on the body, CW agents consist of choking, nerve, blood, blister, and incapacitating agents (see *Potential Military Chemical/Biological Agents and Compounds* for more information on CW agents). Virtually all weapons systems, from howitzers to aerial bombs and missiles, can be used to deliver CW agents over a wide area. Terrorists and insurgents can use spray systems or other devices in localized attacks.

b. Biological Warfare (BW) Agents and Delivery Means. BW is the use of pathogens or toxins as weapons. BW agents include anthrax, plague, cholera, smallpox, ricin toxin, botulinum toxin, mycotoxin, aflatoxin, and many others. Conventional munitions, such as aerial bombs and missile warheads, can be modified to deliver BW agents. Other delivery means include spray devices affixed to manned aircraft or aerial drones and ground-based aerosol generators.

c. Radiological Dispersal Devices (RDDs). RDDs scatter radiological material without a nuclear explosion. The material is dispersed by a small blast to contaminate and deny access to terrain or facilities, which slows military operations. "Dirty bomb" is a common term for an RDD.

d. Nuclear Weapons. Nuclear weapons can be delivered by conventional or unconventional means. Weapons effects can cause significant residual radiation hazards.

e. TIM. Industry develops and produces TIM for industrial operations or for research by industry, government, and academia. These TIM are not manufactured to produce human casualties or to contaminate equipment and facilities. Nevertheless, TIM can be highly dangerous and lethal. Rapid industrialization in the developing world is seldom accompanied by the safety and regulatory regimes found in the United States and Western Europe. Hazards from TIM can occur through collateral damage to industrial facilities or through the acquisition and use of these chemicals by opposing forces. These TIM include hydrogen cyanide, cyanogens chloride, phosgene, and chloropicrin. Many herbicides and pesticides are TIM that could also present a contamination hazard.

3. Concepts—Combat Operations

Decontamination is necessary to allow personnel to remove their protective gear and resume normal operations after they become contaminated. Weathering is the most desirable means of decontamination. However, time and operational needs may not permit this option.

a. Decontamination Purpose and Operational Impact. Decontamination is the removal or neutralization of hazardous levels of contamination from personnel, equipment, materiel, and terrain. The ultimate purpose of decontamination is to restore full combat power in the shortest possible time.

b. Principles of Decontamination Operations. Decontaminate immediately for an agent on the skin. Perform higher levels of decontamination as a result of risk assessment. Personnel should consider the following:

(1) Speed. Personnel should conduct decontamination operations as quickly as possible. Direct exposure to some CBRN, toxic industrial chemicals (TIC), or TIM agents will create casualties and could be fatal within minutes. The sooner equipment is decontaminated, the less likely it is to absorb the agent or spread to other surfaces.

(2) Need. Decontaminate only what is necessary. Personnel have a limited amount of resources available and should expend resources only where they are needed.

(3) Priority. Decontaminate the most essential items first; foremost will be the skin if contact occurs. Once wearing protective equipment, personnel should begin decontamination operations on clothing, equipment, and vehicles.

(4) Limited Area. Personnel should perform decontamination near the area where the contamination occurs. This limits the spread of contamination to other areas and reduces the time spent traveling.

c. Response—Wartime Operations. When a CBRN incident occurs, the commander must decide whether decontamination is required to restore combat power and, if so, what level of decontamination is required (see Table I-1 and Table I-2). Immediate and operational decontamination are time-critical. These levels of decontamination save lives and help to regenerate and maintain combat power. The units and activities affected will continue their primary mission. However, the level of effort required for thorough and clearance decontamination will remove the unit (for an extended period of time) from the primary mission. Decontamination is not a sequential process that requires the conduct (in order) of immediate, operational, and thorough decontamination. For example, weathering may alleviate the requirement to conduct thorough decontamination. See Appendix C for further information on the decontaminants that can be used for the different levels of decontamination.

(1) Immediate. Immediate decontamination is carried out to save lives and reduce penetration of agent into surfaces. This may include decontamination of personnel, clothing, and equipment. Immediate decontamination will help prevent casualties and permit the use of individual equipment and key systems.

(a) Skin decontamination is a basic survival skill and should be performed within 1 minute of being contaminated. Decontamination of the eyes is an immediate decontamination action that involves flushing the eyes with water as soon as possible following contamination (see Chapter III).

(b) Personal wipe down should be performed within 15 minutes. This is done to remove contamination from individual equipment. Use detector paper or an improved chemical-agent monitor (ICAM) to locate the agent. Use a radiac set to locate radiological contamination; and then brush, wipe, or shake it off.

Table I-1. Decontamination Levels and Techniques

Levels	Techniques[1]	Purpose	Best Start Time	Performed By
Immediate	Skin decontamination	Saves lives	Before 1 minute	Individual
	Personal wipe down	Stops agent from penetrating	Within 15 minutes	Individual or buddy
	Operator wipe down	Limits agent spread	Within 15 minutes	Individual or crew
	Spot decontamination	Limits agent spread	Within 15 minutes	Individual or crew
Operational	MOPP gear exchange[2]	Provides temporary relief from MOPP4	Within 6 hours	Unit
	Vehicle wash down	Limits agent spread	Within 1 hour (CARC) or within 6 hours (non-CARC)	Battalion crew or decontamination platoon
Thorough	DED and DAD	Provides probability of long-term MOPP reduction	When mission allows reconstitution	Decontamination platoon
	DTD			Contaminated unit
Clearance	Unrestricted use of resources	METT-TC depending on the type of equipment contaminated	When mission permits	Supporting strategic resources

[1] The techniques become less effective the longer they are delayed.
[2] Performance degradation and risk assessment must be considered when exceeding 6 hours. See *Multiservice Tactics, Techniques, and Procedures for Nuclear, Biological, and Chemical (NBC) Protection*.

Table I-2. Special Medical Considerations

Levels	Techniques	Purpose	Best Start Time	Performed By
Operational (Patient)	Complete decontamination of contaminated areas of patient's MOPP prior to evacuation or return to duty, without removing MOPP.	Reduces the spread of contamination inside ground, water, and air ambulances	Before transport on "dirty" evacuation vehicle	Unit Buddy
Thorough (Patient)	Remove patient's clothing and decontaminate the skin. This may involve decontaminating only the contaminated areas of the skin (especially if water is scarce) or a full-body wash. Clean the patient and put him in patient protective wrap if he is to be transported through a contaminated area.	Removes contamination on patients prior to admission to a clean MTF or USAF aeromedical aircraft	Prior to entry into a clean MTF or USAF aircraft	Medical unit with augmentees

(c) Operator wipe down should be done within 15 minutes. Operators use the M100 Sorbent Decontamination System (SDS) to decontaminate the surfaces they need to touch or contact to operate the equipment. Radiological contamination in the form of dust particles may be wiped, scraped, or brushed off.

NOTE: The M100 SDS is not authorized for use on Naval aircraft.

(2) Operational. Operational decontamination is carried out by contaminated units (with possible assistance from a decontamination unit). It is restricted to the specific parts of contaminated, operationally essential equipment, material and work areas to minimize contact and transfer hazards and to sustain operations. This may include individual decontamination beyond the scope of immediate decontamination, decontamination of mission-essential equipment, and limited terrain decontamination. Operational decontamination reduces the level of contamination, thus lessening the chance of spread and transfer. When combined with weathering, MOPP levels may be reduced without further decontamination, depending on the surface or material being decontaminated and the agent. See Appendix D for more information on the decontamination of specific surfaces.

(a) A MOPP gear exchange should be performed within 6 hours of being contaminated due to the performance degradation that occurs when a unit is in MOPP4. A MOPP gear exchange allows a unit to remove the gross contamination from personnel and equipment, which provides temporary relief from MOPP4 and a return to an increased operating tempo (OPTEMPO) in pursuit of mission accomplishment.

(b) Vehicle wash down should be performed—

- Within 1 hour of contamination for equipment that is not painted with chemical agent-resistant coating (CARC).
- Within 6 hours of contamination for CARC-painted equipment
- When the mission does not permit a thorough decontamination.

(3) Thorough. DED and DAD are conducted as part of a reconstitution effort during breaks in combat operations. These operations require immense logistical support and are manpower-intensive. Thorough decontamination is carried out to reduce contamination on personnel, equipment, materiel, and work areas. This permits the partial or total removal of individual protective equipment (IPE) and maintains operations with minimum degradation. While conducting thorough decontamination, contaminated units will be non-mission-capable. The resulting decrease in MOPP will allow the unit to operate with restored effectiveness.

(a) The DED and DAD restore items so that they can be used without protective equipment. As a safety measure, some services require the use of protective gloves until clearance decontamination has been completed. These operations require support from a CBRN decontamination unit or element.

(b) Representative actions that may follow a thorough decontamination include the following:

- Replacing personnel who may have become injured or ill during decontamination operations.
- Reordering supplies (e.g., detector paper, decontamination solution, decontamination kits and apparatuses).
- Maintaining or repairing vehicles and equipment, including recalibration or replacement of detectors and alarms.

- Marking used decontamination sites and selecting new decontamination sites, reporting old and new decontamination sites, and recording and reporting previously contaminated personnel and equipment.
- Documenting resource expenditures.
- Conducting force health protection (FHP).
- Preparing after-action reviews.

(4) Clearance. Clearance decontamination of equipment and personnel allows the operation to continue unrestricted. Decontamination at this level will probably be conducted at or near a shipyard, advanced base, or other industrial facility. Clearance decontamination involves factors such as suspending normal activities, withdrawing personnel, and having materials and facilities not normally present. Essentially, resources from an industrial base (e.g., Army Materiel Command, Air Force Material Command, Naval Sea Systems Command, and Marine Corps Systems Command [MARCORSYSCOM]) will be required. During clearance decontamination, resource expenditures are documented, FHP measures are conducted, and after-action reviews are prepared.

d. Decontamination Decisions.

(1) The decision to decontaminate is a risk assessment and is made within the context of mission, enemy, terrain and weather, time, troops available and civilian (METT-TC) considerations, and the resources available (see Figure I-1, page I-8).

NOTE: The USMC uses the term mission, enemy, terrain and weather, troops and support available—time available (METT-T) vice the Army's use of METT-TC. Civilian considerations are inherently measured within the context of this acronym.

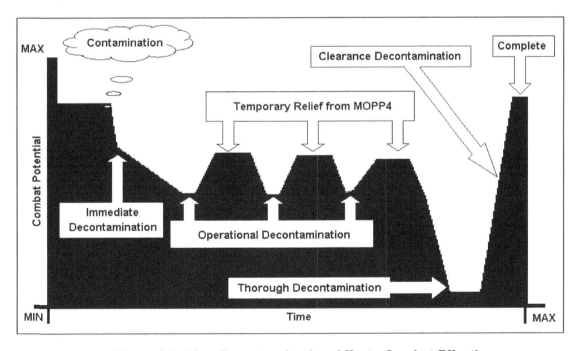

Figure I-1. How Decontamination Affects Combat Effectiveness

(a) The individual or crew decision to conduct immediate decontamination will minimize casualties and limit the contact hazard. This applies the speed and need principles of decontamination. Following decontamination, the unit continues to "fight dirty." The unit's MOPP provides protection; however, continued wearing of MOPP gear causes performance degradation.

(b) The unit or activity decision to conduct operational decontamination will provide temporary relief from MOPP4 and limit the spread of contamination. Operational decontamination supports sustained unit operations for prolonged periods and is conducted as far forward as possible.

(c) The command decision to conduct thorough decontamination should reduce contamination below the detectable level with tactical-level detection equipment. Caution should be exercised. Current tactical detectors are not sensitive enough to ensure that the item does not off-gas when the temperature rises. Units can operate at this temperature without the degradation imposed by higher MOPP levels. The commander determines which assets are critical for a subsequent mission and allocates the resources to conduct DED and DTD. The commander accepts the trade-off that the contaminated assets will not be available for the period of time required to conduct a thorough decontamination.

(2) The commander applies METT-TC considerations to the risk assessment process to determine if and where operational or thorough decontamination is required. For example, weathering may reduce contamination below detectable levels. Additionally, thorough decontamination may be deferred until the operational situation or resources are available to support the process. Furthermore, unique requirements such as decontamination of electronic equipment or depleted uranium (DU) contamination may have special considerations (see Appendix E for more information).

(3) Risk assessment is a continuous process. Low-level residual contamination may remain following weathering or decontamination. The contamination may also not be detectable by tactical-level detection devices (see Appendix F for a summary of how the environment could impact decontamination operations). Medical surveillance (MEDSURV), conducted by preventive medicine (PVNTMED) personnel, is an FHP measure to identify medical threats for personnel who may be exposed.

4. Concepts—Homeland Security

HLS missions may require that defense decontamination support be furnished for the two component parts of HLS—homeland defense (HLD) and CS. Decontamination support will follow a process that essentially involves preparation, response, recovery, and restoration. (Chapter XI provides more detailed information on decontamination support for HLS.) CBRN decontamination operations conducted in support of HLS will comply with 29 Code of Federal Regulations (CFR) 1910.120, *Hazardous Waste Operations and Emergency Response,* within the United States, its territories, and possessions.

a. **Preparation Phase.** Military units tasked to assist local or state responders must become intimately familiar with the National Response Plan (NRP) and coordinate and train closely with local civilian emergency response agencies so that protocols and procedures are coordinated, understood, and practiced before an actual event occurs in the community. Whether preparing for HLS or combat operations, US military forces maintain the capability to conduct or support decontamination based on unit capabilities. Unit or activity HLS preparatory actions are similar to other contingencies. Representative actions include—

- Planning contingency operations.
- Preparing standard operating procedures (SOPs).
- Conducting liaison with applicable organizations.
- Establishing memorandums of agreement (MOAs) with appropriate authorities.
- Establishing and maintaining required certifications.
- Conducting training and exercises.
- Obtaining required equipment (commercial or government) to accomplish primary or collateral missions (e.g., patient decontamination).

b. Response Phase. When a threat or an actual occurrence of a CBRN incident requires HLD or CS decontamination support, DOD resources with decontamination capabilities may respond. The required missions may include mass and casualty decontamination, or technical assistance for decontamination (see Chapter XI for more information on these missions). Personnel performing decontamination operations in support of HLS must be trained and certified to the first-responder operations level as defined in 29 CFR 1910.120, *Hazardous Waste Operations and Emergency Response*.

c. Recovery Phase. For CS, recovery, transition, and redeployment operations start when civil authorities or other designated agencies relieve the commander of selected decontamination-related tasks. The operational duration of the response mission is determined by the requirements established by the appropriate authority. The requirement for mass and casualty decontamination will likely end following the response phase. The requirement for technical decontamination to support first-responder operations in a hot zone may continue. Military units with decontamination capabilities may redeploy during this phase or be assigned other responsibilities. A transition plan is implemented and tasks are transferred from the commander to the appropriate civil authorities. Nongovernmental organizations (NGOs) and contracted services may augment these civil authorities. Upon completion of the required recovery support, the commander executes a transition and redeploys.

d. Restoration Phase. Restoration constitutes those actions necessary to return the decontamination section or unit to its full operational capability. Restoration actions will generally be done at a unit's home station. Restoration actions may include the following:

(1) Replacing personnel who may have become injured/ill during decontamination operations.

(2) Reordering supplies (e.g., detector paper, decontamination solution, decontamination kits and apparatuses).

(3) Maintaining and repairing vehicles and equipment, including recalibration or replacement of detectors and alarms.

(4) Marking used decontamination sites and selecting new decontamination sites.

(5) Documenting personnel and equipment expenditures, event logs, and MEDSURV.

(6) Concluding outstanding agreements with civil authorities or CS organizations.

5. Service Capabilities

All services have varying levels of CBRN decontamination capabilities. All US forces at the individual warfighter level must have immediate decontamination capabilities. Most US military units at the major subordinate command level (e.g., brigade, regiment, wing, shipboard) have operational and thorough decontamination capabilities. Clearance decontamination will normally be conducted at the Unified Combatant Command level (i.e., Central Command [CENTCOM]) with the assistance of multiple agencies within the command.

6. Training and Exercises

Individual and joint unit decontamination training across the force ensures the readiness to fight and win should an adversary employ CBRN weapons. Training is a responsibility shared by combatant commands, services, and a number of DOD agencies. Training and exercise programs must incorporate the principles for operations in CBRN environments and include realistic consideration of CBRN weapons effects on sustained combat operations.

a. Training. Training opportunities exist both internally and externally and should include the following:

- Initial and sustainment training.
- Individual, collective, and unit training.
- Intra-agency and interagency training.

b. Exercises. Exercises provide the opportunity to interact with other units or services and federal, state, or local agencies. Exercises developed by non-DOD agencies provide an opportunity to improve military capabilities for support of HLS operations with minimal resources. These exercises emphasize interoperability requirements and stress staff coordination. They also serve to identify shortfalls in communications or other capabilities that must be corrected.

Chapter II

DECONTAMINATION OPERATIONS: PLAN, PREPARE, AND EXECUTE

1. Background

Decontamination planning provides recommendations for commanders' guidance. This helps ensure that forces and facilities are prepared to operate in CBRN environments; supports the commander's decision-making requirements; and identifies, assesses, and estimates the enemy's CBRN capabilities, intentions, and most likely courses of action (COAs).

2. Decontamination Planning

The decontamination planner must consider the hazards that may result from CBRN or TIM contamination. Decontamination assessments include mission analysis, COA development, and the analysis and comparison of enemy and friendly COAs. Decontamination planning is dynamic and continuous from preattack to postattack, through recovery operations.

NOTE: TIC and other hazardous materials [HAZMAT] are considered TIM throughout this manual.

The unit CBRN defense personnel and staff work together to ensure that decontamination planning is fully integrated into deliberate and crisis action planning. They accomplish this through wargaming friendly versus enemy COAs and by mutually developing products designed to assist the service components, multinational partners, and joint force commanders (JFCs) decision-making processes.

a. Commanders, with input from their staffs, assess their vulnerability to CBRN attacks. Commanders determine the required protection for their units by assessing the capabilities of the enemy. They estimate the likely impact of CBRN attacks and, based on the concept of operations (CONOPS), determine the methods to reduce the impact and allow for mission accomplishment. This includes MOPP acclimatization training and decontamination planning to mitigate the affects of a CBRN attack. See *Multiservice Tactics, Techniques, and Procedures for Nuclear, Biological, and Chemical Vulnerability Assessment* for further information on CBRN vulnerability assessment (VA).

b. The CBRN planner writes a decontamination plan as part of a CBRN defense annex of the operation order (OPORD).

(1) In preparing the decontamination portion of the CBRN defense annex, the planner assesses the likelihood that decontamination operations will be required, the probable extent of those operations, and the best procedures for execution.

(2) In preparing the decontamination portion of the CBRN defense annex, the planner should consider the following questions:

- Does the enemy possess CBRN weapons and has he demonstrated the intent to use them?
- Does the unit's mission bring it into likely contact with TIM hazards?

- What is the unit's decontamination capability (see Appendixes G and H for a summary of decontamination capabilities for the services)?

- Does weather and terrain favor enemy use of CBRN weapons? (For terrain decontamination, see Appendix I.)

- What are the unit's logistics requirements?

- What is the unit's level of decontamination training?

- Is contamination avoidance possible?

- What decontamination assets are available?

- What likely decontamination sites are available (through map reconnaissance)?

(3) During the plan preparation, all factors of the METT-TC considerations are measured. The METT-TC considerations will impact the representative planning areas (e.g., decontamination sites, priorities of effort, decontamination decisions, and decontamination triage).

(a) The preselection of decontamination sites is essentially a map reconnaissance that is based on the supported commander's plan. (Detailed information on a potential site may be determined from intelligence assets.) Preselected sites should be within an avenue of approach, but just off main routes for easy access. Close proximity to rivers, streams, or other water sources is also important. In conducting a map reconnaissance, consider the following:

- Probable level of decontamination that will be conducted.

- Terrain (soil composition).

- Mission.

- Cover and concealment.

- Water sources.

- Drainage.

- Presence or absence of contamination.

- Road network that facilitates the movement in and out of the site for both the contaminated unit and the resupply squad.

- Adequate area for the dispersal of equipment before, during, and after decontamination.

- Location of downwind friendly personnel.

(b) The commander will establish priorities of effort that determine which contaminated units are decontaminated first. Since decontamination assets are limited, the commander must establish a priority of decontamination support. The priority of effort lists the units in the order they will receive decontamination support. This can change from phase to phase during an operation. The CBRN staff develops the priority of effort based on an understanding of the commander's intent.

(c) The commander decides when and where operational and thorough decontamination will occur according to METT-TC. Note that the different levels of immediate decontamination always occur as battle drills at the prescribed times following a CBRN attack.

(d) Planning to decontaminate what is necessary ensures that units or activities understand the decontamination triage (identifying clean and dirty elements). Even though a unit has been identified for decontamination, it does not follow that each individual, vehicle, or item belonging to that unit is contaminated. Decontamination triage is the process of identifying those individuals, vehicles, aircraft, ships, ships spaces, or items of equipment that require decontamination. Only the identified elements are to be processed through the decontamination site. The commander may then employ his uncontaminated elements to support the decontamination operation.

c. Plans for decontamination operations will be included in the CBRN defense annex to the operation plan (OPLAN) or OPORD. In preparing the decontamination portion of the CBRN defense annexes, the planner must assess the disposition of forces and assets available for CBRN reconnaissance and decontamination. It must identify locations for preselected decontamination sites and linkup points and the missions for the CBRN decontamination assets. It must also identify plans for divert airfields and/or naval vessels for recovery operations and identify contingency plans for stations, ports, airfields, forward arming and refueling points (FARPs), and facilities to receive contaminated aircraft and ships with personnel and cargo aboard.

3. Wartime Planning Considerations

Multiple factors must be considered when planning CBRN decontamination during wartime.

a. Joint or Combined Operations. These factors include the following:

- Intelligence collection, analysis, and production.
- Situational awareness (SA).
- Common planning, training, and equipment standards.
- Health service support (HSS).
- Protection of the joint rear area (JRA) and theater sustainment capabilities.
- Priorities.
- Minimum essential requirements for the decontamination.
- Human factor effects of the MOPP.
- Logistics burden of CBRN decontamination.
- Effect of the CBRN attack on the C2 systems.
- Capabilities and limitations of US, multinational, and host nation (HN) decontamination assets.
- Consequence management (CM) support outside the continental United States (OCONUS), its territories, and possessions.
- Mortuary affairs.

(1) SA. Adequate SA is a central concern for decontamination planning. An integrated warning and reporting system provides a significant measure of protection by allowing friendly forces to minimize exposure to the hazard. Accurate and timely understanding of the hazard and its effect minimizes the possibility of having excessive or inadequate force protection (FP). Warning system provisions also address the need to warn personnel, based on an alarm, thus causing units to increase their protective posture, and can act as a warning order (WARNORD) for dedicated decontamination assets.

(2) Common Planning, Training, and Equipment Standards. Common standards for CBRN decontamination (especially training, exercises, and equipment maintenance) enhance joint force capabilities.

(3) HSS. Key elements of HSS include casualty estimation, chemoprophylaxis and immunizations, MEDSURV, PVNTMED, diagnostics, mass casualty management, evacuation, and patient decontamination requirements. HSS planning addresses decontamination considerations. Unit plans should recognize that CBRN attacks have the potential to create mass casualties. The treatment and evacuation of CBRN patients will be difficult and hazardous to the patients, medical personnel, and medical treatment facilities (MTFs). HSS CBRN defense planning includes appropriate liaison with affected and supportive civilian HSS MTFs and an assessment of the capabilities and limitations of those MTFs.

(4) Protection of the JRA and Theater Sustainment Capabilities. The JRA and theater sustainment capabilities must be protected. A successful adversary CBRN attack on a critical logistics facility or a major TIM attack near it may degrade OPTEMPO and force generation capabilities. Mitigation and decontamination measures focus on maintaining support to combat operations and rapidly restoring the degraded capabilities. Alternate sites are designated and exercised in advance to ensure uninterrupted JRA operations and theater sustainment capabilities.

(5) Priorities. In wartime, manpower and time are critical resources that cannot be wasted on nonessential tasks. Therefore, the decontamination of areas, facilities, and equipment will be prioritized and limited by necessity, to allow resumption of operations by protected personnel. Priorities will be directly impacted by the mission with the realization that protected personnel can work with contaminated equipment. Therefore, decontamination must be aimed at restoring mission capability rather than totally minimizing hazards. If decontamination is not possible or needed, non-mission-essential areas may be marked and restricted from use. The first priority will be given to personal decontamination to prevent casualties and reduce manpower losses. The second priority will be the decontamination of equipment and material or facilities necessary to meet mission requirements as established by the commander. During wartime, decontamination operations will be expedited as the situation requires. Primary considerations will be for effective accomplishment of the mission.

(6) Minimum Essential Requirements. The minimal conditions that should be met in planning decontamination operations are as follows:

- Identification of contamination.
- Designation and marking of contaminated area.
- Identification of facilities, equipment, and material that have been contaminated.

- Availability of personnel to fully operate each decontamination station.
- Number and deployment or utilization of decontamination personnel.
- Selection of appropriate decontaminant and decontamination equipment.
- Selection of an effective method of decontamination.
- Selection of a site for decontamination of equipment, supplies, and personnel.

(7) Human Factor Effects of MOPP.

(a) Physiological and psychological stress will occur during decontamination operations. Body temperature must be maintained within a narrow limit for optimum physical and mental performance. MOPP gear restricts the heat loss mechanisms because of its high insulation and low permeability to water vapor. In addition, physical work requires more effort when personnel wear protective clothing because of its added weight and restricted movement. Work intensity, which is managed by leaders, is also a major contributing factor to heat stress.

(b) Military personnel wearing MOPP while conducting decontamination may experience heat stress. To prevent heat stress from resulting in injuries, they follow a prescribed cycle of work and rest periods. See Table II-1 for work/rest cycles and water replacement guidelines. The work/rest cycles are based on the environment (temperature, humidity, and solar load), the workload of the individual, and the clothing ensemble being worn. These work/rest cycles are usually described in terms of minutes of work allowed per hour. The remainder of the hour (after completing the work allowed) is used for rest, allowing heat to dissipate and allowing the individual to cool down. The local application of work/rest cycles is directly influenced by METT-TC.

Table II-1. Work/Rest Cycles and Water Replacement Guidelines

Heat Category	WBGT Index (°F)[1,2]	Light (Easy) Work		Moderate Work		Hard (Heavy) Work	
		Work/Rest (minutes)[4,5]	Water Intake (qt/hr)[3]	Work/Rest (minutes)[4,5]	Water Intake (qt/hr)[3]	Work/Rest (minutes)	Water Intake (qt/hr)
1	78–81.9	No limit	½	No limit	¾	40/20	¾
2 (Green)	82–84.9	No limit	½	50/10	¾	30/30	1
3 (Yellow)	85–87.9	No limit	¾	40/20	¾	30/30	1
4 (Red)	88–89.9	No limit	¾	30/30	¾	20/40	1
5 (Black)	More than 90	50/10	1	20/40	1	10/50	1

[1] Wearing all MOPP overgarments (MOPP4) adds 10°F to the WBGT index.
[2] If wearing body armor, add 5°F to WBGT in humid climates.
[3] Hourly fluid intake should not exceed 1¼ quarts, and daily fluid intake should not exceed 12 liters.
[4] Rest means minimal physical activity (sitting or standing), accomplished in the shade if possible. The information pertains to acclimated service personnel.
[5] The work/rest time and fluid replacement volumes will sustain performance and hydration for at least 4 hours of work in the specified heat category. Individual water needs will vary ±¼ qt/hr.

(c) The incidence of heat casualties can be reduced if personnel are allowed to lower their work intensity and take frequent rest breaks.

(8) Logistics Burden of CBRN Attacks. See *Multiservice Tactics, Techniques and Procedures for Nuclear, Biological, and Chemical Protection.*

(9) Effects of CBRN Attacks on C2 Systems. CBRN attacks can degrade C2 systems. Effective decontamination operations rely on a C2 system that keeps the commander informed and communicates the commander's intent. For example, being notified of the commander's priorities for decontamination is critical for ensuring that support is synchronized.

(10) Capabilities and Limitations of US, Multinational, and HN Decontamination Assets. In preparation for multinational operations, unit planners assess coalition member CBRN capabilities for decontamination and interoperability with US forces. The planning process should consider the implications and feasibility of diverting US assets and capabilities to support HN and other multinational members in accomplishing the required decontamination objectives.

(11) OCONUS CM Support. OCONUS CM support will generally be characterized by crisis action planning. A CBRN or TIM incident may result in US forces providing OCONUS decontamination support. The support would probably be for a short duration and would require extensive coordination and liaison with the HN.

b. International Coalition Operations. Decontamination may be conducted within the context of multinational arrangements. Planning is accomplished through both US and multinational channels. Coordinated CBRN defense planning is essential to the unity effort (e.g., operations; logistics (including infrastructure); intelligence; deception; decontamination; warning, detection, and monitoring; CM; and CBRN interoperability). Supporting plans that address coordination and liaison, host nation support (HNS), and the provision of mutual support are examples of the essential tasks that must be accomplished.

4. Homeland Security Planning Considerations

Decontamination support for HLS and CS present unique planning considerations. CBRN decontamination planning ranges from planning to provide technical assistance and recommendations to planning for resources for mass decontamination. The following are examples of planning considerations that apply for HLS and CS:

- CBRN specialists and planners understand and can operate within the civilian based incident command system (ICS).

- CBRN specialists and planners understand the terms of reference used to support first-responder decontamination operations.

- CBRN specialists conduct planning with civilian counterparts at the federal, state, or local level, as applicable.

- CBRN specialists and planners train and exercise for support of HLS or CS operations.

- CBRN specialists, as required, maintain the required certification to operate in a CS mission with civilian first responders.

- Military issue of the IPE (MOPP ensembles) do not meet Occupational Safety and Health Administration (OSHA) Level C requirements.

5. Preattack Decontamination Operations

Preattack decontamination actions are taken to increase readiness.

a. **Preattack Considerations.** Preattack considerations extend from the present until the first enemy weapon effects occur within the theater of operations.

(1) Commanders will conduct VA and estimate the need for decontamination based on the threat, the resources available for decontamination, and the potential results of this operation. Preattack actions also consider the following:

- Assessing the CBRN threat.
- Identifying and preparing collective protective shelters (CPSs) and MTFs.
- Ensuring the proficiency in CBRN decontamination procedures and methods.
- Preparing to conduct decontamination operations (based on the nature and extent of contamination and resources available for decontamination).
- Preparing to conduct response procedures (before and after a CBRN attack). Guidance must be based on the concept that there may be no warning before an attack and that all attacks in a high-threat area may contain CBRN agents.
- Providing instructions for a warning unit or the base populace.
- Notifying key personnel of an attack, of procedures for the activation of preselected CPSs, and of the need to don the protective clothing.
- Decontaminating mission-essential facilities (see Appendix I for information on terrain decontamination).
- Identifying recovery actions that must begin as soon as possible after the attack.

(2) Subordinate units and activities must support and comply with the commander's intent. They develop contingency plans for CBRN defense actions that support missions conducted within the theater assigned. Plans must address CBRN detection, warning, reporting, and decontaminating procedures and a rapid transition into a CBRN defensive posture.

(3) Specialized CBRN teams will be formed from existing personnel resources to detect, identify, and decontaminate CBRN contamination and to operate protective shelters.

(4) Each soldier must be trained to perform decontamination of his own body, clothing, personal equipment, individual weapons, and casualties.

b. **Reconnaissance/Site Survey of Decontamination Sites.** Decontamination site selection is necessary during preattack operational and thorough decontamination planning. The following criteria should be considered for decontamination site selection:

- Wind direction (to include downwind direction from friendly personnel).
- Water supply.
- Overhead concealment.

- Maximum use of existing facilities.
- Drainage.
- Trafficability. The path or road must be able to withstand large amounts of water being placed on it.
- Accessibility. The site should be accessible to the largest vehicle in the contaminated unit.
- Size. The area must be large enough to handle all stations of the level of decontamination being conducted, especially Station 3 of thorough decontamination.

c. Site and Linkup Point Selection.

(1) The controlling headquarters (HQ) selects the potential decontamination sites as part of mission planning. More than likely, this HQ will only be capable of a map reconnaissance. For decontamination sites on the friendly side of the forward line of own troops (FLOT), every effort must be made to conduct a ground reconnaissance of the site. For thorough decontamination and supported operational decontamination, it is imperative that these sites be further reconnaissanced by the supporting decontamination unit. For example, when an operational decontamination is executed by an Army battalion, the battalion CBRN noncommissioned officer (NCO) should make every attempt to reconnoiter these sites.

(2) As decontamination sites are selected (during the map reconnaissance), one or more linkup points are chosen to support each site. Linkup at the designated point includes establishing security, positioning the necessary marshalling areas, camouflaging the entry and exit points, designating the direction of flow into and out of the site, and ensuring that the unit's supply or prestaged embarked assets have sufficient replacement MOPP gear.

d. Coordination.

(1) The individual in charge of decontamination must make careful coordination with those elements involved to ensure the successful completion of the operation. The unit to be decontaminated must be aware of linkup points, times, and its own responsibilities for the procedure.

(2) Much of the coordination will be arranged through the decontamination element or the unit's higher echelon, particularly when involving the following:

- Power-driven decontamination equipment (PDDE) support.
- Engineer support for site preparation and closure.
- Supply and transportation for linkup with bulk water trucks.
- Air defense and security forces for security when those elements are required.
- HSS.
- Augmentee support.
- Support of medical patient decontamination operations (if the MTF is colocated adjacent to troop decontamination).

e. Communications. Primary communications between the decontamination element and the supported unit will be via radio. Therefore, signal operating instructions (SOI) should be included in the supported unit's initial request for decontamination support.

f. Maintaining SA.

(1) Warnings. Warnings of CBRN contamination are conveyed by alarms and signals. Units use easily recognizable and reliable alarm methods to respond quickly and reliably to CBRN hazards. Standard alarms, the Nuclear, Biological, and Chemical Warning and Reporting System (NBCWRS), and contamination markers help give orderly warning that may also require a change of MOPP level. Alarms and signals may include the following:

- Audible alarms.
- Automatic alarms.
- Visual signals.

(2) Markings. Contamination is marked to warn friendly personnel. Units or CBRN reconnaissance teams mark the likely entry points into the area and report contamination to higher HQ. The only exception is when marking would help the enemy. In this event, the hazard is reported to higher HQ as an unmarked contaminated area. When a unit enters a previously marked contaminated area, personnel check the extent of contamination and adjust plans as necessary. As the hazard area changes, the unit relocates the signs. When the hazard passes, the unit removes the signs. The unit reports all changes to higher HQ. The decontamination site noncommissioned officer in charge (NCOIC) ensures that his team properly marks the decontamination site with the standard markings and sends the NBC5 (areas of actual contamination) report forward.

(3) Control Measures.

(a) Ensure that drivers of contaminated vehicles know when to move into position at the wash-down location.

(b) Ensure that the contaminated unit has provided site security.

(c) See Appendix J for thorough decontamination station signs used as control measures.

(4) Wide-area data flow (Web site) provides up-to-date status, information, and conditions across a broad spectrum.

g. Maintenance of Decontamination Equipment. A thorough operator level maintenance should be done on all decontamination equipment. If no mission-capable equipment is found, all the shortcomings should be forwarded to higher echelons so that the force commander is aware of the full decontamination capability.

h. Pre-positioning of Logistics. Units will need to pre-position the replacement IPE for issue at the end of the DED as part of the thorough decontamination. If replacement IPE is needed during operational decontamination, the unit should pre-position the IPE for use during MOPP gear exchange. As the CBRN threat rises, IPE and chemical decontamination equipment should be pre-positioned forward to ensure timely delivery to units for operational and thorough decontamination.

i. Other Preattack Actions. Other key preattack actions are included in Table II-2.

Table II-2. Preattack Decontamination Actions

• Know the current and future missions.
• Outline the capabilities of the unit or activity.
• Know the external support available from CBRN units.
• Know the decontamination support available to detached/remote elements.
• Designate the decontamination sites.
• Employ avoidance (whenever possible) within the context of the mission.
• Designate the TFAs.
• Establish and exercise the CBRN warning and reporting system.

6. Execution

Actions necessary to successfully execute decontamination operations include establishing a C2 site, establishing clean areas or zones, ensuring security, providing proper and detailed reporting, ensuring the availability of resources, and controlling and documenting personnel exposure.

a. Decontamination Site C2. In a thorough decontamination, the supported unit is responsible for overall control. The level that an operational decontamination operation is being conducted determines C2 for the decontamination site. There are different levels (or techniques) of control when conducting operational decontamination.

(1) Decentralized Operational Decontamination. The unit commander requests decontamination equipment support, selects the decontamination site, links up with the decontamination element, and conducts the decontamination.

(2) Centralized Operational Decontamination. The CBRN staff controls the decontamination. The commander selects the site, and the battalion CBRN staff directs site setup and security and provides C2. The CBRN staff officer or NCO travels with the decontamination element and communicates via radio.

b. Establishment of Clean Areas and Zones. A predecontamination staging area is established downwind of the decontamination site. In the predecontamination staging area, the supported commander segregates vehicles by checking for contamination. Clean areas must be provided to avoid recontaminating personnel and equipment as they finish the decontamination process. The decontamination element should be set upwind of the decontamination site entrance. The MOPP gear exchange should be in place upwind and at a 45° angle of vehicle wash down. After processing, the vehicles should marshal in a postdecontamination assembly area (AA) upwind of the DTD and DED areas.

c. Security. Security ensures that the decontamination operation is conducted without interference. The supported unit is responsible for site security. Cover and concealment must be considered in decontamination site selection. Traffic control is another component of security. Linkup points and the entrances to AAs should be controlled to ensure that uncontaminated personnel or vehicles do not enter.

d. Reporting. Proper and detailed reporting is critical to the success of the decontamination operation and to the restoration operations that will occur at the end of the conflict. At the end of the decontamination operation, several things must be reported.

The CBRN unit will be responsible for submitting a complete NBC5 report after the site is closed. The supported unit will report the following to its higher HQ:

- Quantity and types of vehicles decontaminated.
- Number of personnel decontaminated through the DTD.
- Number of causalities.
- Time decontamination site was opened and closed.

 e. Consumption Rates. Decontamination operations expend resources. The chemical unit must plan to have enough of the proper supplies on hand to perform its mission. For information on consumption rates, see Chapter XII.

 f. Resupply. After a decontamination operation, the CBRN unit must restore itself to mission-capable status. While the supported unit has the requirement to keep on-hand supplies to conduct a DTD, the supporting CBRN unit may supply the majority of the equipment and supplies expended. Likewise, while the supported unit is required to provide the chemical unit with replacement supplies and material at the end of a DED, the CBRN unit should make its material requirements known to the maneuver forces logistics staff. The logistics staff may then arrange for decontamination supplies to be issued, often in "push" packages.

 g. Personnel Exposure Control and Documentation. During decontamination operations, steps should be taken to limit the exposure of personnel to the contamination. Such measures include the decontamination crews wearing toxicological aprons or wet-weather gear over MOPP gear and locating post decontamination AAs upwind. The accurate documentation of individual exposure to contaminants will be essential for proper medical treatment should those personnel become injured.

7. Postdecontamination Operations

Postdecontamination operations provide for the restoration of combat power to the commander.

 a. Immediately following an attack, recovery operations will be initiated. Operations related to mission-essential operations may continue in a contaminated environment. Those personnel not immediately required to ensure the continuation of mission-essential activities will likely remain in their shelters until the hazard dissipates or decontamination efforts allow resumption of their normal duties.

 b. Postattack operations involve assessing the degree of mission degradation after the attack and reporting postattack readiness.

 c. Commanders will ensure that postattack operations emphasize those actions necessary to restore mission and support functions. Representative postattack actions include the following:

- Assessing damage and casualties.
- Restoring communications for C2.
- Detecting, identifying, marking, isolating, decontaminating, and reporting contaminated areas and equipment.
- Performing casualty decontamination.

d. After completion of operational or thorough decontamination, units close out the sites used for MOPP gear exchange, vehicle wash down, DED, and DTD. In a thorough decontamination, the DED is closed first. The CBRN unit then processes through the DTD and the DTD is closed. Then the CBRN unit marks the area as a contaminated area and reports its exact location to the supported unit using an NBC4 report. See Chapters IV and V for procedures to close a site.

Chapter III
IMMEDIATE DECONTAMINATION

1. Background

Once aware of chemical-biological (CB) contamination on the bare skin, initiate immediate decontamination techniques, without command, by using the personal skin decontamination kit (SDK). Decontaminate the hood, mask, gloves, and weapon using the individual equipment decontamination kit (IEDK). To remove radiological contamination from equipment and personnel, brush it off and wash the area with soap and water.

NOTE: Throughout this manual, SDK refers to the M291 kit and IEDK refers to the M295 kit.

2. Skin Decontamination

Start the skin decontamination techniques within 1 minute of becoming contaminated. Some toxic chemical agents, especially nerve agents, kill within minutes.

a. Chemical.

(1) Use the SDK within 1 minute of contamination of the exposed skin. Instructions for its use are listed on the individual packet within the kit. Flushing the eyes with water is also a critical immediate decontamination action and should occur as soon as possible following contamination.

(2) If an SDK is not available, chemical contamination may be blotted from the skin with a cloth and flushed with water from a canteen. Soap (if available) can be used to wash the agent from the skin. Washing with soap and water (preferably warm water) is the best method for toxic-agent removal if SDKs are not available, but this method is not as effective as using the decontamination kits.

b. Biological. Immediately decontaminate using soap and water when there is a suspected exposure to a BW agent. Careful washing removes nearly all the agent from the skin's surface. Hypochlorite solution or other disinfectants are reserved for gross contamination (e.g., following the spill of a solid or liquid agent from a munition directly onto the skin). Grossly contaminated skin surfaces should be washed with a 0.5 percent chlorine solution, if available, with a contact time of 10 to 15 minutes. See Appendix C for details on how to make this solution.

c. Radiological. To remove radiological dust particles, brush, wash, or wipe them off. If MOPP gear is wet, conduct a MOPP gear exchange as soon as possible because brushing or shaking will not remove the contamination. Wash the exposed areas of the skin with soap and water, and pay particular attention to the hair and fingernails.

3. Personal Wipe Down

The personal wipe down technique is most effective when done within 15 minutes of being contaminated. Using the IEDK, wipe down the mask, hood, gloves, and other essential gear. Use the M295 IEDK, an M291 SDK pad, a stick, or any stiff device to remove the gross contamination from the protective overgarment. Scrape any clumps off the material. Brush off radiological contamination or frozen chemical-agent contamination. See *Multiservice Tactics, Techniques, and Procedures for Nuclear, Biological, and Chemical (NBC) Protection* for detailed information on overgarment protective qualities.

    a. **Chemical.** Decontaminate individual equipment using the IEDKs. The ICAMs, chemical-agent monitors (CAMs), and M8/M9 detector paper are used to detect contamination and monitor the level of contamination on the equipment.

    b. **Biological.** Wash with soap and water. If water is not available, use IEDKs in the same manner as described for chemical-agent decontamination.

    c. **Radiological.** Locate radiological contamination with monitoring equipment and remove by brushing or shaking it off. Avoid breathing the dust particles by wearing the protective mask or a piece of cloth over the nose and mouth. Wipe off the equipment with soapy water (preferably warm) using rags or damp paper towels.

4. Operator Wipe Down

Decontaminate other mission-essential surfaces of the equipment before continuing the mission. Operators wipe down is most effective when done within 15 minutes of contamination.

    a. **Chemical.**

        (1) Decontaminate the surfaces that must be touched on the exterior of the vehicle or the equipment with the M100 SDS. If the M100 SDS is unavailable, scrub the surfaces with super tropical bleach (STB) to decontaminate the equipment.

NOTE: The M100 has not been authorized for use on USN or USMC aircraft. Use hot, soapy water to perform operator's wipe down on all aircraft. Also, STB should not be used to decontaminate aircraft surfaces.

        (2) Scrub STB dry mix or slurry onto the exterior surface with brushes (if available). Wait 30 minutes, and then wash it off. If necessary, use the nonstandard decontaminants that are discussed in Appendix C. The ICAM, CAM, and M8/M9 detector paper are used to determine what surfaces require decontamination.

    b. **Biological.** For decontamination of equipment, a 0.5 percent chlorine solution should be used, if available. A contact time of 30 minutes prior to normal cleaning is required. Bleach is corrosive to most metals and fabrics so rinse thoroughly and oil the metal surfaces after completion. Other nonstandard biological decontaminants are described in Appendix C.

NOTE: Bleach has not been authorized for use on USN or USMC aircraft. Use hot soapy water to perform operators wipe down on all aircraft.

    c. **Radiological.** If surfaces are contaminated by fallout, rain out, neutron-induced contaminations, or any type of radiological agent, use the monitoring equipment to help locate it and then decontaminate the surfaces as required. Decontaminate if detection equipment is not available and contamination is suspected. Radiological contamination can usually be removed by brushing or scraping. Water is effective for flushing away radiological contamination; however, use drainage ditches that flow into a sump to control the runoff. Remember, the contamination has not been destroyed, it has just been moved. The runoff will still be hazardous. If time permits, brush or scoop away the top inch of soil from the fighting position to lower the effects of radiological contamination.

5. Spot Decontamination

a. Purpose. Aircrews and aircraft ground support crews can use spot decontamination as an immediate measure to remove contamination from critical locations. Spot decontamination is performed to limit the spread of contamination on aircraft that requires servicing between sorties, to support ingress and egress of aircraft by crews and passengers, and when performing pre- and postflight inspections. Spot decontamination reduces the contamination on the areas that must be touched during servicing.

b. Procedures.

(1) Ensure that sufficient quantities of soapy water or applicable aircraft cleaner and fresh water are available.

(2) Scrub service areas with soapy water using brushes, rags, or sponges until deposited material, dirt, and grime are removed.

(3) Rinse areas with fresh water from a bucket or hose.

(4) Ensure that service providers decontaminate gloves (SDK, soapy water, or high-test hypochlorite [HTH] solution).

(5) Perform service on the aircraft.

(6) Decontaminate runoff by applying a standard or nonstandard decontaminant to the deck/ground/airfield. Runoff can be hosed overboard or into collection sumps. If runoff is hosed without prior decontamination, it should be treated as contaminated.

THIS PAGE IS INTENTIONALLY LEFT BLANK.

Chapter IV
OPERATIONAL DECONTAMINATION

1. Background

Operational decontamination limits the spread and transfer of contamination, allows temporary relief from MOPP4, and facilitates additional decontamination requirements. By speeding up the weathering process, the need for a thorough decontamination may be eliminated. This chapter focuses on land forces operational decontamination TTP. This process will likely require about a 120-square-yard area (depending on the number of contaminated vehicles) and may not require a nearby water source. An operational decontamination consists of a vehicle wash down and a MOPP gear exchange. The techniques that may be used to conduct an operational decontamination include the following:

- Decentralized control for a company-size unit.
- Centralized control for a battalion-size unit.
- Centralized control for a brigade-size unit.

NOTES:

1. See Naval Ships Technical Manual (NSTM) 470 and NSTM 070 for operational decontamination procedures and Naval Air (NAVAIR) 00-80T-121 for TTP on USN and USMC aircrews, aircraft, and support equipment.

2. See *Recovery Operations in a Chemical, Biological, Radiological, and Nuclear (CBRN) Environment* for other information on USN and USMC operational decontamination procedures.

3. See Chapters VIII and IX for additional information on aviation and shipboard decontamination, respectively.

4. Aircrew CBRN IPE/advanced logistics support site (ALSS) configurations for the operational decontamination technique do not allow MOPP gear exchange. See NAVAIR 00-80T-121 for procedures to doff contaminated aircrew CBRN IPE and ALSS.

5. See Air Force Manual (AFMAN) 32-4005, AFMAN 32-4017, AFMAN 10-2602, and USAF Technical Order (TO) 11C15-1-3 for TTP on USAF main operating base (MOB), colocated operating base (COB), and bare operating base operational decontamination.

6. See Chapter VII for further information on fixed-site, port, and airfield decontamination.

2. Planning

Operational decontamination requires a well-thought-out plan to be successful. The advantages and disadvantages of operational decontamination techniques are listed in Table IV-1, page IV-2.

Table IV-1. Advantages and Disadvantages of Operational Decontamination Techniques

	Decentralized Control (Company-Size)	Centralized Control (Battalion-Size)	Centralized Control (Brigade-Size)
Advantages	Flexibility Dispersion	C2 Flexibility Dispersion Planning Sustained operations	C2 Synchronized support assets Rehearsal Time required Planning Sustained operations
Disadvantages	C2 Synchronized support assets Rehearsal Time required Planning Sustained operations	Synchronized support assets Rehearsal Time required	Flexibility Dispersion

a. Decentralized control of a company-size element undergoing decontamination is provided by the contaminated unit's commander. The advantages of this method are that it is flexible and it conforms to the METT-TC conditions. It also disperses the units over a large area, making them less vulnerable to attack by the enemy. The disadvantages are that C2 is more difficult, it is difficult to synchronize the support assets to one location, it may require rehearsal time, it takes more time overall, planning assets are not available at that level, and the company cannot sustain operations without additional support from higher HQ.

b. Centralized control of a battalion-size unit is similar to the above except that the unit CBRN NCO controls the decontamination. The unit commander and the CBRN NCO direct the site setup and provide security and C2 for the selected site. The CBRN NCO travels with the decontamination element and communicates via the radio.

c. Centralized control for a brigade-size unit is done when decontamination assets within the brigade have been consolidated. In this technique, the brigade CBRN NCO performs those functions described for the battalion CBRN NCO.

3. Phases

The three phases for an operational decontamination are preparation, execution, and site clearance (see Table IV-2).

Table IV-2. Operational Decontamination Phases

Area	Actions
Preparation	
Decontamination assessment	Identify the personnel and equipment to be decontaminated.
Coordination	Request decontamination support. The CBRNE section conducts coordination with the contaminated unit on the linkup point. Decontamination operations should be done between 1 and 6 hours after becoming contaminated.

Table IV-2. Operational Decontamination Phases (Continued)

Area	Actions
Preparation	
Site selection (selected by the controlling HQ)	Ensure that the site is off the main route but has easy access. Ensure that the site has a large enough area (120 square yards per site for a squad-size element). Ensure that the site has good overhead concealment. Ensure that the site has food and water sources (plan for 100 gallons of water per vehicle). Ensure that the site has good drainage.
Linkup	Ensure that the NCOIC knows where to link up with the contaminated unit and knows the location for site setup. Radio communication is essential for the operations.
Site setup	Ensure that the decontamination element is positioned properly and ready to dispense hot, soapy water. Ensure that the contaminated unit sets up and operates the MOPP gear exchange at the same time as the vehicle wash down. Consider contamination runoff when positioning the decontamination element.
Execution	
Site control	Ensure that the drivers of the contaminated vehicles know when to move into position at the wash-down location. Ensure that the contaminated unit has provided site security.
Vehicle spray down	Ensure that the decontamination site NCOIC is processing vehicles at a rate of 2 to 3 minutes per vehicle.
MOPP gear exchange (buddy team)	Ensure that personnel are going through the MOPP gear exchange at the rate of 60 minutes per squad/crew.
Site Clearance	
Cleanup	Ensure that the MOPP gear exchange area is cleaned up (NCOIC).
Marking	Ensure that the team properly marks the decontamination site (NCOIC).
Reporting	Send the NBC5 report forward (NCOIC).

a. Preparation.

(1) The preparation phase starts with the decision to conduct an operational decontamination and ends with a site that is set up and ready for operation. The ICAM/CAM is used to identify which vehicles need decontaminating, and decontamination support is requested.

(2) Coordination with higher HQ includes identifying the linkup point and the unit that will provide the decontamination support. SOI are exchanged, and the technique (decentralized company-size control, centralized battalion size control, or centralized brigade-size control) is selected. The number and type of vehicles and the number of personnel for a MOPP gear exchange are provided.

(3) Site selection is done by the controlling HQ. The site may have been designated in the OPORD or selected based on the current METT-TC.

(4) Linkup at the designated point includes establishing security, positioning necessary marshalling areas, camouflaging removal points, designating the direction of flow into and out of the site, and ensuring that unit supply has sufficient replacement MOPP gear.

(5) Site setup requires the decontamination crew to position itself upwind from the entrance, set up the MOPP gear exchange about 164 feet upwind from the vehicle wash down at a 45° angle, and notify the contaminated unit when the site is ready.

b. Execution.

(1) The execution phase starts with establishing positive control over the site and ends with processing the last contaminated vehicle and person through the site. Vehicles move from the predecontamination area to the site upon order or by watching the vehicle ahead. The assistant driver leaves the vehicle and proceeds to the MOPP gear exchange point. The contaminated unit provides security. Throughout the execution phase, periodic wind checks should be performed to ensure that the wind has not shifted and placed the soldiers conducting the MOPP gear exchange in a CBRN hazard.

(2) Each vehicle receives a 2- to 4-minute wash down with hot, soapy water and moves to a point near the MOPP gear exchange area. Vehicles can be washed with cold, soapy water or only cold water when hot, soapy water is not available. Any remaining personnel requiring a MOPP gear exchange will get one then. When the squad or crew has finished, personnel remount the vehicles and move into an after-decontamination AA to await further instructions or move to their next battle position.

(3) Vehicle Wash Down.

(a) A vehicle wash down may be conducted with or without standard decontamination equipment in a one- or two-lane configuration. An unsupported wash down requires the contaminated unit to use its assigned decontamination apparatuses or other alternate washing equipment that can produce 60 to 120 pounds per square inch (psi) of water pressure. The capacity to heat water and inject soap increases the effectiveness. A supported wash down requires decontamination equipment assets that are organic to the unit or from a supporting decontamination unit. A two-lane wash down is simply two one-lane wash downs parallel to each other (see Figure IV-1).

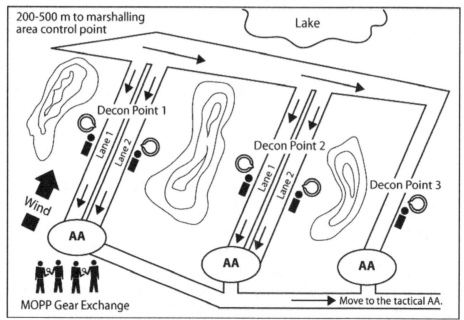

Figure IV-1. Two-Lane Wash Down

(b) Other configurations are limited only by the constraints of the METT-TC. Figure IV-2 illustrates a dispersed operational decontamination setup. Table IV-3, page IV-6, describes the vehicle wash-down process.

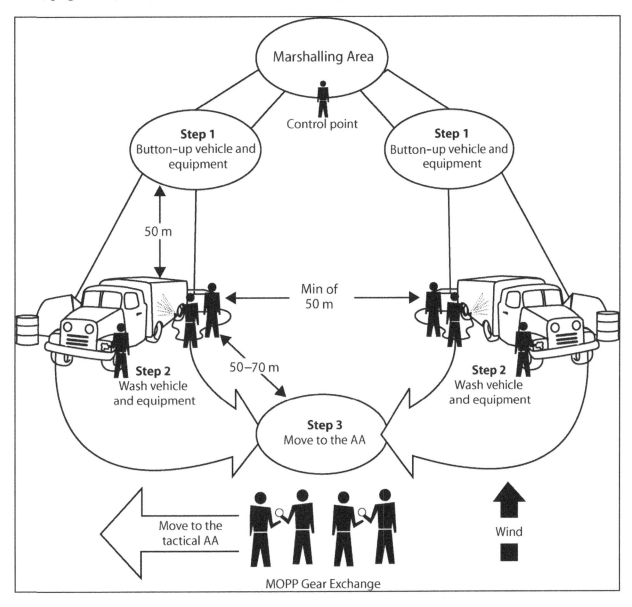

Figure IV-2. Dispersed Operational-Decontamination Setup

Table IV-3. Vehicle Wash-Down Process

Steps	Equipment	Procedures
1. Marshal the area. The unit is tactically dispersed. Personnel at the control point direct movement.	None	Personnel at the control point supervise the preparation of vehicles and direct movement out of the AA.
2. Button up.	None	The crew closes all access doors, hatches, windows, and other openings. They remove camouflage and cover muzzles. If required, they (less drivers) move to the MOPP gear exchange area. They move to the wash area on order.
3. Wash down.	Delivery system (such as the M12, M17, MPDS, 65- or 125-GPM pump, firefighting equipment, and so forth) that delivers hot, soapy water at 60 to 120 psi. Sufficient water, fuel, and detergent for vehicles.	Personnel wash equipment from top to bottom. The decontamination crew wears a TAP or wet-weather gear over MOPP gear.
4. Move to AA.	None	Vehicles move to the MOPP gear exchange area (if required) or the next battle position.

(4) MOPP Gear Exchange. A MOPP gear exchange can be done with a buddy team, a triple buddy team, or an individual (emergency). For planning purposes, estimate 30 minutes for a squad or a platoon-size element to complete the exchange. Since individual performance is severely degraded after 6 hours at MOPP4, the MOPP gear exchange should be scheduled before that time.

(a) Buddy Team Method. This method uses pairs of warfighters under the supervision of their squad leader/team leader (TL) to conduct the buddy team MOPP gear exchange. See Table IV-4 for the procedures for the buddy team method MOPP gear exchange with the joint-service, lightweight, integrated suit technology (JSLIST). See Table IV-5, page IV-11, for BDO MOPP gear exchange steps. See Table IV-6, page IV-19, for the step-by-step procedures for units equipped with the combat vehicle crewman uniform system (CVCUS)/chemical protective undergarment (CPU).

(b) Triple Buddy Team Method. This method is used by personnel equipped with the M40A1, M42, or M43 mask with the quick-doff hood. A third person is needed to hold the filter canister and hose to prevent pulling the mask away from the person's face. See Table IV-7, page IV-23, for the step-by-step procedures for this method. For units equipped with the CVCUS/CPU, see Table IV-8, page IV-28.

(c) Individual (Emergency) Method. This method is used only when a person does not have a buddy to help him and the risk of MOPP gear failure demands that an exchange occur. See Table IV-9, page IV-32, for the step-by-step procedures for this method. For units equipped with the CVCUS/CPU, see Table IV-10, page IV-36. For the procedures for the individual (emergency) method of MOPP gear exchange with the JSLIST, see Table IV-11, page IV-39.

c. **Site Clearance.** The site clearance phase includes cleanup, marking, and reporting. METT-TC will dictate the cleanup requirements. Contaminated waste is collected from the operational decontamination. See Appendix K for information on site clearance procedures.

Table IV-4. Steps for the Buddy Team Method of MOPP Gear Exchange With the JSLIST Chemical-Protective Ensemble

Required Steps	Contamination Type	Required Equipment	Required Procedures
1. Decontaminate gear (removes gross contamination from individual gear [weapon, helmet, load-bearing equipment, and mask carrier]).	All	Four long-handled brushes A large piece of plastic (poncho or similar material) STB (bulk) Shovel	The individual mixes three parts earth to two parts STB.
	CB	One 30-gallon container STB dry mix One IEDK	The individual removes and discards the chemical-protective helmet cover. He brushes or rubs STB onto his individual gear (helmet and mask carrier) and the hose of the M42 or M43 mask if worn. He gently shakes off any excess STB and sets aside his gear on an uncontaminated surface.
	Radiological	Hot, soapy water	The individual brushes or wipes radiological contamination from his individual gear. He washes it with hot, soapy water (if available) and then sets it aside to dry on an uncontaminated surface (plastic, poncho, or similar material).
2. Prepare to decontaminate (facilitates later removal of overgarment trousers and overboots).	All	Cutting tool	Buddy 1 removes the M9 paper from Buddy 2's overgarment. He unties the bow in Buddy 2's coat retention cord if tied. He unfastens the webbing-strip snap at the bottom front of Buddy 2's coat and releases the coat retention-cord loop at the waist. Buddy 1 then loosens the bottom of the coat by pulling the material away from Buddy 2's body. **NOTES: 1. If wearing the M43 protective mask, tie the microphone cord to the hose of the mask. 2. The M40 voice amplifier (M7) and the M42 detachable microphone cannot be decontaminated and will be disposed of as contaminated waste; however, ensure that these items are contaminated before disposing of them.** Buddy 1 unfastens and loosely refastens the hook-and-pile fasteners at Buddy 2's wrists and ankles. He unfastens or cuts the fasteners on Buddy 2's overboots. **NOTE: A person can do this step by himself or with the help of his buddy.**

Table IV-4. Steps for the Buddy Team Method of MOPP Gear Exchange With the JSLIST Chemical-Protective Ensemble (Continued)

Required Steps	Contamination Type	Required Equipment	Required Procedures
3. Decontaminate mask and hood (removes gross contamination).	CB	Two IEDKs per person	Buddy 1 instructs Buddy 2 to decontaminate his own gloves using an IEDK. Buddy 1 instructs Buddy 2 to place two fingers (thumb and forefinger) on his own voicemitter to ensure the mask-to-face integrity. Buddy 1 uses and IEDK to wipe Buddy 2's eye lens outserts from the top, down **NOTE: Do not press so hard that you break Buddy 2's face mask seal. If wearing the JSLIST hood, stop here and move on to Step 4.** If wearing the one-piece hood or the quick-doff hood, Buddy 1 wipes the rest of Buddy 2's hood from the top of the head to the bottom of the hood. After he has finished wiping Buddy 2's mask and hood, he must wipe his own gloves in preparation for rolling Buddy 2's hood. He starts from the rear and rolls Buddy 2's hood, using 2-inch tucks, until it reaches the center of his head. He rolls the front of Buddy 2's hood tightly under the outlet valve and filter. He ensures that the hood is off Buddy 2's garment.
	Radiological	Three containers (about 3-gallon capacity) Two sponges Soapy water Rinse water Paper towels or similar drying material	Buddy 1 wipes Buddy 2's mask and hood (if wearing the one-piece or quick-doff hood) with a sponge dipped in hot, soapy water and rinses them with a sponge dipped in clean water. He dries Buddy 2's mask and hood with paper towels or rags. Buddy 2 wipes his own gloves. **NOTE: Cool, soapy water is not as effective for removing contamination, but it can be used if you scrub longer. If the water supply is limited, use drinking water from a canteen and a wet sponge or cloth. If water is not available, brush off the radioactive dust particles.**
4. Remove chemical-protective coat (limits the spread of agents and helps prevent agents from penetrating through to the undergarments or the skin).	All	Two discard containers (e.g., plastic bags)	Buddy 2 locates the suspender snap couplers on the outside of his coat and releases them. If Buddy 2 is wearing the JSLIST hood, then Buddy 1 unties Buddy 2's draw cord, presses the barrel lock release, and unsnaps the barrel lock. **NOTE: If Buddy 1 has difficulty grasping the barrel lock, he should use the draw cord to pull the barrel lock away from the mask. This will allow him to grasp and unfasten the barrel lock without touching the interior of the hood.** Buddy 1 unfastens Buddy 2's front closure flap and pulls the slide fastener down from the chin to the bottom of the coat. Buddy 1 instructs Buddy 2 to turn around. Buddy 1 grasps Buddy 2's hood, rolls it inside out, and pulls it off Buddy 2's head. Buddy 1 grasps Buddy 2's coat at the shoulders, instructs him to make a fist to prevent the chemical-protective gloves from coming off, and pulls the coat down and away from him, ensuring that the black part of the coat is not touched. **NOTE: If there is difficulty removing the coat in this manner, Buddy 2 should pull one arm out at a time.** Buddy 1 lays the coat on the ground, black side up. **NOTE: Buddy 2 will use the coat later as an uncontaminated surface to stand on when putting on his new overgarment.**

Table IV-4. Steps for the Buddy Team Method of MOPP Gear Exchange With the JSLIST Chemical-Protective Ensemble (Continued)

Required Steps	Contamination Type	Required Equipment	Required Procedures
5. Remove chemical-protective trousers.	All	Two discard containers (from step 4)	Buddy 1 unfastens Buddy 2's hook-and-pile fastener at the waistband, unfastens the two front closure snaps, and opens the fly slide fastener on the front of the trousers. Buddy 1 grasps Buddy 2's trousers at the hips and pulls them down to his knees. Buddy 1 instructs Buddy 2 to lift one leg (with the foot pointed down and bent slightly at the knee for stability). Buddy 1 grasps the trouser leg near Buddy 2's elevated foot with a hand on each side and pulls the trouser leg in an alternating motion until Buddy 2 can step out of it. Repeat the process for the other leg. Buddy 1 discards the trousers. **CAUTION** Care must be taken to avoid contaminating Buddy 2's clothing or skin.
6. Remove chemical-protective overboots.	All	Two discard containers (from step 4)	Buddy 1 Instructs Buddy 2 to loosen his overboots by alternately stepping on each heel and pulling up on his foot. Buddy 1 pulls off Buddy 2's overboots (one overboot at a time), and Buddy 2 steps directly onto the coat spread on the ground as each foot is withdrawn from the overboot. **NOTE: Buddy 2 may put his hand on Buddy 1 for balance but must then decontaminate his gloves.** Buddy 1 discards the overboots.
7. Remove chemical-protective gloves and liners.	All	Two discard containers (from step 4)	Buddy 2 holds the fingertips of his gloves and partially slides his hand out. When the fingers of both hands are free, he holds his arms away from his body and lets the gloves drop off, away from the black side of the coat. Buddy 2 removes the glove liners. Buddy 1 discards the chemical-protective gloves and liners. **NOTE: If Buddy 2 has difficulty removing the gloves, then Buddy 1 can assist.** **CAUTION** Buddy 1 and Buddy 2 must take care to avoid letting their gloves come in contact with the coat spread on the ground.
8. Put on chemical-protective trousers.	All	One JSLIST chemical-protective ensemble per person	Buddy 1 opens the package containing the new trousers without touching the inside of the package. Buddy 2 removes the trousers. While standing on an uncontaminated surface, Buddy 2 puts on his trousers, closes the slide fastener, and fastens the two fly opening snaps. He pulls his suspenders over his shoulders and fastens the snap couplers. He adjusts the length of the suspenders to ensure a comfortable fit. He adjusts the hook-and-pile fastener at the waistband for a snug fit. **CAUTION** Buddy 2 must take care to ensure that the trousers touch only the uncontaminated surface.

Table IV-4. Steps for the Buddy Team Method of MOPP Gear Exchange With the JSLIST Chemical-Protective Ensemble (Continued)

Required Steps	Contamination Type	Required Equipment	Required Procedures
9. Put on chemical-protective coat.	All	One JSLIST chemical-protective ensemble per person	Buddy 1 opens the package containing the new coat without touching the inside of the package. Buddy 2 removes the coat without touching the outside of the package. He puts on the coat, pulls the slide fastener up as far as his chest, and secures the front closure hook-and-pile fastener on the front flap up as far as his chest. He pulls the bottom of the coat down over his trousers. He grasps the loop on the back of the overgarment, pulls the loop away from the coat, and brings the loop forward between his legs, pulling on it so that the bottom of the coat fits snugly over the trousers. He places the loop over the webbing-strip snap and fastens it. He adjusts the coat retention cord if necessary and ties the excess cord in a bow.
10. Put on chemical-protective overboots.	All	One set of chemical-protective overboots per person	Buddy 1 opens the package containing the new overboots without touching the inside of the package. Buddy 2 removes the overboots without touching the outside of the package. He puts the overboots on over his combat boots and secures the fasteners. He pulls his trouser legs over the overboots and secures the two hook-and-pile fasteners on each ankle so that they fit snugly around the overboots.
11. Put on chemical-protective hood.	All	One JSLIST chemical-protective ensemble per person	Buddy 2 puts the hood on his head. He completely closes the front slide fastener on the coat and secures the hook-and-pile fastener on the front flap as far as the top of the slide fastener. He places the edge of the hood around the edge of the mask and secures the hook-and-pile fastener on the hood. **WARNING** The barrel lock release button must face away from the rear of the user when worn to avoid the barrel lock from unfastening and possibly exposing the user to contamination. He pulls the draw cord tight around the edge of the mask, snaps the ends of the barrel lock together, squeezes both ends of the barrel lock while pulling the draw cord, and slides the barrel lock up under his chin to keep the cord in place. Without touching Buddy 2, Buddy 1 inspects the hood and mask to ensure that the hood is positioned properly and the skin is not exposed. Buddy 2 adjusts the hood and mask as directed. If Buddy 1's assistance is required for proper adjustment, Buddy 2 will decontaminate Buddy 1's gloves before he touches the hood or mask.

Table IV-4. Steps for the Buddy Team Method of MOPP Gear Exchange With the JSLIST Chemical-Protective Ensemble (Continued)

Required Steps	Contamination Type	Required Equipment	Required Procedures
12. Put on chemical-protective gloves and liners.	All	One set of chemical-protective gloves with liners per person (correct size) M9 detector paper	Buddy 1 opens the package containing the new chemical-protective gloves and liners without touching the inside of the package. Buddy 2 removes the gloves and liners without touching the outside of the package. He puts on the gloves and liners, pulls the cuffs of the coat over the chemical-protective gloves, and fastens the hook-and-pile fasteners on each sleeve of the coat. He puts the M9 detector paper on as required by the SOP.
13. Reverse roles.	All	One JSLIST chemical-protective ensemble per person One set of chemical-protective gloves with liners per person (correct size)	Buddy 1 and Buddy 2 reverse roles and repeat steps 2 through 13.
14. Secure gear.	All	One chemical-protective helmet cover per person	Buddy 1 places the new chemical-protective helmet cover on the PASGT helmet if used. He uses the buddy system to check the fit of all secured gear.

Table IV-5. Steps for the BDO MOPP Gear Exchange

Required Steps	Contamination Type	Required Equipment	Required Procedures
1. Decontaminate gear (removes gross contamination from individual gear [weapons, helmet, load-bearing equipment, and mask carrier]).	All	Four long-handled brushes A large piece of plastic (poncho or similar material) Shovels	The individual mixes three parts earth to two parts STB.
	CB	One 30-gallon container STB dry mix One IEDK	The individual removes and discards the chemical-protective helmet cover if worn. He brushes or rubs STB onto his individual gear (helmet and mask carrier) and the hose of the M42 or M43 mask if worn. He gently shakes off any excess STB and sets aside his gear on an uncontaminated surface.
	Radiological	Hot, soapy water	The individual brushes or wipes radiological contamination from his individual gear. He washes it with hot, soapy water (if available) and then sets it aside to dry on an uncontaminated surface (plastic, poncho, or similar material).

Table IV-5 Steps for the BDO MOPP Gear Exchange (Continued)

Required Steps	Contamination Type	Required Equipment	Required Procedures
2. Prepare to decontaminate (facilitates later removal of BDO trousers and overboots).	All	Cutting tool	Buddy 1 unfastens the shoulder straps on Buddy 2's hood, pulls them over his shoulder, and reattaches them to the hook-and-pile fasteners. He loosens the draw cord on Buddy 2's hood. The M40 voice amplifier (M7) and the M42A2 detachable microphone cannot be decontaminated and will be disposed of as contaminated waste; however, ensure that these items are contaminated before disposing of them. Buddy 1 removes the M9 detector paper from Buddy 2's overgarment. He unties Buddy 2's draw cords on the trouser legs. He unzips Buddy 2's trouser legs and rolls a cuff in each trouser leg, ensuring that the cuffs do not come above the tops of his overboots (see Figure IV-3). He unfastens or cuts the fasteners on Buddy 2's overboots. When wearing overboots, he unsnaps both quick releases on Buddy 2's overboots. **NOTE: An individual can do this step by himself or with the help of his buddy.**

Figure IV-3. Rolling the Cuff in the Trouser

Table IV-5. Steps for the BDO MOPP Gear Exchange (Continued)

Required Steps	Contamination Type	Required Equipment	Required Procedures
3. Decontaminate mask and hood (removes gross contamination).	CB	Two IEDKs per person	Buddy 1 uses an IEDK to wipe Buddy 2's eye lens outserts from the top, down. **NOTE: Do not press so hard that you break Buddy 2's face mask seal.** Buddy 1 then wipes the rest of Buddy 2's hood from the top of the head to the bottom of the hood (see Figure IV-4). After he has finished wiping Buddy 2's mask, he must wipe his own gloves in preparation for rolling Buddy 2's hood. He starts at the rear and rolls Buddy 2's hood, using 2-inch tucks, until it reaches the center of his head (see Figure IV-5, page IV-14). He rolls the front of Buddy 2's hood tightly under the outlet valve and filter. He ensures that the hood is off of Buddy 2's BDO. **CAUTION** Place two fingers on the voicemitter to prevent the mask seal from breaking.
	Radiological	Two containers (about 4-gallon capacity) Two sponges Soapy water Rinse water Paper towels or similar drying material	Buddy 1 wipes Buddy 2's mask and hood with a sponge dipped in hot, soapy water and rinses them with a sponge dipped in clean water. He dries Buddy 2's mask and hood with paper towels or rags. Buddy 2 wipes his own gloves. **NOTES: 1. Cool, soapy water is not as effective for removing contamination, but it can be used if you scrub longer. If the water supply is limited, use drinking water from a canteen and wet a sponge or cloth. If water is not available, brush off the radioactive dust particles. 2. Do not reverse roles. Only Buddy 2's hood will be decontaminated and rolled at this time.**

Figure IV-4. Wiping From the Head to the Bottom of the Hood

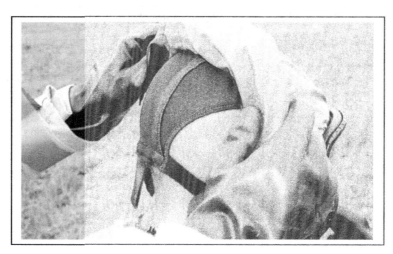

Figure IV-5. Rolling the Hood to the Center of the Head

Table IV-5. Steps for the BDO MOPP Gear Exchange (Continued)

Required Steps	Contamination Type	Required Equipment	Required Procedures
4. Remove BDO and overboots (limits the spread of agents and helps prevent agents from penetrating through to the undergarments or the skin).	All	Two discard containers (e.g., plastic bags)	Buddy 1 grasps Buddy 2's BDO jacket, unsnaps the snaps individually (see Figure IV-6), and unties the draw cord at the bottom of the jacket. He unfastens the hook-and-pile fasteners at the wrist of Buddy 2's jacket and then refastens them. He unfastens the hook-and-pile fastener over the zippered front of Buddy 2's jacket and unzips the jacket. He grasps Buddy 2's jacket at the shoulders and instructs him to make a fist. He then pulls Buddy 2's jacket down and away from him, ensuring that the black part of the jacket is not touched (see Figure IV-7). He lays Buddy 2's BDO jacket on the ground, black side up (it will be used to stand on later). He carefully unfastens and unzips Buddy 2's trousers. **NOTE: Do not loosen Buddy 2's waist tabs.** He instructs Buddy 2 to loosen his overboots by alternately stepping on each heel and pulling up on his foot (see Figure IV-8). He grasps Buddy 2's trousers and pulls them down to his knees. He instructs Buddy 2 to walk out of his trousers and overboots simultaneously and step onto the black side of the jacket (see Figure IV-9, page IV-16). Buddy 2 should step onto the jacket wearing his mask, BDU, combat boots, and gloves.

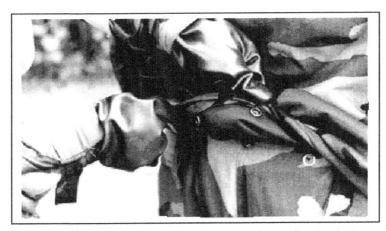

Figure IV-6. Unsnapping the Trousers from the Jacket

Figure IV-7. Pulling the Jacket Down and Away

Figure IV-8. Loosening the Overboots

Figure IV-9. Stepping on the Black Lining of the Jacket

Table IV-5. Steps for the BDO MOPP Gear Exchange (Continued)

Required Steps	Contamination Type	Required Equipment	Required Procedures
5. Remove gloves.	All	Two discard containers (from step 4)	The individual holds the fingertips of his gloves and partially slides his hand out. When the fingers of both hands are free, he holds his arms away from his body and lets the gloves drop (see Figure IV-10).
6. Put on BDO.	All	One set of CPOs per person	Buddy 1 opens the package containing the new BDO without touching the inside of the package. Buddy 2 pulls out the BDO without touching the outside of the package. He puts on the BDO and fastens it, leaving the trouser legs open (see Figure IV-11). **NOTE: Do not reverse roles. Only Buddy 2 will put on the clean overgarment at this time.**

Figure IV-10. Removing the Gloves

Figure IV-11. Putting on the New BDO

Table IV-5. Steps for the BDO MOPP Gear Exchange (Continued)

Required Steps	Contamination Type	Required Equipment	Required Procedures
7. Put on overboots and gloves.	All	One set of chemical-protective overboots per person One set of chemical-protective gloves per person (correct size) M9 detector paper	Buddy 1 opens the package of clean overboots without touching the inside of the package. Buddy 2 removes the overboots from the package without touching the outside of the package, puts them on, and fastens his trouser legs. Buddy 1 opens the package of clean gloves without touching the inside of the package. Buddy 2 removes the gloves from the package without touching the outside of the package and puts them on. Buddy 2 puts on the M9 detector paper (see Figure IV-12, page IV-18). **NOTE: Do not reverse roles. Only Buddy 2 will put on the clean overboots and gloves at this time. The gloves and overboots will have a light powdery coating. This is normal. It is not necessary to remove it. It will not affect the protective qualities.**
8. Secure hood.	All	One IEDK	Buddy 1 uses an IEDK to wipe Buddy 2's gloves. He unrolls Buddy 2's hood, attaches the straps, and tightens the neck cord. Buddy 1 and Buddy 2 reverse roles and repeat steps 2 through 8.

Table IV-5. Steps for the BDO MOPP Gear Exchange (Continued)

Required Steps	Contamination Type	Required Equipment	Required Procedures
9. Secure gear.	All	One chemical-protective helmet cover per person	Each individual secures his individual gear and puts it back on. He puts on a new chemical-protective helmet cover and moves to the area of assembly. He uses the Buddy system to check the fit of all secured gear.

Figure IV-12. Putting on M9 Detector Paper

Table IV-6. Steps for the CVCUS and CPU (Buddy Team Method) MOPP Gear Exchange

Required Steps	Contamination Type	Required Equipment	Required Procedures
1. Decontaminate gear (removes gross contamination from individual gear [weapons, helmet, load-bearing equipment, and mask carrier]).	All	Four long-handled brushes A large piece of plastic (poncho or similar material) STB (bulk) Shovel	The individual mixes three parts earth to two parts STB.
	CB	One 30-gallon container STB dry mix One IEDK	The individual removes and discards the chemical-protective helmet cover. He brushes or rubs the STB onto his individual gear (helmet and mask carrier) and the hose of the M42 or M43 mask if worn. He gently shakes off any excess STB and sets aside his gear on an uncontaminated surface.
	Radiological	Hot, soapy water	The individual brushes or wipes radiological contamination from his individual gear. He washes it with hot, soapy water (if available) and then sets it aside to dry on an uncontaminated surface (plastic, poncho, or similar material).

Table IV-6. Steps for the CVCUS and CPU (Buddy Team Method) MOPP Gear Exchange (Continued)

Required Steps	Contamination Type	Required Equipment	Required Procedures
2. Prepare to decontaminate (facilitates MOPP gear removal).	All	Cutting tool	Buddy 1 unfastens the shoulder straps on Buddy 2's hood, pulls them over his shoulder, and reattaches them to the hook-and-pile fastener. He loosens the draw cord on Buddy 2's hood. He removes the M9 detector paper from Buddy 2's CVCUS. He unzips the ankles on both legs of Buddy 2's CVCUS. He unfastens or cuts the fasteners on Buddy 2's overboots. **NOTE: A person can do this step by himself or with the help of his buddy.**
3. Decontaminate mask and hood (removes gross contamination).	CB	Two IEDKs per person	Buddy 1 instructs Buddy 2 to decontaminate his own gloves using an IEDK. Buddy 1 instructs Buddy 2 to place two fingers (thumb and forefinger) to his own front voicemitter to secure the mask to his face for seal integrity. Buddy 1 uses an IEDK to wipe Buddy 2's eye lens outserts from the top, down. **NOTE: Do not press so hard that you break Buddy 2's face mask seal.** He then wipes the rest of Buddy 2's hood from the top of the head to the bottom of the hood (see Figure IV-4, page IV-13). After he has finished wiping Buddy 2's mask, he must wipe his own gloves in preparation for rolling Buddy 2's hood. He starts from the rear and rolls Buddy 2's hood, using 2-inch tucks, until it reaches the center of his head (see Figure IV-5, page IV-14). He rolls the front of Buddy 2's hood tightly under the outlet valve and filter. He ensures that the hood is off of Buddy 2's garment.
	Radiological	Three containers (about 4-gallon capacity) Two sponges Soapy water Rinse water Paper towels or similar drying material	Buddy 1 wipes Buddy 2's mask and hood with a sponge dipped in hot, soapy water and rinses them with a sponge dipped in clean water. He dries Buddy 2's mask and hood with paper towels or rags. Buddy 2 wipes his own gloves. **NOTE: Cool, soapy water is not as effective for removing contamination, but it can be used if scrubbed longer. If the water supply is limited, use drinking water from a canteen and wet a sponge or cloth. If water is not available, brush off the radioactive dust particles.** Only Buddy 2's mask and hood will be decontaminated and rolled at this time.
4. Remove CVCUS and overboots (limits the spread of contamination).	All	Two discard containers (e.g., plastic bags)	Buddy 1 opens all the zippers on Buddy 2's CVCUS in the following order: wrist, ankles, and front. While standing behind Buddy 2, Buddy 1 grasps the shoulders of Buddy 2's CVCUS and instructs him to make a fist to ensure that his gloves do not come off. He then pulls Buddy 2's CVCUS down below his knees, turning it inside out. Buddy 1 unzips Buddy 2's CPU jacket and removes it by grasping it at the shoulders, pulling it down, and turning it inside out (see Figure IV-13). He places it along side Buddy 2 with the clean side up.

Table IV-6. Steps for the CVCUS/CPU (Buddy Team Method) MOPP Gear Exchange (Continued)

Required Steps	Contamination Type	Required Equipment	Required Procedures
5. Remove overboots and gloves.	All	Two discard containers (from step 4)	Buddy 2 partially removes his overboots by alternately stepping on each heel and pulling up on his foot. Buddy 1 grasps one leg of Buddy 2's CVCUS and his overboot and instructs him to remove his leg and foot simultaneously. As Buddy 2 removes each leg and foot, he steps directly onto the clean inside of the CPU jacket (see Figure IV-14). Buddy 1 discards the overboots. Buddy 2 holds the fingertips of his gloves and partially slides his hand out. When the fingers of both hands are free, he holds his arm away from his body and lets the gloves drop. Buddy 2 removes his protective glove liners. Buddy 1 discards the chemical-protective gloves and liners.

Figure IV-13. Removing the Garment and Turning it Inside Out

Figure IV-14. Removing Your Leg and Foot From the Garment

Table IV-6. Steps for the CVCUS and CPU (Buddy Team Method) MOPP Gear Exchange (Continued)

Steps	Contamination Type	Required Equipment	Required Procedures
6. Remove CPU trousers and combat boots.	All	Two discard containers	Buddy 2 partially removes his boots by alternately stepping on each heel and pulling up on his foot. Buddy 2 removes his foot, stepping directly onto the clean side of the CPU jacket. Repeat the procedure for the other foot. Next, Buddy 1 will remove Buddy 2's CPU trousers by pulling down on the sides and turning them inside out. Buddy 2 is now stripped to his underwear and mask and is ready to put on new clothing. Combat boots should remain beside Buddy 2 on the clean area of the CPU jacket. Buddy 1 discards the CVCUS and CPU trousers. **CAUTION** Use extreme caution to ensure that the outside of the CPU does not touch the skin or underclothing of Buddy 2 or the combat boots.
7. Put on CPU and CVCUS.	All	One CPU and CVCUS per person	Buddy 1 opens the package containing the new CPU without touching the inside of the package. Buddy 2 pulls out the CPU without touching the outside of the package. He puts on the new clothing in the following order: CPU trousers, CPU jacket, combat boots, and CVCUS (over the CPU).
8. Put on overboots and gloves.	All	One set of chemical-protective overboots per person One set of chemical-protective gloves per person M9 detector paper	Buddy 1 opens the package of clean overboots without touching the inside of the package. Buddy 2 removes the overboots without touching the outside of the package and puts them on. Buddy 1 opens the package of clean gloves without touching the inside. Buddy 2 removes the gloves without touching the outside of the package and puts them on. Buddy 2 puts on the M9 detector paper (see Figure IV-15). **NOTE: The gloves and overboots will have a light powdery coating. This is normal. It is not necessary to remove it. It will not affect the protective qualities.**

Figure IV-15. Reapplying the M9 Detector Paper

Table IV-6. Steps for the CVCUS and CPU (Buddy Team Method) MOPP Gear Exchange (Continued)

Steps	Contamination Type	Required Equipment	Required Procedures
9. Secure hood.	CB	One IEDK	Buddy 1 wipes his rubber gloves with an IEDK. He unrolls Buddy 2's hood, attaches the straps, and tightens the neck cord. Buddy 1 and Buddy 2 reverse roles and repeat steps 2 through 9.
10. Secure gear.	All	One chemical-protective helmet cover per person	Each individual secures his individual gear and puts it back on. He puts on a new chemical-protective helmet cover and moves to the area of assembly. He uses the buddy system to check the fit of all secured gear.

Table IV-7. Steps for the Triple Buddy Method of MOPP Gear Exchange With the M40A1 and M42

Steps	Contamination Type	Required Equipment	Required Procedures
1. Decontaminate gear (removes gross contamination from individual gear [weapons, helmet, load-bearing equipment, and mask carrier]).	All	Four long-handled brushes A large piece of plastic (poncho or similar material) STB (bulk) Shovel	The individual mixes three parts earth to two parts STB.
	CB	One 30-gallon container STB dry mix One IEDK	The individual removes and discards the chemical-protective helmet cover if worn. He brushes or rubs STB onto his individual gear (helmet and mask carrier) and the hose of the M42 or M43 mask if worn. He gently shakes off any excess STB and sets aside his gear on an uncontaminated surface.
	Radiological	Hot, soapy water	The individual brushes or wipes radiological contamination from his individual gear. He washes it with hot, soapy water (if available) and then sets it aside to dry on an uncontaminated surface (plastic, poncho, or similar material).

Table IV-7. Steps for the Triple Buddy Method of MOPP Gear Exchange With the M40A1 and M42 (Continued)

Steps	Contamination Type	Required Equipment	Required Procedures
2. Prepare to decontaminate (facilitates later removal of overgarment trousers and overboots).	All	Cutting tool	Buddy 3 unfastens the shoulder and waist straps of the M42 canister carrier from Buddy 2. Once the canister and canister carrier are removed, Buddy 3 holds or tends to the canister throughout the MOPP gear exchange. **NOTE: The canister is attached to the mask by a hose; ensure that the hose does not become fully extended, potentially causing a break in the seal of Buddy 2's mask.** Buddy 1 unfastens the shoulder straps on Buddy 2's hood, pulls them over his shoulder, and reattaches them to the hook-and-pile fastener. He loosens the draw cord on Buddy 2's hood and ties the microphone cord to the hose of his mask (see Figure IV-16). He removes the M9 detector paper. He unzips Buddy 2's trouser legs and rolls a cuff in each, ensuring that the cuffs do not come above the tops of his overboots. He unfastens or cuts the fasteners on Buddy 2's overboots.

Figure IV-16. Tying the Microphone Cord to the Hose of the Mask

Table IV-7. Steps for the Triple Buddy Method of MOPP Gear Exchange With the M40A1 and M42 (Continued)

Steps	Contamination Type	Required Equipment	Required Procedures
3. Decontaminate mask and hood (removes gross contamination).	CB	Two IEDKs per person	Buddy 3 continues to hold the canister. Buddy 1 uses an IEDK to wipe Buddy 2's eye lens outserts from the top, down. **NOTE: Do not press so hard that Buddy 2's face mask seal is broken. Buddy 3 continues to hold the canister.** Buddy 1 then wipes the rest of Buddy 2's hood from the top of the head to the bottom of the hood (see Figure IV-4, page IV-13). After he has finished wiping the mask, he must wipe his own gloves in preparation for rolling Buddy 2's hood, using 2-inch tucks, until it reaches the center of his head (see Figure IV-5, page IV-14). He rolls the front of the hood tightly under the outlet valve and star knob. He ensures that the hood is off of Buddy 2's garment.
	Radiological	Three containers (about 4-gallon capacity) Two sponges Soapy water Rinse water Paper towels or similar drying material	Buddy 3 continues to hold the canister. Buddy 1 wipes Buddy 2's mask and hood with a sponge dipped in hot, soapy water and rinses them with a sponge dipped in clean water. He dries Buddy 2's mask and hood with paper towels or rags. Buddy 2 wipes his own gloves. **NOTE: Cool, soapy water is not as effective for removing contamination, but it can be used if you scrub longer. If the water supply is limited, use drinking water from a canteen and wet a sponge or cloth.** Only Buddy 2's mask and hood will be decontaminated and rolled at this time.

Table IV-7. Steps for the Triple Buddy Method of MOPP Gear Exchange With the M40A1 and M42 (Continued)

Steps	Contamination Type	Required Equipment	Required Procedures
4. Remove overgarments and overboots (limits the spread of agents and helps prevent agents from penetrating through to the undergarments or the skin).	All	Two discard containers (e.g., plastic bags)	Buddy 3 continues to hold the canister. Buddy 1 grasps Buddy 2's outside overgarment jacket, unsnaps the snaps individually, and unties the draw cord at the bottom of the jacket. He unfastens the hook-and-pile fastener at the wrist of Buddy 2's jacket and then refastens it. He unfastens the hook-and-pile fastener over the zippered front of Buddy 2's jacket and unzips the jacket. Buddy 1 grasps Buddy 2's jacket by the shoulders and instructs him to make a fist. He then pulls the jacket down and away from Buddy 2, ensuring that the black part of the jacket is not touched (see Figure IV-17). He lays Buddy 2's overgarment jacket on the ground (it will be used to stand on later). Buddy 1 carefully unfastens and unzips Buddy 2's trousers. **NOTE: Do not loosen Buddy 2's waist tabs. Buddy 2 breaks the seals on his overboots by alternately stepping on each heel and pulling up on his foot.** He grasps his trousers and pulls them down to his knees. Buddy 1 instructs Buddy 2 to walk out of his trousers and overboots, taking care not to step on the contaminated side of the overgarment. If Buddy 2 is wearing overboots, Buddy 1 removes Buddy 2's trousers first and then helps him step out of his overboots onto the black side of the jacket. Buddy 2 steps onto the jacket wearing his mask, BDU, combat boots, and gloves.

Figure IV-17. Removing the Outer Garment

Table IV-7. Steps for the Triple Buddy Method of MOPP Gear Exchange With the M40A1 and M42 (Continued)

Steps	Contamination Type	Required Equipment	Required Procedures
5. Remove gloves.	All	Discard containers (from step 4)	Buddy 3 continues to hold the canister. Buddy 2 holds the fingertips of his gloves and partially slides his hand out. When the fingers of both hands are free, he holds his arms away from his body and lets the gloves drop.
6. Put on the overgarment.	All	One set of chemical-protective overgarments per person	Buddy 3 continues to hold the canister. Buddy 1 opens the package containing the new overgarment without touching the inside of the package. Buddy 2 pulls out the overgarment without touching the outside of the package. He puts on the overgarment and fastens it, leaving the trouser legs open. **NOTE: Do not reverse roles. Only Buddy 2 will put on the clean overgarments at this time.**
7. Put on overboots and gloves.	All	One set of chemical-protective overboots per person One set of chemical-protective gloves per person M9 detector paper	Buddy 3 continues to hold the canister. Buddy 1 opens the package of clean overboots without touching the inside of the package. Buddy 2 removes the overboots without touching the outside of the package, puts them on, and fastens his trouser legs. Buddy 1 opens the package of clean gloves without touching the inside of the package. Buddy 2 removes the gloves without touching the outside of the package and puts them on. Buddy 2 puts on the M9 detector paper. Do not reverse roles. **NOTES: 1. Only Buddy 2 will put on clean overboots and gloves at this time. 2. The gloves and overboots will have a light powdery coating. This is normal. It is not necessary to remove it. It will not affect the protective qualities.**
8. Secure hood.	All	One IEDK	Buddy 3 continues to hold the canister. Buddy 1 wipes his rubber gloves with an IEDK. He unrolls Buddy 2's hood, attaches the straps, and tightens the neck cord. He checks the clips and neck cord on Buddy 2's hood. Buddy 3 returns the canister to Buddy 2 and assists with securing the canister carrier straps. Buddy 1, Buddy 2, and Buddy 3 rotate roles and repeat steps 2 through 8. They rotate roles a third time for the final buddy.
9. Secure gear.	All	One chemical-protective helmet cover per person	Each individual secures his individual gear and puts it back on. He puts on a new chemical-protective helmet cover and moves to the AA. He uses the buddy system to check the fit of all secured gear.

Table IV-8. Steps for the CVCUS and CPU (Triple Buddy Method) MOPP Gear Exchange With the M40A1, M42, and M43 (Aviation and Armor)

Steps	Contamination Type	Required Equipment	Required Procedures
1. Decontaminate gear (removes gross contamination from individual gear [weapons, helmet, load-bearing equipment, and mask carrier]).	All	Four long-handled brushes A large piece of plastic (poncho or similar material) STB (bulk) Shovel	The individual mixes three parts earth to two parts STB.
	CB	One 30-gallon container STB dry mix One IEDK	The individual removes and discards the chemical-protective helmet cover if worn. He brushes or rubs STB onto his individual gear (helmet and mask carrier) and the hose of the M43 mask if worn. He gently shakes off any excess STB and sets aside his gear on an uncontaminated surface.
	Radiological	Hot, soapy water	The individual brushes or wipes radiological contamination from his individual gear. He washes it with hot, soapy water (if available) and sets it aside to dry on an uncontaminated surface (plastic, poncho, or similar material).
2. Prepare to decontaminate (facilitates later removal of overgarment trousers and overboots).	All	Cutting tool	Buddy 3 unfastens the shoulder and waist straps of the M42 canister carrier from Buddy 2. Once the canister and canister carrier are removed, Buddy 3 holds or tends the canister throughout the MOPP gear exchange. **NOTE: The canister is attached to the mask by a hose; ensure that the hose does not become fully extended, potentially causing a break in the seal of Buddy 2's mask.** Buddy 1 unfastens the shoulder straps on Buddy 2's hood, pulls them over his shoulder, and reattaches them to the hook-and-pile fastener. He loosens the draw cord on Buddy 2's hood and ties the microphone cord to the hose of his mask. He removes the M9 detector paper from Buddy 2's trouser legs and rolls a cuff in each, ensuring that the cuffs do not come above the tops of his overboots. He unfastens or cuts the fasteners on Buddy 2's overboots.

Table IV-8. Steps for the CVCUS and CPU (Triple Buddy Method) MOPP Gear Exchange With the M40A1, M42, and M43 (Aviation and Armor) (Continued)

Steps	Contamination Type	Required Equipment	Required Procedures
3. Decontaminate mask and hood (removes gross contamination).	CB	Two IEDKs per person	Buddy 1 uses an IEDK to wipe Buddy 2's hood, mask, and canister and the hose of the M42 or M43 mask. **NOTE: Do not press so hard that Buddy 2's face mask seal is broken.** Buddy 3 continues to hold the canister. After Buddy 1 wipes Buddy 2's mask and his own gloves, he rolls Buddy 2's hood. He starts from the rear and rolls Buddy 2's hood, using 2-inch tucks, until it reaches the center of his head (see Figure IV-5, page IV-14). He rolls the front of Buddy 2's hood tightly under the outlet valve and star knob. He ensures that the hood is off of Buddy 2's garment.
	Radiological	Three containers (about 4-gallon capacity) Two sponges Soapy water Rinse water Paper towels or similar drying material	Buddy 3 continues to hold the canister. Buddy 1 wipes Buddy 2's mask and hood with a sponge dipped in hot, soapy water and rinses them with a sponge dipped in clean water. He dries Buddy 2's mask and hood with paper towels or rags. Buddy 2 wipes his own gloves. **NOTES: 1. Cool, soapy water is not as effective for removing contamination, but it can be used if you scrub longer. If the water supply is limited, use drinking water from a canteen and wet a sponge or cloth. If water is not available, brush off the radioactive dust particles. Do not reverse roles. 2. Only Buddy 2's hood will be decontaminated and rolled at this time.**
4. Remove CVCUS overboots (limits the spread of contamination).	All	Two discard containers (e.g., plastic bags)	Buddy 3 continues to hold the canister. Buddy 1 opens all the zippers on Buddy 2's CVCUS in the following order: wrist, ankles, and front. While standing behind Buddy 2, Buddy 1 grasps the shoulders of Buddy 2's CVCUS and instructs him to make a fist to ensure that his gloves do not come off. He then pulls Buddy 2's CVCUS down below his knees, turning it inside out. Buddy 1 unzips Buddy 2's CPU jacket and removes it by grasping it at the shoulders, pulling it down, and turning it inside out. He places it beside Buddy 2 with the clean side up.

Table IV-8. Steps for the CVCUS and CPU (Triple Buddy Method) MOPP Gear Exchange With the M40A1, M42, and M43 (Aviation and Armor) (Continued)

Steps	Contamination Type	Required Equipment	Required Procedures
5. Remove CPU jacket and gloves.	All	Two discard containers (from step 4)	Buddy 3 continues to hold the canister. Buddy 1 has Buddy 2 partially remove his overboots by alternately stepping on each heel and pulling up on his foot. Buddy 1 grasps one leg of Buddy 2's CVCUS and his overboot and instructs him to remove his leg and foot simultaneously. As Buddy 2 removes each leg and foot, he steps onto the clean side of the CPU jacket. Buddy 1 discards the overboots. Buddy 2 holds the fingertips of his gloves and partially slides his hand out. When the fingers of both hands are free, he holds his arms away from his body and lets the gloves drop. Buddy 2 removes his protective glove liners.
6. Remove combat boots and CPU trousers.	All	Two discard containers (from step 4)	Buddy 3 continues to hold the canister. Buddy 2 partially removes his boots by alternately stepping on each heel and pulling up on his foot. Buddy 1 grasps one of Buddy 2's boots and instructs him to remove his foot. As Buddy 2 removes his foot, he steps directly onto the clean side of the CPU jacket. He repeats the procedure on the other foot. Next, Buddy 1 removes Buddy 2's CPU trousers by pulling down on the sides and turning them inside out. Buddy 2 is now stripped to his underwear and mask and is ready to put on new clothing. Combat boots should remain beside Buddy 2 on the clean area of the CPU jacket. Buddy 1 discards the CVCUS and CPU trousers. **CAUTION** Use extreme care to ensure that the outside of the CPU does not touch the skin, underclothing, or combat boots of Buddy 2.
7. Put on CPU and CVCUS.	All	One CVCUS and CPU per person	Buddy 3 continues to hold the canister. Buddy 1 opens the package containing the new CPU without touching the inside of the package. Buddy 2 pulls out the CPU without touching the outside of the package. He puts on the new clothing in the following order: CPU trousers, CPU jacket, combat boots, and CVCUS (over the CPU).

Table IV-8. Steps for the CVCUS/CPU (Triple Buddy Method) MOPP Gear Exchange With the M40A1, M42, and M43 (Aviation and Armor) (Continued)

Steps	Contamination Type	Required Equipment	Required Procedures
8. Put on overboots and gloves.	All	One set of chemical-protective overboots per person One set of chemical-protective gloves per person M9 detector paper	Buddy 3 continues to hold the canister. Buddy 1 opens the package of clean overboots without touching the inside of the package. Buddy 2 removes the overboots without touching the outside of the package and puts them on. Buddy 1 opens the package of clean gloves without touching the inside of the package. Buddy 2 removes the gloves without touching the outside of the package and puts them on. Buddy 2 puts on the M9 detector paper. **NOTE: The gloves and overboots will have a light powdery coating. This is normal. It is not necessary to remove it. It will not affect the protective qualities.**
9. Secure hood.	CB	One IEDK	Buddy 3 continues to hold the canister. Buddy 1 wipes his rubber gloves with an IEDK. He unrolls Buddy 2 hood, attaches the straps, and tightens the neck cord. He checks the snaps and neck cord on Buddy 2's hood to ensure that they are closed. Buddy 3 returns the canister to Buddy 2 and assists with securing the canister carrier straps. Buddy 1, Buddy 2, and Buddy 3 rotate rolls and repeat steps 2 through 9. They rotate roles a third time for the final buddy.
10. Secure gear.	All	One chemical-protective helmet cover per person	Each individual secures his individual gear and puts it back on. He puts on a new chemical-protective helmet cover and moves to the AA. He uses the buddy system to check the fit of all secured gear.

Table IV-9. Steps for the JSLIST, Individual (Emergency Method) MOPP Gear Exchange

Steps	Contamination Type	Required Equipment	Required Procedures
1. Decontaminate gear (removes gross contamination from individual gear [weapons, helmet, load-bearing equipment, and mask carrier]).	CB	One IEDK	Use M8 detector paper to determine the areas of gross contamination. Use field-expedient absorbents (sand, dirt, or rags) to remove gross liquid contamination. Take special care to avoid touching these areas during overgarment removal. Use an IEDK to decontaminate individual gear.
	Radiological	Hot, soapy water	Remove and discard the chemical-protective helmet cover. Brush or wipe radiological contamination from the individual gear. Wash it with hot, soapy water (if available), and then set it aside to dry on an uncontaminated surface (plastic, poncho, or similar material).
2. Prepare to decontaminate (facilitates later removal of overgarment trousers and overboots).	All	Cutting tool	Remove the M9 detector paper from the overgarment. Untie the coat retention cord if tied. Unfasten the webbing-strip snap at the bottom front of your coat and release the coat retention-cord loop at your waist. Loosen the bottom of your coat by pulling the material away from your body. **NOTE: If wearing the M43 protective mask, tie the microphone cord to the hose of the mask.** Unfasten and loosely refasten the hook-and-pile fasteners at your wrists and ankles. Unfasten or cut the fasteners on the overboots. **NOTE: The M40 voice amplifier (M7) and the M42A2 detachable microphone cannot be decontaminated and will be disposed of as contaminated waste; however, ensure that these items are contaminated before disposing of them.**
3. Decontaminate the mask and hood (removes gross contamination).	CB	Two IEDKS per person	Use an IEDK to decontamination the exposed parts of your mask. Start at the eye lens outserts and wipe down. Wipe all the exposed parts of the mask. Wipe the front edge of the hood, including the barrel lock and fasteners under your chin. Decontaminate the gloves in preparation to release the hood seal. **NOTE: Pay particular attention to the areas between your fingers when decontaminating the gloves.**
	Radiological	Three containers (about 3-gallon capacity) Two sponges Soapy water Rinse water Paper towels or similar drying material	Wipe the mask and hood with a sponge dipped in hot, soapy water and rinse them with a sponge dipped in clean water. Dry the mask and hood with paper towels or rags. Wipe the gloves. **NOTE: Cool, soapy water is not as effective for removing contamination, but it can be used if you scrub longer. If the water supply is limited, use drinking water from a canteen and wet a sponge or cloth. If water is not available, brush off the radioactive dust particles.**

Table IV-9. Steps for the JSLIST, Individual (Emergency Method) MOPP Gear Exchange (Continued)

Steps	Contamination Type	Required Equipment	Required Procedures
4. Remove chemical-protective coat (limits the spread of agents and helps prevent agents from penetrating through to the undergarments or the skin).	All	Two discard containers (e.g., plastic bags)	Feel for and locate the suspender snap couplers on the outside of your coat and releases them. Untie the draw cord if tied, press the barrel lock release, and unsnap the barrel lock. **NOTE: If it is difficult to grasp the barrel lock, use the draw cord to pull it away from the mask, allowing you to grasp and unfasten it without touching the interior of the hood.** Unfasten the front closure flap, and pull the slide fastener from your chin to the bottom of the coat. Grasp the hood by the outside surface near each end of the barrel lock, lift it off your head, and reverse-roll the hood one time while pulling the hood towards the back of your head to remove it. Grasp the front side of the coat, and pull it back until it is off your shoulders. Put your arms behind your back, and work your arms out of the sleeves. **NOTE: Ensure that the outside of the coat does not touch your body.** Lay the coat on the ground, black side up. **NOTE: Use the coat later as an uncontaminated surface to stand on when putting on the new overgarment.** **CAUTION** Take care to avoid contaminating the inside surface of the coat.
5. Remove chemical-protective trousers and overboots.	All	Two discard containers (from step 4)	Unfasten the hook-and-pile fasteners at the waistband, unfasten the two front closure snaps, and open the fly slide fastener on the front of the trousers. Loosen the overboots by alternately stepping on each heel and pulling up the foot. Grasp the trousers, and push them down to the knees. Walk out of the trousers and overboots simultaneously, and step onto the black side of the coat. **CAUTION** Take care to avoid contaminating the clothing and skin.

Table IV-9. Steps for the JSLIST, Individual (Emergency Method) MOPP Gear Exchange (Continued)

Steps	Contamination Type	Required Equipment	Required Procedures
6. Remove chemical-protective gloves and liners.	All	Two discard containers (from step 4)	Wipe around the edges of the packages containing the new items (gloves, overgarments, and overboots) with an IEDK, and then open them. Hold the fingertips of the gloves, and partially slide your hands out. When the fingers of both hands are free, hold your arms away from your body and let the gloves drop. Remove the protective glove liners and discard them. **CAUTION** Take care to avoid letting the gloves come in contact with the coat spread on the ground.
7. Put on chemical-protective trousers.	All	One JSLIST chemical-protective ensemble per person	Remove the trousers from the package without touching the outside. Put them on, close the slide fastener, and fasten the two fly opening snaps. Pull the suspenders over your shoulders, and fasten the snap couplers. Adjust the length of the suspenders to ensure a comfortable fit. Adjust the hook-and-pile fastener at the waistband for a snug fit.
8. Put on chemical-protective coat.	All	One JSLIST chemical-protective ensemble per person	Remove the coat from the package without touching the outside. Put on the coat, close the slide fastener up as far as the chest, and secure the front closure hook-and-pile fastener on the front flap up as far as your chest. Pull the bottom of the coat down over the trousers. Grasp the loop on the back of the coat and pull it out and away from the back of the coat. Bring the loop forward between your legs, pulling on it so that the bottom of the coat fits snugly over the trousers. Place the loop over the webbing-strip snap on the front of the coat, and fasten it. Adjust the retention cord, if necessary, and tie the excessive cord in a bow. **CAUTION** Take care to ensure that the body and clothing touch only the inner surface of the coat.

Table IV-9. Steps for the JSLIST, Individual (Emergency Method) MOPP Gear Exchange (Continued)

Steps	Contamination Type	Required Equipment	Required Procedures
9. Put on chemical-protective overboots.	All	One set of chemical-protective overboots per person	Remove the overboots from the package without touching the outside. Put the overboots on over the combat boots, adjust and secure the fasteners, pull the trouser legs over the overboots, and secure the two hook-and-pile fasteners on each ankle so that they fit snugly around the overboot.
10. Put on chemical-protective hood.	All	One JSLIST chemical-protective ensemble per person	Put the hood on your head, completely close the front slide fastener on the coat, and secure the hook-and-pile fastener on the front flap as far as the top of the slide fastener. Place the edge of the hood around the edge of the mask, and secure the hook-and-pile fastener on the hood. Pull the draw cord tight around the edge of the mask, snap the ends of the barrel lock together, squeeze both ends of the barrel lock while pulling the draw cord, slide the barrel lock up under the chin to keep the cord in place, and tie off the draw cord if needed.
			WARNING The barrel lock release button must face away from the user to avoid the barrel lock from unfastening and possibly exposing the user to contamination.
			CAUTION Take care to ensure that the trousers touch only the uncontaminated surface.
11. Put on chemical-protective gloves and liners.	All	One set of chemical-protective gloves with liners per person (correct size)	Remove the gloves and liners from the package without touching the outside. Put on the liners and gloves, pull the cuffs of the coat over the gloves, and fasten the hook-and-pile fasteners on each sleeve of the coat. Put on the M9 detector paper as required by the SOP.
12. Secure gear.	All contamination	One chemical-protective helmet cover per person	Place the new chemical-protective helmet cover on the PASGT helmet if used. Check the fit of all secured gear.

Table IV-10. Steps for the Individual (Emergency Method) BDO MOPP Gear Exchange

Steps	Contamination Type	Required Equipment	Required Procedures
1. Decontaminate gear (removes gross contamination from individual gear [weapon, helmet, load-bearing equipment, and mask carrier]).	CB	One SDK	Use M8 detector paper to determine the areas of gross contamination. Use field-expedient absorbents (sand, dirt, or rags) to remove gross liquid contamination. Take special care to avoid touching these areas during overgarment removal. Use an IEDK to decontaminate individual gear.
	Radiological	Hot, soapy water	Brush or wipe radiological contamination from the individual gear. Wash it with hot, soapy water (if available), and then set it aside to dry on an uncontaminated surface (plastic, poncho, or similar material).
2. Prepare to decontaminate (facilitates removal of overgarment trousers and overboots).	All	Cutting tool	Unfasten the shoulder straps on the hood, pull them over your shoulders, and reattach them. Loosen the draw cord on the hood of the protective mask. **NOTE: If wearing the M43 protective mask, tie the microphone cord to the hose of the mask.** Remove the M9 detector paper from the overgarment, and untie or cut the draw cords on the trouser legs of the overgarment. Unzip the trouser legs, and roll a cuff in each trouser leg, ensuring that the cuffs do not come above the top of the overboots. Unfasten or cut the fasteners on the overboots.

Table IV-10. Steps for the Individual (Emergency Method) BDO MOPP Gear Exchange (Continued)

Steps	Contamination Type	Required Equipment	Required Procedures
3. Decontaminate mask and hood (removes gross contamination from the mask and hood).	CB	One IEDK	Wipe the eye lens outserts on the mask from the top, down. Wipe the mask and gloves, and roll the hood. Grasp the straps of the hood, and lift the hood off your shoulders and partially over your head until most of the back of the head is exposed. Roll the hood, starting at the chin, and work around the entire mask until the rolled hood will stay up and off of your shoulders. Tuck the straps and neck cord into the roll. Roll the hood tightly against the mask without pulling the hood off the back of the head. Tuck the tail between the upper part of the canister and the mask. **NOTE: Tie the tail over and under the hose for the M42 mask.** Remove the applicator mitt from the package with your nondominant hand. Making a V, wipe down the dominant hand, paying particular attention to areas between your fingers. Once the dominant hand is thoroughly wiped down, insert it into the applicator mitt and thoroughly wipe down the nondominant hand. Gently pat the voicemitter with black powder until it is covered. Start at the top of the hood and wipe down and away, patting until the surface of the hood is covered by the black powder. Rewipe the gloves, starting with the nondominant hand. Lift the hood off your shoulders by grasping the shoulder straps in one hand and placing the other hand on top of your head and pulling the hood over your head until the elastic band is over the knuckles and most of the back of your head is exposed. Do not expose your ears or pull the hood completely over your face or mask. Tuck the shoulder straps, underarm straps, and rolled portion of the hood under the elastic band. When using the M40A1 mask with the quick-doff hood, remove the underarm straps from the front of the hood and place them over your shoulders. Refasten them on the front of the hood. **NOTE: Place two fingers on the voicemitter of the mask to prevent accidental breakage of the seal.**
	Radiological	Three containers (about 4-gallon capacity) Two sponges Soapy water Rinse water Paper towels or similar drying material	Wipe the mask and hood with a sponge dipped in hot, soapy water and rinse them with a sponge dipped in clean water. Dry the mask and hood with paper towels or rags. **NOTE: Cool, soapy water is not as effective for removing contamination, but it can be used if you scrub longer. If water is not available, brush off the radioactive dust particles.**

Table IV-10. Steps for the Individual (Emergency Method) BDO MOPP Gear Exchange (Continued)

Steps	Contamination Type	Required Equipment	Required Procedures
4. Remove overgarment and overboots (prevents agent from penetrating through to the undergarments or the skin).	All	Two discard containers (e.g., plastic bags) Chemical-protective suit with protective gloves and overboots	Grasp the overgarment jacket, and unsnap the snaps individually. Untie the draw cord at the bottom of the jacket. Unfasten the hook-and-pile fastener at the waist, and then refasten it. Unfastens the hook-and-pile fastener over the zippered front of the jacket, and unzip the jacket. Grasp the front of the jacket and pull the jacket back until it is off your shoulders. Put your arms behind your back, and work your arms out of the sleeves. Do not let the outside of the jacket touch the body. When the jacket is off, lay it on the ground with the black side up. Unfasten and unzip the trousers. Do not loosen the waist tabs. Loosen the overboots by alternately stepping on each heel and pulling up on the foot. Grasp the trousers, and push them down to the knees. Walk out of the trousers and overboots simultaneously, and step onto the black side of the jacket. Step onto the jacket wearing the mask, BDU, combat boots, and gloves.
5. Remove gloves.	All	Two discard containers (from step 4) One IEDK	Wipe around the edges of the packages containing the new items (gloves, overgarments, and overboots) with an IEDK. Open the new packages. Hold the fingertips of the gloves, and partially slide your hands out. When the fingers of both hands are free, hold your arms away from your body and let the gloves drop.
6. Put on overgarment.	All	One set of chemical-protective overgarments per person One IEDK	Remove the overgarment from its package without touching the outside of the package. Put on the overgarment and fasten it, leaving the trouser legs open until you put on the new overboots.
7. Put on overboots and gloves.	All	One set of chemical-protective overboots per person One set of chemical-protective gloves per person	Remove the overboots (one at a time) from their package without touching the outside, and put them on. Remove the gloves from their package without touching the outside, put them on, and fasten the trouser legs. **NOTE: The gloves and overboots will have a light powdery coating. This is normal. Do not remove it. It will not affect the protective qualities.**
8. Secure hood.	All	One chemical-protective helmet cover per person	Secure individual gear, and put it back on. Put on a new chemical-protective helmet cover and move to the AA.

Table IV-11. Steps for the CVCUS and CPU, Individual (Emergency Method) MOPP Gear Exchange

Steps	Contamination Type	Required Equipment	Required Procedures
1. Decontaminate gear (removes gross contamination from individual gear [weapon, helmet, load-bearing equipment, and mask carrier]).	CB	One SDK	Use M8 detector paper to determine the areas of gross contamination. Use field-expedient absorbents (sand, dirt, or rags) to remove gross liquid contamination. Take special care to avoid touching these areas during overgarment removal. Use an IEDK to decontaminate the individual gear.
	Radiological	Hot, soapy water	Brush or wipe radiological contamination from the individual gear. Wash it with hot, soapy water (if available), and then set it aside to dry on an uncontaminated surface (plastic, poncho, or similar material).
2. Prepare to decontaminate (facilitates removal of overgarment trousers and overboots).	All	Cutting tool	Unfasten the shoulder straps on the hood, pull them over the shoulders, and reattach them to the front of the hood. Loosen the draw cord on the hood of the protective mask. **NOTE: If wearing the M43 protective mask, tie the microphone cord to the hose of the mask.** Remove the M9 detector paper from the overgarment, and untie or cut the draw cords on the trouser legs of the overgarment. Unzip the trouser legs, and roll a cuff in each trouser leg, ensuring that the cuffs do not come above the top of the overboots. Unfasten or cut the fasteners on the overboots.
3. Decontaminate mask and hood (removes gross contamination from the mask and hood).	CB	One IEDK	Wipe the eye lens outserts on the mask from the top, down. Wipe the mask and gloves, and roll the hood. Grasp the straps of the hood, and lift the hood off your shoulders and partially over your head until most of the back of your head is exposed. Roll the hood, starting at the chin, and work around the entire mask until the rolled hood will stay up and off your shoulders. Tuck the straps and neck cord into the roll. Roll the hood tightly against the mask without pulling the hood off the back of your head. Tuck the tail between the upper part of the canister and the mask. **NOTE: Tie the tail over and under the hose for the M42 mask.**

Table IV-11. Steps for the CVCUS/CPU, Individual (Emergency Method) MOPP Gear Exchange (Continued)

Steps	Contamination Type	Required Equipment	Required Procedures
3. Decontaminate mask and hood (continued)	CB		Remove the applicator mitt from the package with the nondominant hand. Making a V, wipe down the dominant hand, paying particular attention to the areas between your fingers. Once the dominant hand is thoroughly wiped down, insert it into the applicator mitt and thoroughly wipe down the other hand. Gently pat the voicemitter with black powder until it has been covered. Start at the top of the hood and wipe down and away, patting until the surface of the hood is covered by the black powder. Rewipe the gloves, starting with the nondominant hand. Lift the hood off your shoulders by grasping the shoulder straps in one hand and placing the other hand on top of your head and pulling the hood over your head until the elastic band is over your knuckles and most of the back of your head is exposed. Do not expose your ears or pull the hood completely over your face or mask. Tuck the shoulder straps, underarm straps, and rolled portion of the hood under the elastic band. When using the M40A1 mask with the quick-doff hood, remove the underarm straps from the front of the hood and place them over your shoulders. Refasten them on the front of the hood. **NOTE: Place two fingers on the voicemitter of the mask to prevent accidental breakage of the seal.**
	Radiological	Three containers (about 4-gallon capacity) Two sponges Soapy water Rinse water Paper towels or similar drying material	Wipe the mask and hood with a sponge dipped in hot, soapy water, and rinse them with a sponge dipped in clean water. Dry the mask and hood with paper towels or rags. **NOTE: Cool, soapy water is not as effective for removing contamination, but it can be used if you scrub longer. If water is not available, brush off the radioactive dust particles.**
4. Remove CVCUS and overboots.	All	Two discard containers (e.g., plastic bags)	Open all the zippers on the CVCUS in the following order: wrists, ankles, and front. While standing adjacent to the clean area, grasp the front of the CVCUS and pull it off your shoulders. Make a fist to ensure that the gloves do not come off when removing the CVCUS. Put your arms behind your back, and work your arms out of the sleeves. Loosen the overboots by alternately stepping on each heel and pulling up on the foot. Pull the CVCUS down below the knees, turning it inside out. Do not let the outside of the CVCUS touch your body. Walk out of the CVCUS and overboots simultaneously, and step onto the clean area.

Table IV-11 Steps for the CVCUS/CPU, Individual (Emergency Method) MOPP Gear Exchange (Continued)

Steps	Contamination Type	Required Equipment	Required Procedures
5. Remove jacket and gloves.	All	Two discard containers (from step 4)	Wipe the gloves and around the edges of the packages containing the new items (gloves, undergarments, and overboots) with an IEDK. Open the new packages. Hold the fingertips of the gloves, and partially slide your hands out. When the fingers of both hands are free, hold your arms away from your body and let the gloves drop. Open all hook-and-pile wrist fasteners, and unzip the CPU jacket. Remove the CPU jacket by grasping it at the shoulders and pulling it down, turning it inside out. Place the jacket on a clean area with the clean side up. Remove the protective glove inserts.
6. Remove combat boots and CPU pants.	All	Two discard containers (from step 4)	Unlace the combat boots, remove them, and step directly onto the CPU jacket. Take off the CPU drawers by placing the hands beneath the waistband and removing them, turning them inside out. If wearing the BDU, stand on the clean area (but not on the CPU jacket), and unlace the combat boots. Partially remove the boots by alternately stepping on each heel and pulling up on your foot. Step out of each trouser leg and combat boot simultaneously, and step directly onto the clean side of the CPU jacket.
7. Put on CPU.	All	One set of chemical-protective undergarments per person	Remove the undergarment from the package without touching the outside. Put on the undergarment in the following order: CPU trousers, CPU jacket, combat boots, and CVCUS (over the CPU trousers).
8. Put on overboots and gloves.	CB	One set of chemical-protective overboots per person One set of chemical-protective gloves per person M9 detector paper	Remove the overboots from their package without touching the outside, and put them on. Remove the gloves from their package without touching the outside, and put them on. Put on the M9 detector paper. **NOTE: The gloves and overboots will have a light powdery coating. This is normal. It is not necessary to remove it. It will not affect the protective qualities.**
9. Secure hood.	CB	One IEDK	Wipe the rubber gloves with an IEDK. Unroll the hood, attach the straps, and tighten the neck cord.
10. Secure gear.	All	One chemical-protective helmet cover per person	Secure individual gear, and put it back on. Put on a new chemical-protective helmet cover, and move to the AA.

Chapter V
THOROUGH DECONTAMINATION

1. Background

a. Thorough decontamination operations reduce and sometimes eliminate contamination from equipment and personnel. This allows the MOPP level to be reduced. Operators and crew members must perform periodic checks on their equipment since there is a risk of residual contamination. Operators make these checks with standard detectors (e.g., M8/M9 paper, ICAM/CAM) and the M256A1 kit. This chapter focuses on land force decontamination operations as part of ongoing combat operations or reconstitution operations.

b. Combat service support (CSS) elements replenish combat stocks, refit equipment, and replace personnel and equipment, as required. The contaminated unit, with some assistance from a decontamination unit, performs the DTD.

NOTE: The USN and the USMC do not have standing CBRN support units to perform decontamination. See Appendix G for service CBRN decontamination capabilities.

c. A supporting CBRN unit performs the DED or DAD. The planning considerations that are required to conduct a thorough decontamination operation and the methods that various decontamination units use to conduct DTD/DED are discussed in this chapter. The exact layout of a thorough decontamination site is determined by the METT-TC. After a thorough decontamination operation, the unit moves out of the decontamination site into a tactical AA. The unit, while in this tactical assembly, may undergo reconstitution or may prepare for future operations.

NOTES:

1. See NSTM 470 and NSTM 070 for thorough decontamination procedures.

2. See NAVAIR 00-80T-121 for USN and USMC aircrews, aircraft, and support equipment.

3. See Chapters VIII and IX for additional information on aviation and shipboard decontamination.

4. See *Recovery Operations in a Chemical, Biological, Radiological, and Nuclear (CBRN) Environment* for other information on USN and USMC thorough decontamination.

5. See AFMAN 32-4005, AFMAN 32-4017, AFMAN 10-2602, and AFTO 11C15-1-3 for USAF MOB, COB, and BB operating thorough decontamination TTP.

6. See Chapter VII for further information on fixed-site, port, and airfield decontamination TTP.

2. Planning

Thorough decontamination is the most effective type of decontamination, but it is the most resource-intensive.

a. Thorough decontamination operations are conducted beyond the range of enemy direct-fire systems. If a contaminated unit requires a thorough decontamination as part of its reconstitution operations, the decontamination site is established near the reconstitution area or the parent unit rear area. Company-size units are usually reconstituted in the brigade rear area while battalion-level units are reconstituted in the division rear area.

b. All echelons prepare for thorough decontamination operations as part of the overall planning process. The CBRN staff can begin to develop the decontamination plan from the commander's general guidance. Coordination with higher HQ is required to determine the availability of engineer support for site preparation and closure. Engineers provide support for sumps and drainage ditches. They also coordinate with the civil affairs office for HNS (personnel, equipment, and supplies) and for environmental requirements and restrictions.

c. The CBRN staff selects possible lineup points throughout the unit area of operation (AO) based on such factors as the decontamination type, terrain, mission, threat, road network, and availability of water. Decontamination site locations that support these lineup points are finalized after reconnaissance of the sites by the decontamination platoon. After the decontamination sites are selected, linkup points are chosen to support each site. A site may have more than one linkup point.

d. Since decontamination assets are limited, the commander must establish priorities of decontamination support and list the units in the order they will be decontaminated. This can change from phase to phase during an operation. The CBRN staff develops the priority of support based on an understanding of the commander's intent.

e. Giving the priority of support to the lead task force during the assault phase may not be the best choice since the contaminated elements will not stop for decontamination until after the assault is complete. The commander should establish a priority of work that specifies the order in which equipment will be decontaminated. (For example, a priority of work may be in this order: engineer equipment, artillery pieces, main battle tanks, and long-haul vehicles.) Ships with embarked amphibious and aviation units will have to prioritize similarly, as will aviation units operating ashore. A limiting factor is the availability of water. A typical vehicle requires 500 gallons of water during the DED. The actual amount of water required varies by the vehicle and its contamination level. The supported unit CBRN staff must develop a water resupply plan for thorough decontamination operations.

f. A water resupply plan can be as simple as selecting a series of linkup points along a route where the chemical unit can link up with a bulk water truck. More complex water resupply plans include caching water throughout the AO, coordinating for the movement of water bladders by aircraft, and identifying water sources in the unit AO. The use of nonpotable, salt, and brackish waters should be considered. See Table V-1 for the planning factors for the rinse station.

NOTE: Naval aircraft exposed to salt water require emergency reclamation per *Aircraft Weapons System Cleaning and Corrosion Control,* and *Avionics Cleaning and Corrosion Prevention/Control.*

Table V-1. Planning Factors for the Rinse Station

Equipment	M12A1 PDDA Rinse		M17 LDS Rinse	
	Gallons Applied	Minutes Applied	Gallons Applied	Minutes Applied
M1 Tank	325	12	57	14
M2 BFV	325	12	57	14
M113 APC	203	9	38	10
M109A Paladin	325	12	57	14
HEMTT	180	8	30	12
5-Ton Truck	158	7	42	11
HMMWV	90	4	23	6
NOTE: The rinse is done with the spray wand for the M17.				

3. Preparation

Units prepare for thorough decontamination to be successful.

a. Subordinate units review their higher HQ decontamination plan. If additional decontamination sites or assets are required, they request them from the higher HQ. The supporting decontamination leader conducts a reconnaissance of the designated decontamination sites. Since the decontamination sites are initially selected by map reconnaissance, the actual site may not be suitable. If the selected site cannot support decontamination operations, the CBRN unit leader attempts to find another site close to the original site and notifies the supported unit and higher HQ of the change.

b. The decontamination unit leader determines the support requirements that are needed to operate the decontamination site. Engineers are required to dig sumps, improve access to the site, and dig ditches for runoff. Air defense and military police are required to provide security. Medical support is also required. Depending on the operational situation and the threat, some DED sites may be prepared in advance. Routes must be established and published in the OPORD, leading the contaminated unit to the linkup point.

NOTE: Inform units not to proceed directly to the decontamination site.

4. Execution

The actual decontamination operation begins once a contaminated unit requests decontamination support. The unit leader must assess the situation and accurately report it to the HQ. This situation report (SITREP) should include the type and extent of contamination, the current location, the unit's ability to perform the current mission while contaminated, and the time the unit will become ineffective in combat. The contaminated unit should perform immediate decontamination techniques to increase its survivability and to limit the spread of contamination. An operational decontamination should also be considered and performed, as appropriate. The request for decontamination support must contain several essential elements of information to assist the CBRN staff and the decontamination unit leader in coordinating the decontamination operation. These essential elements of information include the following:

- Designation of the contaminated unit.
- Location of the contaminated unit.
- Time the unit became contaminated.

- Time the unit can move and begin decontamination.
- Type of contamination.
- Number and type of vehicles contaminated.
- Special requirements (e.g., patient decontamination station, recovery assets, unit decontamination team).
- Supported unit's frequency and call sign to facilitate initial linkup.

a. The supporting decontamination unit is given a WARNORD to conduct a decontamination operation. Subsequent WARNORDs provide more detailed information. After requesting decontamination support, the supported unit issues an OPORD/fragmentary order (FRAGORD) to the chemical unit.

b. The supporting decontamination unit must coordinate the movement of the contaminated unit to the linkup point. If the contaminated unit is out of the supported unit AO, the move must be coordinated with the higher HQ.

c. Once the chemical unit is set up, the decontamination unit leader moves to the linkup point. Other elements may provide assets to support the decontamination operations, such as medical, engineer, air defense, and military police. These elements link up with the chemical unit before the arrival of the contaminated unit (see Table V-2).

d. The supported unit is responsible for site security and overall control. The decontamination leader is responsible for operating the predecontamination area and for processing vehicles.

e. After linkup is achieved and all support assets are in position, the actual decontamination operation begins. The decontamination platoon leader, with help from the commander of the contaminated unit or the supported unit C2 cell, supervises the decontamination operation. All equipment not necessary for decontamination operations should be located in an uncontaminated area to limit the spread of contamination.

Table V-2. Thorough Decontamination Support Matrix (Land Forces)

Tasks	Division CMO	Division	Brigade	DISCOM	FSB	Chemical Unit	Contaminated Unit	Battalion
Preparation Phase								
Request	S	N/A	N/A	N/A	N/A	N/A	P	S
Coordination	S	N/A	S	N/A	N/A	N/A	N/A	P
Site selection	N/A	S or P		N/A	N/A	P	N/A	N/A
Advance-party linkup	N/A	N/A	N/A	N/A	N/A	S	P	S
Site setup	N/A	N/A	N/A	S	S	P	N/A	N/A
Execution Phase								
Site control/security	N/A	N/A	N/A	N/A	N/A	S	P	N/A
Predecontamination actions	N/A	N/A	N/A	N/A	N/A	P	S	N/A
Processing	N/A	N/A	N/A	N/A	N/A	P	S	N/A

Table V-2. Thorough Decontamination Support Matrix (Land Forces) (Continued)

Tasks	Division CMO	Division	Brigade	DISCOM	FSB	Chemical Unit	Contaminated Unit	Battalion
Site Clearance Phase								
Cleanup	N/A	N/A	N/A	N/A	N/A	P	P	N/A
Marking and reporting	N/A	N/A	N/A	N/A	N/A	P	N/A	N/A
Legend: P=primary; S=supporting								

    f.   A thorough decontamination site consists of the following areas:

- Predecontamination staging area.
- DED area.
- DTD area.
- Postdecontamination AA.

    g.   There should be an alternate route for vehicles that have been decontaminated but did not pass the M8 paper or ICAM test. This limits the spread of contamination by not exposing clean vehicles with vehicles that might need to be reprocessed back though the DED. The chemical unit leader selects these areas based on operational guidance, the road network, available cover and concealment, and the water supply. The contaminated unit uses the predecontamination staging area to ready itself. The postdecontamination AA is the location where the vehicles and personnel exiting the DED and DTD areas are linked up before moving from the decontamination site (see Figure V-1).

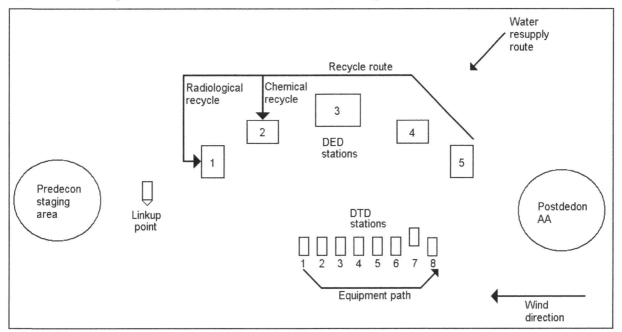

Figure V-1. Thorough Decontamination Site

5. Predecontamination Staging Area

The contaminated unit moves to the predecontamination staging area about 500 meters downwind of the thorough decontamination site. The contaminated unit performs predecontamination actions, to include segregating vehicles by checking for contamination.

   a. For chemical contamination, use the ICAM/CAM and the M8/M9 detector paper. When monitoring vehicles for contamination, there should be about 15 meters between each vehicle to prevent false positive readings with the ICAM. For radiological contamination, use the AN/PDR-77, AN/VDR-2, or ADM-300 radiac detector.

   b. If the vehicle only has isolated areas of contamination, use the M100 to decontaminate those areas. Recheck for contamination, and consider the vehicle clean if contamination is not detected.

NOTE: Do not use the M100 on sensitive items.

6. Vehicle Crews

Vehicle crews play an integral part in the thorough decontamination process.

   a. The vehicle crews, except for the drivers, dismount. As the crews dismount, they remove all contaminated equipment, including sensitive items (i.e. electro-optical), from the top and sides of the vehicles. Once the crews have exited the vehicle, they will not reenter. This prevents contamination from being spread into the vehicle interior.

   b. Using the pioneer tools from the contaminated vehicles, the crew removes all heavy mud and debris. They concentrate on the undercarriage, which would be the most likely place for contamination to collect and the hardest place to decontaminate. Once the crew is finished with the pioneer tools, they are placed back on the vehicle. The initial removal of the mud and debris makes it more likely that the decontamination wash will remove any remaining contamination.

   c. Seat covers (when applicable), canvas items, camouflage netting, wooden rails, and any other material that can absorb liquid contamination are removed. These items create a potential transfer hazard and are not easily decontaminated. Left untreated, absorbed chemical agents will desorb after being decontaminated and will create a vapor hazard. The crew removes the items that cannot be decontaminated by the standard methods used in the DTD and places them at the collection point. Decontamination unit personnel provide advice concerning the decontamination or disposal of these items.

   d. Design vehicle-loading plans to minimize the amount of equipment carried on the outside of the vehicle that cannot be readily decontaminated. Whenever possible, CBRN covers should be used when a chemical attack is expected (see *Multiservice Tactics, Techniques, and Procedures for Nuclear, Biological, and Chemical Protection*). All CBRN covers are removed and disposed of as contaminated waste during the predecontamination actions.

   e. Equipment and supplies that are exposed after removal of coverings should be checked for contamination. If the items that can be removed are uncontaminated, they should be moved via a clean route to the postdecontamination area. Contaminated equipment and supplies will be decontaminated or disposed of properly.

7. Detailed Equipment Decontamination and Detailed Troop Decontamination Areas

In coordination with the CBRN unit leader operating the decontamination site, the contaminated unit begins sending contaminated vehicles by priority for processing. Communication is maintained between the predecontamination staging area and the CBRN unit leaders. All assistant vehicle drivers are the first individuals sent through the DTD to ensure that there is a driver exchange at Station 3. See Appendix J for a series of charts to support DED station attendants and supervisors.

a. Postdecontamination AA. The CBRN unit leader selects the general location for the post decontamination AA. It must be big enough to hold the entire unit and to provide the proper cover and concealment while undergoing the thorough decontamination. The postdecontamination AA is located about 1 kilometer (km) upwind from the DED and DTD areas. The unit assembles in the postdecontamination AA after completing the DTD and DED operations. The unit occupies the postdecontamination AA until the entire unit has gone through decontamination and will then be instructed to move to a reconstitution location or a tactical AA to prepare for future operations.

b. Decontamination Sumps. The construction of decontamination sumps will be required to control the wastewater runoff from various stations in the DED and for the disposal of expendable supplies from the DED or DTD. The sumps should be of an appropriate size and volume for the station that requires the sump. To prevent the spread of contamination into the ground and to assist in the weathering process, each sump should be lined with a sufficient amount of STB. See Appendix K for a discussion on contaminated-waste disposal.

c. DTD. The contaminated unit or its higher HQ is responsible for setting up, operating, manning, and closing the DTD area at the thorough-decontamination site. The CBRN unit leader determines the general location of the DTD within the decontamination site and provides technical advice on setting up, operating, and closing the DTD area. The supervisor of the DTD must establish a work/rest cycle. There are eight stations for a DTD. Spacing between the stations is approximately 5 meters (see Figure V-2, page V-8). A summary of personnel and equipment for a DTD is provided in Table V-3, page V-8. Whenever possible, personnel should process through the DTD in buddy teams. If a buddy is not available, the station attendant will provide assistance.

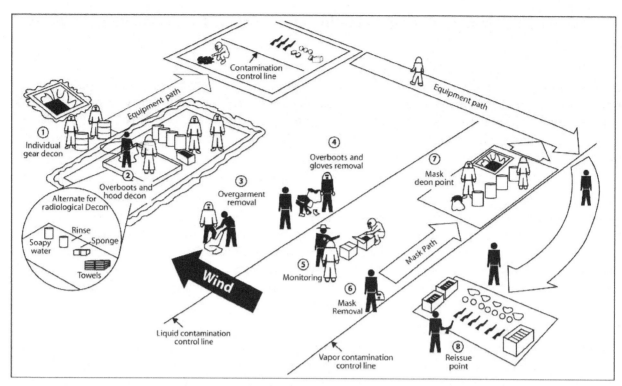

Figure V-2. DTD Layout

Table V-3. DTD Personnel and Equipment Recapitulation

Station	Personnel	Equipment and Supplies
Station 1—individual-gear decontamination	1 monitor (CAM/ICAM operator) 2 attendants	4 30-gallon containers 2 long-handled brushes 2 ponchos or plastic sheets 1 CAM/ICAM 8 books of M8 detector paper 4 M256A1 detector kits 100 plastic trash bags Sufficient STB slurry mix Rinse water *Hot, soapy water *AN/VDR-2 *Sponge
Station 2—overboots and hood decontamination	1 attendant	1 cutting tool 1 SDK or IEDK per person Large plastic sheet Plastic trash bags (as required) 10 drums of STB 1 shovel
Station 3—overgarment removal	1 attendant	2 30-gallon containers 100 plastic trash bags 10 boxes of SDKs

Table V-3. DTD Personnel and Equipment Recapitulation (Continued)

Station	Personnel	Equipment and Supplies
Station 4—overboots and gloves removal	3 attendants	8 30-gallon containers 2 long-handled brushes M8 detector paper (as required) 1 immersion heater 100 plastic trash bags 1 CAM/ICAM Engineer tape 1 cutting tool 2 ponchos or large plastic sheets 5 percent STB/HTH solution Hot, soapy water Cold rinse water
Station 5—monitoring	1 attendant (CAM/ICAM operator) 1 trauma specialist (or combat lifesaver)	1 CAM/ICAM First aid supplies 5 books of M8 detector papers 1 box of SDKs
Station 6—mask removal	2 attendants	1 M8A1 or M22 ACAA Engineer tape
Station 7—mask decontamination point	2 attendants 1 monitor	1 30-gallon container 4 3-gallon containers 1 CAM/ICAM 2 sponges 1 case of paper towels 1 immersion heater Mask sanitizing solution Hot, soapy water Rinse water
Station 8—reissue point	Unit CBRN NCO/supply sergeant	Mask PLL
* Denotes the equipment needed for radiological contamination. NOTE: Assume that an operational decontamination was done before the thorough decontamination.		

(1) Station 1—Individual-Gear Decontamination. At this station, contamination is removed from individual gear (load-bearing equipment, mask carrier, helmet, and weapon). The individual gear is checked with the ICAM or M256 kit to ensure the completeness of the decontamination.

(a) Preparation. At this station, the following equipment and supplies are needed: four 30-gallon containers for each two decontamination lanes used; two long-handled brushes for each two decontamination lanes used; sufficient STB slurry mix for chemical contamination; hot, soapy water and a sponge for radiological contamination; rinse water; two ponchos or plastic sheets; and engineer tape.

- Dig a sump that is 6 feet long, 6 feet wide, and 4 feet deep (minimum). Place four 30-gallon containers near the sump for easy changing. Fill two containers with the STB slurry mix. Fill the other two containers with clean water for rinsing, and place them about 3 feet forward of the STB containers. Place two long-handled scrub brushes at each container of STB slurry.

- Prepare the slurry. Mix 100 pounds of STB with 20 gallons of hot water. (The decontamination unit provides the hot water.) Change the mixture after 20 personnel have decontaminated their gear, and change the rinse water after every 10 personnel or when it appears dirty. Dump the old rinse water and used STB in the sump.

- Place a poncho or a plastic sheet on the ground at the checkpoint. Using engineer tape, divide the poncho or sheet in half (this is the contamination control line). Ensure that the checkpoint is a minimum of 10 feet from the other stations in order to get a true reading on the detection equipment. Place the following equipment at the checkpoint for an average company-size unit: one ICAM, eight books of M8 detector paper, four M256A1 detector kits, 100 plastic trash bags, and one AN/VDR-2 for radiological contamination. An additional CAM/ICAM may be required in the event of saturation of the ion chamber.

(b) Execution. The contaminated person decontaminates his gear by washing and scrubbing it for 6 minutes in the container with hot, soapy water or an STB slurry mix (see Figure V-3). If he is wearing the M42 mask, he should use hot, soapy water and a sponge or an STB slurry mix to decontaminate the hose and canister.

Figure V-3. Decontaminating Individual Equipment

- The contaminated person dips his gear into the clean-water container, rinses it for 4 minutes, hands it to the attendant, and then proceeds to the next station. The attendant takes the gear to the equipment checkpoint, places the decontaminated gear on the "dirty" side of the contamination control line, and returns to the container to pick up more gear. The monitor at the checkpoint checks the gear using the appropriate detection device and the procedures associated with that device. If residual contamination is detected, the attendant recycles the gear and decontaminates it again. If the gear passes the check, the attendant places it on the clean side of the contamination control line. The attendant carries the equipment to the reissue point.

- The contaminated gear may go through more extensive washing and checking procedures if time allows. The longer the gear is washed or left out in the air after washing, the lower the contamination level will be. The gear may be put in closed areas or plastic bags and checked for hazardous vapors with the M256A1 detector kit or the CAM. The CAM only detects the G- and V-series nerve-agent vapors and the H-series blister-agent vapors.

(c) Risk. If these procedures are done improperly, contamination may remain on the equipment. The resulting vapor hazard could cause casualties to unmasked personnel, particularly in closed areas (vehicle interiors) or heavily wooded areas where air circulation is poor.

(2) Station 2—Overboots and Hood Decontamination. At this station, gross contamination on overboots, trouser legs, mask, and hood is neutralized. If ample hoods are available at the reissue point, the hood should be cut away.

(a) Preparation. The following equipment and supplies are needed for the mask and the shuffle pit: one cutting tool for each decontamination lane used, one SDK or IEDK per person, plastic trash bags (as required), ten drums of STB, and one shovel. One person is required to operate this station. The attendant directs and observes the contaminated personnel as they decontaminate their overboots and hoods.

- Prepare a shuffle pit by digging a shallow pit about 3 feet long, 3 feet wide, and 6 inches deep.

- Fill the shuffle pit with STB dry mix or STB slurry, depending on the availability of water.

- Prepare the STB dry mix by mixing three parts of earth to two parts of STB.

- Prepare the STB slurry as at Station 1.

- Add more STB to the mix after ten people have processed through the shuffle pit. The CBRN unit will provide ten drums of STB for every company-size unit that goes through the station.

(b) Execution. The contaminated person walks into the shuffle pit, spreads his legs apart (double shoulder-width), bends at the waist, and uses his hands to thoroughly rub the STB dry mix or the STB slurry on his overboots and lower trouser legs (see Figure V-4, page V-12). He takes special care to rub the rear of his overboots and also removes any excess decontaminant from his gloves.

Figure V-4. Shuffle Pit Decontamination

- If a replacement hood is available, remove the hood as follows: Buddy 1 cuts the shoulder straps and draw cord on Buddy 2's hood. Buddy 1 pulls Buddy 2's hood inside out over the front of the mask, being careful not to touch the exposed neck or head. Buddy 1 gathers Buddy 2's hood in one hand and, using a cutting tool, cuts away the hood as close as possible to the eye lens outsert, voicemitter, and inlet valve covers. Make sure that nothing is left dangling below the bottom of the mask.

- If a replacement hood is not available, Buddy 1 decontaminates and rolls Buddy 2's hood in the same manner as for a MOPP gear exchange (see Chapter III). When the task is completed, Buddy 1 and Buddy 2 reverse roles.

NOTE: Personnel should check their overboots, rubber gloves, and overgarment for damage. Any rips, tears, or punctures in these items should be reported to the monitor at Station 5. This allows the monitor to check personnel for chemical-agent symptoms and check their clothing for possible contamination.

- Buddy 1 decontaminates his own gloves. He loosens Buddy 2's overgarment hood by unfastening the barrel lock. (**NOTE: If there is difficulty unfastening the barrel lock, loosen the draw cord.**) He then loosens the draw cord around the edge of the hood and unfastens the hook-and-pile fastener at the chin. Buddy 1 must take care to avoid touching Buddy 2's skin and throat.

- Buddy 1 removes Buddy 2's overgarment hood by opening the front closure flap and pulling the slide fastener from the chin down to the chest. Buddy 1 instructs Buddy 2 to turn around. Buddy 1 grasps the back of Buddy 2's hood, rolls the hood inside out (being careful not to contaminate the inner garment), and pulls the hood off.

(c) Risk. If these procedures are done improperly, contamination can be transferred from the hood to the combat boots, head, and neck.

(3) Station 3—Overgarment Removal.

(a) Preparation. At this station, the contaminated overgarments are removed before the agent penetrates the overgarment material and touches the undergarments or the skin. The following equipment and supplies are needed: two 30-gallon containers for each two decontamination lanes, 100 plastic trash bags (or about one per person), and ten boxes of SDKs. One person is required to operate this station. He directs and monitors personnel as they remove their overgarments in the same manner as a MOPP gear exchange (see Chapter III).

(b) Execution.

NOTE: The attendant avoids touching the person's skin or inner clothing. If contact is made, decontaminate immediately and then proceed with the overgarment removal.

- The attendant assists the contaminated person in removing his overgarment. The contaminated person locates his trouser suspender snap-couplers by feeling for them on the outside of his jacket and releases them. The attendant cuts and removes the M9 detector paper from around the person's wrist. He unfastens the hook-and-pile fastener over the jacket zipper, waist cord, and wrist straps on the jacket. The attendant unfastens the front-closure flap on the front of the jacket and pulls the slide fastener from the top of the chest down to the bottom of the jacket. He unfastens the webbing-strip snaps at the bottom of the jacket and releases the coat retention cord. He unfastens the back snaps and instructs the person to make a fist. Touching only the outside surface of the jacket, the attendant loosens the bottom of the jacket by pulling the material away from the body. He then pulls the jacket down and away from him (see Figure V-5).

Figure V-5. Removing the Overgarment Jacket

- The attendant instructs the person to turn around, extend his arms in front of him, and make a fist to prevent the removal of his chemical protective gloves. The attendant grasps the jacket near the shoulders and removes it by pulling it down and away from the body.

NOTE: If there is difficulty removing the jacket in this manner, pull one arm out at a time.

- The attendant cuts and removes the M9 detector paper from the trousers. He unfastens the hook-and-pile fasteners and zippers on the cuffs of the trousers. He also unfastens the front waist snaps and unzips the front zipper. He has the person lift one leg and point that foot down and bend slightly at the knees for stability. The attendant grasps the cuff of the elevated foot with a hand on each side and pulls the cuff in an alternating, jerking motion until the person can step out of the trouser leg. The process is repeated on the other leg.

NOTE: The attendant ensures that the person steps wide enough so that he will not rub his clean leg against the contaminated boot and overgarment.

(4) Station 4—Overboots and Gloves Removal. At this station, contaminated overboots and gloves are removed to limit the spread of contamination. The overboots and gloves may also be decontaminated for reissue.

(a) Preparation. At this station, the following equipment and supplies are needed for every two lanes used: engineer tape, two cutting tools, and 100 plastic trash bags (or about one per person).

- If the overboots and gloves are not being decontaminated, two 30-gallon containers are needed.

- If the overboots and gloves are being decontaminated, the following items are needed: eight 30-gallon containers; two long-handled brushes; two ponchos or large plastic sheets; one CAM; one AN/VDR-2 (for radiological contamination); four M256A1 detection kits; one immersion heater; 100 plastic trash bags; M8 detector paper, as required; 10 percent STB/HTH solution; hot, soapy water; and cold rinse water.

- If replacement overboots and gloves are available, establish a liquid contamination control line and set two 30-gallon containers 1 foot back from the line (see Figure V-6). Personnel should support themselves using the containers and discard their overgarments into the containers. An attendant directs and monitors the personnel as they remove their overboots and gloves in the same manner as a MOPP gear exchange (see Chapter III); however, the person steps over the control line instead of onto a jacket.

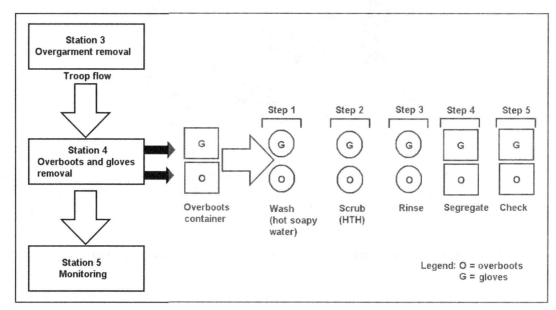

Figure V-6. Station 4 Layout

- If replacement overboots and gloves are not available, fill two 30-gallon containers with hot, soapy water; two 30-gallon containers with a 10 percent STB/HTH solution, placing two scrub brushes near the containers; and then fill two 30-gallon containers with cold rinse water. One attendant supervises and assists the personnel wearing the M42 mask. The other two attendants decontaminate the overboots and the gloves; one processes the overboots, while the other processes the gloves.

NOTE: Replace the water in all the containers once 20 items have been processed. When available, the decontamination platoon will assist with the water requirements.

- Use engineer tape to mark the liquid-contamination control line on the ground. Place the cutting tools, two dirty containers, and plastic bags on the dirty side of the liquid contamination control line. The liquid contamination control line separates the dirty and clean areas. No liquid agent should be tracked on the ground beyond the liquid contamination control line.

(b) Execution. The attendant unfastens or cuts the elastic closures on the overboots. The contaminated person faces the liquid contamination control line and steps back about 12 inches. The attendant steps on the back of the overboot and instructs him to lift his heel and work his foot out of the overboot and step across the liquid contamination control line (see Figure V-7). Repeat the process on the other foot. If this process cannot remove the overboot, the attendant cuts it off and discards it in the designated container. The person holds the fingertips of his gloves and partially slides his hands out. The attendant removes the gloves. If the contaminated person is wearing the M42 protective mask, the attendant from Station 6 carries the filter canister until it is removed. The overboots and gloves are decontaminated using the following steps:

Figure V-7. Liquid Contamination Control Line

NOTES:

1. Check all items for holes, tears, and punctures; and discard any item with a defect. Do not decontaminate any item that is unserviceable.

2. The attendant at Station 4 performs his duty from the dirty side of the liquid contamination control line.

- Step 1. Submerge the gloves and overboots in their respective container of hot, soapy water. (Some of the contamination is removed during this step.)

When the overboots and gloves are removed from the container, ensure that no water remains inside them.

- Step 2. Submerge the gloves and overboots in their respective containers of STB/HTH solution. Thoroughly scrub the items until no visible contamination remains. After scrubbing, submerge each item once more before transferring it to the rinse container.

- Step 3. Thoroughly rinse the scrubbed items, making sure that they are rinsed inside and out.

- Step 4. Place the usable items on a poncho or a plastic sheet to air-dry and weather.

- Step 5. Place the usable items in a plastic trash bag along with an M256A1 detector kit. If the detector kit shows that contamination remains, the attendants can recycle the items or discard them. However, if the kit shows no contamination, the items can be reused.

(c) Risk. If the overboots are improperly removed, the combat boots may become contaminated and contamination may be spread to the clean areas. If the gloves are not properly removed, the undergarments and skin may become contaminated.

(5) Station 5—Monitoring. At this station, contamination on personnel is identified, spot decontamination is provided, and medical aid is provided, as required.

(a) Preparation. The following equipment and supplies are needed for the attendant and health care provider: first aid supplies, one CAM/ICAM, one AN/VDR-2 (for radiological contamination), five books of M8 detector paper per 100 people, and one case of SDKs. A health care provider should be present to treat any casualties suffering from chemical-agent symptoms. If a health care provider is unavailable, a combat lifesaver should be present.

(b) Execution. The attendant checks personnel for agent vapor contamination using the CAM/ICAM (see Figure V-8). The attendant uses M8 paper to detect liquid agents. Symptoms of agent poisoning are the most obvious indication of skin contamination. At this station, the trauma specialist checks each person for symptoms of agent poisoning and treats them, as required. Personnel should report damage to their MOPP gear that was identified at Stations 2, 3, and 4. The attendant can then decontaminate the identified areas with the SDK. Personnel are remonitored after decontamination. It is possible that all liquid chemical contamination is absorbed into the clothing. If so, M8/M9 detector paper will indicate negative, even though there is a hazard.

Figure V-8. Checking for Contamination

(c) Risk. If this station is omitted, the contaminated personnel could become a casualty. After this station, the personnel will not be checked for contamination or decontaminated again. Commanders can choose to conduct a more extensive contamination check here if medical assistance and time are available. This decreases the risk of casualties.

(6) Station 6—Mask Removal. At this station, the mask is removed without contaminating the person. The mask is taken to a mask decontamination point, limiting agent transfer at the station.

(a) Preparation. The M8A1 or M22 automatic chemical-agent detector alarm (ACADA) and engineer tape are needed. Two people are needed to operate this station. They remove and carry the masks to Station 7.

(b) Execution.

- If the hood is still attached to the mask, the attendant pulls the hood over the front of the mask, grabs the mask by the voicemitter cover, and pulls the mask off the person. The person holds his breath as the mask is removed. If the mask has optical inserts, the attendant holds the mask open so that the person can remove the inserts without touching the outside of the mask. The person walks upwind 5 meters, crosses the vapor contamination control line, and then resumes breathing. The attendant brings the mask to Station 7.

NOTE: The attendant should show the individual the exit route before he removes his mask and closes his eyes.

- If the wind direction remains constant, no chemical vapor hazard is expected beyond the vapor contamination control line. Position the M8A1 or the M22 ACADA upwind of the station to warn of vapor hazards. The person getting decontaminated moves straight ahead; while his mask, which may still give off vapors, is held on the dirty side of the vapor contamination control line and taken to Station 7 where it is decontaminated.

(c) Risk. If the mask is removed improperly, the person can breathe toxic vapors. There is a high probability that the vapor hazard is still present on the mask and the hood after it is decontaminated. The person must not touch the outside of the mask because it could contaminate his bare hands. (The person then proceeds to Station 8.)

(7) Station 7—Mask Decontamination Point. At this station, all the contamination is removed from the mask.

NOTE: Once 20 items have been processed in the wash containers, replace the water. Once 10 items have been processed in the rinse water, replace it. Place the contaminated waste into the sump.

(a) Preparation.

- At this station, the following materials and equipment are needed: four containers (about a 3-gallon capacity); one CAM (for chemical only); hot, soapy water; rinse water; mask-sanitizing solution; one immersion heater; one 30-gallon container; two sponges; and one case of paper towels per company.

- Dig a sump that is 4 feet long, 4 feet wide, and 4 feet deep to discard the used filters and canisters. Place the equipment and materials as shown in Figure V-3, page V-8. Three people are needed to operate this station. Two people strip, wash, rinse, sanitize, and dry the masks. The other person checks the masks and carries them to the reissue point.

(b) Execution. Remove the eye lens outserts and the hood (if the hood was not cut off at Station 2). Remove and discard the filters or canisters. Put the items into the properly marked containers. Wash the mask, hood, eye lens outserts, and hoses on the M42 and M43 masks in hot, soapy water. Rinse these items in clean water, dip them into the sanitizing solution, agitate them for 5 minutes, and then rinse them again in clean water. Ensure that two different buckets of water are used for rinsing. Add one tube of mask-sanitizing solution (HTH) for each quart of water. Wipe the masks with rags until they are almost dry. Discard each container of mask-sanitizing solution into a sump after every ten masks. Check the masks for contamination with a CAM. If the masks are still contaminated, recycle them for more decontamination and then decontaminate your rubber gloves. If the masks are not contaminated, take the masks to the reissue point. Take care not to become contaminated or to contaminate the reissue point.

(c) Risk. If these procedures are done improperly, personnel may become contaminated when the masks are reissued at the reissue point. Even if they are done correctly, there is still a possible danger when many masks are stacked together. Small amounts of residual vapor from each mask can become potentially dangerous.

NOTE: Runners between Stations 7 and 8 are in MOPP2 and are prepared to go to MOPP4.

(8) Station 8—Reissue Point. At this station, the mask and its components are provided to personnel for reassembly and decontaminated individual equipment from Station 1 is reissued.

(a) Preparation. At this station, the protective mask prescribed load list parts are needed. The unit CBRN NCO or supply sergeant sets up the reissue point to provide personnel with replacement parts for all types of protective masks and to assist in mask maintenance. If M42 or M43 masks are used, the unit CBRN NCO must be at this station.

(b) Execution. The mask and its components are reissued to the person who assembles it in the AA. The unit CBRN NCO affixes canisters to the cleaned M42 and

M43 hoses. The person picks up their individual gear and moves to the postdecontamination AA.

(c) Risk. If these procedures are done improperly, personnel may be inadequately equipped for future operations.

NOTE: If time is critical, the CBRN NCO will have replacement chemical suits, overboots, and gloves at this station for reissue. If time is available, personnel will receive this equipment at the postdecontamination AA.

d. Resupply Support Responsibilities. The supporting decontamination unit must supply most of the equipment and supplies that are required to operate the DTD. This does not relieve the supported unit of the requirement to maintain adequate supplies to conduct DTD procedures.

(1) A decontamination unit will continue to receive support from its parent organization. The supported unit provides the decontamination unit with replacements, supplies, and material at the end of the DED. This shortens the time that the decontamination unit is not mission-capable following the DED. The supported unit must coordinate for supplies and equipment necessary to operate the DTD. Three people are at the station for proper operation.

- One person supervises the decontamination of the individual gear and takes the decontaminated equipment to the checkpoint. He also prepares a new slurry mixture as necessary.

- One person remains at the checkpoint and checks the gear using the detection equipment to ensure that it is decontaminated.

- One person transports the decontaminated gear to the reissue point.

(2) Typical nondecontamination units do not have more than two CAMs per company-size unit. However, the DTD requires a minimum of three CAMs. The supporting HQ may need to provide additional CAMs. The division support command (DISCOM) sustains the division decontamination units. A decontamination unit attached to a maneuver force identifies the resources that are needed to accomplish the mission and passes these requirements to the maneuver staff supply officer (S-4)/component logistics staff officer (G-4). The S-4 and G-4 then coordinate with the supporting CSS element to fill the requirement. The supply units that operate the Class II points issue the protective masks and overgarments. They normally package protective clothing as complete sets of MOPP equipment to support a predetermined number of personnel. Decontamination supplies may be issued in preconfigured "push" packages.

e. DED. Decontamination units are responsible for setting up, operating, and closing the DED portion of the thorough decontamination operation. The DED for CB contamination is comprised of five stations. For radiological contamination, the DED uses all but Station 2. Stations are normally 50 meters apart; however, spacing is METT-TC-dependent. Resupply procedures are of critical importance. Resupply vehicles typically operate independently and need to maintain communications with the platoon HQ in the event that the platoon relocates or needs to change linkup locations or the mission requirements change.

CAUTION

Do not kneel or touch the ground while attempting to remove contamination.

---

(1) Station 1—Primary Wash.

(a) At this station, the gross contamination and dirt are removed from the vehicle. Spray the vehicle for 2 to 3 minutes with hot, soapy water, and scrub it to help remove caked-on dirt. The mechanical action of scrubbing also helps remove thickened chemical agents. Although the undersurfaces are difficult to reach, try to remove as much dirt as possible. After scrubbing the vehicle, spray it again for 2 to 3 minutes to remove loosened dirt and contamination. This station uses about 250 gallons of water per vehicle. Larger vehicles with large quantities of dirt use more water. The runoff from this station is contaminated and must be treated as hazardous. The contaminated runoff must be controlled; if available, engineer support may be used to construct a sump. This station requires high water pressure systems (M12A1 power-driven decontamination apparatus [PDDA], M17 lightweight decontamination system [LDS], or multipurpose decontamination system [MPDS]) rather than low water volume systems (65-gallon-per-minute [GPM] pumps).

NOTE: Use 35 cubic feet of space per 250 gallons of liquid runoff when calculating the size for the drainage sump.

(b) The effectiveness of the wash depends on the type of wash (hot, soapy water; hot water; cold water; or steam). The relative effectiveness rankings for selected surfaces are listed in Table V-4. Hot, soapy water is heated from about 120°F to 140°F to and a detergent is added to reduce surface tension. The detergent removes the agent by emulsification, which is followed by the mechanical displacement of the suspension. Hot water alone is less effective than hot, soapy water. For some chemical agents, cold water exhibits better solvent characteristics. Because of the high temperature, some agents are best removed by steam through vaporization. See *Potential Military Chemical/Biological Agents and Compounds,* for the chemical and physical properties of CW agents.

Table V-4. Effectiveness of Types of Wash

Agents/Surfaces	Type of Wash
TGD on alkyd-painted metal	Hot water and/or steam; hot or cold, soapy water
TGD on CARC-painted metal	Hot, soapy water; hot water and/or steam; cold water
TGD on canvas or webbing	Steam; hot water and/or hot, soapy water; cold water
THD on alkyd-painted metal	Hot water and/or steam; hot, soapy water; cold water
THD on CARC-painted metal	Hot, soapy water; hot water and/or steam; cold water
THD on canvas or webbing	Steam; hot, soapy water; cold water; hot water
HD on alkyd-painted metal	Hot, soapy water; hot water and/or steam; cold water
HD on CARC-painted metal	Hot, soapy water and/or steam; cold water; hot water
HD on canvas or webbing	Steam; hot water; hot, soapy water; cold water
VX on alkyd-painted metal	Steam; cold water; hot water and/or hot, soapy water
VX on canvas or webbing	Steam; hot water and/or hot, soapy water; cold water
GD on canvas or webbing	Steam; hot, soapy water and/or hot water; cold water
NOTE: The types of wash are listed in the order of effectiveness, starting with the most effective to the least effective.	

(2) Station 2—Decontaminant Application.

(a) At this station, a decontaminant is applied to the entire vehicle. The vehicle is divided into four parts, and a member of the scrubbing team is assigned to each part. This limits the workload of each member of the scrubbing team and avoids duplication of work. STB slurry, STB dry mix (if the temperature is below 0°F), or another approved decontaminant is applied starting at the top of the vehicle and working toward the undercarriage. Every effort is made to apply the decontaminant to the undercarriage, especially if the vehicle has crossed a contaminated area.

(b) Before starting the decontamination operation, the decontamination crew prepares the slurry mix in the M12 PDDA or by mixing 100 pounds of STB with 20 gallons of hot water in 30-gallon containers. Each member of the scrubbing team wears a toxicological agent-protective (TAP) apron or wet-weather gear to protect him and his clothing from being saturated with water, decontaminant, or agent.

NOTE: Use 35 cubic feet of space per 250 gallons of liquid runoff when calculating the size for the drainage sump.

(c) Ensure that there is a sufficient amount of decontaminant on the item being decontaminated for neutralization to occur.

(3) Station 3—Contact Time/Interior Decontamination.

(a) At this station, the decontaminant is allowed to completely neutralize the chemical agent and the interior of the vehicle is decontaminated. Vehicles are moved to a concealed position. The attendant tracks the time each vehicle enters and exits this site to ensure that at least 30 minutes has passed. When there is a 30-minute contact time, there should be no desorption for most chemical agents. The attendant also tracks whether any contamination is found on the inside of the vehicle. This information may be needed for redeployment as part of the clearance decontamination.

(b) While the vehicle is held at this station for the decontaminant to completely react, the driver inspects the interior of the vehicle for liquid contamination. The driver is given M8 detector paper to check for chemical contamination. If he identifies contamination, he is given decontamination supplies to decontaminate the interior of the vehicle. The best decontamination solution for use in the interior of vehicles is a 5 percent solution of HTH or STB. The driver wipes all reasonably accessible surfaces with a rag or sponge soaked in the HTH or STB solution. He should not attempt to decontaminate areas where there is little likelihood of contamination (electrical assemblies, the area beneath the turret floor, etc.).

(c) Once the interior decontamination is complete, the driver places covers over the seats and floor of the vehicle. (This prevents the assistant driver from soaking excess decontaminant into his MOPP gear.) The driver dismounts the vehicle and proceeds to the start of the DTD. The assistant driver, having completed the DTD, checks with the attendant to ensure that at least 30 minutes have passed, mounts the vehicle, and moves it to the next station. All drivers must exercise caution when entering or exiting the vehicle.

(d) For radiological contamination, use an AN/PDR-77 or AN/VDR-2 radiac detector to determine the extent and location of contamination inside the vehicle. If there is contamination, determine the intensity of the contamination. If the contamination is greater than 0.33 centigray (cGy), the interior of the vehicle must be decontaminated. Use a wet sponge to wipe the interior of the vehicle.

(4) Station 4—Rinse. At this station, the decontaminant is removed from the vehicle. Spray the vehicle with water from the top to the bottom. Take care to rinse the undercarriage. This station uses about 200 gallons of water per vehicle. Failure to remove all the decontaminant from the vehicle may cause a false positive reading at Station 5. If high water pressure systems (M12A1 PDDA, M17 LDS, or MPDS) are not available, large-volume water pumps (65- and 125-GPM) should be used at this station. The driver removes plastic or other material (if present) covering the seats and floor and disposes of it as hazardous waste.

(5) Station 5—Check. At this station, the vehicle is checked to see if it has a negligible contamination level or if it still has significant contamination remaining. Detection procedures will vary depending on the type of contamination. If significant contamination is found on the vehicle, the vehicle is recycled to Station 2 for chemical contamination or to Station 1 for radiological contamination. (See Figure V-1, page V-5, for a suggested layout of the recycle route.) Caution must be exercised to prevent the vehicle from contaminating clean areas. If the vehicle cannot be recycled, the commander must decide what to do with the vehicle; at a minimum it should be segregated from the clean troops and vehicles for weathering to occur. Personnel operating the vehicle must remain in elevated MOPP. If sufficient resources and time are available, the vehicle should be placed back into a through decontamination line.

(a) Chemical (CAM Interferents).

- The ICAM/CAM is used to check for the presence of vapor from residual liquid contamination. A one-bar or lower reading on the ICAM/CAM indicates a negligible contamination level. Once the ICAM/CAM indicates the presence of vapor contamination, M8 detector paper is used to verify the presence of liquid contamination. If it is suspected that the ICAM/CAM and M8 detector paper are producing false positive results, use an M256A1 detector kit near the area to verify the presence of contamination. See Table V-5 for a list of common interferents that can cause false positive readings on the CAM. If the vehicle has significant contamination remaining, recycle it to Station 2 for chemical contamination or to Station 1 for radiological contamination. The commander may modify the recycle criteria based on mission requirements.

Table V-5. Common Interferents for the CAM

Interferents	G Agent Bar Response	H Agent Bar Response
Insect repellent	Low to very high	N/A
Brake fluid	High to very high	Very high
General-purpose cleaner	High	N/A
Burning kerosene	N/A	High
Breath mints	High	N/A
Gasoline vapors	Low	Low
Burning grass	Low to high	Low
Burning gas	Low	N/A
Green smoke	Low	Low to high
Break-free oil	Low	N/A
Ammonia	Very high	N/A

- There will be desorption of chemical agents from the surfaces after decontamination. The desorption of vapors on surfaces painted with the CARC will stop sooner than it will on surfaces painted with alkyd. Consider this when checking decontaminated items for overall decontamination effectiveness.

(b) Radiological. Use the AN/PDR-77, ADM-300, or AN/VDR-2 to determine if any contamination remains. If there is contamination remaining, determine the intensity of the contamination inside and outside the vehicle. If the contamination is greater than 0.33 centigray per hour (cGy/hr), the vehicle is then recycled to Station 1.

f. Recycle Criteria. The commander, with the CBRN unit leader's help, establishes the recycle criteria before starting the decontamination operations. The recycle criteria determine which vehicles will return to Station 1 after contamination is detected. If the unit has sufficient time and resources, any vehicle having more contamination than the acceptable level should be recycled. However, time and resources are usually limited and not all vehicles can be recycled. The recycle criteria are based on the weathering effects.

g. Reconstitution Criteria. The operational and thorough decontamination operations that are performed on vehicles or major equipment will be recorded on the *Operator's Inspection Guide and Trouble Report (General-Purpose Vehicles)*. This information will become a permanent record for these vehicles or major equipment. The entries that are required on this form are the type of decontamination performed, decontaminant used, date-time group (DTG) completed, location of the decontamination site, and type of monitoring equipment used to verify decontamination completeness. This information will assist with reconstitution operations once the conflict or war has ended.

h. DED Layouts.

(1) Decontamination units establish thorough decontamination sites differently because of organization and equipment differences. The optimum layout for each type unit is described in the following paragraphs. This layout provides the maximum output for units at 100 percent personnel and equipment strength. The equipment and personnel requirements for the optimum layout are identified for the decontamination unit and the supported unit (augmenter) (see Table V-6, page V-24).

Table V-6. Personnel and Equipment Requirements for the Optimum DED Layout of an M12A1 PDDA-Equipped Unit

Stations	Personnel		Equipment and Supplies
	Decontamination platoon	**Augmentees**	
Station 1—Primary wash	1 squad leader 1 PDDE operator 2 sprayers	4 scrubbers	1 M12A1 PDDA 1 3,000-gallon tank 2 65-/125-GPM pumps 6 long-handled brushes 4 TAP aprons Liquid detergent 1 TPU 2 flashlights
Station 2—Decontaminant application	1 squad leader 1 PDDE operator 2 sprayers	8 scrubbers	1 M12A1 PDDA 1 3,000-gallon tank 18 long-handled brushes 9 mops with extra mop heads 3 30-gallon containers Sufficient STB 4 TAP aprons 1 TPU 2 flashlights
Station 3—Contact time/interior decontamination	1 NCO	2 assistants	2 AN/VDR-2s 3 TAP aprons 6 30-gallon containers 10 books of M8 detector paper 30 sponges 8 M256A1 detector kits 50 trash bags 1 clipboard 1 pen 1 stopwatch
Station 4—Rinse	1 squad leader 1 PDDE operator 2 pump operators	2 sprayers	1 M12A1 PDDA 1 3,000-gallon tank 3 65-/125-GPM pumps 1 TPU 2 TAP aprons 2 flashlights
Station 5—Check	2 NCOs or CAM operators	None	2 CAMs 10 M256A1 detector kits 20 books of M8 detector paper 2 AN/VDR-2s 2 M8A1 or M22 ACAAs
C2	1 PL 1 PSG	None	1 HMMWV with a radio 3 NBC marking kits
Total Personnel	17	16	N/A

(2) Since it is unlikely that all units will be at 100 percent strength, alternate layouts are discussed. For each alternate layout, decontamination unit equipment requirements are identified. However, personnel requirements are not identified by the

chemical unit and supported unit. The total number of personnel that are needed is identified, with a minimum number of decontamination unit personnel.

i. Alternate-Layout Planning Considerations. CBRN unit leaders use METT-TC to determine the best possible DED layout to execute their mission. When determining alternate DED layouts, they use the following guidelines:

(1) The ability to spray hot, soapy water or steam under pressure must be retained at Station 1.

(2) The largest number of people is required at Station 2.

(3) Experienced and qualified ICAM/CAM operators are required at Station 5.

(4) Water does not have to be hot to rinse off the decontaminant; however, the lower the water pressure, the greater the amount of water required for the rinse.

j. Decontamination Unit (M12A1).

(1) The optimum DED layout for an M12A1 PDDA-equipped decontamination unit requires the use of all authorized equipment and personnel. While this DED layout is manpower- and equipment-intensive, it provides for the rapid decontamination of vehicles and equipment (eight vehicles processed per hour). This layout uses dual lanes at Stations 1, 4, and 5 to process two vehicles at a time. Since the most time- and labor-intensive work takes place at Station 3, this station is designed to process three vehicles at a time.

(2) It may not be possible for an M12A1 PDDA-equipped decontamination unit to use the optimum DED layout. Limited personnel or equipment will affect the DED layout. See Table V-7 for an alternate layout. The processing rate using this layout will be affected by work/rest cycles (see Table V-8, page V-26).

Table V-7. Personnel and Equipment Requirements for the Alternate DED Layout of an M12A1 PDDA-Equipped Unit

Stations	Personnel	Equipment and Supplies
Station 1—Primary wash	1 NCOIC* 1 PDDE operator* 2 sprayers 2 scrubbers	1 M12A1 PDDA 1 3,000-gallon tank 2 65-/125-GPM pumps 4 long-handled brushes 4 TAP aprons Liquid detergent 1 TPU 2 flashlights
Station 2—Decontaminant application	1 NCOIC* 1 PDDE operator* 2 sprayers 8 scrubbers	1 M12A1 PDDA 1 3,000-gallon tank 12 long-handled brushes 4 mops with extra mop heads 3 30-gallon containers Sufficient STB 1 TPU 4 TAP aprons 2 flashlights

Table V-7. Personnel and Equipment Requirements for the Alternate DED Layout of an M12A1 PDDA-Equipped Unit (Continued)

Stations	Personnel	Equipment and Supplies
Station 3—Contact time/interior decontamination	1 NCO* 2 interior decontamination assistants	2 AN/VDR-2s 3 TAP aprons 6 30-gallon containers 10 books of M8 detector paper 30 sponges 8 M256A1 detector kits 50 trash bags 1 clipboard 1 pen 1 stopwatch
Station 4—Rinse	1 NCOIC* 1 PDDE operator* 2 sprayers	1 M12A1 PDDA 1 3,000-gallon tank 3 65-/125-GPM pumps 1 TPU 2 TAP aprons 2 flashlights
Station 5—Check	2 NCOs or CAM operators*	2 CAMs 10 M256A1 detector kits 20 books of M8 detector paper 2 AN/VDR-2s 2 M8A1 or M22 ACAAs
C2	1 PL* 1 PSG*	1 HMMWV with a radio 3 NBC marking kits
Total Personnel	29	N/A

*Denotes personnel from the decontamination unit.

Table V-8. Recommended Work/Rest Cycles for DED

Temperatures	Stations and Workload				
	Station 1 Primary Wash	Station 2 Decontaminant Application	Station 3 Contact Time/Interior Decontamination	Station 4 Rinse	Station 5 Check
	Physical Exertion				
	Moderate	Heavy	Moderate	Moderate	Light
Cool (less than 68°F)	60 work 15 rest	30 work 30 rest	60 work 15 rest	60 work 15 rest	60 work 15 rest
Warm (68°–74°F)	45 work 45 rest	20 work 20 rest	45 work 45 rest	45 work 45 rest	50 work 50 rest
Hot (74°–84°F)	30 work 60 rest	15 work 30 rest	30 work 60 rest	30 work 60 rest	40 work 80 rest
Very hot (greater than 84°F)	20 work 60 rest	10 work 30 rest	20 work 60 rest	20 work 60 rest	25 work 75 rest

NOTE: When operating in temperatures above 75°F, consider the ability of the personnel to accomplish the mission. Once the personnel have reached their maximum workload for heat stress, they cannot recover quickly enough to accomplish the decontamination mission. A viable option is to postpone the decontamination operation until a cooler part of the day or evening. This will reduce the heat stress load on the personnel and increase the probability of mission success.

k. Decontamination Platoon (M17 LDS or MPDS).

(1) The decontamination units equipped with the M17 LDS or MPDS will set up the DED differently than the decontamination units equipped with the M12A1 PDDA (see Table V-9). While the optimum DED layout is manpower- and equipment-intensive, it provides for the rapid decontamination of vehicles and equipment (eight vehicles processed per hour). The layout uses dual lanes at Stations 1, 4, and 5 to process two vehicles at a time. Since the most time- and labor-intensive work takes place at Station 3, this station is designed to process three vehicles at a time. The processing rate of this layout will be affected by any work/rest cycles.

Table V-9. Personnel and Equipment Requirements for the Optimum DED Layout of an M17 LDS-Equipped Unit

Stations	Personnel		Equipment and Supplies
	Decontamination platoon	**Augmenter**	
Station 1—Primary wash	1 squad leader 4 sprayers 2 scrubbers	2 scrubbers	2 M17 LDSs 2 3,000-gallon tanks 2 65-/125-GPM pumps 6 long-handled brushes 8 TAP aprons Liquid detergent 2 flashlights
Station 2—Decontaminant application	1 squad leader 3 appliers/mixers	8 appliers	2 65-/125-GPM pumps 1 3,000-gallon tank 18 long-handled brushes 9 mops with extra mop heads 6 30-gallon containers Sufficient STB 2 flashlights
Station 3—Contact time/interior decontamination	1 NCO 2 assistants	None	2 AN/VDR-2s 3 TAP aprons 6 30-gallon containers 10 books of M8 detector paper 30 sponges 8 M256A1 detector kits 50 trash bags 1 clipboard 1 pen 1 stopwatch
Station 4—Rinse	1 squad leader 4 sprayers	2 sprayers	1 M12A1 PDDA 1 3,000-gallon tank 3 65-/125-GPM pumps 2 TPUs 2 TAP aprons 2 flashlights

Table V-9. Personnel and Equipment Requirements for the Optimum DED Layout of an M17 LDS-Equipped Unit (Continued)

Stations	Personnel		Equipment and Supplies
	Decontamination platoon	Augmenter	
Station 5—Check	2 NCOs or CAM operators	None	2 CAMs 10 M256A1 detector kits 20 books of M8 detector paper 2 AN/VDR-2s 2 M8A1 or M22 ACAAs
C2	1 PL 1 PSG	None	1 HMMWV with a radio 3 NBC marking kits
Total Personnel	**23**	**12**	**N/A**

(2) It may not be possible for an M17 LDS- or MPDS-equipped decontamination unit to use the optimum DED layout. Limited personnel or equipment will affect the DED layout. See Table V-10 for an alternate layout.

Table V-10. Personnel and Equipment Requirements for the Alternate DED Layout of an M17 LDS-Equipped Unit

Stations	Personnel	Equipment and Supplies
Station 1—Primary wash	1 NCOIC* 4 sprayers 4 scrubbers	2 M17 LDSs or MPDSs 1 3,000-gallon tank 2 65-/125-GPM pumps 4 long-handled brushes 8 TAP aprons Liquid detergent 2 flashlights
Station 2—Decontaminant application	1 NCOIC* 8 scrubbers/mixers	2 65-/125-GPM pumps 1 3,000-gallon tank 12 long-handled brushes 8 mops with extra mop heads 3 30-gallon containers Sufficient STB 2 flashlights
Station 3—Contact time/interior decontamination	1 NCO* 2 interior decontamination assistants	2 AN/VDR-2s 3 TAP aprons 6 30-gallon containers 10 books of M8 detector paper 30 sponges 8 M256A1 detector kits 50 trash bags 1 clipboard 1 pen 1 stopwatch
Station 4—Rinse	1 NCOIC* 4 sprayers	2 M17 LDSs or MPDSs 1 3,000-gallon tank 2 65-/125-GPM pumps 4 TAP aprons 2 flashlights

Table V-10. Personnel and Equipment Requirements for the Alternate DED Layout of an M17 LDS-Equipped Unit (Continued)

Stations	Personnel	Equipment and Supplies
Station 5—Check	2 NCOs or CAM operators*	2 CAMs 10 M256A1 detector kits 20 books of M8 detector paper 2 AN/VDR-2s 2 M8A1 or M22 ACAAs
C2	1 PL* 1 PSG*	1 HMMWV with a radio 3 NBC marking kits
Total Personnel	30	N/A
*Denotes personnel from the decontamination unit.		

l. Thorough Decontamination Site Closure. Once all vehicles and personnel from the contaminated unit have processed through the thorough decontamination site, the site can be closed. Coordination with the supported unit is necessary before actually closing the site to ensure that all contaminated elements have been processed. The decontamination unit closes the DED first. Once the DED is closed, the decontamination unit processes through the DTD. After the chemical unit has processed through the DTD, the DTD is closed. At this point, the decontamination unit marks the area as a contaminated area and reports its exact location to the supported unit using an NBC5 Report.

(1) Closing the DED Area. The DED is closed in sequence, starting at Station 1. All vehicles, equipment, and nonexpendable supplies are inspected for contamination. If contamination is found on an item, it is decontaminated.

(a) Station 1—Primary Wash. Spray all vehicles and equipment with hot, soapy water to remove any contamination that could have been transferred during the primary wash operations. Drain the water billets or fabric tanks of water. Inspect all equipment and vehicles for contamination using the appropriate detection equipment.

(b) Station 2—Decontaminant Application. Throw the mops and brushes that were used in applying the decontaminant into a sump or bury them. Inspect the unused decontaminant, and load it on a vehicle.

(c) Station 3—Contact Time/Interior Decontamination. Inspect any unused supplies and equipment for contamination. If no contamination is detected, load the equipment and supplies on a vehicle. Throw all contaminated supplies into the nearest sump.

(d) Station 4—Rinse. Spray all vehicles and equipment with hot, soapy water to remove any contamination that could have been transferred during the rinse operations. Drain the water billets or fabric tanks. Inspect all the equipment and vehicles for contamination using the appropriate detection equipment. If no contamination is detected, load the equipment onto the vehicles. Spread one can of STB dry mix into each of the sumps and then cover them. Post NBC hazard markers near the covered sumps.

(e) Station 5—Check. Ensure that all equipment has been checked for contamination. If it is not contaminated, load it onto a vehicle. If it is contaminated, decontaminate it according to the appropriate technical manual (TM). Throw any contaminated supplies into the nearest sump. Move all vehicles upwind of Station 5 and inspect them again for contamination. If any contamination is detected, use the M100 to decontaminate the identified areas. Once the vehicles are staged, all personnel proceed to the DTD.

(2) Closing the DTD Area. Once all personnel from the DED have processed through the DTD, it may be closed. After the last person has exited the DTD—

(a) Pick up all used supplies from Station 7, and put them in the Station 7 sump. Remove the contamination control line. If engineer tape was used, dispose of it in the Station 7 sump.

(b) Move all usable supplies and equipment from all stations to Station 1. Discard all unusable supplies from Stations 3, 4, and 5 in the Station 1 sump.

(c) Decontaminate all supplies and equipment collected at Station 1 using the decontamination and rinse water at Station 1. Pour the decontamination and rinse water from the station into the sump, and decontaminate the containers.

(d) Mark the entire decontamination area. Remove your overgarment using the MOPP gear exchange technique, and dispose of it in the sump at Station 1.

(e) Move any equipment used to fill the sump upwind of the decontamination area. Decontaminate rubber gloves, and move all remaining equipment and supplies at Station 1 upwind of the decontamination area. Keep this equipment and supplies separate from that used to fill the sump.

NOTE: See Appendix K for detailed procedures on the disposal of contaminated waste.

8. Thorough Decontamination Under Unusual Conditions

Decontamination operations are not restricted to daylight hours. The enemy may employ CBRN weapons at night, since weather conditions are usually more favorable for their employment. Consequently, CBRN contamination encountered at night may require decontamination before daylight.

a. Conducting decontamination operations at night is a challenge. "White light" cannot be used without possibly revealing your location. However, decontamination personnel must have illumination to perform essential decontamination tasks such as spraying water, applying decontaminants, using detection equipment, and doffing the MOPP gear.

b. Use M8/M9 detector paper to check for chemical contamination and to see how well the chemical decontamination was performed. If contamination is present, the paper color changes to red, which cannot be seen if red-filtered light is used. The CAM and M256A1 detector kit can be used to identify and detect chemical agents, but they require a light source to obtain a reading.

c. Several vehicles waiting for or undergoing decontamination present a significant infrared signature because of the hot engines. Entering, exiting, and moving within the decontamination site is difficult under blackout conditions.

d. Night-decontamination operations are difficult, but they can be accomplished. Conduct thorough decontamination operations in built-up areas, whenever possible. Use a building for DTD operations and a warehouse for DED operations, if available. This allows the use of white light. Personnel can see what they are decontaminating, see where they are going, and read the color changes of the M8/M9 detector paper.

e. There will be a need for additional people to act as ground guides in the DED area. The NCOICs of Stations 1, 2, and 4 will inspect each vehicle with a flashlight or chemical light before the vehicle can proceed to the next station. There should be at least two flashlights at each station in the DED and DTD areas.

9. Colocation of Patient Decontamination With Troop Decontamination

The decontamination of patients for entry into an MTF or while they are awaiting evacuation in clean vehicles for transport to an MTF can be established adjacent to a DTD area. Close coordination needs to be maintained between medical personnel supervising the patient decontamination and personnel supervising the DTD. This offers benefits to both units.

NOTE: See Chapter X and FM 4-02.7 for more information.

THIS PAGE IS INTENTIONALLY LEFT BLANK.

Chapter VI
CLEARANCE DECONTAMINATION

1. Background

a. Clearance decontamination is the final level of decontamination. It is the most resource-intensive. It requires command involvement, guidance, and decisions on the disposition of possible mission-essential equipment.

b. Clearance decontamination provides the decontamination of equipment and personnel to a level that allows unrestricted transportation, maintenance, employment and disposal. Clearance decontamination can be used to prepare organizations or individual units for return to their home garrisons, whether within the United States, its territories, or possessions. At the end of a conflict or at normal rotation during peacekeeping or nation-building operations, a unit may be ordered to return to garrison. US military assets may also be required to support clearance decontamination to support HLS/HLD requirements.

c. Tasks given to CBRN defense personnel or elements supporting clearance decontamination may involve the physical status of the unit or activity itself, or they may involve the fulfillment of obligations under a treaty or memorandum of understanding (MOU) to the HN. These tasks may include the following:

- Recordkeeping.
- Postconflict intelligence preparation of the battlespace (IPB).
- FP.
- Decontamination.
- Containment of residual hazards.
- Recovery and control of enemy CBRN capabilities.
- FHP.
- Coordination with multinational forces or nonmilitary entities.
- Contaminated material retrogradation.

c. Most of the specified and implied tasks of CBRN defense personnel supporting clearance decontamination are simultaneous and interdependent. For example, post conflict IPB supports FP, containment of residual hazards, and contaminated material retrogradation. Clearance decontamination may include supporting recovery and control of the enemy CBRN hazards (see Figure VI-1, page VI-2). Recordkeeping supports virtually all other tasks. Recovery operations are closely related to conflict termination.

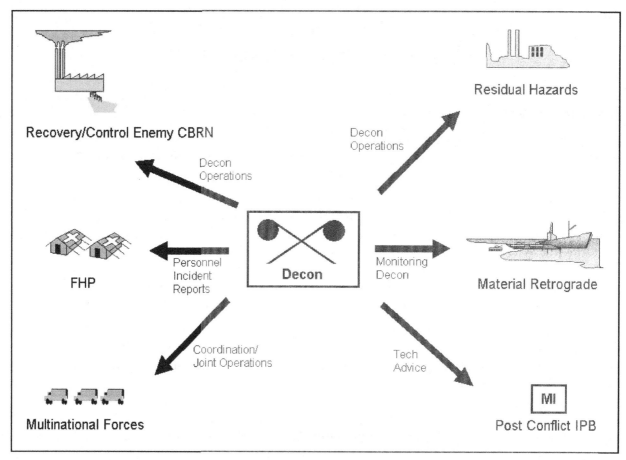

Figure VI-1. Decontamination Support

e. Clearance decontamination requires a significant level of effort. The resources needed to conduct clearance decontamination (i.e., low-level CBRN or TIM monitoring capabilities, decontamination units, MEDSURV, supplies, and equipment) require coordination from the unit level through the combatant command level.

2. Postconflict Intelligence Preparation of the Battlespace

As a conflict ends, there remain significant IPB-related functions that may continue to require decontamination support.

a. Even when the conflict has terminated, the continued presence of threat CBRN weapons, contaminated areas, and TIM hazards presents volatile situations. This may be particularly true as HN and international relief agencies enter the area. CBRN defense assets may be tasked to support intelligence collection on enemy CBRN weapons that are assessed to exist but which have not been captured or destroyed. In such cases, intelligence will attempt to develop a complete picture of the enemy's residual CBRN assets and capabilities—including probable locations and dispositions of weapons and agents, research and production facilities, documentation, key enemy military and civilian personnel, and possible reaction from residual enemy forces.

b. The CBRN defense personnel may also be tasked to assess the hazards from indigenous TIM facilities that have suffered collateral damage and to be prepared to deal with the release of TIM from those facilities.

3. Force Protection

During conflict termination, FP measures still deter, detect, contain, and mitigate the possible effects of CBRN attacks and threats. Unit draw-down may invite strikes by residual enemy forces or terrorists to punish and inflict revenge on the United States and coalition forces. Planning for decontamination operations, therefore, must continue. Decontamination site selection can now be based on internal lines of communication (LOCs) rather than the axis of advance, which facilitates logistics and transportation. Other site selection considerations (such as road network accessibility, water sources and drainage, and likely wind direction) still apply.

4. Decontamination

Clearance decontamination may be required as part of a supported unit's restoration operations. For example, a unit may now have time to conduct clearance decontamination that was deferred during previous operations. Decontamination elements may also be tasked to support the decontamination of civilian personnel, equipment, facilities or terrain in coordination with HN authorities. See *Multiservice Tactics, Techniques, and Procedures for NBC Defense of Theater Fixed Sites, Ports, and Airfields* for more information on clearance decontamination procedures.

5. Containment of Residual Hazards

Expect to receive taskings to identify, assess, and mitigate contamination hazards that may remain at the end of the conflict. An assessment based on the accurate records of known hazards will help determine what actions are necessary (e.g., isolation, weathering, decontamination, containerization). Decontamination may be required, and decontaminated materials may be transferred to the HN or to follow-on forces.

6. Recovery and Control of Enemy Chemical, Biological, Radiological, and Nuclear Capabilities

Emphasis will be placed on identifying and securing enemy CBRN capabilities. As enemy CBRN weapons, agents, and facilities are discovered, they will likely be disabled, destroyed, or isolated. Decontamination elements can expect taskings to support the recovery and control of enemy CBRN capabilities.

a. As in combat operations, prior planning will facilitate decontamination support and ensure that the mission is successful. Decontamination elements should maintain close coordination with those forces searching for and assessing residual enemy CBRN capabilities (particularly the types of agents, locations, and size of facilities). This coordination will enable decontamination planners to anticipate logistics, transportation, and personnel requirements.

b. A search and recovery task force (S/RTF), formed to gain timely control over enemy CBRN capabilities, may include a decontamination specialist to advise on how items, facilities, or hazard areas may be decontaminated or advise on the practicality of decontamination. This specialist would provide vital planning information to the decontamination element.

c. The S/RTF would also provide emergency responses to CBRN incidents or accidents, resulting in an emergency response from the supporting decontamination element. This requires the decontamination element to maintain close coordination with its higher HQ and supporting transportation and logistics elements.

7. Force Health Protection

a. The services use MEDSURV systems to identify outbreaks of illness, which can help in the assessment and identification of potential BW casualties. Medical teams can identify, treat, and handle CBRN casualties. MTFs have personnel who are trained in decontamination procedures so that only clean patients will enter and be admitted to hospitals. Biologically contagious patients can be treated under isolation conditions. HSS systems also conduct health risk assessments for CBRN and TIM exposure and monitor individual exposure as part of their recordkeeping. For more information, see FM 4-02.7.

b. Records kept by decontamination elements also contribute to the surveillance process. When coordinated with health service units is maintained, useful information on individual exposure and decontamination (such as the type of agent, level of radiation exposure, number of exposed individuals, dates and times of exposure events) can be provided to assess the patient's condition and short- and long-term treatment requirements.

8. Coordination With Multinational Forces or Nonmilitary Entities

a. As combat operations terminate, multinational forces or HN elements may arrive and assume missions from redeploying US units. The activities of these forces and organizations may include the decontamination and management of contaminated areas. The US decontamination elements may be tasked to take the lead or to assist in these activities. Working relationships with these elements should be defined by a treaty or MOU.

b. Incoming personnel must be briefed on multinational or HN procedures, equipment, and training. In any case, ensure that the responsibilities of each element and the procedures to be used are agreed to and clearly understood by all parties.

9. Contaminated Materials Retrogradation

As a part of unit redeployment, some equipment to be redeployed (retrograded) may have potential residual or low-level contamination. Suspected equipment may be identified through the records made during operational and thorough decontamination operations. Also, any vehicle or piece of equipment that was present in an attack or a downwind hazard area may have residual contamination.

a. If equipment is to be retrograded under nonemergency conditions, then it is assumed that there will be time for thorough and clearance decontamination and weathering. Redeployment planning should specify consolidation points in the JRA for equipment suspected of residual contamination. Specialized detectors and monitors may be needed for clearance decontamination to confirm and monitor for contamination. As suspected equipment is consolidated for monitoring, decontamination, and weathering, security and buffer zones around the site provide an additional contamination control measure. Personnel engaged in monitoring, preparation, and clearance decontamination of equipment will require stringent personal protection and specialized detectors. This process may continue for weeks or months.

b. Even after thorough decontamination, potential vapor and contact hazards will likely remain. The risk increases as contaminated equipment is consolidated and as personnel work around the equipment for extended periods. The risk increases again as equipment is disassembled for maintenance or containerization (therefore, the need for clearance decontamination). However, given the limitations of decontamination technology, some items of equipment may require extensive weathering before retrogradation, or may have to be destroyed.

c. Once in the continental United States (CONUS), an item of equipment with a contamination history will require precautionary measures throughout its remaining life cycle. Guidance on the eventual disposition of previously contaminated equipment should be provided from the strategic level.

d. Accurate record keeping is crucial to a successful clearance decontamination operation. Messages sent or received via the NBCWRS; records of personnel and equipment undergoing operational, thorough, and clearance decontamination; and photographic or video records will be referred to again in assessing a unit's requirements during clearance decontamination operations and in evaluating the (former) battlespace for residual CBRN and TIM hazards. Especially important are NBC 4, 5, and 6 reports, which may also be used to report TIM hazards. There may be a requirement to share information on contaminated areas (contained in NBC 4, 5, and 6 reports) with the HN. (The security that surrounded an NBC5 report during operations may no longer be required when hostilities have ceased.) These reports may also form the basis for new CBRN reconnaissance and monitoring missions at the end of hostilities.

(1) Records pertaining to personnel and equipment that have undergone operational and thorough decontamination are also necessary for assessing the unit undergoing clearance decontamination. These records are made at the predecontamination triage (they identify elements that required decontamination and identify uncontaminated elements that were sent ahead to the postdecontamination AA) and should contain vehicle and equipment identification numbers. While the contaminated unit is responsible for maintaining an accurate decontamination record, it is useful for the supporting decontamination element to keep a duplicate record. For example, such records can be used to justify the expenditure of decontamination materials and the reordering of supplies. In the context of clearance decontamination operations, the decontamination element may be required to account for decontaminated personnel and equipment, even those that belong to a supported unit.

(2) Prepare follow-up reports as the conflict nears an end. Prepare summaries that outline when, where, and how CBRN attacks or TIM incidents occurred. These records will facilitate many of the tasks associated with clearance decontamination operations, particularly postconflict IPB and the containment of residual hazards. Site incident reports involving personnel will be useful in evaluating long-term health issues that could be operationally related and will contribute to overall FHP.

THIS PAGE IS INTENTIONALLY LEFT BLANK.

Chapter VII

FIXED-SITE, PORT, AND AIRFIELD DECONTAMINATION

1. Background

a. This chapter addresses fixed-site decontamination, capabilities, and organization. It also discusses the procedures for processing personnel on a fixed site for chemical and radiological decontamination. See *Multiservice Tactics, Techniques, and Procedures for Chemical, Biological, Radiological, and Nuclear Defense of Fixed Sites, Ports, and Airfields* for more detailed information on CBRN decontamination operations for fixed sites. Decontamination is necessary when protective items cannot be worn to perform the mission, or when long-term occupancy is anticipated. Examples of fixed sites include the following:

- Command, control, communications, and intelligence facilities.
- Ports and airfields.
- Temporary key structures for reserve and large troop concentration.
- Supply installations, and depots.
- Pre-positioning of material configured to unit sets (POMCUS) storage locations, airfields, water terminals, and rail terminals.
- MTFs.
- Ammunition supply points and petroleum, oils, and lubricants (POL) points.
- Maintenance sites.

b. Decontaminate as soon as possible. Remove any contamination that forces personnel into a higher MOPP level. The first steps in recovering mission effectiveness are personnel decontaminating themselves, their personal equipment, and critical, mission-essential equipment.

c. Decontaminate only what is necessary. For fixed sites, decontamination is more of a manpower resource constraint rather than a time constraint. Decontaminate only mission-essential equipment, and mark contamination appropriately. An example of this principle is the loading and unloading of supplies on a boxcar at a site with railheads. Since fixed-site personnel do not have the capability to decontaminate the entire boxcar, only those parts that are touched, such as the door, are decontaminated.

d. Decontaminate by priority. The commander must establish a set of priorities. These priorities may be broken down by functional area if the site performs missions such as maintenance (light and heavy), ammunition repair and supply, and general supply. Items such as wheeled vehicles, forklifts, and railcars, which are critical to the overall mission, should be decontaminated first.

e. Limit the spread of contamination. Units should conduct decontamination (operational and thorough) outside the contaminated area but near where the contamination occurred. This reduces the risk of spreading contamination to other areas and reduces travel time.

2. Assessing Capability

Fixed-site decontamination capabilities must be adapted for each fixed site. Mobile decontamination equipment capabilities may be available at a fixed site to decontaminate equipment, roads, and buildings. Loading docks, entries and exits, and building exteriors can be decontaminated with more conventional methods such as using STB and soap and water. Equipment such as fire trucks could also be used. Commanders should identify all systems that are capable of contributing to the decontamination effort (e.g., fire trucks, steam cleaners, water pumps). Decontamination equipment can be retrofitted to accommodate the throughput of each work area. For instance, rest-and-relief shelters need rapid personnel decontamination systems, and supply operations need a decontamination system that can handle moderate-size pieces of equipment at a high volume.

3. Organizing for Decontamination

The commander should designate and train teams that can perform decontamination for fixed-site operations. The following are fixed-site decontamination techniques that the teams could apply:

a. Decontamination can be conducted at contaminated entry and exit points to sustain the mission. This concept is more practical and efficient when employing limited decontaminated assets. The STB application could be conducted 3 meters on each side of the entry and exit points. Transfer hazard will remain a problem until all parts of the area have weathered. Buildings entries and exits must be decontaminated accordingly.

b. To decontaminate helipads and similar sites, spray STB on entry and exit approaches or on paths in an event that chemical contamination occurs. Airborne STB particles can damage sensitive aircraft components so the area should be washed with water prior to landing helicopters.

c. In POMCUS sites, decontaminate entry and exit approaches to limit contamination. Exposed vehicles in motor parks will get contaminated, but most likely there will not be enough personnel to drive the vehicles to a decontamination station. Decontaminate parked equipment by spraying them with STB or hot, soapy water. Driving other vehicles around the parked vehicles and equipment will get the outside air flowing and will accelerate the weathering process of the chemical agents.

d. Establish a patient transfer zone for medical assets where designated dirty ambulances coming from the contaminated area can transfer patients to clean ambulances for patient movement to the MTF.

4. Buildings and Mission-Essential Operating Areas and Surfaces

The decontamination of buildings and mission-essential surfaces and equipment requires a well-thought-out process.

a. Buildings. The decontamination of a building consists of two parts—interior and exterior.

(1) Interior. When conducting decontamination of the interior of a building, the following activities must occur:

- Secure the facility.
- Sample to confirm and determine the extent of the contamination.

- Evaluate the sampling results.
- Isolate the areas to prevent the spread of the contamination.
- Remove critical objects for special decontamination procedures. Take care to ensure that contamination is not spread or transferred during movement.
- Decontaminate localized areas of the contamination.
- Continue monitoring and protecting against low-level exposure risks.
- Document and record the decontamination operations.

(2) Exterior. When decontaminating the exterior of a building, see Appendix D to determine how to decontaminate specific building surfaces (e.g., roofing material and wood). Many materials may absorb contamination and may not be completely decontaminated. The removal or sealing (painting) of these surfaces may be required to reduce the hazard. Continue monitoring the decontaminated surfaces until the detector indicates there is no more off-gassing. As temperatures rise, off-gassing of previously contaminated surfaces may occur at detectable levels. A point detection device (e.g., ICAM/CAM) should be used to monitor contaminated surfaces.

b. Mission-Essential Operating Surfaces and Equipment.

(1) On- and Off-Loading Ramps and Piers. Use Appendix D to determine how to decontaminate the surfaces of on- and off-loading ramps and piers.

(2) Helipads. Use Appendix D to determine how to decontaminate helipad surfaces.

(3) Lines of Communications. See Appendix I for information on terrain decontamination.

(4) Staging Areas. Staging areas pose a unique opportunity for the enemy to contaminate large amounts of personnel and equipment. Commanders and their CBRN staffs must ensure that they can effectively identify contaminated personnel and equipment. Decontaminating only those personnel and equipment that have been contaminated saves resources and time. The decontamination of staging areas can be critical to operations. In addition to the personnel and equipment contaminated, contaminated routes in and out of staging areas must be decontaminated to reduce the likelihood of the spread of the contamination. See *Multiservice Tactics, Techniques, and Procedures for Nuclear, Biological, and Chemical Reconnaissance* for methods to determine the location and extent of contamination.

(5) Terrain. Terrain decontamination is covered in Appendix I of this manual.

5. Personnel Processing Procedures (Chemical)

A comprehensive CBRN VA can help determine a suitable location for the fixed-site contamination control area (CCA) and the toxic-free area (TFA) complexes. The next consideration is determining how large an area will be needed. The CCA and TFA may be off or on the installation. The location of the CCA and TFA will depend on feedback from the CBRN VA.

a. **Off Site.** The decision to site CCA and TFA complexes off the installation (probably at preselected sites located at least 10 km from the installation) should work if the following parameters are present:

(1) The sites are located at least 15 km away from populated areas, and the proposed routes to the CCA and TFA complexes are not intersected by potential civilian evacuation routes.

(2) Locations provide adequate space, multiple access routes, sufficient water and utility support, communications (primarily back to the main installation C2 and warning and notification networks), and a degree of personnel protection (from elements and hostile attack).

(3) Civilian populations are not located downwind within 15 km of the CCA complex, to include the aeration area and contaminated-waste disposal area.

(4) There is an exceptionally limited or nonexistent ground threat, to include activities from terrorists.

(5) The installation possesses sufficient resources to execute the plan.

b. **On Site.** Finding and utilizing clean areas for CCA and TFA operations within the installation perimeter is preferable when—

(1) The installation is near heavily populated civilian areas or near a potential civilian evacuation route (there may be resulting traffic jams that would probably result in making off-base CCA and TFA complexes unreachable).

(2) A ground threat exists.

(3) The population is resource-constrained in regards to transportation. Communications limitations are also a factor.

(4) The installation is large enough to possess areas outside the target-rich environment associated with the industrial and main housing areas.

(5) The installation possesses a reliable detection network. The potential risk to personnel as a result of changing weather conditions and certain terrain features is increased if the installation cannot field an effective detection system. For example, because agents tend to follow the low-lying areas of the ground, an installation may establish CCAs and TFAs on uncontaminated hilltops, ridges, or multistoried buildings. It is possible that the concentrations of an agent at these levels (verified through the use of detectors) are such that rest and relief may be obtained by "going up."

c. **Combined Approach.** A combined approach of site selection may be the best methodology. The prioritization for site selection should be—

(1) On site with a ground level arrangement.

(2) On site with a vertical arrangement (space permitting).

(3) Off site.

d. **Space Requirement.** The requirement for space is a factor associated with selecting the site for CCA and TFA complexes. The minimum size for CCA and TFA sites is 500 square meters. Once a processing line is established and people are moving through it (i.e., as one person leaves a station, another person steps up), a relatively smooth flow will begin to take place. Each of the CCA and TFA complex subcomponents has accompanying space requirements, and there are several variables.

(1) CCA Entrance. A single entrance area can be used for multiple processing lines. However, the size needed for the entrance area depends on the number of personnel the installation is expecting to process at any given time. This number will also drive the sizes of the transportation point, CCA, and holding area where personnel can rest while waiting for their turn to process.

(2) CCA Processing Lines. The CCA processing lines will take a large amount of space in order to optimize processing and FP ideals. Spread out the distance between processing stations as far as reasonably possible. If space permits, stations should be spaced approximately 18 meters apart and areas within each station should be 9 meters apart. Establish the lines in an angular, staggered fashion as opposed to a straight line. The line angle should be 20°. When using this method, the concentration of trailing vapor hazards washing over people downwind of each processing station is significantly reduced.

(3) Mask Refurbishment Area. Lay the out-processing lines with plenty of space for the mask refurbishment area located in the contact hazard area (CHA). The mask refurbishment area requires sufficient space for working; a disposal area for detection kits, decontamination kits, hoods, and eye lens outserts; a stock of spare parts; and a holding area for masks waiting to be checked.

(4) Ground Chemical Ensemble (GCE) Aeration and the Contaminated-Waste Disposal Area. The aeration and disposal areas have the potential to be as large or larger than the processing lines. Therefore, an area of approximately 200 square meters is recommended. This area should be separate from the CCA lines and the TFA by approximately 50 meters.

(5) Buffer or Transition Area. Once monitored, personnel remove their masks and proceed to the TFA. At least 25 meters is recommended from the end of the vapor hazard area (VHA) to the TFA.

(6) TFA. The size of the TFA is the largest variable of all. An area of 500 square meters is recommended. The main housing portion of the TFA should be separated from the CCA processing lines by the maximum distance available. A separation of at least 100 meters is recommended. A chemical-vapor detection network should exist between the TFA and the CCA. See *Multiservice Tactics, Techniques, and Procedures for Nuclear, Biological, and Chemical Reconnaissance* for guidance on setting up a chemical detection network.

e. Other CCA and TFA Consideration Factors. The selection process involves numerous factors, to include the availability of areas that are upwind and a safe distance from contamination, areas accessible by ground transportation, and areas offering as much privacy and concealment as possible. Selecting locations that are out in the open may invite secondary attacks and the unwanted curiosity of others. Additional considerations include areas where localized weather conditions and wind patterns remain consistent, areas away from valley and ridgelines, areas offering the most inherent necessities, and areas within walking distance of the personnel shelter portion of the TFA. It will do no good to decontaminate crew members if they cannot get to a clean area to rest and debrief. If the shelter is not in the immediate area, arrange transportation.

(1) The locations must also offer the best possible options for disposing of or removing contaminated waste. Always coordinate the disposal of hazardous waste with CBRN specialists.

(2) For an airbase (AB), choosing a site near the ground personnel processing line will facilitate resupply and provide better security. However, a potential secondary hazard exists with this technique since ground crew personnel are more likely to encounter contamination. However, the aircrew ensemble, by design, does not provide protection from liquid contamination. They should not process through the ground crew CCA.

(3) Multiple site locations should be chosen to ensure the coverage of threat contingencies.

(4) Other considerations during the site selection process are site security, communications, the slope of the terrain, and the presence of other natural features. The protection of equipment from temperature extremes, rain, and pilferage is also required.

(5) For an AB, the decontamination site must be capable of accommodating the appropriate aircraft type in the required numbers. It should be relatively secure but close enough to refueling and rearming points to permit a reasonably quick turnaround if required. The site should have sufficient terrain flight routes within 2 to 3 km to facilitate entry and exit. A slight slope to the terrain is desirable but must remain within aircraft limits. It is preferable to sequence groups of aircraft through the decontamination site to prevent arriving or departing aircraft from interfering with decontamination operations. Depending on the personnel and resources available, it may be possible to clean several aircraft simultaneously.

f. CCA and TFA Patient Decontamination Sites. Optimal requirements for a decontamination site include the following:

(1) Colocation with the supported MTF (not closer than 75 meters downwind or crosswind and situated so that arriving vehicles and casualties can reach it without approaching the MTF).

(2) Access to water (free of CBRN contaminants but not necessarily potable).

(3) Hookup to electricity or an electric generator for water pump operation and lighting.

(4) Approximately a 60-meter controlled perimeter and ground or floor gradient sufficient to facilitate the drainage of contaminated water away from the decontamination facility and MTF.

NOTE: For detailed instructions on patient decontamination, see Chapter X and FM 4-02.7. Patient spot decontamination can be performed at the CHA with transport to an MTF that has a patient decontamination station (PDS).

g. Decontamination Site Layout. The CCA and TFA complexes are composed of subelements; each is connected in some way and can only be successfully accomplished through cohesive, integrated operations. See Figure VII-1 for an example of a decontamination site layout.

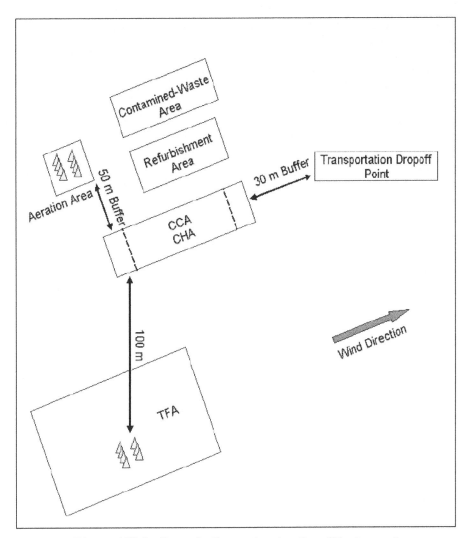

Figure VII-1. Sample Decontamination Site Layout

(1) The transportation drop-off point should be located on the downwind side of the CCA (approximately 30 meters). Establish a wind device (i.e., windsock) to monitor the wind direction. It is in this area that the first active efforts are taken by individuals to reduce contact and vapor hazards. As personnel leave the transportation drop-off point, they should be directed (by a sign or by an attendant) to the CCA.

(2) The entrance to the CCA includes the following areas: arrival and initial decontamination, weapons clearing, wash and holding, and external equipment removal. Use this CCA entrance for the following:

(a) To perform the initial decontamination of each person and his buddy prior to entering the CHA.

(b) To inform personnel of the sequence of events and emergency response procedures.

(c) To provide a covered area for rest and relief while waiting to process.

(d) To allow for the turn-in of weapons and the removal of external personal equipment other than the overgarment (i.e., helmet, vest [aircrew], web gear, mask carrier, flak vest, and cold/wet weather gear). Most of this equipment cannot be decontaminated to safe levels.

(3) The CHA is where individuals remove their overgarments. The goals of the CHA are contamination reduction in regards to processing personnel and the containment of all contact hazards (i.e., agents in liquid or solid form) within the CCA. See Figure VII-2 and VII-3 (pages VII-9 and VII-10) for examples of a CCA layout for ground crew and aircrew operations.

(4) The overgarment removal area may not be necessary if the chemical threat is low, the unit is sufficiently stocked with suits, and the resupply line is functioning. In this case, previously used suits could be sent directly to the contaminated-waste disposal area. However, if the threat of multiple CBRN attacks is probable, suits are in short supply, or there is not a realistic resupply capability, then the removal area is critical to mission sustainment. Units must perform a risk assessment before establishing an overgarment aeration area. Personnel should consider the following when selecting a site:

(a) Locate the removal area as close to the CHA as possible. However, ensure that the aeration area is downwind from the CHA and VHA transition point. Also, ensure that the aeration area is far enough from the TFA and mask removal point that it does not present a threat to unprotected personnel. The vapor hazard must be constantly monitored because the collection of contaminated suits in a single area will create an artificial hot spot.

(b) Ensure access to the suits for egress.

(c) Optimize the effects of weathering. Expose the suits to high temperatures, sunlight, and high winds; and also provide overhead cover to prevent inadvertent recontamination.

(d) Secure the area using available resources.

(5) It is probable that at least two contaminated-waste areas will be required—one within the MOB area and one in conjunction with the CCA function. Site selection should be based on prevailing winds for the season, and the site should be located downwind of all personnel housing and rest-and-relief locations. If sufficient equipment exists, place automatic vapor alarms around or downwind of the area. CBRN reconnaissance personnel should periodically monitor outside the area with a handheld vapor detection device, such as the ICAM or the M256.

(6) The VHA provides the last chance for the CCA staff to verify that processing personnel are free of contamination before transitioning to the TFA. In the case of open-air processing, there should be at least a 15-meter buffer zone between the end of the CHA and the monitoring station. At the end of the VHA, attendants should verify that the chemical vapor concentrations are at safe levels before they let personnel remove their mask. A decision to remove the mask will be based on the recommended safe levels provided. Consequently, the two-stage approach of clothing removal and monitoring is executed throughout this area.

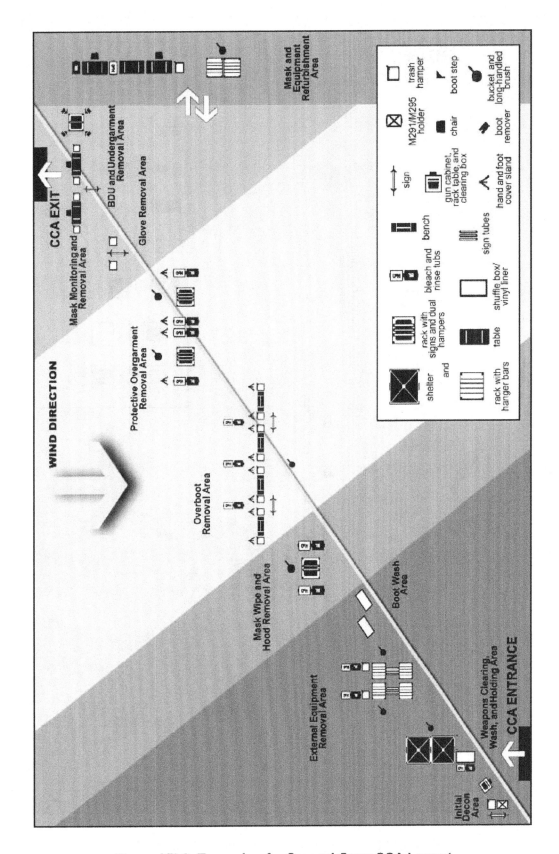

Figure VII-2. Example of a Ground Crew CCA Layout

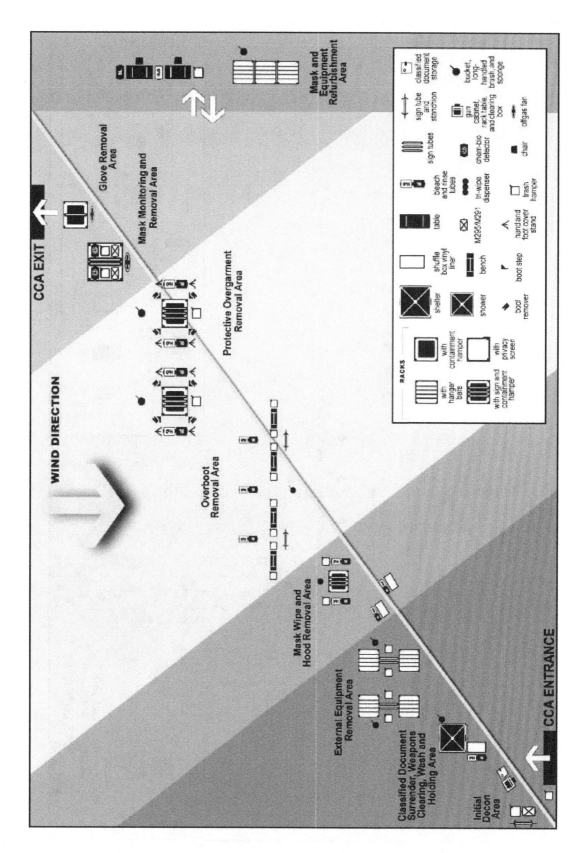

Figure V-3. Example of an Aircrew CCA Layout

(a) Personnel must remove clothing that could be "off-gassing" in the VHA prior to entering the TFA. Personnel should not be allowed to automatically transition into the TFA wearing their underwear if they were not using the battle dress uniform (BDU) option since that layer of protection would be missing. Consequently, each installation must develop a workable CONOPS for clothing replacement.

(b) If the threat dictates, personnel should be monitored with the ICAM for "dusty" contamination within the VHA. The attendants' sight and the use of M8/M9 paper are not effective, especially in the case of dusty mustard. In order to provide the highest degree of protection for personnel, VHA attendants must routinely monitor the air at the mask removal point.

(7) The purpose of the mission-critical equipment (MCE) refurbishment area is to decontaminate MCE and return it to the warfighter as quickly as possible. This area includes refurbishment of the ground crew, firefighters, and explosive ordnance disposal (EOD) equipment. To prevent bottlenecks during this process, this function should have dedicated personnel when the CCA is fully operational. Regardless of whether it is a single activity or several line-by-line activities, the personnel will require large supplies of plastic bags, M8 paper, M291/M295 decontamination kits, sponges, and bleach. The refurbishment area should be located outside the CCA processing lines. The refurbishment duties are split between the CHA and the VHA. Ensure that adequate space, dedicated personnel, and supplies are available for this tasking.

(a) Personnel in the TFA will remain vulnerable to a new CBRN attack and radical wind shift until their masks are returned.

(b) Untrained personnel may inadvertently be the cause of casualties. Extreme attention to detail is required regarding contamination identification, mask decontamination (if appropriate), mask cleansing, and filter replacement. The eyes are the most vulnerable part of the body, and the slightest mistake on the part of the mask refurbishment team may result in vision problems and the immediate loss of productivity.

(8) The transition buffer zone between the CCA and the TFA is the area where personnel remove their masks prior to entering the TFA.

(9) The TFA includes accountability and logistics resupply points.

(a) In open-air processing, the rest-and-relief area of the TFA is located at least 200 yards outside the CCA boundary. Shifting wind directions or the accumulation of contaminated materials (potential hazard effects from off-gassing or agent resuspension) necessitate the need to establish the TFA far from the CCA in an open-air environment. When overpressure systems are used, the entire structure beyond the point of the air lock is the TFA.

(b) There is a requirement for the installation to operate egress processing lines. Adequate space must be provided for sufficient egress lines to allow personnel to process out of the TFA while keeping with shift change requirements. CCAs should accommodate simultaneous ingress and egress lines and inhibit cross contamination of egressing personnel. In a worst-case scenario, many lines may be necessary because personnel would have to utilize previously used overgarments, combat boots, and clothing. In this scenario, space would also have to exist to store these items along the egress processing lines. There is also a space requirement for the storage of individual equipment (i.e., web belts, canteens, first aid kits, helmets, M9 paper).

(c) The size of the supply transition point depends on the wings CCA implementation philosophy and the degree of contamination control utilized prior to the attack.

(d) The size of the TFA is the largest variable of all. An area of 200 square meters is recommended. The main housing portion of the TFA should be separated from the CCA processing lines by the maximum distance available. A separation of at least 100 meters is recommended. A chemical-vapor detection network should exist between the TFA and the CCA.

(10) Other considerations during the site selection process are site security, communications, terrain slope, and the presence of other natural features.

(11) Optimal requirements for the CCA and TFA patient decontamination sites include the following:

(a) Colocation with the supported MTF (not closer than 75 meters downwind or crosswind and situated so that arriving vehicles and casualties can reach it without approaching the MTF).

(b) Access to water (free of CBRN contaminants but not necessarily potable).

(c) Hookup to an electricity source for water pump operation and lighting.

(d) Approximately a 60-meter controlled perimeter and ground or floor gradient sufficient to facilitate the drainage of contaminated water away from the decontamination facility and MTF.

(e) Protection of the equipment from temperature extremes, rain, and pilferage is required.

6. Personnel Processing Procedures (Radiological)

Prossessing personnel prior to actually sending them to decontamination can, in some cases, help alleviate the need for decontamination altogether.

a. Site Selection of the Contamination Control Station (CCS). The following considerations apply for CCS site selection:

- Locate the CCS downwind of the entry control point and operating areas, no closer than 300 feet to the nearest hazard.

- Select an area that is free of weeds, brush, and rocks. A paved area is preferred.

- Ensure that the CCS team members monitor a 25-square-foot area around the selected site.

CAUTION

The runoff of removed material should be carefully contained since it will remain a radiological hazard.

b. CCS Setup.

(1) Setup procedures will begin after the area is monitored and deemed clear of contamination.

(2) Individuals setting up the CCS will don protective equipment and will tape-up, ensuring that no skin is exposed, and determine and record background readings.

(3) Administrative personnel will log all personnel in and out of the area and inspect all personnel entering the area to ensure that they are properly dressed.

(4) The team chief will inspect all CCS members and personnel processing into the CCS for holes and tape.

c. CCS Activation.

(1) As soon as it is determined that there is contamination and that personnel are returning to the CCS, personnel in the CCS will don their masks and tape-up, ensure that the area is cleared of unnecessary personnel and material, contact the rear line, and report the area "hot." The CCS is now ready for processing.

(2) The team chief will ensure that personnel are processed by priority (e.g., injured, TLs), move throughout the area, and monitor all actions in the CCS.

d. Personnel Processing.

(1) Personnel will be processed on a priority basis.

(2) Injured personnel will be processed as follows:

- If by ambulance, the vehicle will be allowed to leave and the route taken will be closed, monitored, and cleaned if it is found to be contaminated.

- If by litter, the person will be wrapped in a blanket and the litter will be passed over the hot line and put into an ambulance on the clean side.

(3) All equipment and documents will be dropped on the hot side of the equipment drop table. Any contaminated item that needs to leave the area will be bagged. The person requiring the item will pick it up after it has processed through the CCS. All tape (except tape around wrists) will be removed and placed in the tape barrel (use the buddy system).

(a) Station 1.

NOTE: The person being processed is seated.

- Remove the bootie nearest the hot line, and place the bootie in the barrel.

- Ensure that the foot is held in the air to be monitored for radiological contamination.

- Place the boot down on the clean side of the hot line if the boot is clean.

- Remove and remonitor the boot if it is contaminated.

- Repeat procedures for the other foot.

- Instruct the person not to leave the mat until directed.

- Stand up on the clean side of the hot line, and proceed to the next station.

(b) Station 2.

NOTE: The person being processed will stand spread-eagle.

- Conduct whole-body monitoring for alpha, beta, and gamma rays.
- Monitor one side of the body for alpha rays and the other side for beta and gamma rays.
- Instruct the person to turn around 180° and repeat the monitoring.
- Start monitoring at the inlet valve or filter inlet on the mask.
- Monitor the rest of the head and shoulders.
- Monitor the body trunk with a large X formation.
- Instruct the individual to proceed to the medical station for processing if no contamination is found.
- Instruct the individual to proceed to Station 3 if contamination is found.

(c) Station 3.

- Remove the hood from the head. If the hood unfastens from the suit, take it off and put it in the barrel.
- Remove the protective clothing.
- Place the clothing in the barrel.
- Proceed to Station 4.

(d) Station 4.

- Use the same procedures as Station 2.
- Have the person remove his outer clothing and place it in the barrel at Station 3 if contamination is found.
- Have the person return to Station 4 for remonitoring if contamination is found.
- Have the person remove his mask and proceed to the medical station if no contamination is found.
- Have the person put on clean protective clothing, and transport him to the supporting MTF for decontamination if contamination is still found.
- Ensure that all personnel exit through the medical station.

e. Area Expansion. Establish another personnel processing line or a new area if the existing area becomes too congested.

f. CCS Shutdown. Use the following procedures for shutdown:

- Monitor, clean, and discard (as required) all area equipment and material.
- Monitor the area for remaining contamination.
- Request assistance from specialized teams if the area is still contaminated.

Chapter VIII
AIRCRAFT AND AIRCREW DECONTAMINATION

1. Background

This chapter addresses aircraft and aircraft cargo decontamination (i.e., general planning, aircraft decontamination planning, aircraft decontamination levels and procedures, civil air fleet and contract airlift decontamination, aircraft munitions decontamination, and air cargo decontamination). For more detailed TTP for air and naval forces aircraft and aircrew decontamination, see AFMAN 10-2602.

2. General Planning

The protection of aircraft and aircrews is of utmost importance during a CBRN threat. The ultimate goal is to minimize sortie generation degradation (by limiting the number of personnel that are exposed, the amount of equipment exposed to the contamination, and the time spent in IPE). The following factors should be considered during decontamination planning:

a. Combatant commanders have the responsibility to designate a decontamination location and coordinate approval with the HNs. AB, airfield, and FARP commanders and officers in charge must organize the capabilities and personnel of permanent, tenant, and transient organizations to support decontamination operations.

(1) Infrastructure factors that should be considered during the site selection process include the adequacy of the aircraft ramp area, access to water (free of contaminants but not necessarily potable), prevailing winds, the slope of the terrain, security, and hookup to electricity or an electric generator (for water pump operation, lighting, billeting, communications, etc.).

(2) The goal is to eliminate or reduce the contamination and restore the mission-critical resources to a condition that permits unrestricted use, handling, and operation.

(3) Thorough decontamination operations will be conducted after hostile actions have terminated, when the commander determines it is in the unit's best interest, or when directed by higher authority.

b. Operational units shall coordinate locations for parking the contaminated and uncontaminated aircraft, the location of aircraft and aircrew decontamination sites, maintenance personnel decontamination sites, and the retrogradation or disposal of contaminated equipment and consumables with host commands.

c. Aircraft are most vulnerable while they are on the ground and not protected by overhead cover. For this reason, taxi time should be minimized and every effort made to take advantage of available cover.

d. Units and activities place special emphasis on securing the aircraft points of ingress and egress by closing or covering cockpits, doors, and ramps when the aircraft is not in use and prior to decontamination.

e. The priority of the decontamination should support sortie generation. Maintenance procedures shall address the decontamination considerations (such as covered areas for parking, inspections, servicing, munitions/pod/tank loading and unloading, arming and dearming, and washing) prior to maintenance. The predecontamination procedures focus on the following areas:

(1) Protecting critical assets, using detection devices, marking and segregating contaminated equipment, and removing and replacing contaminated coverings. Commanders should use the contaminated equipment for contaminated operations.

(2) Receiving and providing disposition of contaminated equipment or products (e.g., support equipment, munitions, fuel, and spare parts). Actions may include moving equipment and aircraft through a decontamination line or outside of the maintenance areas for weathering.

f. Aircraft returning from missions may present little or no threat of contamination to the airfield or facility. Contaminated aircraft will be directed to an alternate (contaminated) airfield before landing (if possible). The following actions are applicable in a CBRN environment:

(1) Use monitoring equipment to detect contamination on the aircraft and aircrew, and report the results.

(2) Remain in IPE until decontaminated.

(3) Complete the immediate decontamination efforts as quickly as possible once contamination is detected. Decontamination activities must be completed before the agent absorbs into the surface (typically within minutes from the time of agent contact).

(a) Be aware of the locations of nonporous surfaces where the liquid may stay. Though these surfaces are the most receptive to decontamination, they also represent the most dangerous areas for liquid transfer and vapor hazard.

(b) Avoid exposing personnel to porous surfaces (e.g., painted metal or rubber) that will sorb chemical agents. Although sorption minimizes the liquid transfer hazard, the vapor hazard remains.

(4) Perform the required servicing on the aircraft.

g. Special Considerations.

(1) Operational and thorough decontamination procedures are similar to aircraft maintenance corrosion control.

(2) Key leadership and installation personnel must realize that there are limitations associated with decontamination efforts and form realistic expectations for an effective decontamination.

(3) CBRN agents can infiltrate the aircraft interior through the aircraft environmental control system and contaminate the cockpit area and avionics bay. The principal chemical-agent challenge to avionics components is vapor, regardless of the type of agent.

(4) The sensitivity of electrical equipment to chlorine or other water-based solutions severely limits its feasibility for decontamination.

(5) Units conduct operational and thorough decontamination planning by identifying C2 relationships, team requirements, equipment requirements, decontamination assets, and contaminated-waste collection points. Team checklists guide the decontamination team activities. These plans and checklists are focused on the unit tasks (such as critical cargo movement and postconflict decontamination operations). Requirements that exceed the unit or activity resources are included in the resource requests.

(6) No effective chemical compound is available for thorough aircraft decontamination. STB corrodes the metal components and the aircraft skin. Immediate decontamination may be performed using the service-authorized decontamination kits or solutions.

3. Aircraft Decontamination Levels and Procedures

The levels of decontamination for aircraft are the same as those described in Chapter I (immediate, operational, thorough, and clearance). However, this section will address only the first three levels. Aircrew decontamination procedures are outlined in Chapters III, IV, and VII.

a. Immediate Decontamination. There are three components of immediate decontamination. They are skin decontamination, personal wipe down, and spot decontamination. Skin decontamination and personal wipe down are described in Chapter III.

b. Spot Decontamination. Spot decontamination is an immediate decontamination technique that will normally be performed on aircraft that have been recovered and will be quickly turned around for continued flight operations. Spot decontamination reduces the contamination on areas that must be touched during an operation and while servicing the aircraft. Conducting spot decontamination will reduce contamination and limit its spread. The following steps should be used for conducting spot decontamination ashore or afloat:

(1) Spot Decontamination of Fixed-Wing Ejection Seat Aircraft and Helicopters.

(a) Determine a location for the decontamination. The location to conduct spot decontamination depends on the operating cycle, the space available (ship or facility), and the size of the aircraft being decontaminated.

(b) Spot decontamination should be performed by the crew, division, team, or work section responsible for the service being performed. All personnel involved in spot decontamination shall wear appropriate nonaircrew MOPP gear. Wet-weather clothing may be worn over MOPP gear to prevent the saturation of the nonaircrew protective ensemble. Table VIII-1 (page VIII-4) and the following list, provide a baseline for the areas that should be decontaminated prior to servicing the aircraft:

- Refueling access.
- Ordnance, armament, and equipment.
- Ingress and egress (ladders, handholds, footholds, steps, etc.).
- Preflight and postflight check areas.
- Inspection areas.

- Canopies, windscreens, windows, and optical sensors.
- Support equipment (seats, controls, chocks, chains, etc.).
- Aircraft tie-down and tow points.

Table VIII-1. Aircraft Spot Decontamination

Action and Location	Areas to Decontaminate	Personnel Responsible	Decontaminants	Procedures	Remarks
Refueling at the refueling point	Fuel ports, hatches, and all areas that FARP personnel touch	POL handler	Diesel fuel; JP8; or hot, soapy water	Wipe the fuel ports and hatches with a sponge dipped in the decontaminant. Do not allow the decontaminant to enter the fuel system. Control the runoff because the agent will not be neutralized. This method simply flushes the contamination from the surface.	Refueling personnel should conduct an operational decontamination after servicing contaminated aircraft.
Arming at the rearming point	Armament system	Ammunition handler	JP8 or hot, soapy water	Wipe the armament system with a sponge dipped in the decontaminant. Control the runoff because the agent will not be neutralized. This method simply flushes the contamination from the surface.	**CAUTION** Take care to prevent certain areas of the armament system from being exposed to the decontaminant. Check the armament system TM for more information.

Table VIII-1. Aircraft Spot Decontamination (Continued)

Action and Location	Areas to Decontaminate	Personnel Responsible	Decontaminants	Procedures	Remarks
Entering and exiting the aircraft anywhere	Door handles, steps, ladders, handholds, and all areas that may be touched by aircrews	Crew members, POL handlers, and rearming personnel	JP8 or hot, soapy water	Apply the decontaminant. Prevent the spread of liquid contamination from the outside of the aircraft to the inside. Control the runoff because the agent will not be neutralized. This method simply flushes the contamination from the surface.	Procedures should be developed for each type of aircraft. Before entering the aircraft, use an IEDK on boots and gloves.
Preflight and postflight checks anywhere Maintenance inpections at aviation intermediate maintenance facilities	Areas that must be touched as part of the inspection	Aircrew	Diesel fuel; JP8; or hot, soapy water on exterior surfaces Hot air for interiors or areas that are not compatible with decontaminants or liquids	Wipe the areas that are required to be touched for the preflight and postflight checks with a sponge dipped in the decontaminant. Wash gloves in the decontaminant before touching uncontaminated surfaces. Decontaminate gloves with an IEDK after the inspection is complete. Control runoff because the agent will not be neutralized. This method simply flushes contamination from the surface.	Overheated air should not be used directly on instrumentation. The crew may want to wear wet-weather gear to prevent the contamination of overgarments.

Table VIII-1. Aircraft Spot Decontamination (Continued)

Action and Location	Areas to Decontaminate	Personnel Responsible	Decontaminants	Procedures	Remarks
Repair and recovery anywhere	The parts or areas that need to be decontaminated depending on the situation	Maintenance personnel (someone who knows what assembly or parts are needed)	Diesel fuel; 5% chlorine solution; or hot, soapy water on exterior parts or surfaces. Hot air on interior parts that are not compatible with liquids or corrosive decontaminants.	Decontaminate only those parts or assemblies that need to be touched during cannibalization.	Caustic decontaminants should be used only on those areas that have been removed from the aircraft. Assemblies must be rinsed thoroughly before replacing.
Overhaul at maintenance facilities	All areas and equipment required to be worked on during the overhaul	Maintenance personnel or a decontamination unit	Diesel fuel; 5% chlorine solution; or hot, soapy water. Hot air for surfaces that are easily destroyed by liquid or corrosion	Wash with diesel fuel; wash with hot, soapy water; and then rinse. Check for contamination with M8 detector paper or the ICAM/CAM. If time permits, allow the equipment to weather.	Caustic decontaminants should only be used on the assemblies that have been removed from the aircraft. The assemblies must be rinsed thoroughly before replacing. This will have the same result as a thorough decontamination.

  (c) The procedures for spot decontamination are as follows:

- Make available sufficient quantities of soapy water or applicable aircraft cleaner and fresh water.

- Scrub the service areas using brushes, rags, or sponges with soapy water until deposited CB material, dirt, and grime are removed.

- Rinse with fresh water from a bucket or hose.

- Decontaminate gloves.

- Perform service.

- Decontaminate runoff cleaner by applying standard or nonstandard decontaminant to the deck, ground, and airfield; and then hose overboard or into collection sumps. If runoff is hosed without prior decontamination, it should be treated as contaminated.

  (2) Spot Decontamination of Large-Frame, Fixed-Wing, Nonejection Aircraft. If mission requirements do not allow ample time for operational decontamination or weathering, provide spot decontamination of large-frame aircraft. Large-frame aircraft (i.e., C-5, C-17, C130, and C141) will normally operate from an open ramp without cover while on the ground for a short period of time. Their vulnerability to CBRN contamination on the ground will result from being outside and unprotected at the time of a chemical attack. Additionally, the size of the aircraft makes spot decontamination a much larger

task. Contamination can also transfer from contaminated personnel or cargo allowed on the aircraft.

NOTE: These procedures are written in generic form to cover all large-frame aircraft and require the user's knowledge of the applicable aircraft. For example, the C-5 user would understand that decontamination of the cargo ramp area would include both forward and aft ramps while the C-17, C-130, and C-141 users would only be concerned with single aft ramps.

> **CAUTION**
> Ensure that all decontaminants used in these procedures are authorized in appropriate aircraft and maintenance manuals before execution. Failure to do so may violate maintenance instructions and damage the aircraft.

(a) A TL directs the efforts of two-person teams as they decontaminate the aircraft. The TL can be any maintenance specialty code, military occupational specialty (MOS), or Navy enlisted classification (NEC); but it is recommended that a qualified aircraft crew chief be used. The mechanics performing as members of the two-person teams can be any maintenance specialty code, MOS, or NEC provided they are familiar with the ground handling and flight line safety procedures for the applicable aircraft and can work in full MOPP gear.

(b) Three two-person teams designated as Teams A, B, and C are recommended. The number of personnel can be adjusted based on the availability and workload, provided the two-person team concept is not violated. Tasks are designated by the letter (A, B, or C) of the team doing the work, but these team designations are optional if more or less personnel are used.

(c) The TL assembles the full team at the nose of the aircraft for a situation and safety briefing. He uses the applicable aircraft ground handling TM or TO to make the aircraft safe for maintenance. He briefs personnel on the absolute necessity of operating in two-person teams and the use of the "buddy system" to enhance personal decontamination and safety throughout the operation. The TL also performs the following duties:

- Ensures that the required supplies are available (such as M295 kits, M9 tape, shuffle box, logbook, bags, heavy-duty plastic).

- Ensures that the required equipment is available (such as handheld radios and ICAMs/CAMs).

- Uses M295 kits to spot-decontaminate ground fire extinguisher(s) to ensure that they are available in an emergency.

- Assigns two-person inspection teams to inspect and spot-decontaminate portions of the aircraft interior and exterior.

(d) Team A performs the following duties:

- Inspects (using the appropriate detection device) and spot-decontaminates the crew entry area. Pays particular attention to the crew entry doors, ladder, and handrail.

- Places the shuffle box with absorbent at the foot of the ladder.

- Cleans feet in the shuffle box prior to entering the aircraft, checks each other for contamination (decontaminate if necessary), and proceeds up the ladder into the aircraft.

- Inspects and decontaminates any contamination present onboard in the crew entry area, to include the galley and closest floorboards.

- Exits the aircraft and reports the findings to the TL for entry into the log.

- Disposes of the waste in the garbage bag.

- Inspects (using ICAMs/CAMs or the appropriate detection device) and spot-decontaminates the ground interphone connection/door. Pays particular attention to the cable connection area and door latches.

- Reports the findings to the TL for entry into the log.

- Disposes of the waste in the garbage bag.

- Inspect (using ICAMs/CAMs or the appropriate detection device) the main landing gear (MLG) wheel wells.

- Enters the MLG wheel wells. Records the detector reading in the front and rear of each MLG wheel well.

- Spot-decontaminates (as needed) any safety down-lock pins and wheel chocks.

- Reports the findings to the TL for entry into the log.

(e) Team B performs the following duties:

- Inspects (using ICAMs/CAMs or the appropriate detection device) and spot-decontaminates the ground power unit (GPU) and aircraft ground power receptacle. Pays particular attention to the electrical plug area, the pintle hook area, and all knobs and switches. Reports the findings to the TL for entry into the log. Disposes of the waste in the garbage bag.

- Inspects (using ICAMs/CAMs or the appropriate detection device) and spot-decontaminates any ground servicing points that will be accessed prior to launch (i.e., oxygen, hydraulic, and latrine servicing ports). Pays particular attention to the connection areas, doors and latches, and all knobs and switches. Reports the findings to the TL for entry into the log. Disposes of the waste in the garbage bag.

- Inspects (using ICAMs/CAMs or the appropriate detection device) the nose landing gear (NLG) wheel well. Enters the NLG wheel well and records the detector reading in the front and rear of the wheel well. Decontaminates (as needed) any safety down-lock pins and wheel chocks. Reports the findings to the TL for entry into the log.

(f) Team C performs the following tasks:

- Inspects (using ICAMs/CAMs or the appropriate detection device) and spot-decontaminates the fuel truck and hoses, and the aircraft fuel servicing ports (filler caps if used) and fuel servicing panels. Pays particular attention to the hose connections, all knobs and switches, and the driver's-side door area. Reports the findings to the TL for entry into the log. Disposes of the waste in the garbage bag.

- Inspects (using ICAMs/CAMs or the appropriate detection device) and spot-decontaminates the aircraft ramp areas. Cleans feet in the shuffle box prior to entering the aircraft, checks each other for contamination (decontaminates if necessary), and enters the aircraft through the crew entry door after using the shuffle box. Pays close attention to the ramp control panel and the ramp hinge areas. Decontaminates all knobs, switches, and handles as appropriate. Reports the findings to the TL for entry into the log. Disposes of the waste in the garbage bag.

(g) The TL reviews the aircraft forms and directs the teams to spot-decontaminate any areas of the aircraft requiring access for maintenance (engine nacelle latches, access panels, tires). The TL reports any abnormal findings or actions to the maintenance and operations sections. He also accounts for all team members.

c. Operational Decontamination. The goal of operational decontamination is to limit the spread of contamination and to minimize the hazards to personnel, while allowing operations to continue. The following procedures apply to ejection seat aircraft, large-frame aircraft, and helicopters. Detailed aspects of specific operational personnel and equipment procedures for air and naval forces are addressed in AFMAN 10-2602.

(1) Responsibilities. Aerial ports of embarkation (APOEs) and APODs will concentrate the decontamination efforts on operational decontamination during hostilities. Thorough and clearance decontamination are generally conducted following the end of hostilities. The magnitude of this effort will depend upon the type and concentration of contamination, mission requirements, and available resources. Commanders conduct operational decontamination to minimize contact hazards, accelerate the weathering process, and limit cross contamination of mission-critical resources. Performing aircraft wash down within 1 to 6 hours of contamination will speed the weathering process and may allow the aircraft to be operated and maintained in reduced aircrew IPE or MOPP levels. Aircraft operational decontamination is accomplished by decontaminating surfaces (exterior and interior) that must be touched during aircraft servicing and operations.

(2) Preparation.

(a) Areas. Multiple areas will need to be set up, marked, and maintained within zones to effectively control or eliminate the potential for cross contamination. The locations depend on the operating cycle, the space available (facility or ship), and the type of aircraft being decontaminated. Figures VIII-1 and VIII-2 (page VIII-10) depict examples of stationary aircraft decontamination areas.

(b) Water. The site must have sufficient fresh water to wet the entire exterior of the aircraft. For planning purposes, the following recommendations are provided: CH46E, 250 gallons; CH53E, 350 gallons; F/A18, 300 gallons; and C130, 800 gallons.

NOTE: Water requirements are approximations. The water requirements for specific aircraft should be based on the surface area compared to the recommended water volumes provided above.

(c) Equipment. Washing equipment that can produce 60 to 120 psi of water pressure is preferred. The capacity to heat water and inject soap increases the effectiveness. The lack of pressurized washing equipment decreases the effectiveness of the wash down and may require scrubbing to achieve the desired effect. The M17 lightweight decontamination systems (USMC), M12 PDDA, standard water pumps, and pressure washers, and firefighting equipment are examples of standard and field-expedient equipment.

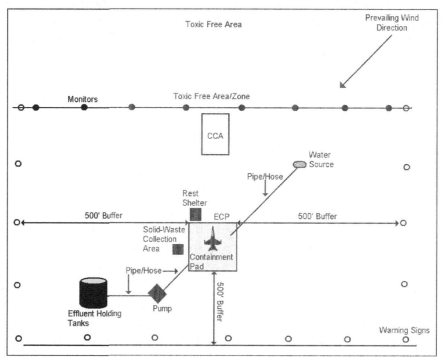

Figure VIII-1. Aircraft Operational Decontamination Site Layout

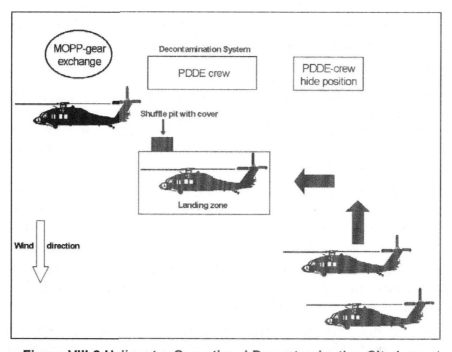

Figure VIII-2 Helicopter Operational Decontamination Site Layout

(d) Decontamination Area or Pad. A suitable remote site that is at least 500 feet away from all other flight line activities must be selected to conduct aircraft decontamination. The decontamination pad must have enough space so that all of the drainage and wastewater runoff is collected and contained. The establishment and enforcement of an entry control point is required to control and monitor access to the decontamination pad.

(e) Containment Area. An aircraft decontamination containment area should be large enough to completely cover the ground under the entire aircraft and catch all the contaminated runoff water. The construction of the pad should be of a waterproof material (vinyl, plastic, or tarp) with suitable sides (berm) to control and contain the water or decontaminant runoff. Operational decontamination sites established at wash racks will require a containment feature (such as sandbags, sand-filled fire hoses, or commercially available containment berms or pools) that is large enough to accommodate the aircraft being washed and to prevent runoff from spreading contamination. The pad size will vary based on the type of aircraft requiring decontamination and must be built to accommodate the largest known contaminated aircraft. Sample aircraft sizes and recommended pad containment areas are given in Table VIII-2.

Table VIII-2. Sample Aircraft Sizes and Recommended Pad Containment Areas

Aircraft	Length	Wingspan	Recommended Pad
C-5	247' 10"	222' 9"	270' x 250'
C-17	173' 11"	170' 9"	200' x 200'
C-141	168' 4"	160'	180' x 180'
KC-135E	136' 3"	130' 10"	160' x 160'
C-130	97' 9"	132' 7"	125' x 160'

(f) Overspray or Splatter Hazard Area. Another factor to consider is the potential for an overspray or splatter hazard during decontamination operations. The liquid containment system associated with a ground barrier is designed to allow the wastewater to be collected in an appropriate container, pending further analysis and proper disposal. If possible, establish the decontamination area at a 20° angle to the prevailing winds. Using this method, the concentration of trailing vapor hazards will be significantly reduced.

(g) Site. Sewer drains must be plugged, and a system for containing discarded wastewater must be established using a temporary berm. Ensure that the ground slope allows the runoff to flow to the downwind side of the washing operation but still be retained in the area so that it will not cross contaminate other areas. All wastewater used in the decontamination process will need to be collected and tested.

(h) Wastewater Storage. Wastewater storage tanks should be available to store runoff. In areas where sufficient natural drainage exists to carry wastewater away from the operation, wastewater lagoons could be constructed to provide a holding area for the wastewater, pending proper disposal. If lagoons are utilized, they must be established downwind of the decontamination area, properly marked, and fenced. Because of the large construction requirements, lagoons should only be used as a last resort.

(i.) Collection System. The design of the collection system largely depends on the specific site conditions such as the slope of the land, soil composition, and wind direction. Planners must also consider piping and sump pumps to move contaminated water into storage tanks or a holding lagoon. The quantity and selection of piping and pumps depend on the slope and distance from the decontamination pad to the holding tanks.

(3) Procedures. Aircraft wash-down techniques are employed to reduce the levels of contamination on the aircraft between sorties (when time allows). An aircraft wash down should be performed as a minimum contamination reduction measure when time does not permit a more extensive decontamination.

(a) All personnel involved in the aircraft wash down shall wear the appropriate MOPP gear prior to the aircraft entering the decontamination site. Wet-weather clothing or TAP aprons worn over MOPP gear is recommended to prevent the saturation of the nonaircrew protective ensemble.

(b) Personnel place the appropriate barrier and contamination hazard markings prior to commencing the wash down. They erect barriers to isolate the decontamination site. Appropriate (CB) North Atlantic Treaty Organization (NATO) contamination markers should be attached to the rope barrier to warn personnel of a contamination hazard.

(c) Aircraft stands or ladders should be available to the spray areas inaccessible from the ground or deck. As a last resort, decontamination personnel can climb on the aircraft.

(d) The aircraft is towed or taxied into position.

(e) The aircrew egress. If contaminated, the aircrew must remain with the aircraft in IPE or may be directed to a personnel decontamination site (shore-based) or CCA (ship) for the removal of contaminated IPE and flight gear.

(f) The crew closes all of the hatches, doors, and windows on the aircraft.

(g) Warm, soapy water is applied to the aircraft. Spray should be applied to the aircraft working upwind to downwind and top to bottom. Do not neglect the landing gear and the belly of the aircraft. Angle the spray streams from 15° to 30° in order to avoid water being introduced behind the hatch and cover seams that house the sensitive aircraft components. Control the overspray to avoid transferring the contaminated runoff to personnel or to areas outside the decontamination barrier.

> **CAUTION**
> Consult the appropriate aircraft maintenance publications for areas that could be damaged by the application of water spray. Prepare these areas for aircraft wash down as specified in TMs for normal washing. The spray streams should be angled from 15° to 30° in order to avoid water being introduced behind the hatch and cover seams that house the sensitive aircraft components. Ensure that only approved aircraft cleaners are used. The overspray should be controlled to avoid transferring contaminated runoff to personnel or to areas outside of the decontamination barrier.

(h) Rinse. Perform this optional step for corrosion control purposes if time allows.

(i) Check the interior for liquid or solid contamination. If contamination is discovered, spot-decontaminate by wiping with rags dipped in warm, soapy water or another approved aircraft cleaner.

(j) Move the aircraft to an area where it can weather.

(k) Repeat steps 3 (a) through (j) as required.

(4) Site Close-Out. At the end of the decontamination procedures, the decontamination pad must be cleaned with a standard or nonstandard decontamination solution to ensure that all traces of contamination have been neutralized. Additionally, the planners should consider that all joint- or crack-sealing material will need to be removed and replaced.

d. Thorough Decontamination. The goal of a thorough decontamination is to reduce contamination to negligible levels or to eliminate it so that aircraft can be operated and maintained safely for extended periods of time without aircrew IPE or nonaircrew IPE. Thorough decontamination consists of personnel and equipment decontamination. Detailed aspects of specific thorough personnel and equipment decontamination for air and naval forces are addressed in AFMAN 10-2602. This section primarily addresses thorough aircraft decontamination procedures for forces operating ashore. Thorough personnel decontamination is outlined in Chapter V.

(1) The DAD restores items so that they can be used without aircrew IPE or nonaircrew IPE. Normally, the DED and the DAD are conducted as part of a reconstitution or during breaks in combat operations.

(2) The thorough decontamination of aircraft is costly in terms of time and resources. A critical limitation to aircraft thorough decontamination is decontamination of the interior. Electronics, electrical systems, and other sensitive components of cockpits, flight decks, and cargo areas can become damaged if subjected to the volume of water that would have to be introduced in order to effectively remove contamination from these areas. As discussed, there are currently no available decontamination technologies, other than using standard aircraft soaps and cleaners to displace contamination from an aircraft. Therefore, in considering thorough decontamination of an aircraft, commanders must first determine the extent of the contamination to the interior spaces of the aircraft. If these spaces are heavily contaminated, it may make more sense to operationally decontaminate the exterior of the aircraft, spot-decontaminate the interior of the aircraft, and allow the aircraft to weather to an acceptable level instead of spending the resources to conduct a thorough decontamination of the exterior, knowing that spot decontamination of the interior is the best that can be achieved with the current decontamination technology.

(3) The procedures for DAD are similar to those for operational decontamination. The principal difference between the two techniques is the amount of time that is required. There is a stationary, single-station method and a five-station method for conducting DAD. In either method, DAD will take longer because of the requirement to scrub the aircraft. Scrubbing the aircraft with soap will assist with the contaminant removal process and increase the effectiveness of decontamination. All personnel involved in the DAD may wear the appropriate rain gear. Rain gear is recommended to prevent the saturation of the nonaircrew protective ensemble.

(a) Determine the Location for the Decontamination. The location to conduct aircraft decontamination is dependent on the operating cycle, space available at the facility, and the type of aircraft being decontaminated.

(b) Conduct Site Preparation. Considerations for selecting a thorough decontamination site and the preparation of that site are similar to those discussed in operational decontamination (paragraph 3c). Thorough decontamination will require more logistics support. For planning purposes, the following recommendations are provided: CH-46E, 500 gallons; CH-53E, 700 gallons; and C130, 1600 gallons. Containment at the DAD will have to be increased to hold the additional runoff.

NOTE: Water requirements are approximations. The water requirements for specific aircraft should be based on the surface area compared to the recommended water volumes provided above.

(c) Perform Single-Station Procedures.

- Tow or taxi the aircraft into position; and close all of the hatches, doors, and windows on the aircraft. Prepare the aircraft the same as for a normal washing, and then initiate the decontamination process.

- Apply warm, soapy water to the outside of the aircraft. Spray should be applied to the aircraft, working from upwind to downwind and top to bottom.

> **CAUTION**
> Consult appropriate aircraft maintenance publications for areas that could be damaged by the application of water spray. Prepare these areas for aircraft wash down as specified in TMs for normal washing. Spray streams should be angled from 15° to 30° in order to avoid water being introduced behind the hatch and cover seams that house sensitive aircraft components. Ensure that only approved aircraft cleaners are used. The overspray should be controlled to avoid transferring contaminated runoff to other personnel or to areas outside of the decontamination barrier.

- Apply appropriate aircraft cleaner or soap to the exterior of the aircraft using long-handled brushes or nonabrasive scrub pads. Scrub the soap into the exterior surfaces of the aircraft, working from upwind to downwind and top to bottom. Pay particular attention to the areas where contamination tends to accumulate, such as landing gear, landing gear bays, tires, and areas with POL.

- Check the interior spaces with a CAM/ICAM or M8 paper. If contamination is discovered or suspected, spot-decontaminate these areas with rags or sponges dipped in warm, soapy water or with another approved aircraft cleaner. Wring-out the excess water to avoid contaminated runoff. Porous material such as cargo straps, seats, and seat belts cannot be effectively spot-decontaminated. These items and other porous items should be removed and weathered or discarded. Personnel performing the interior decontamination must ensure that they are not transferring contamination inside of the aircraft. If necessary, decontaminate the footgear and gloves before entering the aircraft.

• Apply rinse water to the outside of the aircraft. Spray should be applied to the aircraft, working from upwind to downwind and top to bottom. Heated water will aid in contamination removal.

> **WARNING**
> **Overspray should be controlled to avoid transferring the contaminated runoff to personnel or to areas outside of the decontamination barrier.**

> **CAUTION**
> Consult the appropriate aircraft maintenance publications for areas that could be damaged by the application of water spray. Spray streams should be angled from 15° to 30° to avoid water being introduced behind the hatch and cover seams that house the sensitive aircraft components.

• Check for contamination. Use the CAM/ICAM, M8A1, M22 ACADA, MK26 Ship ACADA, M256/M256A1, or biological handheld assay (HHA) (as required) to check the exterior for contamination. If contamination is found, recycle the aircraft according to the command guidance or segregate the aircraft from personnel and other aircraft for the weathering process to lower contamination levels.

(d) Perform Five-Station Procedures.

• CBRN units may set up, operate, and close the DAD portion of the thorough decontamination operation. Table VIII-3 (page VIII-16) shows the personnel and equipment requirements for the five-station DAD. The site setup is the same for CBR. The DAD area is composed of primary wash, decontaminant solution application, contact time and interior decontamination, rinse, and check stations (see Figure VIII-3, page VIII-17).

Table VIII-3. Personnel Requirements for DAD

Stations	Personnel - Decontamination Unit	Personnel - Augmentees	Equipment/Supplies
Station 1—Primary wash	1 TL 1 PDDE operator 1 sprayer	2 scrubbers	1 PDDE 1 3,000-gallon tank 2 65-GPM pumps 6 long-handled brushes 5 TAP aprons Liquid detergent
Station 2—Decontaminant application	1 TL 2 appliers 2 sprayers 1 PDDE operator	4 appliers	1 PDDE 18 long-handled brushes 9 mops with extra heads 5 TAP aprons Liquid detergent
Station 3—Interior decontamination/wait	1 NCO (ICAM/CAM operator)	2 assistants	2 AN/VDR-2s or AN/PDR-77s 2 TAP aprons 6 30-gallon containers 10 books of M8 paper 30 sponges 8 M256A1 detector kits 50 plastic trash bags 1 clipboard with pen 1 stopwatch 1 ICAM/CAM
Station 4—Rinse	1 TL 1 PDDE operator 2 sprayers	None	1 PDDE 1 3,000-gallon tank 3 65-GPM pumps 1 TPU 2 TAP aprons
Station 5—Check	1 TL 2 CAM/ICAM operators	None	1 CAM/ICAM 10 M256A1 detector kits 20 books of M8 paper 2 AN/VDR-2s or AN/PDR-77s 1 M8A1 or M22 ACADA
C2	1 TL 1 assistant	None	1 HMMWV 3 marking kits
Aircraft moving team	None	6 drivers 18 ground guides	None
Total Personnel	**19**	**32**	**N/A**

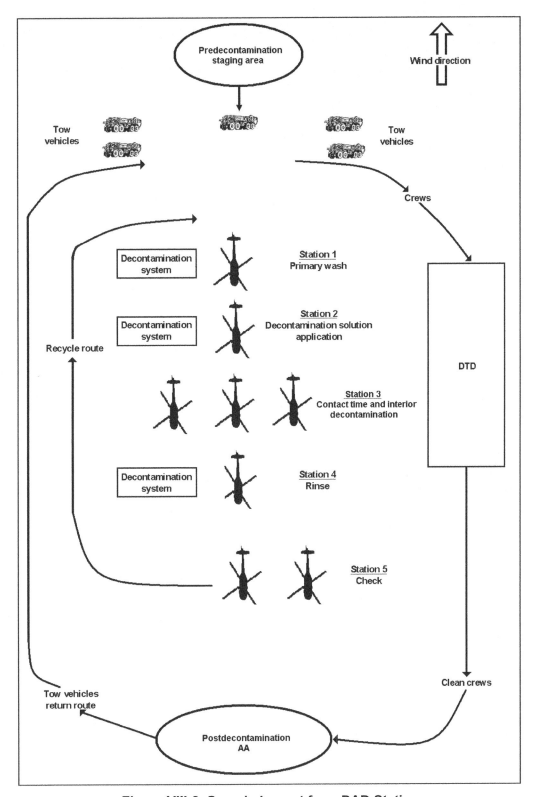

Figure VIII-3. Sample Layout for a DAD Station

- The representative actions that are taken at each station are as follows:

    o Station 1: Primary Wash. At this station, gross contamination is removed from the aircraft. The aircraft is sprayed for 2 to 3 minutes with hot, soapy water.

> **WARNING**
> To prevent damage, avoid hitting the aircraft's skin at a 90° angle. Also avoid the sensitive areas shown in Figures VIII-4 and VIII-5.

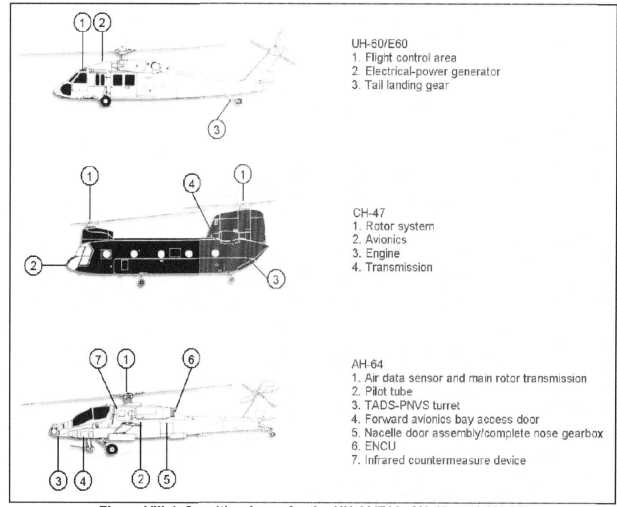

Figure VIII-4. Sensitive Areas for the UH-60/E60, CH-47, and AH-64

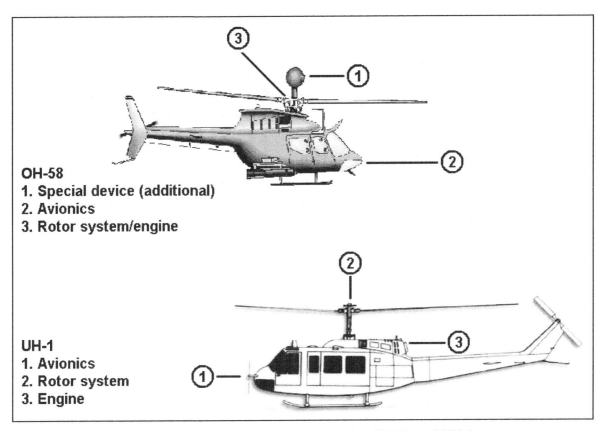

Figure VIII-5. Sensitive Areas for the OH-58 and UH-1

o   Station 2: Decontaminant Application. At this station, a decontamination solution is applied using a decontamination apparatus such as the M12A1 PDDE or the M17 LDS (in the siphon injector mode). After the solution is applied, a member of the scrubbing team scrubs the aircraft skin. This allows the chemical agent to mix with the decontamination solution (especially when thickened chemical agents are present). STB and HTH should not be used because of their corrosive nature.

o   Station 3: Contact Time and Interior Decontamination. At this station, the decontamination solution is allowed to completely neutralize the chemical agent; also, the interior of the aircraft is decontaminated (if necessary). The aircraft will remain in Station 3 at least 30 minutes. The decontamination solution reacts with most chemical agents within 5 minutes. However, allowing the decontamination solution to remain on the contaminated surface for 30 minutes should ensure a complete neutralization.

➢   Inspect the interior of the aircraft for liquid contamination using the CAM/ICAM and M8 detector paper. If a liquid-chemical contamination is identified, decontaminate the interior of the aircraft.

WARNING
Personnel should not be in the aircraft during this operation.

> Decontaminate the aircraft's interior with hot, soapy water as long as maintenance personnel approve the use of it on certain pieces of equipment. Use IEDKs or damp, soapy washcloths to decontaminate optical and electrical equipment and instruments.

NOTE: The IEDK leaves a charcoal residue on surfaces.

> Use a radiac meter for radiological contamination to determine the extent and location of the contamination inside the aircraft. If there is contamination, determine the intensity of the contamination. If the contamination has an intensity greater than 0.33 cGy, decontaminate the interior of the aircraft. Use hot, soapy water to wash the contaminated areas and a sponge to mop up the water and the contamination.

o Station 4: Rinse. Removed the decontamination solution is from the aircraft. Spray the aircraft with water from top to bottom. Take care not to damage the aircraft skin. This station will use about 250 gallons of water.

CAUTION
Failure to remove all of the decontamination solution from the aircraft skin may cause corrosion.

---

o Station 5: Check. At this station, the completeness of the decontamination is checked. Detection procedures vary depending on the type of contamination. If significant contamination is found on the aircraft, recycle it to Station 2 for chemical contamination or to Station 1 for radiological contamination.

> Use the ICAM to check for the presence of vapors. If the ICAM indicates the presence of vapors, use the M8 detector paper to check for liquid contamination. If it is suspected that these are producing a false positive, use an M256A1 detector kit to confirm or deny the presence of contamination. If the aircraft has significant contamination remaining, recycle it. Desorption of chemical agents may occur after the decontamination. On CARC-painted surfaces, the desorption of vapors will stop sooner than on alkyd-painted surfaces.

> Use the radiac meter to determine if any contamination remains. If so, determine the intensity of the contamination.

- The commander establishes the recycle criteria before starting a decontamination operation. If contamination is detected at Station 5, the recycle criteria are used to determine which aircraft are returned to Station 2 or, if radiologically contaminated, to Station 1. If the unit has sufficient time and resources available, the aircraft still having detectable levels of contamination should be recycled. However, time and resources are usually limited and not all aircraft can be recycled.

e. Operational and Thorough Decontamination. Operational and thorough decontamination sites for aircraft must be selected with care. The decontamination area must be large enough for the required number of aircraft, have an available water source, and allow for adequate drainage. The sites should be relatively secure; however, they should be close enough to the AOs to allow for a reasonably quick turnaround of the aircraft. The sites should not have less than a 5 percent slope. Decontamination sites should be integrated into the tactical plan.

4. Civil Reserve Air Fleet and Contract Airlift Operations

The Civil Reserve Air Fleet (CRAF) and contract airlift crews are provided ground crew CW defense ensembles for emergency use. Crews receive just-in-time training in order to quickly and properly don the suit and proceed to a protective shelter. Civil crews are not expected to sustain operations in a CB environment. Therefore, they have no decontamination capability.

    a.   Civil aircraft are not usually modified for operations in a CBRN environment.

    b.   Civil aircrews are not obligated or trained to fly into a contaminated environment. The CRAF will not intentionally operate in a known contaminated environment.

    c.   If an aircraft becomes contaminated while on the ground, the crew will be evacuated by the first available means and the aircraft will be grounded until it is decontaminated.

5. Aircraft Munitions Decontamination

This paragraph addresses aircraft munitions; specifically, contaminated munitions assets, the decontamination of munitions assets, and the handling of contaminated waste.

    a.   Munitions personnel must possess an immediate decontamination capability for themselves (M291 and M295 decontamination kits, and glove and boot decontamination troughs with 5 percent chlorine solutions) and an operational decontamination capability for munitions, assets, and vehicles. For the decontamination operations to be beneficial, the site personnel must initiate the decontamination shortly after the onset of contamination since there will not be sufficient time for off-site personnel to arrive and conduct the decontamination operations.

    b.   If the aircraft munitions are contaminated while in the storage area, the munitions handlers maintain MOPP4 (even if the aircraft parking area and other resources are uncontaminated). If dealing with contaminated individually wrapped trailers in the flight line weapons storage area, the weapons load crew removes the barrier material and disposes of it as contaminated waste before transporting the load to the aircraft parking area. However, if positioning the weapons without overhead cover for more than 1 hour at (or in the immediate vicinity of) the aircraft parking area, the weapons load crew replaces the barrier material before leaving for the site.

    (1)   Because of the hazard that is imbedded in contaminated munitions equipment and weapons, munitions personnel must conspicuously identify the contaminated assets and keep them separated from the uncontaminated resources (whenever possible). Contaminated munitions remain hazardous to unprotected personnel for extended periods.

    (2)   Contaminated munitions should be hung on the contaminated aircraft. If it is necessary to use the contaminated munitions on uncontaminated aircraft, ordnance shall be decontaminated before applying it to an aircraft.

(3) If the munitions area is contaminated and the weapons build process did not have an overhead cover, the commanders should determine the need for additional weapons during this period. If the munitions operation built enough weapons for the next 24 hours, it may not be necessary to continue building bombs in the first few hours after an attack. Munitions work crews should conduct decontamination of the munitions area, munitions equipment, and munitions.

(4) The supervisors and munitions work crews shall ensure that the contamination status of munitions and equipment is clearly marked.

c. For the decontamination operations to be beneficial, the individual vehicle and equipment operators must immediately decontaminate the parts of the munitions assets that will be touched within 15 minutes of being contaminated. Units may organize and equip contamination control teams to support sustained operations. They use the team concept (normally two members) to assist unit personnel in developing and executing the immediate decontamination measures, resupplying the unit with decontaminants, and collecting and disposing of contaminated waste.

(1) There is no need for extensive decontamination of each contaminated piece of ordnance, vehicle, or equipment (trailer, bomb loader, etc.) as long as the personnel clearly identify the contaminated assets as containing a residual hazard. The operator's or work center's accomplishment of the immediate decontamination using M295 decontamination kits will suffice to continue the mission operations. The decontamination operations will not produce significant results once the agent has sorbed into the paint or other absorbent surfaces. Depending on the surface, this sorption takes place in periods ranging from less than 1 minute up to 1 hour. Regardless of the decontamination technique used, it will be relatively easy to remove agents from the smooth panels before they absorb into the surface. However, the CBRN agents will tend to remain at low levels in crevices, rivet heads, and joints.

(2) The majority of munitions assets on installations use paint with polyurethane compounds. Chemical agents readily sorb into this type of paint. Thus, the decontamination operations will not have a significant effect unless they take place within minutes after the time of contamination. Timely decontamination will reduce the residual contact hazard. Impermeable surfaces (arming wires and other unpainted metal components) do not allow the agent to penetrate. Therefore, these locations represent the most dangerous areas on the contaminated assets.

(3) Plastic and rubber components are porous materials, and the agents easily soak into these components. While the use of the M295 decontamination kit or a 5 percent chlorine solution will effectively reduce or eliminate the operational contact hazard, the agent will remain imbedded in the material and an off-gassing hazard will remain.

(4) There are no effective, operationally feasible methods for completely decontaminating canvas storage covers, webbing, and other textile materials contaminated with liquid chemical agents. These items will have to be weathered or removed and treated as contaminated waste.

6. Air Cargo Movement Decontamination

Contamination can significantly disrupt the air and ground cargo movements if the cargo handlers do not plan and execute preattack and postattack actions. The commanders must identify and coordinate the task priorities, obtaining additional support when needed.

a. Cargo handlers must effectively employ preattack and postattack measures to minimize mission degradation and enable sustained operations. This includes the coordinated use of a system that balances the mission criticality level (importance) of the cargo with the hazard category (residual danger) associated with the materials to determine the appropriate action. The cargo handlers will require assistance from their unit CBRN reconnaissance team and CBRN specialists to determine the degree of contamination that is present on the cargo, cargo storage areas, and cargo movement areas. Personnel controlling the cargo movement will use Table VIII-4 to identify the mission criticality of the material and will conspicuously mark the relative code on the cargo.

Table VIII-4. Cargo Movement Mission Criticality Level

Mission Criticality Level	Definition
C—Critical	The cargo is sufficiently important that it must be transported within 4 hours, regardless of the existence of contamination.
P—Priority	The cargo is sufficiently important that it must be transported within 12 hours, regardless of the existence of contamination.
A—Accelerated	The cargo is sufficiently important that it must be transported within 24 hours, regardless of the existence of contamination.
R—Routine	The mission can be delayed until contamination levels, such as MOPP4 are not required, regardless of how long it takes the contamination to dissipate.
N—Negligible	The mission can be delayed until there is no measurable contamination. This type of cargo should not be accepted inside the cargo movement area. Room must be saved for higher priority cargo.

b. Table VIII-5 may be used to determine the hazard category associated with the cargo.

Table VIII-5. Cargo Movement Hazard Category

Hazard Category	Definition
1	Actual or suspected surface disposition of biological pathogens
2	HD, L, or GB vapor present without contact hazard
3	VL or L contact hazard present without measurable vapor hazard
4	HD or GB contact hazard combined with a medium level of danger associated with vapor concentrations (4 to 5 CAM/ICAM bars with HD and up to 6 CAM/ICAM bars with GB)
5	HD, L, GB, or VX contact hazard combined with a high level of danger associated with vapor concentrations (6 or more ICAM/CAM bars with HD, positive M256A1 tab for L, 7 or more ICAM/CAM bars with GB, or 6 or more CAM/ICAM bars with VX) **NOTE: In the case of GB, high vapor hazard alone can drive this category designation.**

c. In addition to the required CBRN reconnaissance, self-aid, and buddy care activities, cargo handlers accomplish the following actions. The timing of the postattack reconnaissance and self-aid buddy care activities depend on the situation, the direction from the installation, and the unit chain of command. Unless otherwise directed, do not accomplish the following actions until after the liquid deposition phase of the attack has ended.

   (1)   Determine the contamination status of each individual cargo pallet. Annotate and report the results to the commander.

   (2)   Remove and replace the covering within 6 hours (the sooner the better) if a single sheet of plastic is protecting the contaminated assets. Carefully remove the outer layer and replace it as time permits if a double or triple sheet of plastic or canvas is protecting the contaminated assets,. Carefully roll the material so that the contaminated side is rolled to the inside, and discard the material as contaminated waste.

   (3)   Mark the item as contaminated according to the unit marking procedures (NBC marking kit, signs on all sides) if barrier material is not protecting the contaminated cargo. Attach each type of signs to the cargo if it is contaminated with more than one type of agent (e.g., CB).

   (4)   Annotate the front of the appropriate NBC marking kit sign with the mission criticality and hazard category designator for prioritizing the cargo movement. The code for the mission criticality designator will be the first letter of the appropriate word (i.e., "C" represents critical and "N" represents negligible). The code for the hazard category is the number designator itself (i.e., "3" represents a contact hazard without a measurable vapor hazard).

   (5)   Annotate the specific agent, date, time of marking, and temperature (F or Celsius [C]) at the time of the marking operation on the rear of the marking sign. If using the DOD sampling kits (biological-agent samplers), annotate on the rear of the sign whether the HHA tests are positive or negative.

   (6)   Report the contamination status of each pallet to the unit operations center.

   (7)   Use Table VIII-6 to determine what decontamination actions, if any, are necessary based on the mission criticality level and hazard category of the contaminated cargo.

Table VIII-6. Cargo Decontamination Actions (Negligible)

Mission Criticality Level	Hazard Category	Recommended Action
Critical	1	Spray the cargo with water if it will not damage the contents. Triple-wrap and mark "C1."
Critical	2	Aerate for 30 minutes if the surrounding environment is clean. Triple-wrap and mark "C2."
Critical	3	Decontaminate with an IEDK. Triple-wrap and mark "C3."
Critical	4	Decontaminate with an IEDK. Aerate for 30 minutes if GB is the agent and the surrounding area is clean. Triple-wrap and mark "C4."
Critical	5	Decontaminate with an IEDK. Aerate for 30 minutes if GB is the agent and the surrounding area is clean. Triple-wrap and mark "C5."

Table VIII-6. Cargo Decontamination Actions (Negligible) (Continued)

Mission Criticality Level	Hazard Category	Recommended Action
Priority	1	Same as "Critical 1." In addition, wipe down the cargo with a dust remover, reset the cargo with HHA, triple-wrap, and mark "P1."
Priority	2	Aerate for 6 hours if the surrounding area is clean. Triple-wrap and mark "P2."
Priority	3	Decontaminate with an IEDK, recheck with the M8 paper, and use an IEDK again if necessary. Triple-wrap and mark "P3."
Priority	4	Aerate for 6 hours if the surrounding area is clean, decontaminate with an IEDK, triple-wrap, and mark "P4."
Priority	5	Aerate for 6 hours if the surrounding area is clean, decontaminate with an IEDK, triple-wrap, and mark "P5."
Accelerated	1	Same as "Priority 1." In addition, expose the cargo to sunlight for 4 hours, attempt a wash down, and conduct the wipe-down procedures again if the second HHA test was positive. Triple-wrap and mark "A1."
Accelerated	2	Aerate for 12 hours if the surrounding environment is clean, triple-wrap, and mark as "A2."
Accelerated	3	Same as "Priority 3." In addition, aerate for 12 hours before the decontamination process, recheck with the M8 paper, and decontaminate with an IEDK as often as necessary or until time no longer permits. Triple-wrap and mark "A3."
Accelerated	4	Same as "Priority 4." In addition, aeration time should be extended to 12 hours. Recheck with the M8 paper following the initial IEDK decontamination action. Repeat the IEDK operation if the contact hazard still exists. Triple-wrap and mark "A4."
Accelerated	5	Same as "Priority 4." In addition, aeration time should be extended to 12 hours. Recheck with the M8 paper following the initial IEDK decontamination action. Repeat the IEDK operation if the contact hazard still exists. Triple-wrap and mark "A5."
Routine	1	Same as "Accelerated 1." In addition, continue the weathering and wash-down or wipe-down process until the HHA tests are negative. Triple-wrap and mark "R1"
Routine	2	Same as "Accelerated 2." Triple-wrap and mark "R2."
Routine	3	Same as "Accelerated 3." In addition, aerate for 24 hours before starting the decontamination process. Triple-wrap and mark "R3."

Table VIII-6. Cargo Decontamination Actions (Negligible) (Continued)

Mission Criticality Level	Hazard Category	Recommended Action
Routine	4	Same as "Accelerated 4." In addition, the cargo should not be loaded until the contact hazard has completely dissipated. Triple-wrap and mark "R4."
Routine	5	Same as "Accelerated 5." In addition, the cargo should not be loaded until the contact hazard has completely dissipated. Triple-wrap and mark "R5."
Negligible	1	Same as "Routine 1." Triple-wrap and mark "N1."
Negligible	2	Do not process unless the contamination dissipates or the mission criticality level is upgraded. Triple-wrap and mark "N2."
Negligible	3	Do not process unless the contamination dissipates or the mission criticality level is upgraded. Triple-wrap and mark "N3."
Negligible	4	Do not process unless the contamination dissipates or the mission criticality level is upgraded. Triple-wrap and mark "N4."
Negligible	5	Do not process unless the contamination dissipates or the mission criticality level is upgraded. Triple-wrap and mark "N5."

    d.   Use the following detection guidelines when loading and transporting contaminated cargo:

    (1)   Determine the contamination status of the material handling equipment and the transport vehicles. Determine if the items have measurable amounts of contamination. Attempt to locate the pockets of contamination. This may entail the use of a CAM/ICAM to pinpoint the pockets of dirt and grease that may house the agents in liquid or dusty forms, which the M8 paper does not readily identify.

    (2)   Take the following precautions if the transport vehicle is uncontaminated to keep it clean during the cargo movement process:

    (a)   Conduct immediate decontamination on the portions of the material handling equipment exposed to the cargo pallet or the transport vehicle. Use the M295 decontamination kit or 5 percent chlorine bleach solution to decontaminate.

    (b)   Place plastic or another barrier material in the bed of the transport vehicle over the area where the cargo pallets will sit.

    (c)   Replace the outer layer of barrier material on the cargo pallets (if necessary).

    (d)   Ensure that the transport vehicle operator is the only person in the transport vehicle and that he wears the appropriate level of IPE.

    (e)   Ensure that the local cargo handlers perform the actual cargo loading. The cargo handlers should not touch, stand on, or go inside the vehicle unless absolutely necessary. If it is necessary, they should use the decontamination troughs containing 5 percent chlorine solutions to decontaminate their gloves and boots before making contact.

    (f)   Check the clean the transport vehicle for evidence of cross contamination, and if contaminated, conduct an immediate decontamination.

(g) Seal the vehicle chocks or other transport vehicle accessories that may have come in contact with contaminated surfaces inside a plastic bag prior to loading.

(h) Mark the vehicle and the cargo to clearly identify the hazard associated with the contaminated cargo.

(3) Use the following guidelines when loading and transporting clean cargo after attacks with CB agents:

(a) Determine the contamination status of the material handling equipment and the transport vehicles.

(b) Take the following precautions if the material handling equipment or transport vehicle is contaminated to prevent them from cross-contaminating the cargo pallet during the cargo movement process:

- Conduct immediate decontamination on the portions of the material handling equipment that will come in contact with the cargo pallet.

- Place at least two sheets of plastic or another layer of barrier material in the bed of the transport vehicle over the area that the cargo pallets will sit on.

- Ensure that the pallets have at least a double wrap of barrier material. The transport vehicle operator should be the only person in the transport vehicle, and he must wear the appropriate level of IPE.

- Ensure that the local cargo handlers perform the actual cargo loading. The cargo handlers should not touch, stand on, or go inside the vehicle or vehicles unless absolutely necessary. If necessary, they should use the decontamination troughs containing 5 percent chlorine solutions to decontaminate their gloves and boots after making contact.

- Check the pallets for evidence of cross-contamination, and if contamination is present, immediately decontaminate.

- Appropriately mark the vehicle to clearly identify the associated hazard.

(4) The cargo movement personnel should accomplish the following actions when receiving contaminated cargo from another location:

(a) Acquire the available information concerning the cargo. This includes the following:

- A description of the cargo.

- A description of the suspected contamination on the cargo.

- The physical condition of the cargo.

- The time of the estimated cargo contamination in relation to the anticipated reception time at the installation.

- The status of the vehicle operators.

- Contact information for the CBRN specialists and the unit expecting delivery.

(b) If the cargo does not have a high mission priority (as stated by the receiving unit), assess the ability of the unit or cargo handlers to isolate the cargo upon reception. If choosing the isolation option, clearly cordon off the area surrounding the pallets. Use a cordon radius of 25 feet (or as directed by CBRN personnel).

(c) If the personnel must expediently use the contaminated cargo to facilitate the mission operations, the receiving unit or cargo handlers should take the following actions:

- Ensure that the reception personnel are in the appropriate MOPP (normally MOPP4).

- Remove the layers of the barrier material (if present), cargo nets, or pallet banding; and dispose of these items as contaminated waste.

- Verify the type and level of the contamination (for example, VX in liquid form on metal boxes with no measurable vapor hazard).

- Remove the specific cargo from its packaging configuration (if feasible), and dispose of the packing material as contaminated waste.

- Accomplish the appropriate decontamination activities based on the extent of the contamination, agent present, cargo surface, and time available.

- Mark the contaminated cargo appropriately so that work center personnel will immediately recognize the potential residual hazard.

e. Use the following decontamination guidelines for aircraft pallets:

(1) Determine, report, and annotate the contamination status of each pallet. If a single sheet of barrier material protected the contaminated assets, remove and replace the covering. Accomplish this within 6 hours (the sooner the better). Carefully roll the material so that the contaminated side rolls to the inside, and then dispose of the material as contaminated waste. If a double or triple sheet of plastic or canvas protected the contaminated assets, remove the outer layer and replace it as time permits.

(2) Dispose of the barrier material as contaminated waste in the appropriate predetermined location. If a barrier material did not protect the contaminated property, identify the item as contaminated.

(3) Pay special attention to pallet netting. If the netting was contaminated, it will most likely be impossible to decontaminate over time. Ensure that the contaminated wrapping materials are disposed of in a temporary waste disposal area. Routinely transfer the contaminated waste to the installation contaminated waste disposal site.

Chapter IX
SHIPBOARD/MARITIME DECONTAMINATION

1. Background

This chapter addresses shipboard CBR decontamination and the decontamination aspects of CBRN recovery operations. Recovery operations involve those operations in which military or civilian personnel, equipment, and supplies move from sites off of naval ships (e.g., ashore or on another vessel into amphibious shipping)

2. Shipboard Chemical, Biological, and Radiological Decontamination

Shipboard CBR decontamination requires a well-thought-out plan and organization.

a. Shipboard Organization and Manning. The primary advisor to the commanding officer for CBR decontamination actions is the damage control assistant (DCA). The damage control organization includes the personnel assigned to damage control repair stations, standoff detector operators, countermeasure washdown system operators, ventilation control personnel, on-station monitors, survey teams, decontamination teams, and personnel decontamination station operators coordinated through the damage control center (DCC). Medical personnel are integrated into the shipboard chemical, biological, and radiological defense (CBRD) organization. Shipboard personnel may be required to conduct CBRD actions with a variety of routinely embarked units, including USN staffs, USN aviation squadrons and detachments, USMC units, USN special warfare units, EOD personnel, elements of Naval beach groups (NBGs) assault craft units, USCG law enforcement detachments, and USA units. Minimum damage control repair station manning requirements are outlined in NWP 3-20.31. The number of personnel may be modified by the type of ship. See the commander's repair party manual (Commander Naval Surface Forces Instruction [COMNAVSURFORINST] 3541.1) for a particular ship class.

b. Shipboard Decontamination Techniques and Procedures. Detailed CBR decontamination actions are outlined in NWP 3-20.31, NSTM 470, and NSTM 070. Shipboard CBRD decontamination and contamination control capabilities are focused on the survivability of the unit and are conducted primarily by the shipboard damage control organization.

c. Shipboard Safety Precautions.

(1) Countermeasure Wash Down System (CMWDS). For decontamination with detergents, in the absence of an oxidizer, the contaminants are not chemically neutralized and remain toxic. The possibility exists that the agent-contaminated water may drain or flow in such a way that contamination remains on the ship. Decontamination operations should be planned and conducted so that most of the runoff flows into the sea and that areas of heavy traffic and sensitive areas are not recontaminated. Care should be taken to minimize spraying or splashing of the contaminated liquid.

> **WARNING**
>
> Aircraft subjected to CMWDS will become deadlined due to corrosion control requirements until emergency reclamation maintenance is performed.

(2) Protective Clothing. Full chemical protective clothing shall be worn, and those personnel who might be exposed to contaminated spray should wear wet-weather gear over the JSLIST. However, wearing wet-weather clothing will dramatically increase heat stress. This factor shall be taken into consideration when planning the decontamination efforts.

(3) Surfaces. No decontaminated surface should be assumed to be completely free of CBR hazards until suitable tests are negative. Traces of an agent will often remain trapped in crevices or absorbed into paint even after treatment with an oxidizer. Weathering will reduce contamination over time.

(4) Sensitive-Equipment Decontamination. Most shipboard surfaces can be safely treated with the standard hypochlorite and detergent solution. The solution shall not, however, be used on aircraft, ordnance material, or electronic instruments because of the risk of corrosion damage.

(5) Use of Hypochlorite. Pure, undiluted calcium hypochlorite burns upon contact with many organic compounds (including petroleum products and some chemical agents). Calcium hypochlorite powder shall be added to the water before being used in ship decontamination. The powder shall not be scattered onto shipboard surfaces. See NTRP 3-20.31.470 (NSTM 470) for mixing instructions and NTRP 3-20.31.670 (NSTM 670) for stowage instructions.

d. Decontamination Priorities. Faced with the presence of contamination, the commander must decide to what degree decontamination is required. The best means of contamination prevention or control is achieved through the proper use of the CMWDS. However, aircraft that is exposed to the saltwater spray of the CMWDS will be deadlined until emergency reclamation maintenance is performed. Pockets of contaminants may require an operational or thorough decontamination through the use of fire hoses or other means. Thorough decontamination is extremely labor-intensive. Clearance decontamination is not technically feasible with onboard assets. Effective preparations for CBR decontamination operations must include the designation of those areas for which decontamination is absolutely essential to ensure the mission's sustainability. The decontamination of other areas will be deferred, and the crew will "fight dirty" as required. When the mission permits, the ship should be repositioned to an uncontaminated location. The need for additional decontamination measures should then be evaluated (natural weathering may eliminate much of the hazard). *All clear* should be sounded as soon as possible to allow a reduction in the MOPP level.

e. Decontamination Levels. Decontamination is the primary countermeasure process supporting sustained operations in CBRN environments. Risk management (RM) requires that the decisions regarding the level of decontamination be implemented and the optimum time for such implementation be allowed.

f. Decontamination Materials. Decontamination materials consist of installed systems and shipboard expedients. The installed systems include CMWDS, a fire main system, decontamination stations, and ventilation control systems. Expedients consist of readily available shipboard items such as brushes, buckets, bags, swabs, soap, calcium hypochlorite, and rags (see NSTM 470).

g. CBR Decontamination Actions after Attack.

(1) Chemical. Ship and personnel decontamination procedures will commence as soon as possible. In practice, decontamination is any process that eliminates or substantially reduces the hazards of contaminated surfaces or objects. It includes the physical removal of an agent by wash down, the chemical destruction or neutralization of an agent, or weathering.

(a) Operational Recovery. The restoration of shipboard operations after a chemical attack will be very labor-intensive. Mission intensity is the primary factor in determining personnel availability. Specific priorities must be established based on operational need. As intensity subsides, the priority can shift to more general decontamination activities.

(b) Survey. Once the CW attack has ended and the ship or force is believed to be clear of the agent cloud, survey or monitoring teams will conduct a survey of the entire ship. Vital areas such as ventilation intakes must be free of liquid contamination before commencing *purge ship* procedures. The contaminated areas must be identified and isolated.

(c) Personnel Protection. Personnel protection will gradually be reduced as practical, consistent with shipboard CW hazards and the probability of a subsequent attack. The protective mask is not removed for showering, but is worn until verification that no vapor hazards exist aboard ship and *all clear* is announced ship-wide. Personnel protective measures during decontamination operations are straightforward. Personnel directly involved in the operations must be masked, wearing CBR IPE and foul-weather clothing with all closures fully sealed. Personnel downwind of the operation must remain masked and continue wearing chemical protective clothing.

(d) Personnel Decontamination. Personnel CCAs used aboard the ship are installed or expedient. Installed stations are spaces that by functional design, location, and installed equipment are designated for personnel decontamination. Expedient stations are designated spaces in which the use of improvised procedures and equipment is necessary to meet the practical demands of the situation. It may be necessary to operate several decontamination stations simultaneously if risk to personnel is deemed greater than the current operational requirements. It is desirable to have personnel decontamination facilities capable of processing at least half of the exposed topside personnel at any given time. Refer to NSTM 470 for a detailed description of the decontamination area setup and procedures. Refer to NAVAIR 00-80T-121 for the modifications to standard shipboard contaminated doffing procedures that apply to aircrews.

(e) Surface and Equipment Decontamination. Using the CMWDS and fire hoses are the countermeasures available for general, overall decontamination of the ship's exterior surfaces. Agent depositions remaining after wash down and fire hosing include absorbed and surface depositions. CW agents absorbed into the paint, deck coatings, etc., can usually be left to evaporation and the weathering effects of the environment. Decontamination may still be required after wash down with fire hoses, and splash or spray of contaminant-bearing water can be a hazard to the decontamination personnel or to anyone downwind of the hosing operation.

(f) Interior Decontamination. In the event that interior decontamination is required, the standard decontaminant available on USN ships is calcium hypochlorite mixed with detergent in an aqueous solution. Steaming is an effective alternative means of decontaminating a ship's interior; however, it is recommended that this procedure be conducted at a shipyard. Steaming, which displaces all air from the contaminated compartment, allows the compartment surfaces to be heated to a maximum temperature of approximately 212°F. Agent vapor may discharge from a steamed compartment unchanged, but mixed with the exhaust steam. This could result in a hazard to personnel. Interior decontamination must include ventilation blowers. Blower vanes and the surrounding housing can be expected to be heavily contaminated and must be decontaminated to avoid reevaporation or blow-off hazard to the compartments served.

(g) Final Recovery. Personnel must take precautions to prevent skin contact with decontaminated surfaces, because of the possibility of CW agents desorbing from paint and other coverings. Personnel engaged in decontamination must continue to maintain the maximum levels of protection. Personnel in well-ventilated spaces do not require protection after gross decontamination and purging of the residual vapors has removed vapor hazards. Personnel should exercise caution when working in poorly ventilated spaces.

(2) Biological. The decontamination of vital spaces should be accomplished as soon as possible. It is important to identify the personnel who may have been exposed to the threat. The available shipboard decontaminants should include calcium hypochlorite, topical disinfectants, soap and water, and laundry bleach. The objective following an attack is to ensure that the ship can continue its mission without an excessive risk to the personnel following an attack. Damage control personnel may need to assist with the following:

(a) Ship Decontamination. Follow the standard decontamination procedures using an approved method such as steaming, using decontamination solution, swabbing, and spraying. The DCA must establish a priority list prior to beginning the ship decontamination and concentrate on vital stations and crew living spaces. Industrial facilities may be required for the final decontamination process, depending upon the type and concentration of the agent. After the decontamination is complete and the ship has exited the affected area, the greatest threat of infection will be from contact with exposed individuals. Once infected individuals have been identified (a process that could take several days), they should be isolated from the rest of the crew.

(b) Detection. The decontamination of BW agents is complicated by the fact that portable monitoring equipment is extremely limited. The decontamination may consist of a general scrub-down, concentrating initially on vital or known areas of contamination. Areas of known contamination are identified by the observation of BW agent clouds or the detonation of munitions containing BW agents.

(3) Radiological. Radiological hazards can last a long time and can range in severity from instantaneous casualties to a health hazard that is long-term but of no immediate operational significance. Radiological countermeasures cannot be applied in the same sequence in all situations. Command consideration of the tactical situation and the degree of radiological involvement will influence decisions regarding the countermeasures to be used (when they are used and how long they will remain in effect). When a ship is under attack, the commander must first defend the ship from the attack. If the attack is intense, all radiological countermeasures must wait until the requirements for the essential defense of the ship have subsided.

(a) Operational Recovery. The operational recovery phase of a major radiological involvement starts when emergency actions are discontinued. Maintaining the level of operational capability required to satisfy the existing tactical situation must be the primary objective of this phase. It also needs to include reducing the radiation hazards and repairing the damage. This phase extends over the period of time of decreasing shipboard radiation when vital stations can be operated for limited periods of time without producing casualties. Ship maneuvering, personnel shelter, crew rotation and reduction, and early ship decontamination are applicable countermeasures. In this phase, the command may have to accept some casualties to maintain the required offensive or defensive capability of the ship. Setting the appropriate material condition to secure the ship is essential. When ordered, the closure of fittings will never be given priority over the movement of personnel to sheltered locations. Ventilation ducts, boilers, and air passages should also be checked for the accumulation of contaminants. The contamination of saltwater systems does not present an immediate hazard.

(b) Personnel Decontamination. The adequate decontamination of personnel can be accomplished using decontamination stations, designated washrooms, or showers. Personnel decontamination stations should be located within the ship to afford personnel the best shielding from radiation. The detection of contaminated personnel with a radiac meter is difficult when the intensity of penetrating radiation from other sources is high.

(c) Ship Decontamination. The DCA shall develop a decontamination prioritization list for the vital watch stations. Hosing and manual scrubbing are the most effective decontamination measures suitable for use at sea. Saltwater is the basic material for decontamination of a ship at sea. The institution of decontamination procedures will commence after fallout has ceased and when the tactical and radiological situations permit. A monitoring team shall make a rapid survey of selected topside locations and report the results to aid in the decision to order decontamination.

(d) Final Recovery. The final recovery phase of a major radiological involvement starts after the intensity of radiation has dropped to a level that no longer presents a radiological threat. Minimizing the long-term hazard to the health of the crew is the objective of this phase. Shipboard decontamination and contamination control are applicable measures. The time of cessation can be determined from the plot of intensity versus the time readings plotted by the DCC. When the readings continue to decrease at a steady rate, the assumption can be made that fallout has ceased. When the topside radiation levels are below 5 rads/hour, the period of operationally significant radiological involvement is concluded.

3. Recovery Chemical, Biological, Radiological, and Nuclear Decontamination

Recovery operations are principally intended for the expeditionary strike group (ESG) commanders, amphibious squadron commanders, landing force commanders, embarked units, and staffs performing the recovery operations. When tailored, these principles can also be applied by any size Marine air-ground task force (MAGTF) (e.g., a single-ship MAGTF or an expeditionary strike force or amphibious task force) or by ships responding to a CBRN attack. See *Tactics, Techniques, and Procedures for Recovery Operations in a Chemical, Biological, Radiological, and Nuclear (CBRN) Environment* for detailed information on CBRN recovery operations.

Recovery operations encompass those operations in which military forces and civilian personnel (to include casualties), equipment, and supplies move from naval ships (e.g., ashore or on another vessel) onto amphibious shipping. These operations may include—

- Preplanned amphibious withdrawal of forces subsequent to operations ashore.
- Noncombatant or other evacuations.
- Recovery of personnel and equipment.
- Movement of forces and equipment from shore-to-sea as part of ongoing tactical, humanitarian, or logistical operations.
- Operations undertaken to investigate the nature of materials being transported on a vessel at sea using a ship's boarding party or specialized landing force team.

This section addresses the decontamination procedures required to support retrograding forces, to include their equipment, DOD essential civilians and contractors, and civilians under the protection of an expeditionary force. Paramount to the discussions of recovery operations in a CBRN environment is an understanding that these operations will place extreme demands on a ship's freshwater system to support the effort. Accordingly, commanders at all levels shall institute procedures to conserve water and order that excess water be stored in advance of known or suspected CBRN operations. In completing the requirements for decontaminating personnel and equipment, commanders are not authorized to alter a ship's basic design to reconfigure a space or create accesses; conversely, they may modify the use of a space (e.g., establish an isolation ward).

a. Procedures.

(1) Decontamination Procedures.

(a) Decontamination procedures are generally personnel- and labor-intensive operations. They are largely dependent upon the use of chemical solutions to rid surfaces of contaminants and upon time to complete weathering or decay in order to achieve a state of cleanliness that enables the personnel to perform their assigned duties without the added burden of wearing IPE. The amount of space available to complete the procedures will generally be determined by the class of ship. Commanders of cruisers, destroyers, frigates, and smaller-sized ships should anticipate using their flight deck or fantail areas to support decontamination procedures.

(b) A solution of calcium hypochlorite, detergent, or other soap is used in scrubbing and swabbing. Normally, a 9 percent solution in seawater is used, but a 3 or 5 percent solution can be mixed if calcium hypochlorite is in short supply. Directions for mixing solutions of various strengths are provided in Table 470-7-2 of NSTM 470. If calcium hypochlorite is unavailable, laundry bleach can be used as a substitute. The pattern of swabbing is top to bottom, front to back. The minimum amount of decontamination solution that will adequately cleanse the area should be used. Brisk rubbing and scrubbing should be used to mix the agent thoroughly with the oxidizer so that chemical neutralization can proceed more quickly. After an area is scrubbed and swabbed with the calcium hypochlorite solution or a detergent solution, the area shall be rinsed with seawater or freshwater while continuing to scrub and swab as necessary to remove any residue.

> **CAUTION**
>
> Attention must be given when mixing the solution. The tendency is to make a 10 percent solution. Above 9 percent, the solution becomes caustic and it can degrade or destroy equipment and materials. Calcium hypochlorite is not recommended for use on aircraft.

(c) If calcium hypochlorite is not available and detergent must be used alone, scrubbing and swabbing will only result in the physical removal of the agent, not detoxification. The detergent assists in bringing the agent into solution. The resulting solution contains toxic agents and shall be washed overboard by fire hosing. In areas where fire hosing is not possible, rinse the area with buckets of clean freshwater or seawater and scrub and swab as necessary to remove the toxic solutions.

(d) Harsh detergents and oxidizers cannot be used to decontaminate electronic systems and aircraft without risking damage to the equipment. Instead, only the materials normally used in maintenance and corrosion control on such systems and aircraft shall be used. Care shall be exercised to avoid contact with the runoff or other residue as the toxic properties of the agent are not changed by physical removal methods. The residue or runoff is still toxic.

(2) Decontamination Coordination.

(a) Forces who are retrograding to a ship or directing the movement of contaminated personnel and equipment to a ship shall attempt to reduce the extent of contamination to the lowest possible amount (consistent with the threat and nature of the operation) before embarking the ship. They shall also make every effort to inform and update the receiving platform of the nature of any known or suspected contamination and the degree of decontamination procedures performed.

(b) Commanding officers support and assist in the decontamination of ground forces by ensuring that suitable locations, equipment, and properly trained decontamination teams are on station. Furthermore, they are ultimately responsible for ensuring that recovered personnel have completed the required decontamination procedures before allowing them access to interior spaces. They have the authority to decide what equipment shall be discarded; however, they will coordinate with the commander of troops and the commanders of carrier air wings (CAW), MAGTF, and MAGTF air combat elements (ACEs) to determine the final disposition of recovered landing force vehicles, aircraft, supplies, and equipment.

(c) If the ship is basically clear of contaminants, only the flight deck or well deck are contaminated, and operations must continue, the commanders will work front to back in clearing the hazard and establish a pool of decontaminated craft to assume transport duties for the unaffected personnel and equipment. In some instances, it may be advisable to transfer the unaffected or decontaminated craft to a clean ship to maintain the ability to move both unaffected and contaminated personnel and equipment. In order to minimize the need to repeat decontamination procedures, as long as a need exists to move contaminated personnel, then contaminated or previously contaminated craft will be used to move these individuals and their equipment.

(3) CCA. The establishment of CCAs is critical to the effectiveness of any decontamination effort. The CCA serves as the focal and initial entry point for any effort to bring personnel into the interior of the ship. In well decks, the CCA should be set up as far back as possible, to include on the stern gate if sea states permit and the effort is to support personnel returning in combat rubber raiding craft (CRRCs) or like craft. Similarly, CCAs that are established in hangar bays should be positioned as near an elevator as possible. Containment pits should be set out to capture contaminated water, which will help reduce decontamination efforts that will be required for the deck. The collected water is drained through fire hoses rigged to discharge overboard.

NOTE: Since the hoses will become contaminated and require disposal, ships should maintain a pool of old fire hoses that can be expended under such circumstances.

(4) Decontamination Showers. Aside from the obvious advantage showers afford for removing contaminants from personnel, showers provide two added benefits. They give cooling to individuals suffering from the effects of heat stress and they offer a psychological boost from the feeling of removing the contamination. After showering, personnel should be advised to keep previously exposed portions of their body uncovered as long as possible since clothing will block or reduce the weathering effect. Additionally, wearing clothing on previously exposed skin can drive any residue further into the skin. Ships have the following five basic options for providing showers for personnel:

(a) Established Decontamination Showers. Showers offer the best facility to complete personal decontamination. The ship's decontamination teams can monitor personnel through view ports, and contaminated personnel can be guided in completing the required procedures. However, their location within the ship is not always conducive to providing returning forces an area close to their entry point onto the ship or the CCA, which can lead to increased chances for spreading contaminants or offer challenges for providing safety.

(b) Locally Manufactured Showers. Locally manufactured showers offer the flexibility to meet the design variations within classes of ships, assist in overcoming shortfalls in decontamination station locations and quantities, and complement locally developed plans to process individuals with varying needs. They are dependent upon an undefined quantity of stock material that may or may not be available on the ship to complete such a structure (e.g., spare shower heads, various sized piping and fittings, flexible hose, and fabric to cover the structure to create some semblance of privacy and control the contaminated water residue/spray). Accordingly, locally manufactured showers should be planned in advance. Efforts should be made prior to deploying or entering a CBRN-contaminated area to procure the needed supplies so that multiple units are manufactured and contingency operations are properly supported.

(c) Portable Shower Tents. Portable shower tents offer flexibility for decontaminating a large force or group of civilians. Easy to erect, these portable and self-contained units include all the piping and wastewater containment capability required to complement a CCA. Ships would need to rig a source of freshwater or saltwater and a drainage hose over the side. Consider if the water should be heated and how to heat it if no access to hot, freshwater exists.

(d) Field Showers from Embarked Units. Field showers, designed and utilized by forces ashore, offer yet another option to meet the challenge of decontaminating a large number of personnel. This equipment would most likely be sent to the field in support of the landing force or naval support elements and would be an essential part of the effort to complete their decontamination prior to retrograding to the ship. The ship's use of such equipment would require that an MOU be established in advance of such operations.

(e) Fire Hoses. Rigging fire hoses to create a makeshift shower could serve as a minimal resource for providing a shower to retrograding personnel. Like the field and portable showers, some consideration would have to be made for heating the water. Likewise, personnel manning such stations could be jeopardized by experiencing hypothermia or increased incidences of dehydration and heat stress from wearing wet-weather gear to protect their CBRN suits.

(5) Wash and Gear-Removal Stations. Ships may rig any number of CCAs to enable personnel to ready themselves for being certified safe for entering the interior of the ship. Stations will range from areas where individuals can initially attempt to decontaminate their personal gear and small arms, or to areas that serve as a collection point for these items, to ultimately providing sites where they can doff their IPE before proceeding to the shower. If a ship establishes a CCA in the well deck or the hangar bay and does not have a portable decontamination shower or a locally manufactured shower in close proximity, a process shall be adopted for moving personnel from the CCA to the shower wherein the personnel are afforded some measure of privacy (e.g., ships can rig screening curtains along the route or provide individuals with disposable garments). The principal decontamination solution for personal gear and equipment will be calcium hypochlorite. Calcium hypochlorite solutions and the synonymous HTH solution are prepared in accordance with NSTM 470 by personnel wearing facial shielding, aprons, rubber gloves, and CBR protective gear. Additional guidance for the construction of shuffle pits (boot wash), mask lens wash, scissors wash, etc. is provided within *Recovery Operations in a Chemical, Biological, Radiological, and Nuclear (CBRN) Environment.*

> **CAUTION**
>
> **Do not use saltwater for the mask lens wash because it may scratch the mask lens.**

(6) Shipboard Decontamination of Personnel. The decontamination of retrograding personnel shall follow the established procedures for decontaminating shipboard personnel. Personnel shall be routed to a CCA where the initial decontamination procedures are conducted. Upon completion of the tasks directed at the CCA, personnel shall be routed to a decontamination shower facility. Contaminated personnel should be given step-by-step procedures, read aloud to them where possible, by members of the ship's decontamination station teams. For situations in which escort ships within an ESG or carrier strike group (CSG) are tasked to receive contaminated personnel, ships shall follow the established procedures (see NTSM 470) consistent with decontaminating scrubber or survey teams. However, in order to support the embarkation, it is necessary to establish a CCA in the vicinity of the fantail, for personnel retrograding by small craft; or in the vicinity of the flight deck, if the movement is by helicopter. Personnel will not retrograde to a submarine.

(7) Casualty Treatment/Patient Decontamination. As with shore forces, casualty decontamination should be performed separately from noncasualty

decontamination. A medical staging area or mass casualty area should be placed near the decontamination area, but far enough away so that personnel will not be affected by any contaminant. Refer to NTTP 3-20.31, NSTM 470 and FM 4-02.7.

(8) Decontamination of Other Forces/Special Decontamination Personnel. Some modifications to the shipboard personnel decontamination process may be necessary to accommodate the differences between shipboard protective clothing and equipment and the corresponding items used by other organizations. Shipboard decontamination station personnel need to be aware of the differences. *Multiservice Tactics, Techniques, and Procedures for Nuclear, Biological, and Chemical Protection* describes Army protective clothing and equipment that may also be worn by USMC and USN beachmasters and construction personnel. The following items differ from the shipboard counterparts as indicated:

- The BDO is a two-piece ensemble with slide fastener closures used by ground forces. It cannot be decontaminated. The newer JSLIST suit is similar.

- The USA M-40 series masks are worn by ground forces with a hood that extends downward over the shoulders. The hood is not part of the overgarment.

- Green or black vinyl overshoes are used with the BDO. They are worn over combat boots for chemical protection and can be decontaminated and recovered.

- The USA has a suit, contamination avoidance, liquid protection (SCALP) that may be worn over the BDO for up to 1 hour for protection from gross liquid decontamination. The SCALP is a lightweight, disposable suit consisting of a jacket, trousers, and footwear covers.

- USA aircrew members may wear the aircrew uniform integrated for the battlefield, a two-piece uniform with hook-and-pile closures. In addition to providing CBRN protection, it also provides flame protection; it replaces the standard flight suit and the BDO.

- The chemical protective gloves used by these personnel are similar to the shipboard item.

The features that differentiate the protective equipment and ALSS used by USN and USMC aircrews are specifically detailed in NAVAIR 00-80T-121 and include the following:

- The A/P22-14 (V) 1-4 aircrew respirators are designed to be compatible with the standard aircrew helmet.

- Blown, filtered air is provided to the mask by a battery-powered pusher fan that is affixed to a C2/C2A1 canister. The pusher fan/canister assembly resides in a pocket attached to the crewman's survival vest or CBR overvest. CBR respirators used by fixed-wing aviators have a second filter canister that connects to the aircraft oxygen systems.

- The aircrew CPU consists of an undershirt and trousers. The fabric is composed of a nonwoven material with encapsulated carbon in a stretchable matrix. It is worn under the flight suit. The set can be washed once and reused if it is not contaminated. This undergarment cannot be decontaminated.

- A disposable plastic cape can be worn over the flight suit for protection from liquid agents.

- Chemical protective socks are worn under standard aircrew flight boots; disposable plastic overboots may be worn over the flight boots.

- The chemical protective gloves worn by aircrew personnel are of three varieties, two of which are similar to the shipboard item. The third is made of a gore-type material. Nomex™ flyers gloves are worn over the chemical protective gloves.

> **WARNING**
>
> Operational decontamination procedures for contaminated ground force personnel are not adequate to allow them entry into the ship. Personnel must complete the thorough decontamination procedures before being permitted to enter the interior spaces.

b. Flight Deck Operations. Aviation operations in a contaminated environment create challenges for a ship's aviation department. The aviation department head and commanding officer of an embarking aviation unit shall establish MOUs during predeployment to set policies for such contingencies. They must also arrange for frequent training to attain mission-essential task list standards will be necessary. Plans must be developed for conducting extended flight operations, thus necessitating a possible requirement for additional personnel trained to support flight deck operations. General statements such as "personnel are not transported after dark" will be negated by operational and tactical requirements, and such approval can be granted by the MAGTF commander. One option to meeting these challenges may be to reduce the number of aircraft operated, with a corresponding reduction in the number of flight deck spots used. Still, supervisors will need to anticipate a requirement for additional flight deck colored shirts, additional vests, an increase in the amount of IPE, and foul-weather gear. Some items may be capable of being laundered, but personnel may be required to don contaminated equipment over their IPE in the interest of following recognized safety procedures and to limit the contamination of clean equipment. Recovery operations will require considerable space to support the collection, separation, weathering, and off-gassing of equipment, weapons, flight deck jerseys, float coats, ordnance, etc. Likewise, depending upon environmental conditions, added restrictions may be enacted that limit work periods to correspond with the heat stress work restrictions.

> **WARNING**
>
> **Commands shall not attempt to minimize contamination to aircraft by stationing personnel with energized fire hoses on the flight deck and directing the aircraft to hover or pass through a "wall of water," even if it is only freshwater that is streamed toward the aircraft. The combination of rotor wash and the potential for aircraft ingesting water into the air intakes or damage by too strong a stream of water striking the aircraft present too great a risk for personal injury or damage to the aircraft.**

Because flight operations are normally conducted when winds are off the bow, commanding officers should endeavor to maintain a wind off the starboard bow to reduce the area potentially contaminated by a CBRN hazard. Ships should anticipate using their high-reach equipment and cranes as part of the plan to detect and clean contaminated areas. The use of the mechanical deck scrubber is not recommended because of its ability to be decontaminated is highly suspect.

(1) Moving Aircrews. Because decontaminating the interior of aircraft is difficult, care must be exercised when moving pilots and aircrew from the interior of the ship to their aircraft to avoid contaminating the exterior of their individual protective suits or boots. This can be accomplished through the use of temporary boot covers and the assistance of the flight deck support personnel. Personnel must remain mindful that contaminants can be kicked up by jet exhaust and helicopter rotor wash. Flight crews disembarking from their aircraft will be processed in a manner that is consistent with the procedures used for troops moving from the aircraft.

(2) Moving Troops.

(a) Members of the combat cargo division or flight deck crew will guide retrograding forces from helicopters to the appropriate CCA. If possible, personnel will remain in the helicopter until the rotor blades have ceased turning. Once the blades have stopped turning, personnel will be led in a single file to the designated CCA. If rotor blades must remain engaged, personnel will be directed to move as expeditiously as possible to clear the helicopter while being led to the appropriate CCA (maintaining a single file). The use of lights or other markers should be used to identify the path personnel should attempt to remain within.

(b) For personnel departing the ship on a clean helicopter in a contaminated environment, there is a similar concern as for the aircrew. The outside of the helicopter may be contaminated upon landing on the ship. These personnel would generally have to be encapsulated in their IPE before they could move from the ship's interior to embark their assigned helicopter. Ideally, it would be helpful if these troops could cross the contaminated flight deck and board their externally contaminated helicopter without contaminating their boots or suits. This would in turn require the use of temporary coverings for their boots as they crossed the contaminated deck. The use of large numbers of temporary boot coverings raises concerns about foreign object damage (FOD) to the engines. For this reason, loading might also need to be done prior to the engine startup, giving time to recover stray boot covers. Alternatively, troops could walk across the deck contaminating their boots and then don temporary boot covers as they enter the transport helicopters. This would leave the boots of the vertical assault troops contaminated, which is less than ideal, but would use the temporary covers to protect the floor of the helicopter.

(c) It would be best to protect the troops and the transport helicopter from becoming contaminated. This may require that a pathway be decontaminated on the deck from catwalks to helicopter spotting areas if the temporary boot covers are not used. Still another option to consider is the use of a plastic covering to line the floor of the helicopter. Again, completing such an action will require regard for FOD and a review of all requirements.

(3) Loading and Unloading Aviation Ordnance on Aircraft. Aviation ordnance and ammunition is treated similar to personnel with cargo with regard for minimizing the spread of contaminants. Returned munitions should not be stored in ship's magazines until certified as decontaminated.

(4) Aircraft Decontamination.

(a) If air and ground crews are careful when operating in a contaminated environment, cross contamination from the exterior to the interior can be minimized. In-flight airflow over the aircraft's smooth skin at typical flight speeds facilitates a higher rate of evaporation. Still, some agents will migrate into crevices, rivet heads, and joints and continue to be a hazard. A common area of contamination will also be on the aircraft's tires. Thickened agents evaporate slowly and may remain a hazard even after prolonged flights.

(b) If the interior is determined to be contaminated, flying the aircraft with the doors open can help reduce the hazard. Procedures for decontamination of naval aircraft, aircrews and aviation support personnel are provided in NAVAIR 00-80T-121. Information on emergency reclamation requirements can be found in *Aircraft Weapons Systems Cleaning and Corrosion Control* and *Organizational/Unit Intermediate Maintenance for Avionics Cleaning and Corrosion Prevention/Control.*

CAUTION

Ships are cautioned that improperly sealed flight deck lighting can contribute to contaminants seeping into the interior spaces of the ship.

(c) If time is available and flight operations are secured, aircraft should be moved forward to a wash-down spot consisting of a containment pit and a decontamination team.

NOTE: Ships should try to maintain at least one landing spot of separation between the recovery landing spots and the wash-down sites.

CAUTION

Do not use steam to decontaminate an aircraft. Damage to the composite materials used in the construction of aircraft may result.

(d) An aircraft wash down (i.e., operational decontamination) should be conducted within 6 hours of becoming contaminated, but it is most effective when conducted within 1 hour. Some amount of chemical contamination may remain after the aircraft wash down. The aircrew shall continue to wear their protective masks and rubber gloves for protection until a thorough decontamination is conducted or until the aircraft has weathered and the contamination is below detectable levels.

> **CAUTION**
> Most of the field-expedient decontaminants are corrosive and could cause damage to aircraft materials.

(e) While it is possible to perform a thorough decontamination of individual aircraft, this can be a tedious and time-consuming activity that will require a considerable amount of manpower to accomplish.

c. **Well Deck Operations.** The requirements for well deck and small boat operations in a CBRN environment are similar in nature to those of flight deck crews. The ship's first lieutenant and DCA, working in conjunction with the ships combat cargo officer, coordinate policies for manning requirements and decontamination procedures with the embarked element commanders. Once such operations are directed to occur, the DCA and the ship's first lieutenant brief the assigned personnel on the plan of action for the survey and decontamination procedures, recovery of equipment and personnel, and any offload requirements. All well deck personnel will require IPE consistent with the threat and their duties. Once cleared to disembark their craft, personnel will be led to a CCA to initiate decontamination procedures. Craftmasters shall be advised to maintain loads that were wet during transit to the ship if contamination is known or suspected to exist. It is the responsibility of the craftmasters, coxswains and drivers to keep the CBRN defense cell and well deck control officer advised of the craft's contamination condition. Depending on a variety of factors (e.g., tactical situation, sea state, and craft capabilities) craftmasters, coxswains, and drivers will attempt to decontaminate any known hot spots prior to recovery. They shall also attempt to complete a survey to verify that the decontamination is complete. If the craft is unable to be given a wash down, personnel may be brought into the ship and soaked using the ship's firefighting sprinklers with the aqueous film-forming foam (AFFF) secured. Similarly, the craft can be positioned in close proximity to the ship's quarter and sprayed by personnel with saltwater fire hoses. Once this is completed, a report to the ship shall be made citing that the craft is ready to enter the well. If the environmental conditions permit, and if the procedures exist and can be authorized, a stern gate or sill marriage is preferred. If the sea state conditions do not permit or if a final recovery of the craft is expected, the craft should be brought in using the steepest possible wedge and then be grounded out. All crafts and loads will be rinsed from top to bottom, front to back. Following the decontamination operations and when the landing craft can be directed to exit the well, the ship will flood the well deck to further eliminate any hazards. For the amphibious transport dock (LPD-4) class of ships, energizing the water curtain can be used to isolate the vehicle storage area from the landing craft air cushion (LCAC) to spray and rinse the loads. The recovery and decontamination procedures described in the following paragraphs will be completed for the craft (as applicable).

(1) LCAC.

    (a) The craftmasters shall maneuver their craft to maximize the exposure to sea spray. Propeller reversal, with the craft proceeding downwind and across the wind, is recommended as a minimum. If the craftmaster's survey confirms that the craft is clean, direct the craft to proceed into the well. Conversely, if the craft is still contaminated and the tactical situation and sea state permit, direct the LCAC to go off-cushion astern or alongside the ship. Have the ship's well deck crew hose down the craft with saltwater from the stern or catwalks; avoid hitting the LCAC propellers with a solid stream of water.

> **WARNING**
>
> Spraying water into the moving propellers could produce catastrophic blade failures presenting hazards to personnel. Spraying solid streams of water at stopped propeller blades could result in damage to the propellers and should be avoided.

    (b) If the LCAC is still contaminated and the operational situation permits, bring the LCAC in using the emergency recovery rig and spot it as far behind as possible to reduce the likelihood of spreading the contamination within the well deck. With the crew and troops remaining within the craft, well deck teams will survey the LCAC and decontaminate the hot spots. If the LCAC went over land to recover or deliver its load, contaminants will have been absorbed into permeable material, presenting a long-lasting contact and vapor hazard. At-risk material includes nonskid coverings and the rubber skirt; a thorough decontamination will likely result in their removal and replacement. It is possible that the emergency recovery line might become contaminated through contact with the craft. Following the last evolution, discard the line over the side, ensuring that it does not create a hazard to navigation. If a replacement line is not available, cut off the affected portions and reconstruct the line's features as necessary.

    (c) When bringing a contaminated LCAC into the well deck, every effort should be taken to clear the well deck and wing walls of all porous materials (e.g., lines, fire hoses). Porous materials exposed to the contamination should be jettisoned. Personnel who are exposed to LCAC-generated wind and spray shall don their JSLIST and wet-weather gear. All well deck and vehicle storage supply ventilation shall be turned on high speed, all exhaust ventilation shall be secured, and all vent exhaust intake covers shall be covered to ensure that air is forced toward the rear part of the ship and exits through the stern gate opening. When sea state and weather permit, it may be necessary to deviate from the ship's normal recovery ballast condition in order to minimize the spraying action of the contamination throughout the well deck and wing walls. In such cases, it will then be necessary to complete an emergency recovery of the LCAC using the towing rig with the propellers secured. Ballast the ship to the steepest wedge possible, with the water level at the sill to a minimum of 5 feet. Recover and shut down the LCAC engines. Activate the well deck sprinkler system with the AFFF in the recirculating mode, and operate the system for 2 minutes to wash down any contaminated spray from the craft. Fire hose main pressure should be at the maximum, and all nozzles should be operational to ensure the complete designed coverage. The survey and decontamination teams will then conduct established checks and cleaning procedures that are consistent with the ship's CBRN defense bill.

(2) Landing Craft, Utility (LCU). The LCU initiates active decontamination during transit to the ship, including activation of its CMWDS. Upon nearing the ship, the LCU should be directed to take and maintain its station alongside the ship at the slowest and safest possible speed. Once alongside, the ship's force uses additional fire hoses from the catwalks to concentrate on those areas not fully covered by the LCU system. The LCU crew is then directed to survey their exterior and report results to the ship; any hot spots will be further decontaminated. If agents have been left on the craft for over an hour, the epoxy-based paint may have absorbed them and a thorough decontamination may be required. The ship's force and LCU crews should pay particular attention to the crew cabin ventilation, air conditioning systems, and the large filter units for the engine air intake system. The crew cabin ventilation system can create a serious vapor hazard by blowing the agent vapor into an otherwise sealed compartment. When retrieving an LCU, a stern gate or sill marriage is preferred to minimize the contamination of the ship. Alternatively, bring the LCU in and ground it out without fully deballasting. With the ramp down, the ship's survey team checks the craft for any residual agents and, working with the craft crew, completes the decontamination. Direct disembarking personnel to proceed to the CCA to commence personal decontamination and to receive medical attention (if required). Complete the decontamination of the craft while the well is deballasted, flushing out the well deck in the process.

NOTE: There is a possibility that the steadying lines will be contaminated. Following the last evolution, discard the lines over the side, ensuring that they do not become a hazard to navigation. If replacement lines are not available, cut off the section which came in contact with the craft and resplice the line's eye.

(3) Amphibious assault vehicles (AAVs) essentially complete an external decontamination as a function of their transit to the ship. To further decontaminate the craft, position the personnel in the vicinity of the stern and direct them to hose down the AAV with saltwater prior to signaling it to enter the well. Once in the well, keep the hatches closed, with the crew and troops still inside, stop the AAV in the center of the well, and hose it down again with saltwater from fire hoses on both wing walls. Turn the AAV 180 degrees, and hose it again before backing it into a parked position. Keep the planking wet before and during recovery to avoid or reduce the likelihood of the agent saturating the wood. The AAV platoon commander will initiate the internal decontamination procedures. After a survey and the additional decontamination, permit the crew and troops to exit the vehicle, directing them to the CCA to complete their decontamination and medical assistance before allowing them into the interior of the ship. Setting "Circle William" hinders the ship's ability to ventilate the heavy AAV fumes from some well decks and could contribute to a buildup of fumes in the well deck and contribute to reduced visibility.

(4) Landing Craft, Mechanized (LCM). The procedures are the same as for an LCU, except the craft has no CMWDS and does not use a stern gate or sill marriage.

(5) CRRC. Contaminated CRRCs should be recovered one at a time. When environmental conditions permit, the CRRCs and their crews should remain in the rear section of the well deck during their survey and decontamination. The decontamination team uses portable showers for the crews. Once an initial rinsing has been completed, the personnel are directed to proceed to the CCA for decontamination and medical attention (if required).

(6) Other Small Craft. For davit-hoisted small craft (e.g., motor whaleboats, rigid hull inflatable boats), call the craft alongside for the initial decontamination by the shipboard fire hose teams; take care not to injure the personnel or swamp the boat. Once the craft is at the rail, the personnel disembark, are surveyed, and are directed to the CCA for decontamination and first aid (if required). The craft receives a thorough survey and decontamination prior to being hoisted aboard and secured. If a determination cannot be made that the craft is decontaminated, and if weather permits, it may be left at the rail until further decontamination can be accomplished. The eyes on all of the steadying lines and the sea painter will be dipped into an HTH solution and then cut off and disposed of over the side; new eyes on the lines will be made.

d. Vehicle and Equipment Decontamination Procedures.

(1) Ships generally lack sufficient equipment to conduct a thorough decontamination of vehicles; specifically, they do not carry wash racks to facilitate easy access to the undercarriage of the vehicles. Any effort to embark the contaminated vehicles and cargo into previously uncontaminated amphibious shipping requires a thorough review of all the options available to complete the assigned mission (to include a review of the follow-on mission responsibilities). If the ESG has the option to consolidate the clean cargo and vehicles before loading the contaminated items, such a course of action shall be pursued. If wash ramps are not available, ships with a "false beach" offer the best option for receiving the contaminated vehicles (e.g., LPDs, amphibious assault ships [general purpose and multipurpose, and cargo variant landing ship docks [LSDs]).

(2) In order to accomplish the cleaning, ships should ballast, create a steep wedge, and avoid submerging the false beach. When sea state and wave action in the well deck permit, create a 3- to 5-foot basin of water in the well deck, attach fording gear to the vehicles, and slowly drive them for 5 to 10 minutes in the saltwater. Spray with fire hoses, and use scrubbing teams (as necessary) to decontaminate the unsubmerged areas. Once the vehicle is determined to be free of contaminants, it will be directed to move further up on the false beach and receive a freshwater wash down to minimize corrosion potential. Finally, maintenance personnel should perform the post-saltwater emersion maintenance tasks.

(3) Steam cleaning may be considered as an option for decontaminating vehicles and cargo, but such evolutions are likely to be extremely dangerous and difficult to accomplish. Steam lancing can produce injuries similar to surgical incisions and the risks may far outweigh the potential gains that might be made over attempting to complete the decontamination procedure by creating a pool of water as described above.

e. Force Reconstitution.

(1) Reconstitution is generally beyond the capabilities of an ESG. However, reconstituting and expeditiously returning the force to a full mission readiness standard is the ultimate goal of any decontamination effort. In some instances this will not be possible until a considerable period of time has elapsed (e.g., following a nuclear warfare attack). Should the force be unable to restore itself to a full operational-readiness standard, assistance from outside commands or agencies will be sought, to include replacing contaminated personnel and equipment with assets obtained from the rear area commands. Similarly, in situations where the forces are being maneuvered (i.e., transported) from one landing force objective to another, forces may only be capable of accomplishing a limited operational decontamination. If the forces are unable to complete a thorough

decontamination, the commanders will make every effort to ensure that personnel are afforded the maximum level of support in assuring their comfort. For example, landing forces may be required to remain in the well deck or sequestered on the flight deck, but every effort will be made to afford them with adequate shelter and meals. Commanders may likewise find it more practical to take advantage of consolidating the forces along the lines of their levels of contamination and have one or more of the ships serve as contaminated ships and the remainder as clean ships, thus modifying the landing plan to align with the modified force disposition.

(2) The commanders may reduce the protective postures and allow the unprotected military personnel, DOD essential civilians, and contractors to operate in the proximity of the formerly contaminated material or equipment. This reduction can be made after using the currently fielded and available technologies to validate that the decontamination procedures or weathering have reduced the hazards from material and equipment to nondetectable levels. The commanders will ensure that the equipment and personnel are periodically monitored to determine if signs of a return of the contamination are detected. Should a hazard be identified, commanders will direct that appropriate action be taken to safeguard affected personnel.

> **WARNING**
> **Risks to personnel safety increase as residually contaminated equipment is consolidated and personnel work around this equipment for prolonged periods, particularly in areas with limited air circulation.**

(3) Before initiating the action to recover potentially contaminated equipment to the CONUS for repair, the commanders should coordinate with the JRA coordinator to determine if an emergency condition exists and warrants the risks associated with such an action. Generally, the equipment will not be returned to CONUS until it has been determined to be clear of contamination, even if such an action results in the requirement for an extended period of time for weathering. If the equipment cannot be decontaminated, destruction may be required.

> **CAUTION**
> Civil aircraft will not normally be used to transport the contaminated equipment due to the safety and legal concerns.

Chapter X

PATIENT EVACUATION AND DECONTAMINATION

1. Background

a. The evacuation of patients under CBRN conditions forces the unit commander to consider how he will commit evacuation assets to enter the contaminated area. Generally, if a supported force is operating in a contaminated area, most or all of the medical evacuation assets will operate there also. Efforts should be made to keep some ambulances and aircraft free of contamination. See FM 4-02-7 and FM 8-10.6 for additional information.

b. On the modern battlefield, land forces have three basic modes of evacuating patients (personnel, ground vehicles, and aircraft). Watercrafts may also be used to conduct patient evacuation for waterborne forces (see MCRP 4-11.1E).

c. Cumbersome MOPP gear, climate, increased workloads, and fatigue will greatly reduce the effectiveness of the unit personnel. Using the personnel to physically carry patients incurs a great deal of inherent stress.

d. The evacuation of patients must continue even under CBRN conditions. The medical leader must recognize the constraints that CBRN contamination places on him and then plan and train to overcome them. These constraints include the need for the allocation of dirty evacuation vehicles, patient transfer processes from dirty to clean vehicles, the allocation of personnel and supply resources for PDS operations, and the restricted working conditions of medical personnel wearing MOPP in ambulances with patients who have not been thoroughly decontaminated.

e. When evacuating patients in a CBRN contaminated environment, evacuation considerations should include the following:

(1) Evacuation assets could become contaminated in the course of battle. Optimize the use of contaminated medical and nonmedical resources before employing uncontaminated resources.

(2) Once a vehicle enters a contaminated area, it is highly unlikely that it can be spared long enough to undergo decontamination. This will depend upon the contaminant, the tempo of the battle, and the resources available for patient evacuation. Normally, the contaminated vehicles (air, water, and ground) will be confined to contaminated environments. However, immediate decontamination may be accomplished to reduce the amount of contamination in the patient transport area.

(3) Ground ambulances or other assets that are easy to decontaminate and readily replace should be used versus using air ambulances. However, this does not

preclude the use of aircraft in a contaminated environment or the evacuation of contaminated patients.

(4) If evacuation personnel are sent into radiologically contaminated areas, adhere to the operational exposure guide (OEG). Radiation exposure records must be maintained by the supported unit and made available to the commander, staff, and medical leader. Based on the OEG, the commander (with the assistance of his medical staff), will decide which evacuation elements are sent into the contaminated environment.

(5) The relative positions of the contaminated area, FLOT, threat air defense systems, and the patient's medical condition will determine if and where air ambulances may be used in the evacuation process with minimal air crew exposure. One or more air ambulances may be restricted to the contaminated areas. When possible, use ground vehicles to cross the line separating the contaminated and clean areas.

(6) Patients should receive immediate and patient decontamination at the operational level and first aid and buddy care prior to being placed on evacuation vehicles. To reduce the spread of contamination on ground ambulance wheels for vehicles that have been in the contaminated area, a contamination control line can be established at the edge of the contaminated area where patients can be transferred from the dirty ambulances to clean ambulances that do not contain contamination on their wheels. The clean medical evacuation vehicles would then proceed to a PDS at an MTF. The patients have not been given patient decontamination at the thorough level at this point. The inside of these clean vehicles may become contaminated if patients are not provided with immediate decontamination of their MOPP uniforms to remove most of the contamination. This necessitates that all ambulance crew members wear MOPP while in the field vehicles to protect them from possible cross contamination or vapor hazards from agent on patient MOPP. Another alternative is to determine the specific routes that will be used by dirty medical evacuation vehicles to get to the PDS at an MTF. The routes used by the dirty ground vehicles to cross between contaminated and clean areas are considered dirty routes and are not crossed by clean vehicles. See FM 4-02.7 for the setup of a PDS at an MTF.

(7) When employing ground ambulances, watercraft, or aircraft in a medical evacuation, place plastic sheeting under the litters to prevent transferring contaminants from the patients or litters to the inside of the vehicle. The plastic sheeting can be removed with the patients, thus removing most of the contamination with it. When plastic sheeting is not available, placing a blanket under the litter will reduce the amount of agent that makes contact with the inside of the vehicle.

(8) The rotor wash of the helicopter or turbulence (e.g., prop blast) from wing aircraft must always be kept in mind when evacuating patients, especially in a contaminated environment. The intense winds may disturb contaminants, increasing vapor hazards at the contaminated landing site. The effects of downwash may be reduced by allowing the helicopter to land and reduce to flat pitch before patients are brought near it. Additionally, a helicopter must not land too close to a PDS that is open to the air as it can disturb dust and contaminants that may be in the area. If the PDS operation is in an uncontaminated area and contains contaminated runoff (such as in a bladder to hold contaminated waste), downwash should not be an issue at the PDS.

(9) Casualty protection during an evacuation is critical. Casualties who have been thoroughly decontaminated at a forward MTF and have had their MOPP ensemble removed must be placed in a patient protective wrap (PPW) or have their MOPP ensemble replaced if they are to be transported on a dirty aircraft, watercraft, or ground vehicle or when they are moved across a contaminated area.

(10) Medical evacuation by a fixed-wing aircraft will be severely limited as these assets are few compared with rotor wing and ground ambulance, and they require significant time to decontaminate. Some nations may not allow casualties from contaminated areas to travel through or over their territory. Every effort should be made to thoroughly decontaminate the casualty by removing the contaminated clothing and thoroughly washing the patient at an MTF PDS prior to the casualty reaching the staging area. The patient must undergo a thorough decontamination before entering a fixed-wing aircraft that is designated as clean.

f. Operational decontamination of medical evacuation assets should be accomplished to minimize crew exposure if the mission permits. The unit SOP should include equipment decontamination procedures.

2. Patient Decontamination

a. Contaminated patients potentially create increased hazards to casualty extraction teams, HSS personnel, MTFs, and materiel. Detailed information on patient decontamination is found in FM 4-02.7. This section provides an overview of patient decontamination for the individual services.

b. Personnel who have undergone a CBRN attack may suffer from the effects of a CBRN agent, TIM exposure, a conventional wound, psychological stress reactions, or a combination of these. In addition, some personnel may suffer from heat injuries induced by extended time spent in MOPP4.

c. Patient decontamination supports the decontamination process at the immediate, operational, and thorough levels.

d. The process of patient decontamination begins at the incident site. The contaminated service member performs immediate personal decontamination. If the service member is unable to decontaminate himself due to injury or incapacitation, a buddy performs this function. The contaminated areas on the MOPP ensemble and the exposed skin are decontaminated. For liquid chemical contamination, the M291 SDK is useful. If the M291 SDK is not available, use soap and water or a field-expedient absorbent material (such as clean, dry earth), ensuring that the skin is not abraded during its use. For vapor and aerosol contamination, use soap and water. Immediate decontamination is critical to limit the injury to the contaminated individual. For biological contamination, soap and water will remove these agents, but may not kill all of them. Radioactive contamination can also be removed (but not neutralized) with water or soap and water, by simply brushing dust and debris from the clothing and hair, or vacuuming with a vacuum that is fitted with a high-efficiency particulate air (HEPA) filter.

e. Every attempt must be made to limit the spread of contaminants onto the medical evacuation vehicles. As much contamination as possible must be removed from the patient's MOPP prior to loading him on the evacuation assets to reduce the contamination of these assets and the cross contamination of the other patients and crew. Individuals who are transported to the MTF for care may or may not be contaminated. If feasible, uncontaminated patients should be protected from cross contamination. Ways to reduce cross contamination include the following:

- Designating areas for the contaminated patients on the ambulance.

- Placing the contaminated patients on plastic sheets in the vehicle.

- Identifying separate assets for dirty and clean patients who are transported from the battlefield in MOPP.

- Decontaminating the MOPP of all patients who come from the dirty evacuation assets (ensuring that the MOPP gear is adequately decontaminated reduces cross contamination inside the dirty vehicle).

f. The key in patient decontamination at the thorough level is that the proper decontamination procedures must be followed to limit the spread of contamination so that MTFs and other patients are not compromised through the incapacitation of medical staff who are wearing CBRN protective equipment.

g. Each service follows slightly different procedures for thorough patient decontamination (based on the service's mission and equipment). All services follow similar principles, which include the following:

(1) Medical personnel supervise the patient decontamination operations. Augmentees from the supported units are usually required to assist in the decontamination process and perform patient lifting and washing.

(2) In the triage area outside the PDS, further decontamination of MOPP is performed to limit the spread of contamination (while necessary medical care is provided to stabilize the patient).

(3) Medical triage officers sort patients, considering the priorities for treatment, decontamination, and evacuation, based on the patient's need for care and his ability to benefit from what is available at that MTF.

(4) Those who do not require lifesaving procedures at a smaller MTF may remain in their MOPP4 ensemble on the dirty side of the hot line. There, the patient will be given patient operational decontamination and medical stabilization and returned to duty or evacuated to a larger in-theater MTF (where there is adequate staff to provide patient thorough decontamination to larger numbers of patients).

(5) Patient decontamination at the thorough level is a comprehensive cleaning process that must be carried out prior to a patient being allowed inside any MTF. It involves removing all of the patient's MOPP and any underclothing that is suspected of

being contaminated. Typically, all of the patient's clothing is removed. The patient's skin is then decontaminated. When water resources are limited, only the patient's mask and those areas of suspected skin contamination are decontaminated (pay particular attention to areas where there were breaks in the protective clothing and around wounds). The M291 and soap and water are used for chemical contamination. However, a 0.5 percent hypochlorite solution is useful if water is limited and the M291 kits are not available. Soap and water are best for biological and radiological contamination. For all agents, a complete body wash, using soap and water, can be performed (if adequate resources are available).

(6) Medical care and triage are provided before, during, and after patient decontamination to ensure that the patient remains stable enough to survive the procedure.

(7) Open wounds are irrigated with clean water or saline.

(8) The least desired alternative for skin decontamination is hypochlorite solution. If used, only a 0.5 percent hypochlorite solution is used for patient decontamination. Higher concentrations will irritate and burn the skin and allow some nerve agents to enter the skin more rapidly. During patient decontamination at the thorough level, the only place where 5 percent hypochlorite (full strength liquid bleach) solution is used is to decontaminate plastic mesh litters that are designed to be decontaminated. The litters are rinsed before reuse. The litter washing process is performed away from the patient decontamination area.

(9) All patients who arrive at the PDS wearing protective masks will remain in their masks during the decontamination process and until they are out of the PDS vapor hazard area. Medical personnel may remove the patient's protective mask to intubate the patient. The resuscitation device, individual, chemical (RDIC) is used if there is a vapor hazard in the area of treatment.

(10) Patients who are treated outside the MTF should not have their MOPP removed as long as they do not enter the MTF or a clean area or do not require skin decontamination.

(11) Contaminated bandages and splints are only removed by trained medical personnel. The bandages are removed; the skin is decontaminated and only replaced if bleeding continues. Splints are not removed during the decontamination process; cravat and other strapping material may be removed one item at a time, the skin decontaminated and a new cravat placed on the splint. Repeat this process until the entire splint has been decontaminated.

3. Army Patient Decontamination Procedures

a. The Army is a land-based mobile force, which uses patient decontamination procedures that meet the mission demands. Decontamination equipment is simple, is easy to relocate and set up, can be used in a limited water environment, and takes up relatively little storage space.

b. Each MTF, from Level I to larger, has a patient decontamination medical equipment set. Larger facilities, such as Levels III and IV, have more equipment and staff to handle larger numbers of patients evacuated to them from smaller, forward MTFs.

c. Smaller, battalion level MTFs are not staffed to perform patient thorough decontamination and medical treatment. Therefore, patient thorough decontamination must be performed by nonmedical personnel from the supported units or units located within the base cluster or in vicinity of the MTF. These individuals are supervised by the medical personnel. The minimum number of personnel required for basic PDS operation is 16. Larger MTFs will require greater numbers of personnel as they will need to process greater numbers of patients. Also, additional personnel should be considered to allow for a work-rest rotation of workers. Personnel are split into two categories. The two categories are:

- Nonmedically trained augmentees to assist with ambulatory decontamination and litter decontamination.

- Medically trained personnel serve as medics at the triage area, dirty side emergency medical treatment (EMT) areas, litter and ambulatory decontamination areas, clean side of the hot line, and clean treatment area.

d. If the MTFs are located near the troop decontamination units, coordination can be made to colocate medical patient decontamination and nonmedical troop decontamination side by side to share assets. Brigade is the lowest level that this operation can be effectively planned. However, decontamination support for other unique operational organizations (e.g., SOF) may require execution at a lower level. The operation requires close coordination between the brigade chemical officer, brigade S-4, brigade surgeon, and medical company commander.

e. Army patient thorough decontamination involves decontamination procedures for litter and ambulatory patients. This encompasses a series of specific steps for patient medical stabilization, the removal of clothing, wash down, and mask removal before entry into the MTF. Army field decontamination equipment sets provide buckets, sponges, liquid soap, HTH for a shuffle pit and hypochlorite solution preparation, litters, and litter stands.

f. Detailed step-by-step instructions for the operation of the Army PDS are found in FM 4-02.7.

4. Marine Corps Patient Decontamination Procedures

a. The Marine Corps is an amphibious mobile force that can conduct patient thorough decontamination operations on a ship, according to the Navy shipboard procedures, or on land with procedures similar to those used by the Army. It uses patient decontamination procedures at the thorough level that meet the mission demands. Decontamination equipment is simple, is easy to relocate and set up, can be used in a limited water environment, and takes up relatively little storage space.

b. The Navy MTFs supporting the Marine Corps are not staffed to perform patient thorough decontamination and provide medical treatment. Therefore, the patient thorough decontamination must be performed by nonmedical personnel from the supported units or units located within the base cluster or in vicinity of the MTF. These individuals are supervised by the Navy medical personnel. The minimum number of nonmedical personnel required for a Level I battalion aid station for patient thorough decontamination is identical to the requirements for the Army. The requirements include personnel to assist with ambulatory decontamination, litter decontamination, and hot line management. Navy medical personal minimal requirements would include medics at the triage area, dirty side EMT area, litter and ambulatory decontamination areas, and the hot line. Levels II and larger will require greater numbers of personnel as they will need to process greater numbers of patients at larger Navy medical facilities supporting Marine Corps units. In these cases, additional manpower will be needed to ensure appropriate manpower work-rest rotation.

c. The Marine Corps land-based patient thorough decontamination involves decontamination procedures for litter and ambulatory patients. This encompasses a series of specific steps for patient medical stabilization, the removal of clothing, wash down, and mask removal before entry into the MTF. The equipment and procedures are almost identical to those of the Army, with minor differences in the cutting of clothing procedures for patients.

d. Detailed, step-by-step instructions for the operation of the Marine Corps land-based PDS are found in FM 4-02.7.

5. Navy Patient Decontamination Procedures

a. The Navy is primarily a sea-based force that can conduct patient thorough decontamination operations on a ship (according to Navy shipboard procedures) or on land for land-based Navy MTFs.

b. Ship-based procedures are unique to the Navy due to the architecture and layout of the ship. Contaminated litter casualties are typically triaged, stabilized, and decontaminated above deck and then brought below deck for treatment after they are decontaminated. Some ships may contain decontamination stations built within the ship where patients can be processed below deck.

c. Patient thorough decontamination procedures for land-based Navy MTFs are similar to those of the Army, depending on the decontamination equipment available.

d. Detailed, step-by-step instructions for the operation of the Navy land-based PDS are found in FM 4-02.7.

6. Air Force Patient Decontamination Procedures

The USAF is deployed as a land-based force that projects air power from a stationary site that may become contaminated. USAF patient thorough decontamination procedures are for deployed and CONUS forces in two separate configurations.

a. In deployed environments, the USAF utilizes expeditionary medical decontamination teams (EMDTs). These teams, with equipment and procedures, meet the mission demands for a stationary land support force that must sustain operations in a contaminated environment. Patient thorough decontamination is designed to allow the force to continue limited operations in an environment that becomes contaminated. Patient decontamination equipment is packaged to be air-transportable, ergonomically designed for optimal manning, and rugged for sustained use. USAF patient decontamination assets are only deployed with a chemically protected deployable medical system (CPDEMEDS) 25-bed medical package or larger. Decontamination equipment includes a Small-Shelter, Personnel Decontamination System (SSPDS), which is composed of tentage, a water bladder, a litter roller system, water heaters for handheld soap and water sprayers, and a runoff wastewater collection system. The SSPDS has lanes for both litter and ambulatory patients. Environmental control units regulate the temperature inside the SSPDS and maintain positive air pressure through access doors to the outside so that the unit can operate with contamination outside. The environmental control units also include air locks to the CPDEMEDS MTF. The 19-person manpower detail, which makes up one EMDT, is primarily composed of medical personnel who train together and perform all the decontamination procedures and medical care involved in the patient decontamination process. One EMDT can simultaneously process an average of 15 ambulatory and 15 nonambulatory casualties per hour. Detailed step-by-step instructions for the operation of the EMDT are found in AFI 10-204, with supplemental information found in FM 4-02.7.

    b. Within CONUS, the USAF uses an in-place patient decontamination capability (IPPDC). This is a nondeployable asset that is designed to provide patient thorough decontamination at USAF MTFs. It is designed for patients who self-present or are transported for definitive medical care to the MTF and may have bypassed decontamination at the incident scene. Equipment includes a decontamination tent that can be readily deployed. The entire tent setup includes plumbing, with soap and water sprayers, to decontaminate both litter and ambulatory patients and a roller system for litter patients. It also has water heaters and a runoff water collection system. The plumbing must be connected to a fire hydrant or an outside faucet. The IPPDC decontamination team is typically composed of 12 medical personnel who train as a group. Detailed, step-by-step instructions for the operation of the IPPDC are found in AFI 10-204, with supplemental information found in FM 4-02.7. Many CONUS MTFs have similar nondeployable patient decontamination layouts.

Chapter XI
DECONTAMINATION IN SUPPORT OF HOMELAND SECURITY

1. Background

a. During every incident involving a CBRN release, there is a possibility that the target could be a military installation, unit, or activity or a civilian site. The targets could include critical infrastructures or members of the public. The DOD maintains significant decontamination resources (personnel, equipment, and supplies) that may be used to support a request for federal assistance. Additionally, service decontamination resources may likely be used to respond to an incident or accident at a military installation. This chapter will briefly address how DOD decontamination capabilities could be provided to support HLS. Additionally, this chapter will address decontamination terms, procedures, and planning considerations that could be applicable to an incident or accident supporting HLS.

b. To prevent, prepare for, respond to, and recover from terrorist attacks, major disasters, and other emergencies, the United States Government (USG) has established a comprehensive approach to domestic incident management. The objective of the USG is to ensure that all levels of the government have the capability to work efficiently and effectively together. In order for the government to accomplish this mission it developed the *Federal Response Plan* and later the NRP.

c. For additional information refer to *Multiservice Tactics, Techniques, and Procedures for Nuclear, Biological, and Chemical Aspects of Consequence Management.*

2. Federal Assistance

Providing decontamination assistance to non-DOD government organizations requires detailed coordination.

a. Local and state governments routinely respond to a wide array of domestic emergencies without any federal assistance. Some CBRN incidents may not overwhelm local response capabilities, but may require technical advice and assistance that is not readily available in local or state agencies. However, a large-scale incident may overwhelm local and state responders, requiring considerable federal assistance.

b. Requests for assistance (RFAs) from civil authorities are coordinated through the processes outlined in the NRP. If local or state authorities submit an RFA, the Federal Emergency Management Agency (FEMA) develops a mission assignment and tasks the appropriate primary agency. If the tasked primary agency needs additional assistance, it may request military support through the on-scene defense coordinating officer or the Secretary of Defense (SecDef). The military elements capable of providing the necessary response are then sent to the incident area under the operational control of the defense coordinating officer (DCO) or JTF (during a CBRN incident) to perform the tasks.

c. Under DODD 3025-1, imminently serious conditions resulting from a civil emergency or attack may require immediate action by military commanders or by responsible officials of other DOD agencies to save lives, prevent human suffering, mitigate great property damage, or limit the spread of contamination.

3. Response to a Homeland Security Incident—Decontamination Considerations

There are important differences between a HAZMAT incident and a CBRN incident. Responders must be aware of these differences and take the proper precautions for self-protection, protection of other responders, and protection of the public during response actions. See *Multiservice Tactics, Techniques, and Procedures for Nuclear, Biological, and Chemical Aspects of Consequence Management* for decontamination considerations that apply to consequence management operations.

    a. General Considerations.

    (1) With most CBRN material, responders must complete decontamination swiftly in order to save lives and minimize the number of victims. Although a rapid response is required because of the speed that many of the toxic chemical agents affect the body, responders must resist rushing in to assist until the situation is over.

    (2) The number of expected victims is the first major difference between a standard HAZMAT situation and a CBRN incident. Responders may be required to control, triage, decontaminate, and track a large number of people at the site of a CBRN incident. Scene control may involve a large area, a mass victim situation with numerous responders who want to help, and the press corps seeking information about the incident. A response of this magnitude will require more personnel and material than may be available; therefore, detailed contingency planning, training, and exercising is required in advance.

    (3) A terrorist CBRN incident is a federal crime scene. During the decontamination process, responders must make every effort to preserve evidence for eventual use in apprehending and prosecuting the perpetrators.

    (4) Runoff control is required to reduce the spread of the hazard. Because of its potential toxicity, keep decontamination runoff away from sewer drains, groundwater, streams, and watershed areas. If runoff cannot be controlled, notify the appropriate agencies (e.g., sewer, water, and environmental).

    b. Purposes of Decontamination. The potential for exponentially increasing panic and cross contamination after a CBRN release is staggering. Responders who are called upon to assist in the decontamination process must possess the ability to execute the decontamination procedures properly; thus, negating the exponential effects and enhancing victim confidence.

    c. Decontamination Levels.

    (1) Emergency decontamination can occur at any point during a decontamination operation. Like mass decontamination, it commonly refers to procedures taken for the rapid reduction of agent from the skin. However, when an emergency arises during the decontamination process (e.g., the responder runs out of air during a technical decontamination), quick steps must be taken to alleviate or mitigate the emergency while also practicing contamination avoidance.

    (2) Mass decontamination is a commonly used term referring to the rapid reduction of agent from the skin of many contaminated victims. Mass decontamination is performed as quickly as possible while also practicing contamination avoidance. Other

terms associated with the mass decontamination process are emergency, gross, and immediate decontamination.

(3) Technical decontamination commonly refers to the deliberate decontamination of responders, equipment, and evidence. Technical decontamination can also be performed on a mass contaminated populous if conditions allow. Technical decontamination is performed with the emphasis on neutralization of the agent. Speed is not a factor. Terms that are commonly associated with technical decontamination are detailed, thorough, deliberate, definitive, and responder decontamination.

d. Decontamination Planning Considerations.

(1) Mass decontamination can take many improvised forms, with the intent being the rapid removal of the agent.

(a) Government agencies (e.g., OSHA) recommend a high-volume, low-pressure water system as the default standard for mass decontamination.

(b) High-pressure water systems are discouraged because they may force contaminants through the clothing and increase contamination on the victim.

(c) Field-expedient methods, like the ladder-pipe decontamination system method developed by the Howard County Fire Department for the Baltimore Exercise (BALTEX) V (an emergency response demonstration in Baltimore, Maryland), proved that a multiple-apparatus platform allows responders to create a longer corridor for decontamination that will accommodate a large number of victims.

(d) Commercially available decontamination systems are effective, but most of these systems are trailer-mounted and require transportation to the incident site, causing delays. However, if these systems are centrally located and rapidly deployable, they offer an advantage over other systems because they provide the following:

- Heated showers.
- Cover.
- Systems to control runoff.

(e) The use of chlorinated swimming pools, elevated master nozzles, fog streams, and public-school shower facilities are other improvised methods that meet the intent of emergency decontamination. The objective is the rapid and gross removal of most of the agent involved in the incident.

(2) Emergency decontamination does not require the use of a decontamination corridor, although the nature of the corridor lends itself to an organized and effective decontamination operation.

(3) Weather conditions and the possible requirement of an indoor decontamination site (e.g., school gym with showers, car wash, or community center) are things to keep in mind when choosing a location. Techniques for adjusting water pressure may also come into play when using hose lines and elevated master streams in the decontamination process.

(4) Appropriate personal coverings are provided for persons undergoing decontamination, using items readily available from the local area, such as disposable ponchos, coveralls, and salvage covers. Incident logistics coordinators or responders might

procure blankets, large towels, sheets, and tablecloths from local restaurants, stores, hospitals, and hotels. Consider providing overhead cover to afford additional consideration for modesty.

(5) Establishing a triage, treatment, and transport area in a clean and secure location that is large enough to accommodate all victims must also be considered. Ensure that all responders are aware of the signs and symptoms of CBRN exposure. The use of mechanical ventilation and pharmaceuticals may be required to stabilize victims.

(6) Decontaminated victims and responders must be treated and transported to supporting MTFs immediately following the decontamination. Consider mass transit, when available, to assist in transporting victims.

e. Safety of Responders.

(1) The safety of responders is of the utmost importance. All responders with the potential to encounter contaminated victims or be exposed to contaminated material must wear protective clothing and respiratory protection equal to or one level below the level of protection required for the hazard. Responders can assure maximum consideration for the safety of themselves and victims by instituting and following safety procedures. The following are the levels of protection given in Department of Labor (DOL) Regulation 29 CFR 1910-120:

(a) Level A.

- Positive pressure, full face piece, self-contained breathing apparatus (SCBA) or positive pressure-supplied air respirator with escape SCBA approved by the National Institute for Occupational Safety and Health (NIOSH).

- Totally encapsulating chemical-protective suit.

- Coveralls (optional).

- Long underwear (optional).

- Gloves, outer and inner, chemical-resistant.

- Boots, chemical-resistant, steel toe and shank.

- Hard hat (under suit) (optional).

- Disposable protective suit, gloves and boots (depending on suit construction, may be worn over totally encapsulating suit).

(b) Level B.

- Positive pressure, full face piece SCBA or positive pressure-supplied air respirator with escape SCBA (NIOSH-approved).

- Hooded chemical-resistant clothing (overalls and long-sleeved jacket, coveralls, one- or two-piece chemical-splash suit, disposable chemical-resistant overalls).

- Coveralls (optional).

- Gloves, outer and inner, chemical-resistant.

- Boots, chemical-resistant, steel toe and shank.

- Boot covers, outer, chemical-resistant (disposable) (optional).

- Hard hat (optional).
- Face shield (optional).

(c) Level C.

- Full face piece or half mask, air-purifying respirators (NIOSH-approved).
- Hooded chemical-resistant clothing (overalls, two-piece chemical-splash suit, disposable chemical-resistant overalls).
- Coveralls (optional).
- Gloves, outer and inner, chemical-resistant.
- Boots, chemical-resistant, steel toe and shank (optional).
- Boot covers, outer, chemical-resistant (disposable) (optional).
- Hard hat (optional).
- Escape mask (optional).
- Face shield (optional).

(d) Level D.

- Coveralls.
- Gloves (optional).
- Boots or shoes, chemical-resistant, steel toe and shank.
- Boots, outer, chemical-resistant (disposable) (optional).
- Safety glasses or chemical-splash goggles.
- Hard hat (optional).
- Escape mask (optional).
- Face shield (optional).

(2) If the agent is unknown, Level B is the minimum required protection. Military issue IPE (MOPP ensemble) does not meet OSHA Level C requirements. If wearing MOPP—

- Minimize contact with the victims.
- Practice contamination avoidance.
- Know the agents and the signs and symptoms of their effects.
- Institute the universal safety precautions to better protect operations level responders from blood-borne pathogens.

NOTE: MOPP gear does not provide adequate protection for many TIM.

f. Isolation and Organization of Ambulatory Victims.

(1) Determine the best ways to isolate victims and establish victim control.

(2) Explain to victims that they need help. Provide them with instructions pertaining to what steps need to be taken. This can be done with loudspeakers or public address systems.

(3) Evacuate the victims upwind and uphill of the hazard. Separate the victims who are showing symptoms (symptomatic) from the victims who are not showing symptoms (asymptomatic). Separate men and women. Collect personal items (e.g., use a plastic bag and a method of identification, voucher personal articles for later return).

(4) Provide special consideration to families, small children, the elderly, and special-needs persons.

g. Types of Decontaminants.

(1) While there are numerous types of decontaminants available for use by responders, they fall into three basic categories:

(a) Miscellaneous (Commercial). Available stockpiles of these decontaminants may be quickly expended and not readily replaceable. Therefore, it is important that responders have an understanding of other decontaminants, their sources, and their uses.

(b) Natural. The use of natural decontaminants will reduce the responder time and the use of available decontaminants.

(c) Standard Military. If the military is called in to support the incident, military decontaminants may be available.

(2) Decontaminants should be stocked and stored before any incident. They must be accessible and clearly marked for content. Test decontamination material routinely for viability (strength). Operations level responder training must stress decontaminant use, application, and risk (e.g., agent use and contact time for personnel and equipment).

(3) When capabilities and resources allow, decontaminants of choice are soap and water, water, or household bleach if soap and water are limited. Full strength, 5 percent bleach solution from the bottle should only be applied to equipment (15-minute contact times) and never to skin. It will decontaminate most CB agents. A 5 percent bleach solution followed by a complete flushing is the maximum bleach concentration used for skin and clothing (though not exactly matching the recommended percentages, a standard rule of thumb is 10:1, or 10 parts water to 1 part bleach). Do not apply bleach to a victim's face.

(4) Responders may use commercially available materials (such as absorbents) for the control of liquid contamination at an incident scene and the removal of most gross chemical contamination from surfaces. Contamination will be transferred to the absorbent material, which must be treated as contaminated waste and disposed of accordingly. Since there is no preparation time for absorbent material application, utilize the material as soon as it arrives at the incident scene.

(5) Nonaqueous (without water) methods provide a means for contaminant removal.

(a) The use of dry, gelled, or powdered decontaminating materials to absorb chemical agents is appropriate (if their use is expedient). Commonly available absorbents include dirt, flour, baking powder, sawdust, charcoal, ashes, activated carbon, alumina, silica gels, and clay materials. Although these absorbents may be an expedient means of decontamination, their effectiveness has not been determined. In general, absorbents only remove contamination, they do not always neutralize the agent.

(b) The DOD uses the M291 and M295 SDKs, which employ a charcoal-based resin absorbent and are available for commercial purchase. However, while these kits are effective in removing spots of liquid chemical-agent contamination, they may not be suitable for treating mass casualties. This is due to their potentially limited availability and the relatively high labor requirements because of the size of the decontamination pad and the time it takes to clean large amounts of contamination from the victim.

(6) The use of natural degradation and ultraviolet (UV) light does not require responder preparation or application time. UV light kills most biological agents quickly, but does not kill spores.

h. Decontamination Corridor.

(1) Responders must be prepared to conduct emergency decontamination and to set up a decontamination corridor. To do this, select and secure a large area upwind and uphill of the hot zone. Provide protection for and be able to accommodate the decontamination of large numbers of victims. Base an emergency decontamination operation on speed rather than neatness.

(2) The sooner one begins and completes the decontamination, the better, as time will be a critical element. The decontamination process also has the potential of creating a hazard. Notify the proper authorities downstream if responders cannot confine the runoff to the incident scene. To reduce this hazard, responders must do the following:

(a) Control decontamination runoff as best as possible. Know where it is going, and ensure that it will not flow into clean areas.

(b) Coordinate with local environmental management officials if possible. Confinement may be critical if radiological materials are involved.

(c) Establish measures for the decontamination of fatalities. One method is to establish an additional lane within the decontamination corridor. Consider the psychological implications of the colocation with living victims and the potential need for autopsies for evidence as factors in determining where to establish the decontamination facilities for fatalities.

(3) After establishing the decontamination corridor, responders must effectively communicate to the victims what action can be expected as they pass through the corridor during the decontamination process.

(a) During decontamination, have the victims remove their outer clothing, down to their undergarments to increase the thoroughness of the decontamination process. The removal of clothing removes approximately 50 to 80 percent of the contamination.

(b) Additionally, consider implementing the following techniques:

- Use bags (such as trash bags, biohazard bags, or other bags of suitable size and strength) to collect and identify the individual clothing removed from the victims.

- Place the bagged clothing into a sealed container (tagged for identification) for a more thorough inspection later.

- Wet the victims down before removing their individual clothing (if the hazard is biological or radiological). This will embed the agent on the clothing of the victims and reduce the potential for the biological or radiological agent to adhere to the bodies of the victims or becoming reaerosolized.

- Blot the agent off (using a pinching motion) to remove the liquid (if the hazard is a suspected liquid mustard [blister] agent).

i. Nonambulatory Emergency Decontamination of Patients.

(1) Emergency cutout and decontamination of the nonambulatory victims at a WMD terrorist event presents many challenges to the first responders. Responders must be able to perform cutout procedures efficiently in order to accommodate the numerous victims that will need immediate medical attention. Precautions must be taken to prevent the spread of contamination to the responders, team, victims, and uncontaminated ground.

(2) Minimize responder and victim exposure during the decontamination process by—

- Selecting PPE at a level that protects the responder against the threat (chemical or biological agent). OSHA guidelines state that the PPE level must be at least one level below the contaminated responder's protective level. When the agent is unknown, OSHA requires PPE Level B. However, PPE Level A protection is recommended for additional safety pending the agent identification.

- Wearing positive pressure SCBA.

- Limiting the number of responders that come in physical contact with victims.

(3) Consider the following techniques to provide protection when handling victims:

- Use supports to hold the stretchers and backboards off the ground (e.g., milk crates or sawhorses).

- Keep clothing away from the victim's face during removal (limits the victim breathing the agent).

- Remove or cut the clothing from head to toe, front to back.

(4) Do not cut through holes or tears when removing clothing from victims. These are clues to the event and may prove to be useful evidence.

(5) Control and monitor all responder's activities throughout the incident for accountability and treatment in the event they become contaminated. If responders become contaminated, they may be required to conduct self-decontamination procedures to assure their own safety.

j. Technical Decontamination.

(1) When setting up the technical decontamination corridor, establish it away from the emergency decontamination corridor. During the emergency decontamination process, the emphasis is on speed and CBR agent removal since the victims have no

protection against the agent. Technical decontamination concentrates more on completeness and neutralization since the responders are in protective clothing.

(2) The distance between the stations of the corridor is critical in minimizing the vapor hazard and cross contamination. The distance is most critical at the last station, where personnel remove their respiratory protection and move to the cold zone. The incident commander or HAZMAT technician will establish the distances required between stations based on the weather conditions, the number of victims, space available, the type of agent used, and time restraints.

4. Department of Defense Decontamination Capabilities

See Appendix G for a summary of representative DOD decontamination capabilities.

THIS PAGE IS INTENTIONALLY LEFT BLANK.

Chapter XII
LOGISTICS

1. Background

Many of the materials that are needed to conduct decontamination operations are identified in this chapter.

2. Consumption Rates and Replenishment

Serious consideration must be given to consumption rates and the replenishment of items in order to sustain decontamination operations and remain prepared.

   a. Skin Decontamination and Personal Wipe Down. Each warfighter carries his own SDK. The SDK will be stored in the individual's mask carrier. The basis of issue per individual is two SDKs (12 packets). The unit maintains at least one SDK per assigned person for resupply. Personal wipe down is also done with these kits.

   b. Individual Gear Decontamination. The standard decontamination kit for individual gear is the IEDK. Each warfighter carries an IEDK according to procedures outlined in their unit SOP. The basis of issue per warfighter is one IEDK. Each kit contains four individual decontamination packets, enough to decontaminate two complete sets of individual gear.

   c. Operator Wipe Down. The unit or activity will use the M100 SDS for operator wipe down. The M100 contains two packs of reactive sorbent powder, two wash mitt type sorbent applicators, a case, and two straps. It allows two operators to perform simultaneous decontamination operations.

   d. MOPP Gear Exchange. Each warfighter wears or carries one complete set of MOPP gear. The unit or activity will maintain additional sets of MOPP gear as specified in the service logistics authorization documents. When a unit or activity undergoes a MOPP gear exchange, the unit sends a supply vehicle with the replacement MOPP gear and any decontaminants to rendezvous with the contaminated element at the operational decontamination site. The units or activities will generally maintain a 5 percent overage of MOPP gear, based on their personnel strength or authorization (whichever is greater) to ensure that a complete range of sizes and replacement gear is available. All MOPP gear, serviceable and unserviceable, is handled as organizational clothing and equipment (Class II supplies). The higher HQ is responsible for resupplying these items.

   e. Vehicle Wash Down.

   (1) Vehicle wash down is done in the unit or activity AO by the unit decontamination crew. The crew moves to the operational decontamination site, conducts a rendezvous with the contaminated element, and conducts the wash down. The vehicle wash-down crew may use a PDDE to spray 100 to 150 gallons of hot, soapy water on each vehicle to wash off the gross contamination. For vehicles such as the M1 series armored fighting vehicles, 200 gallons of water may be required per vehicle. Each 100 gallons of water provides a two- to three-minute wash. See Chapter IV for planning, coordinating, and determining the requirements for a vehicle wash down.

(2) A PDDA, such as the M12A1, injects detergent into the water as it operates. It uses 2.5 quarts of detergent for every 1,200 gallons of water (about 1 quart of soap per 450 gallons of water).

f. DTD. Generally, the units or activities conduct the DTD with the support of the CSS assets. Materials for this technique must be requested from the supporting CSS assets. The reconstitution operations should be closely associated with the decontamination operations. An assessment and recovery team ensures that the material and equipment are available for the decontamination operation as a part of the reconstitution effort.

g. DED.

(1) A CBRN unit must have access to a large water source (e.g., rivers, ponds, or a public water system) to conduct a DED. The CBRN unit leader estimates the amount of decontaminants that are needed. A CBRN decontamination unit sets up the DED site, supplies the decontaminants, and conducts the DED. The CBRN decontamination unit should carry enough decontaminants to service one company or squadron size unit. A CBRN decontamination unit that is assigned to conduct a DED for approximately 16 vehicles should carry a minimum of 4 gallons of liquid detergent and thirty 50-pound drums of STB. The CBRN decontamination platoon is usually resupplied through its parent unit. Command assignment relationships can change the resupply channels. (See Table XII-1 for the estimated water consumption guidelines for operational decontamination, DED, and DTD.)

Table XII-1. Estimated Water Consumption

Required Equipment	Time	Water Consumption
Operational Decontamination[1]		
M12A1 PDDA M17 LDS MPDS	1–3 minutes	100–150 gallons per regular vehicle 150–200 gallons per armored or larger vehicle **Example:** 15 (contaminated vehicles) x 150 (gallons of water) = 2,250 gallons [2]
Detailed Equipment Decontamination[3]		
M12A1 PDDA M17 LDS Karcher™ MPDS	Varies, see Chapter IV	Regular vehicles: Station 1 - primary wash, 250 gallons Station 2 - decontaminant application, 10 gallons per vehicle Station 4 - rinse, 200 gallons Armored or larger vehicles: Station 1 - primary wash, 300 gallons Station 2 - decontaminant application, 12.5 gallons per vehicle Station 4 - rinse, 200 gallons **Example:** 6 vehicles x 460 gallons of water = 2,760 gallons 4 tanks x 512.5 gallons of water = 2,050 gallons Total: 4,810 gallons

Table XII-1. Estimated Water Consumption (Continued)

Required Equipment	Time	Water Consumption
Detailed Troop Decontamination		
30-gallon container	Varies, see Chapter IV	The initial setup requires approximately 250 gallons of water. The water must be changed after 10 personnel have been decontaminated through the DTD to avoid the transfer of contamination. Station 1 (120 gallons, four 30-gallon containers)
3-gallon container		Station 2 (6 gallons, two 3-gallon containers)
30-gallon container		Station 4 (180 gallons, six 30-gallon containers)
3-gallon container		Station 7 (12 gallons, four 3-gallon containers) **Example:** About 150 personnel are to be decontaminated through the DTD. Two hundred-fifty gallons of water will be needed for every 10 personnel. 150 (number of personnel) ÷ 10 (required water change) = 15 (the amount of times the water will need to be changed) 15 x 250 (gallons of water for every 10 personnel) = 3,750 gallons of water for 150 personnel
[1] To reduce contamination, conduct operator spray down before the operational decontamination. This process requires less water consumption during a thorough decontamination. [2] Always include a 10% planning factor to the total estimate of the water consumption for the DED and the DTD. Example: 2,250 (gallons of water for the DTD) x 10% = 225 (additional gallons of water). A total of 2,250 + 225 = 2,475 (gallons of water required for the DTD). [3] The planner should consider the vehicle predecontamination action to estimate the water consumption. He should consider the vehicles that were processed through the operational decontamination because they will normally increase the weatherization process and may reduce the water usage.		

(2) See Table XII-2 for the decontamination resources that should be available at each organizational level for the USA unit decontamination requirements. See Table XII-3 (page XII-4) for the USA units estimated requirements for the equipment and supplies that are needed for the decontamination operations. See service logistics and authorization documents for their allocation of decontamination resources. See Table XII-4 (page XII-7) for a listing of the decontamination equipment used at a medical patient decontamination site.

Table XII-2. Decontamination Resources Available at Each Organizational Level (Army)

Organizational Level	Decontamination Resources
Individual	2 SDKs, 1 IEDK
Operators and crews	2 SDKs, 2 IEDKs, 1 onboard decontamination apparatus (M100), soap and water, two 50-pound drums of STB
Companies	2 immersion heaters, two or three 30-gallon containers, six 3-gallon containers, 6 long-handled brushes, 6 sponges, 300 plastic trash bags
Battalion PDDE crews	PDDE (M17 LDS or MPDS), basic load, liquid detergent
Chemical company decontamination squad	PDDE (M12A1 PDDA/M17 LDS/MPDS), basic load, liquid detergent
Chemical company decontamination platoon	PDDE (M12A1 PDDA/M17 LDS/MPDS), sufficient materials to set up a DTD

Table XII-3. Equipment and Supplies Needed for Decontamination Operations (Army)

Minimum Amounts of Equipment and Supplies Needed for Decontamination Techniques								Nomenclature	Class of Supply	Unit of Issue	Basis of Issue (See TO&E for Actual Authorization)[3]
SD[1]	PW[1]	OS[1]	OW[1]	MGX[2]	VW[2]	DTD[3]	DED[3]				
N/A	N/A	N/A	1	N/A	N/A	N/A	N/A	M100 SDS	II	Each	1 per every piece of major equipment
2	1	N/A	N/A	1	N/A	35	N/A	M291 SDK	II	Each	1 per mask
								M295 IEDK	II	Each	1 per person
N/A	N/A	N/A	N/A	N/A	N/A	1	N/A	Filter canister, C2 or C2A1[4]	II	Each	1 per M40 series mask
N/A	N/A	N/A	N/A	N/A	N/A	1	N/A	Hood, M40 mask	II	Each	1 per mask
N/A	N/A	N/A	N/A	1	N/A	2	N/A	Shears	II	Each	As needed
N/A	N/A	N/A	N/A	N/A	N/A	N/A	N/A	Knife	II	Each	As needed
N/A	N/A	N/A	N/A	[3]	N/A	N/A	[3]	Axe, single bit	II	Each	1 per most vehicles
N/A	N/A	N/A	N/A	[3]	N/A	[3]	[3]	Shovel, hand, RD, PT, D handle	VII	Each	1 per most vehicles
N/A	N/A	N/A	N/A	N/A	N/A	N/A	[3]	NAAK, Mark 1	VII	Each	3 per individual
N/A	N/A	N/A	N/A	N/A	N/A	[3]	N/A	Chemical agent nerve antidote	VII	Each	1 per individual 5 per combat lifesaver 10 per trauma specialist or 10 per company/platoon medic
N/A	N/A	N/A	N/A	N/A	N/A	[3]	3	Paper, chemical agent, detector, M9	II	Roll	1 per squad 3 per platoon
N/A	N/A	N/A	N/A	N/A	N/A	[3]	[3]	Paper, chemical agent, detector, M8	II	Book	6 per company
N/A	N/A	N/A	N/A	N/A	N/A	[3]	[3]	Radiac meter, AN/PDR-2	VII	Each	Per TO&E
N/A	N/A	N/A	N/A	N/A	N/A	2	[3]	Radiac meter, IM-93/UD	VII	Each	Per TO&E

Table XII-3. Equipment and Supplies Needed for Decontamination Operations (Army) (Continued)

Minimum Amounts of Equipment and Supplies Needed for Decontamination Techniques								Nomenclature	Class of Supply	Unit of Issue	Basis of Issue (See TO&E for Actual Authorization)[3]
SD[1]	PW[1]	OS[1]	OW[1]	MGX[2]	VW[2]	DTD[3]	DED[3]				
N/A	N/A	N/A	N/A	N/A	N/A	1	2	Alarm, chemical agent, M8A1 or M22	VII / VII	Each / Each	Per TO&E
N/A	N/A	N/A	N/A	N/A	N/A	4	2	CAM	VII	Each	Per TO&E
N/A	N/A	N/A	N/A	N/A	N/A	4	N/A	Detector kit, chemical agent, M256A1	II	Kit	1 per squad
N/A	N/A	N/A	N/A	N/A	N/A	1	N/A	Mask sanitizing solution	III	Tube	4 per 10 masks
N/A	N/A	N/A	N/A	N/A	N/A	[2]	1	Decontaminating agent, STB	III	Drum	3 per company
N/A	N/A	1	N/A	N/A	N/A	2	24	Brush, scrub, long-handled	N/A	N/A	As required
N/A	N/A	N/A	N/A	N/A	N/A	7	N/A	Pail, metal, 14-quart	II	Each	As required
N/A	N/A	N/A	N/A	1	N/A	9	4	Garbage can, galvanized, 30-gallon	II	Each	2 per company
N/A	N/A	N/A	N/A	N/A	N/A	N/A	6	Mop	II	Each	As required
N/A	N/A	N/A	N/A	N/A	N/A	5	N/A	Sponge, cellulose	II	Each	As required
N/A	N/A	N/A	N/A	2	N/A	4	6	Brush, scrub	II	Each	As required
N/A	N/A	N/A	N/A	2	N/A	2	N/A	Towels, paper	II	Box	As required
N/A	N/A	N/A	N/A	1	1	1	1	Detergent, GP, liquid	II	Gallon	As required
N/A	N/A	N/A	N/A	1	N/A	1	1	Bag, plastic	II	Box	125 bags
N/A	N/A	N/A	N/A	N/A	[2]	N/A	10	TAP apron	II	Each	10 per platoon
N/A	N/A	N/A	N/A	1	N/A	1	N/A	Suit, clothing, protective	II	Each	2 per soldier
N/A	N/A	N/A	N/A	1	N/A	1	N/A	Glove set, CP	II	Pair	1 per soldier
N/A	N/A	N/A	N/A	N/A	N/A	N/A	N/A	Cover, helmet, chemical protective	II	Each	1 per soldier
N/A	N/A	N/A	N/A	1	N/A	1	N/A	Overboots	II	Pair	1 per soldier

Table XII-3. Equipment and Supplies Needed for Decontamination Operations (Army) (Continued)

Minimum Amounts of Equipment and Supplies Needed for Decontamination Techniques								Nomenclature	Class of Supply	Unit of Issue	Basis of Issue (See TO&E for Actual Authorization)[3]
SD[1]	PW[1]	OS[1]	OW[1]	MGX[2]	VW[2]	DTD[3]	DED[3]				
N/A	N/A	N/A	N/A	2	2	2	2	NBC marking kit	II	Kit	1 per squad
N/A	N/A	N/A	N/A	N/A	N/A	2	N/A	Immersion heater	II	Each	2 per company

[1]Techniques executed by individual soldiers.
[2]Techniques executed by units.
[3]Amounts vary depending on the situation.
[4]If DF 200 is used, filters must be changed every 12 hours when conducting continuous decontamination operations.

Table XII-4. Medical Equipment Set Chemical-Agent Patient Decontamination

Equipment	Unit of Issue
Scissors bandage, 7.25"	Each
Bag, special, plastic (poly), 12x15 inches, 500 sheets	Package
Syringe, irrigating, 60-ml, 40	Package
Support, litter, folding	Pair
Litter, folding, 91.6"	Each
Chest, No. 4, 30x18x12 inches	Each
Chest, med ins sup, No. 6	Each
Paper, chemical-agent 25 sheets, M8	Book
Disinfectant, 6-ounce	Bottle
Decontaminating kit	Box
Pail, utility, plastic 3-gallon	Each
Pen, ballpoint, black	Dozen
Form, printed	Hundred
Sponge, cellulose	Each
Bag, plastic	Roll
Plastic sheet (poly)	Roll
Scalp suit ,small	Each
Scalp suit, medium/large	Each
Scalp suit, extra large/extra extra large	Each
Glove set, chemical-protective, small	Set
Glove set, chemical-protective, medium	Set
Glove set, chemical-protective, large	Set
Glove inserts, chemical-protective, cotton, small	Pair
Glove inserts, chemical-protective, cotton, large	Pair
Cutter, seat belt	Each
Soap, castile	Bottle

h. Patient Decontamination. See Chapter X.

i. Aircraft Decontamination. See Chapter VIII.

j. Shipboard. See Chapter IX.

k. Mass Casualty. Depending on the type of incident, the resources required could be difficult to plan. Chapter X of this manual discusses patient decontamination.

l. HLS and HLD. The DOD, in conjunction with the local and state responders, will determine the resources that will be required based upon the information available, the type of incident, and other supporting unit capabilities (see Chapter XI).

3. Maintenance Considerations

The disabled equipment or systems located within a contaminated area should not be removed for maintenance or returned to the owning organization until after they have been decontaminated. Minor on-site maintenance of the contaminated equipment or systems may be necessary. All maintenance that is performed on contaminated or potentially contaminated equipment and systems must be coordinated with the owning unit commander and the maintenance unit. If available, decontamination units may assist by providing site and equipment decontamination for the affected area.

THIS PAGE IS INTENTIONALLY LEFT BLANK.

Appendix A
CONVERSIONS AND MEASUREMENTS

This appendix contains the measurements and weights of decontaminant containers that are the replacements for used containers (see Table A-1). It also contains a table of commonly used metric system prefixes (see Table A-2) and a table of conversion factors (see Table A-3, page A-2).

Table A-1. Measurements and Weights of Decontaminant Containers

Containers	Measurements	Weights
Drum, 55-gallon, 16-gauge NSN 8110-00-597-2353	Volume – 12 cubic feet Length – 35 inches Width – 27.5 inches	Empty – 70 pounds Filled with water – 529 pounds Filled with STB (slurry) – 620 pounds
Drum, 55-gallon, 18-gauge NSN 8110-00-292-9783	Volume – 12 cubic feet Length – 35 inches Width – 27.5 inches	Empty – 50 pounds Filled with water – 509 pounds Filled with STB (slurry) – 600 pounds
Ash and garbage can, 32-gallon NSN 7240-00-160-0440	Volume – 7 cubic feet Length – 26.5 inches Width – 20 inches	Empty – 33 pounds Filled with water – 300 pounds Filled with STB (slurry) – 353 pounds
Gasoline can, 5-gallon NSN 7240-00-178-8286	Volume – 1 cubic feet Length – 18.5 inches Width – 6.75 inches	Empty – 10.5 pounds Filled with water – 52 pounds Filled with STB (slurry) – 66 pounds
Drum, 8-gallon, STB, 16-gauge NSN 6850-00-297-6693	Volume – 1.4 cubic feet Length – 14 inches Width – 14 inches	Empty – 11 pounds Filled with water – 78 pounds Filled with STB (slurry) – 91 pounds

Table A-2. Table of Commonly Used Prefixes

Prefix	Symbol	Factor
mega	M	$10^{6} = 1,000,000$
kilo	k	$10^{3} = 1,000$
hecto	h	$10^{2} = 100$
deca	da	$10^{1} = 10$
deci	d	$10^{-1} = 0.1$
centi	c	$10^{-2} = 0.01$
milli	m	$10^{-3} = 0.001$
micro	μ	$10^{-6} = 0.000001$
nano	n	$10^{-9} = 0.000000001$
pico	p	$10^{-12} = 0.000000000001$

Table A-3. Conversion Factors

To Convert	Into	Multiply By	To Convert	Into	Multiply By
Ounces (fluid)	Milliliters	29.573500	Inches	Millimeters	25.4000000
	Liters	0.029570		Centimeters	2.5400000
Ounces (weight)	Grains	437.500000		Meters	0.0254000
	Drams	16.000000		Kilometers	0.0000254
	Pounds	0.062500	Feet	Miles	5,280.0000000
	Grams	28.3495270		Centimeters	30.4800000
	Kilograms	0.028300		Meters	0.3048000
Grains	Ounces	0.002286		Kilometers	0.0003048
Drams	Ounces	0.062500	Yards	Meters	0.9144000
Pounds	Grams	453.592400	Miles	Meters	1,609.0000000
	Kilograms	0.453600		Kilometers	1.6090000
Quarts	Milliliters	946.400000	Centimeters	Inches	0.3937000
	Liters	0.946400		Feet	0.0328100
Milliliters	Ounces (fluid)	0.033800		Meters	0.0100000
	Quarts	0.001057	Millimeters	Inches	0.0393700
Liters	Ounces (fluid)	33.814000	Meters	Inches	39.370000
	Quarts	1.057000		Feet	3.2810000
	Gallons (US)	0.264200		Yards	1.0940000
	Cubic Feet	0.035310		Miles	0.0006214
Grams	Ounces (weight)	0.035270		Kilometers	0.0010000
	Pounds	0.002205	Kilometers	Meters	1,000.0000000
Kilograms	Ounces (weight)	35.274000		Feet	3,281.0000000
	Pounds	2.205000		Miles	0.6214000
Gallon (US)	Gallon (UK)	0.832670	Cubic Feet	Cubic Meters	0.0283200
Gallon (UK)	Gallon (US)	1.200950		Liters	28.3200000
			Cubic Meters	Cubic Feet	35.3100000
			Square Yards	Square Meters	0.8360000
			Square Meters	Square Yards	1.1960000

NOTES:
1. **The avoirdupois system of weights** is used for pounds, ounces, and drams except when specified. The avoirdupois system is the everyday system of weights commonly used in the United States where 16 ounces = 1 pound and 16 drams = 1 ounce. It is considered more modern and standardized than the alternative troy or apothecary system.
2. The US gallon is a different size than the UK gallon, so no liquid measures of the same name are the same size in the US and UK systems.

Appendix B
TECHNICAL ASPECTS OF CHEMICAL, BIOLOGICAL, RADIOLOGICAL, NUCLEAR, AND TOXIC INDUSTRIAL MATERIAL DECONTAMINATION

1. Background

This appendix provides basic information on the technical aspects of CBRN weapon effects and characteristics as it relates to decontamination. It also briefly addresses the decontamination-related aspects of TIM. Many CBRN and TIM substances are airborne hazards and may leave some degree of residual contamination that is hazardous to humans.

2. Nuclear and Radiological Weapons

Radioactive material will remain radioactive for some time and forces use removal or shielding methods to effectively decontaminate.

   a. Nuclear weapons have an enormous potential for physical damage and residual contamination. An RDD is a device that causes the dissemination of radioactive material across an area without a nuclear detonation. An RDD functions by using conventional explosives to blow up and scatter radioactive debris across a targeted area. This type of weapon may also cause conventional casualties to become contaminated with radioactive material and would complicate recovery actions within a contaminated area. Significant amounts of radioactive material may be deposited on surfaces after the use of a nuclear weapon or an RDD. Military operations in these contaminated areas will require an evaluation of the potential hazards and may require protective actions and decontamination. Operations could result in military personnel receiving radiation exposure or contact with particulate contamination, which would warrant medical evaluation and remediation.

   b. Nuclear radiation is characterized as initial or residual. The initial radiation is produced within 1 minute of the explosion. Residual radiation, also referred to as delayed fallout, occurs over a period of time. Fallout is composed of radioactive particles from the bomb and material from the surface of the earth that is carried into the air by the explosion. The larger particles return to the earth within 24 hours, but the smaller dust particles may take several months to fall. Other hazards include the presence of radioactive material on or in exposed sources, such as food and water.

   (1) Little or no fallout is generated by a high-altitude burst.

   (2) Little or no fallout is generated by an airburst. While the fireball is still glowing, a tremendous amount of radioactive energy is released.

   (3) The heaviest amount of fallout from a surface burst occurs within 24 hours in the immediate area of ground zero (GZ). Lighter fallout, in the form of a radioactive cloud, creates a residual radiation hazard (or footprint) that can extend hundreds of kilometers downwind. Table B-1, page B-2, provides representative estimates of the downwind radiation hazards resulting from different sized nuclear weapon detonations.

These estimates are for planning purposes and are subject to change based upon variables such as environmental conditions and the height of the weapon detonation.

Table B-1. Nuclear-Weapon Detonation Downwind Radioactive Fallout Hazard Estimate

Weapon Yield (in kilotons)	Wind Speed (in kilometers per hour)	Downwind Distance (in kilometers)	
		Zone I—Immediate Operational Concern	Zone II—Secondary Hazard
2	10	5	10
	25	8	16
	50	12	24
5	10	8	16
	25	13	26
	50	19	38
30	10	19	38
	25	30	60
	50	42	84
100	10	33	66
	25	55	110
	50	80	160
300	10	55	110
	25	90	180
	50	130	260
1,000	10	100	200
	25	155	310
	50	230	460

c. The types of ionizing radiation are described below.

(1) Alpha particles are charged particles that are approximately four times the mass of a neutron. Because of their size, alpha particles cannot travel far and are stopped by the dead layers of the skin or by a uniform. Alpha particles are a negligible external hazard; but when they are emitted from an internalized source, they can cause significant cellular damage in the region immediately adjacent to their physical location.

(2) Beta particles are very light-charged particles that are found primarily in the fallout radiation. These particles can travel a short distance in the tissue. If large quantities are involved, beta particles can damage the skin and produce a "beta burn" that can appear similar to a thermal burn.

(3) Gamma rays, emitted during a nuclear detonation and from the fallout, are uncharged radiation similar to X-rays. They are highly energetic and pass easily through most material. Because of their high penetration ability, exposure to a gamma radiation source can result in a whole-body exposure.

(4) Neutrons, like gamma rays, are uncharged and are emitted only during a nuclear detonation; they do not present a fallout hazard. Compared to gamma rays, neutrons can cause 20 times more damage to the tissue.

d. The three principle means to mitigate nuclear weapon effects are time, distance, and shielding.

(1) Time. Minimize the exposure times of the personnel conducting the decontamination. Personnel should remain inside unless directed otherwise through the chain of command. See *Multiservice Tactics, Techniques, and Procedures for Nuclear, Biological, and Chemical (NBC) Protection* for information on radiation exposure guidance.

(2) Distance. Maximize the distance from the hazards.

(3) Shielding. Concentrate efforts to prevent physical contact with the fallout. As a minimum, wear the appropriate IPE when outside. The standard-issue chemical protective masks afford protection from the inhalation and ingestion of radioactive material. Remain within the protected areas or shelters until directed otherwise. Perform damage assessment, self-aid, and buddy care and report these actions. Decontaminate when necessary to remove or reduce the contact or long-term exposure hazards from the fallout particles. The units and activities that are exposed to the initial radiation must first identify the intensity (dose rate) of the residual or induced radiation using radiac meters. They will then send the NBC 4 contamination and radiation dose status reports through the command channels. The commanders identify the units that exceed the OEG. They decide whether to withdraw these units and conduct decontamination operations or to continue with the mission. The personnel contaminated by the radioactive dust or debris perform an immediate decontamination by brushing or wiping their bodies and gear. As the mission permits, they can further reduce the radiation exposure by occupying armored vehicles, bunkers, shelters, or buildings. Highly contaminated vehicles and major weapon systems that pose a hazard undergo operational decontamination. This procedure limits the spread of the contamination to other areas and reduces radiation hazards. Early decontamination is necessary to cut down on the cumulative effects of radiation.

3. Biological Warfare Agents

There are many factors that determine how to decontaminate BW agents.

a. BW agents are pathogens or toxins. Some kill, while others incapacitate; some act quickly, while others incubate for several weeks; and some are contagious, while others are not. The pathogens include spore-forming agents (anthrax) that can persist for days in the environment. See Table B-2, page B-4, for information on the properties of selected biological agents.

Table B-2. Survival of Selected Bacterial and Rickettsial Agents in Some Environments

Agent	Glass	Paper	Soil	Seawater	Water	Vegetation
Anthrax (*Bacillus anthracis* spores)	Sprayed on: 56–70 days	Direct sun: December: 6.5 but not 8.5 hours; April: 2.3 but not 3 hours; May: 1.5 but not 2.5 hours	Months to years	Data not available	Data not available	Data not available
Brucellosis (*Brucella abortus*)	Data not available	Data not available	5–180 days	46 days	Lake water: 10 but not 36 days	0–6 days
Brucellosis (*Brucella melitensis*)	Dark: 16 days; Direct sun: 5–90 min	Diffused light: 7 days	6–69 days	11–46 days	Tap water: 20–72 days	6–22 days
Diphtheria (*Corynebacterium diphtheriae*)	Dark: 104–159 days; Direct sun: 2–5 min but not more than 10 min	91–159 days	10-208 days	Data not available	Data not available	Data not available
E. Coli (*Escherichia coli*)	Dried: Direct sun: 1 min but not more than 5 min	Data not available	21 - >80 days	99.998% loss in 5 days	Data not available	Data not available
Tularemia (*Francisella tularensis*)	Data not available	Data not available	Data not available	Data not available	May grow in water	Data not available
Listeriosis (*Listeria monocytogenes*)	Less than 24 hours	Diffused light: 24 but not 48 hours	In sun; soil surface: 12 days (2-3 cm); Buried: 180 days	Data not available	Data not available	Data not available
Tuberculosis (*Mycobacterium tuberculosis*)	Dark: 4 days but not more than 8 days Direct Sun: 15 min not more than 20 min	Data not available	Drop saline on sand: Shade: >4 hours; Sun: 2.5 but not 3.6 hours	Data not available	7–17 but not 25 days	Data not available
Glanders (*Pseudomonas mallei*)	10–15 days	14–16 days	Data not available	Data not available	28 but not 35 days	Data not available
Melioidosis (*Pseudomonas pseudomallei*)	Data not available	9 days	Greater than 27 days	Data not available	Data not available	Data not available
Salmonellosis (*Salmonella paratyphi*)	Data not available	39 days	Shade: 56 but not 70 days; Sun: 14 but not 29 days	18 days	Half life: 16 hours	Data not available
Salmonellosis (*Salmonella typhi*)	Dark: 15–33 hrs Sun: 5–15 min	Data not available	29 – 58 days	9 days	8 days	Data not available

B-2. Survival of Selected Bacterial and Rickettsial Agents in Some Environments[1]
(Continued)

Agent	Glass	Paper	Soil	Seawater	Water	Vegetation
Salmonellosis (*Salmonella typhimurium*)	Data not available	39 days	Shade: 56 but not 70 days Sun: 14 but not 28 days	7–21 days	Data not available	Data not available
Shigellosis (*Shigella dysenteriae*)	Direct sun: 20 but not 30 minutes	Data not available	13–30 days	12 hours	Data not available	Several tropical fruits: 1 hour
Cholera (*Vibrio cholerae*)	Dark: 24 but not 30 hrs Direct sun: 2 but not 8 minutes	1–3 days	Data not available	3–7 days	1 hr–3 days	Data not available
Plague (*Yersinia pestis*)	Dark: 2 to 4.5 days Direct sun: less than 1 to 3.5 hours	Dry: 4 but not 8 days Moist: more than 60 days	Dry: Less than 1 to 3 days Moist: More than 60 days	Data not available	16 days	Data not available
Leptospirosis (*Leptospira interrogans var. Pomona*)	Data not available	Data not available	Dry: 2 hours Moist: 5 days	18–24 hours	-20°C: 58 min 15 to 17°C: 12–42 days 34°C: 2 days	Data not available
Psittacosis (*Chlamydia psittaci*)	15 but not 20 days (4 but not 6 days when mixed with E. coli)	Data not available	Data not available	18–24 hours	Data not available	Yock sac culture on straw, 22°C: 20 but not 25 days When mixed with E. coli: 6 but not 8 days
Q Fever (*Coxiella burnetii*)	Data not available	Data not available	Sandy soil: Shaded Summer: 102 days Winter: 120 days In Sun: Summer: 56 days Winter: 70 days Nonsandy soil: 99.5% loss in 9 minutes Sun dry sterile soil (10^5–10^6 conc), 4-6°C: 210 but not 270 days; 34-36°C: <60 days	Data not available	Tap water: 20–22°C: 160 days	Data not available

b. Knowing how an agent can be disseminated is important to shaping an effective response. The size, shape, intensity, and overall effectiveness of the agent deposition pattern are influenced by the delivery method.

(1) Theater ballistic missiles are a viable means of delivery for many agents and may cause some contamination depending on the type of agent.

(2) The size of the submunition pattern allows the area targets to be more effectively targeted.

(3) Stationary or vehicle-mounted ground sprayers can be used to deliver agents. However, the resulting line source can cover a very large area and may cause some contamination at the point of release for a point source depending on the type of agent.

(4) As an airborne line source, aircraft sprayers may also yield some contamination depending on the type of agent.

(5) In addition to weapons-associated delivery of BW, BW agents can be disseminated through other means such as fomite spread and food or water contamination.

(a) Using inanimate objects (fomites) to spread an agent is another potential way to disseminate a biological agent, such as smallpox.

(b) Food or other products for human consumption are also a group that is vulnerable to BW agent contamination.

(c) Water supplies are a potential means for a biological attack. Some pathogens can grow and survive in water for a considerable length of time. However, the amount of agent required to have an operational impact make this a less likely means of delivery.

c. Environmental Factors.

(1) Environmental factors will dictate the size and shape, dosage at inhalation, height of the agent deposition, and the concentration of the agent deposition patterns on the ground.

(2) The conditions necessary to cause an operationally significant reaerosolization hazard are not completely understood. The form of the agent at the time of delivery is significant. Dry anthrax may be deposited over large areas with relatively small deposition levels on the ground. It is unlikely that reaerosolization of the anthrax from these depositions will generate an operationally significant hazard.

d. Most biological agents are not persistent and will decay within hours or days with exposure to the environment. However, anthrax spores can survive in a nonvegetative state for years if embedded just beneath the surface where they would be shielded from UV radiation, temperature, and humidity effects.

e. The DOD biological sampling kit provides a simple presumptive identification capability for a limited number of biological agents (pathogens and toxins). However, the user will most likely not know what areas are contaminated. BW agents are generally not recognizable in the air or on a surface by the human senses.

(1) Since BW agents are released as small particles and aerosols, they tend to move with the wind. Stronger winds move the clouds faster, resulting in a lower exposure. In calm conditions, the agent cloud stays close to the release site.

(2) A successful attack requires the agent to mix with the air. Stable layers restrict the vertical movement of the agent particles so that the agent released below an inversion remains available for inhalation and causes a higher likelihood of exposure.

(3) Landforms, buildings, and surface coverings (e.g., trees, brush, sand, and asphalt) influence the channeling of the wind and affect the spatial agent distribution.

(4) BW agents decay in the atmosphere at different rates based on heat, humidity, and exposure to UV light. Most BW agents will survive for relatively short

periods of time (minutes to hours) in the open atmosphere. The relatively low rate of biological decay of anthrax spores makes anthrax an attractive BW agent. Anthrax can survive between one and two days in the air.

(5) In a weaponized release, the level of deposition onto ground surfaces is very low. Agent survival on the surfaces is an important characteristic for considering the risk from a reaerosolization and the need for decontamination. Anthrax spores and smallpox virons have been found to be quite stable in soil (for many years).

(6) The time of day affects the operational impacts of an attack because each agent biologically decays at a different rate depending on temperature, humidity, and UV light intensity. In general, night or early morning, with their lower temperatures and UV light, provides the best conditions for a successful BW agent attack because of the lower biological decay. During this period, neutral and inversion conditions (especially with low wind speeds) result in the agent clouds, which maintain lower physical decay (i.e., spreading of the biological agent over time).

4. Chemical Agents

There are many considerations when determining chemical-agent decontamination.

a. Factors such as hazard duration, climactic conditions, the amount and type of contaminated resources, the number of personnel who physically come in contact with contamination, and the type of chemical agent affect, postattack recovery, and medical support activities are all considerations for determining chemical-agent decontamination. The primary CW agents of concern for decontamination are nerve and blister agents. Adversaries may seek to increase their effectiveness of chemical agents by employing them, where possible, under favorable weather conditions. Weather factors that affect chemical-agent employment include wind speed, air stability, temperature, humidity, and precipitation.

b. Chemical agents can adversely affect personnel through three principle routes of entry: inhalation, absorption of liquid or solid agent through the skin, and absorption of vapor through the skin.

c. The following are methods an enemy could use to enhance dissemination.

(1) Chemical agents, such as blister and nerve, have historically been released in neat liquid form, but can be disseminated in thickened or solid particulate (dusty) form. Agents disseminated in neat liquid form initiate a hazard cycle wherein the droplets settle to the ground after detonation, posing a direct contact hazard to people and equipment while the droplets are airborne. The agent is also beginning to evaporate during the droplet fall phase, so a vapor hazard starts to emerge. The largest vapor concentrations and probabilities of cross contamination remain highest while the droplets remain on the surface. In varying degrees of time, the agent will absorb into all but the most nonporous surfaces (e.g., glass, unpainted metal). Once this occurs, the agent may still present a hazard because of the toxic vapors off-gassing from the contaminated surface.

(2) Thickened agents are created by adding small amounts of selected compounds to the agent and thoroughly mixing the substances. Agent thickening may increase the time required for the agent to sorb into major terrain surfaces. During the decontamination process, thickened agents generally require considerably more effort.

(3) Chemical-agent penetration of materials presents challenges that personnel must recognize. Toxic vapors from absorbed liquid agents can penetrate nonporous materials and create a residual vapor hazard, even though physical contact with the liquid agent never occurred. Further, personnel must be aware that chemical agents can penetrate barrier materials, such as plastic sheeting, and release toxic vapors on the underside of the material. Table B-3 provides examples of agent penetration times for common materials. Agent penetration over time is one of the reasons that contaminated barrier materials should be replaced as soon as possible after an attack.

Table B-3. Protective Capability of Common Barrier Material (in Minutes)

Barrier Material	GD	TGD	HD	VX
Wool Blanket	2	84	84	600
Helicopter Cover	29	Data not available	Data not available	600
Heavy Tarp	120	120	120	600
Plastic Pallet Cover	180	180	180	600
NOTE: The criteria for these examples are the penetration of toxic vapor through the material.				

d. Characteristics.

(1) Chemical agents, like all other substances, may exist as solids, liquids, or gases depending on temperature and pressure. Most wartime chemical agents used in munitions are liquids, although some may be in a solid or dusty form. Following a detonation of the munitions container, the agent is primarily dispersed as liquid or aerosol.

(2) Certain chemical agents, such as selected nerve or blister agents, when encountered during the warm months of the year at sea level are liquids, but they are volatile to a certain extent. That is, they volatize or evaporate, just as water or gasoline does, to form an often invisible vapor. A vapor is the gaseous form of a substance at a temperature lower than the substance boiling point (BP) at a given pressure.

(3) The tendency of a chemical agent to evaporate depends not only on its chemical composition, vapor pressure, air temperature, and air pressure, but also on variables such as wind velocity and the nature of the underlying surface with which the agent is in contact. All external factors being equal, because of the respective agents vapor pressures, pure mustard is less volatile than the nerve agent GB, but is more volatile than the nerve agent VX. However, all of these agents evaporate more readily when the temperature rises, a strong wind is blowing, or when they are resting on a nonporous surface rather than on a porous surface.

(4) When a chemical agent is disseminated as a vapor from a bursting munition, the cloud initially expands, grows cooler and heavier, and tends to retain its form. If the vapor density of the released agent is less than the vapor density of the air, the cloud rises, mixes with the surrounding air, and dilutes rapidly. If the agent forms a dense gas (the vapor density of the released agent is greater than the vapor density of air), the cloud flattens, sinks, and flows over the earth's surface.

(5) Aerosols are finely divided liquid or solid substances suspended in the atmosphere. Airborne aerosols behave in the same manner as vaporized agents, but are heavier and tend to retain their forms and settle back to the earth.

(6) When a chemical agent is used for its liquid effect, evaporation also causes the agent to release chemical vapor. The liquid continues to evaporate while the liquid droplets are airborne and for some period of time after reaching the surface. Agent vapor pressure will govern the rate at which the liquid will evaporate. Once the liquid is no longer present on the surface, the desorption (chemical agent vapor returning back into the air) process begins.

(7) Some agents may be in a powder or dusty form. Dusty agents are created by soaking very small particles of inert substances in liquid chemical agents. These solid particles retain about half of the agent that is found in a liquid droplet of the same size.

e. See *Multiservice Tactics, Techniques, and Procedures for Nuclear, Biological, and Chemical Reconnaissance* for detailed information on detector capabilities and employment techniques.

f. Chemical-Agent Response to Decontamination Practices.

(1) When the decontamination process includes scrubbing, decontamination effectiveness is greatly improved. This appears to be true whether the mode of action of the decontaminant is principally chemical or physical because the mechanical action of scrubbing allows a greater amount of agent to react at any given time. For example, testing has shown that scrubbing is indispensable while using soapy water in the decontamination of HD. In general, dissolving the agent in the decontaminant facilitates the rapid destruction of an agent. Additionally, with a longer weathering time before decontamination there is an increase in the decontamination effectiveness because of the evaporation of the CW agent resulting in less CW agent requiring decontamination.

(2) The overall subjective rating of the decontamination effectiveness of hot, cold, or hot soapy water and steam for all surfaces and agents is: steam > hot water $\geq$ hot soapy water > cold soapy water $\geq$ cold water. However, G and V agents are more soluble in cold water than in hot and HD is more soluble in higher water temperatures.

(3) Bleach is effective in removing agents from surfaces; however, it is not able to remove agents that have already penetrated into the paint. Thus, while a bleach wash will remove all the contamination from a painted surface, none is destroyed inside the paint layer. To remove agent H from the paint, an organic solvent in the decontaminant is usually required. Nonsorptive paints, such as CARC, inhibit the penetration of agent into the paint layer, thus allowing the bleach to react with the agent.

5. Toxic Industrial Material

TIM can be found during all types of operations in peacetime or war.

a. A TIM hazard, whether manufactured, stored, distributed, or transported can present hazards to US forces. TIM should be recognized for the hazard they pose and the risks that may result from an explosion or fire. Most present a vapor (inhalation) hazard. This vapor concentration may be very high at or near the point of release. It may also reduce the oxygen concentration below what is required to support life. TIM are generally categorized as shown in Table B-4.

Table B-4. Categories of TIM

Category	Type of Material	Primary Uses
Agriculture	Insecticides, herbicides, and fertilizers	Agriculture and vector control
Industrial	Chemical and radiological material	Manufacturing processes, cleaning, and water treatment
Production and research	Chemical and biological material	Laboratories and storage facilities
Radiological	Nuclear fuel and medical sources	Nuclear power plants, medical facilities, industrial plants, and laboratories

    b. Forces will generally operate in environments where there are TIM. If an uncontrolled or deliberate release occurs, there may be an impact on the full range of military operations. Most TIM are released as vapors. These vapors exhibit the same dissemination characteristics as CW agents. The vapors tend to remain concentrated downwind from the release point (RP) and in natural, low-lying areas such as valleys, ravines, or man-made underground structures. High concentrations may remain in buildings, woods, or any area with low air circulation. Explosions may create and spread liquid hazards, and vapors may condense to liquids in cold air.

    c. The most important action if TIM is released is the immediate evacuation of personnel outside the hazard area. Use the *Emergency Response Guidebook* to identify specific hazards and decontamination implications.

6. Technical Reach-Back

Technical reach-back is the capability to contact a technical SME when an issue exceeds the on-scene subject matter expert's (SMEs) capability. Reach-back should be conducted using established unit protocols. Many of the reach-back resources listed in Table B-5 have other primary missions and are not specifically resourced for reach-back. Issues may include nonstandard agent decontamination of CBRN and TIM. This information could include persistency, medical effects, and decontamination or protection requirements.

Table B-5. Technical Reach-Back POCs

Organization	Telephone
National Response Center, Chemical Terrorism/Chemical Biological Hot Line	1-800-424-8802
Technical Chemical and Biological Assistance Hot Line	1-877-269-4496
DTRA	1-877-244-1187, 1-703-325-2102
AFRRI	1-301-295-0316/0530
USAMRIID	1-888-872-7443
USAMRICD	1-800-424-8802

    a. The National Response Center (NRC) mans the hotline service and serves as an emergency resource for technical assistance. The USCG operates the NRC, and trained operators staff the hotline 7 days a week, 24 hours a day. The CB hotline is a joint effort of the USCG, Federal Bureau of Investigation (FBI), FEMA, Environmental Protection Agency (EPA), Department of Health and Human Services (DHHS), and DOD. Specialty areas include the following:

- Detection equipment.

- PPE.
- Decontamination systems and methods.
- Physical properties of CB agents.
- Toxicology information.
- Medical symptoms from exposure to CB agents.
- Treatment of exposure to CB agents.
- Hazard prediction models.
- Federal response assets.
- Applicable laws and regulations.

   b. The USA Edgewood Chemical and Biological Center (ECBC) hotline provides technical assistance to emergency responders. The hotline is manned and operated 7 days a week, 24 hours a day. Technical CB assistance from ECBC can be obtained by calling 1-877-269-4496.

   c. The Defense Threat Reduction Agency (DTRA) can provide technical reach-back information and services for on-scene personnel. The focal/coordination point for support is through the DTRA Emergency Operations Center (EOC). DTRA can be contacted by calling 1-877-244-1187.

   d. The Armed Forces Radiobiology Research Institute (AFRRI) can provide DOD technical support capability for nuclear/radiological incidents or accidents. AFRRI can be contacted by calling 1-301-295-0316/0530.

   e. The United States Army Medical Research Institute of Infectious Diseases (USAMRIID) provides medical and scientific SMEs and technical guidance to commanders and senior leaders on the prevention and treatment of diseases and the medical management of biological casualties. USAMRIID can be contacted by calling 1-888-872-7443.

   f. The United States Army Medical Research Institute of Chemical Defense (USAMRICD) provides medical and scientific SMEs and technical guidance to commanders and senior leaders on the prevention and treatment of chemical casualties. USAMRICD can be contacted by calling 1-800-424-8802.

THIS PAGE IS INTENTIONALLY LEFT BLANK.

Appendix C
DECONTAMINANTS

1. Background

A decontamination procedure is characterized by the use of specific decontaminants, equipment, or actions to decontaminate an object; one or more modes of decontamination may be involved. Each particular mode of decontamination is determined by the process that best effects decontamination (i.e., chemical, physical, or natural processes). In most decontamination procedures, all three modes of decontamination occur, supplementing each other.

2. Types of Decontaminants

There are three general types of decontaminants—natural, standard, and miscellaneous. There are also developmental decontaminants that are being tested and evaluated.

   a. Natural Decontaminants.

   (1) Weathering. Weathering gradually decomposes CB agents by aeration, hydrolysis, and evaporation. The time necessary for decontamination by weathering depends on the persistency of the agent, its composition, climatic conditions, and the type of surface. Although weathering is the easiest method of decontamination, persistency of an agent is difficult to predict. Therefore, mission deadlines, unfavorable weather conditions, or hazards to unprotected personnel may require the use of a faster method of decontamination. Contaminated surfaces will be posted with standard contamination markers and may be left to the natural decontamination process. Natural weathering of a chemical agent is the simplest method of decontamination and, in some cases, may be the preferred method. If environmental conditions are suitable, weathering is an effective way to decontaminate military materiel, including heavy equipment and vehicles. Increases in the temperature and relative wind speed are the two key facts that accelerate the evaporation of an agent from a contaminated surface. In areas where warm, sunny, windy, and dry weather conditions exist, a substantial amount of agent would evaporate under weathering conditions. On the other hand, evaporation may not be practical for cold-weather or nighttime decontamination if there is a time constraint. Although weathering is recommended for chemical agents with high volatilities, such as GD or GB, their evaporation time frame would change when applied with a thickening agent. If time constraints are of little consequence, evaporative decontamination by weathering is an option for many materials in warm weather. The rate of weathering from surface types examined (bare metal, painted metal surfaces) at approximately 25°C shows the following order of decrease as a function of time: This order for the neat agents parallels what might be expected from examining their vapor pressure (GD > TGD > HD > THD > VX).

      (a) Air. Winds rapidly disperse the vapors of the chemical agents.

      (b) Temperature and Wind. High temperatures speed up the change of state for liquid vapor (evaporation) and hasten the dispersion of chemical agents in the air. The persistency of the liquid chemical agents decreases as the temperature increases. Because the CW agent evaporation rate approximately doubles with each 10°C increase in temperature and because evaporation increases an average of approximately 25 percent with each 1 meter per second wind speed, the blowing of hot winds over CW agent-contaminated areas should hasten the weathering process.

(c) Humidity and Precipitation. Moisture tends to hydrolyze the chemical agents. However, most agents hydrolyze very slowly. Heavy rain aids the decontamination by mechanically removing the agents. However, it may cause a concentration of agents in drainage areas, thus creating another contamination hazard.

(d) Sunlight. Sunlight serves as a decontaminant. Even in cold weather, the direct sun may warm surfaces above air temperature and hasten evaporation and decomposition of the agents. Additionally, the sun's UV radiation will destroy most BW agents.

(2) Earth (Covering). Earth can be used to seal in the contamination or as an absorbent for the contamination. Covering an area with approximately 4 inches of earth gives protection as long as the earth is not disturbed and the chemical agent exposed. Additional protection may be obtained by mixing bleach with the earth. An area treated in this manner may be subjected to light use; however, periodic monitoring will be required.

(3) Fire. The ideal conditions for the use of fire are during periods of lapse temperature gradient with a moderate wind speed away from friendly forces. Burning operations could cause a downwind hazard and should be carried out with caution.

(4) Water.

(a) Flowing water will flush agents from surfaces and will hydrolyze some agents, such as mustard and lewisite. Hydrolysis is a very slow process and should not be used as a primary means for decontamination. Hot water is a much more effective decontaminant than cold water, and the addition of soap produces a more effective decontaminant.

(b) Although water alone will hydrolyze mustards and lewisites, a toxic and blistering residue is formed. Scrubbing with hot, soapy water will physically remove the residue; an alkaline solution will destroy the chemical-agent properties. Therefore, water alone should not be used to decontaminate objects when it is practical to use standard decontaminants.

(c) High-pressure application produces a better cleaning action than low pressure. Flushing will remove the surface contamination but will not affect the agent that is sorbed.

(d) Water used in decontamination operations is contaminated and must not be disposed of in areas where it might flow or be washed into streams or other bodies of water or where it might contaminate groundwater used as a water supply.

(e) Soaking contaminated items in boiling water is an excellent method of decontamination. Soaking them in cold water is less effective. If hot water is not available or if it might cause damage to the item, warm water may be used.

(5) Soil. Soil should be considered a field-expedient decontaminating medium whether or not other decontaminants are available for use. However, the effectiveness of soil as a field-expedient decontaminant remains to be quantified. In all tests using soils or clays as the decontaminating medium, it was concluded that as much material as possible must be used for decontamination and that decontamination must begin as soon as

possible. The use of ample soil will help ensure the absorption of chemical agents and will also reduce the amount of vapor that is released. Soil can be used to remove chemical agents from surfaces by scouring and by sorption. Sorption occurs primarily in the clay and organic soil fractions. In the absence of better absorbents, soil may be used in removing liquid contamination from material; however, the used soil becomes contaminated and must be treated as contaminated waste.

(a) Under various conditions, chemical agents that have been sorbed by clay minerals can desorb, presenting a secondary hazard. Water has a tendency to hinder the sorption process in soil. Water also contributes to the movement and redistribution of chemicals entrapped in soils. The role in sorption and the inactivation of chemical agents by the organic matter in soils is not fully known. Nerve agents are decomposed by naturally occurring processes in the soil. The degradation of mustard also occurs; however, the rates and data on the conditions are very sparse. Studies indicate that mustard is very difficult to degrade by natural processes occurring in soil.

(b) The way agent is held within various soil components is not completely understood. Tests have shown that, following sorption, some agents can be released from the soil; thus, they can contaminate individuals who come in contact with contaminated soil. Work done with organophosphate insecticides indicates that clays will probably not permanently adsorb nerve agents. Certain insecticides, and presumably chemical agents, can remain in soil for long periods. Soil used in decontamination should be marked, dated, and isolated.

(c) Testing has shown that soil can be effective when used simply as a scouring material. However, coarse materials have the least effective surface area for sorption and are, thus, less effective in this role. Clay is the most absorptive portion of the soil. Table C-1 (page C-4) provides guidelines for the use of soil as a decontaminant.

b. Standard Chemical Decontaminants.

(1) STB.

(a) Description and Use. STB is a decontaminating agent for most CW agents. STB is a mixture of chlorinated lime and calcium oxide in a white powder form. STB, in a diluted solution, can be substituted for household bleach. When manufactured, it contains 30 percent available chlorine. Because of this chlorine content, a protective mask and gloves should be worn when handling STB. STB decomposes slowly in storage; this decomposition is easily recognized by the chlorine odor. STB can be expected to cause serious degradation of electronic equipment, it is corrosive to most metals, and it is injurious to most fabrics. It has a slight effect on nonmetals and a moderate effect on sealants.

(b) Chemical Action. STB decontaminates mustard, lewisite, and nerve agents. The vapor given off during the reaction with chemical agents is likely to be toxic. Bleach will produce a strong exothermic reaction with liquid mustard. This reaction may be severe enough to produce a flame. STB may be applied directly to surfaces contaminated with liquid mustard when there is no objection to potentially toxic vapors or if extreme heat would not damage the surface. Mixing STB with water or earth facilitates its distribution and diminishes the temperature resulting from its reaction with liquid mustard. Dry surface and deposits of STB do not react with liquid chemical agents that have been absorbed into the ground or other porous materials, because they do not come into direct contact with the agent. However, as long as STB retains its chlorine content, it serves to neutralize the vapors as they rise from the contaminated surface. Due to the decomposition of STB, the covering should be renewed at least every 24 hours. If the seal is broken by abrasion or traffic, the vapors will again become a hazard and the STB covering must be renewed.

Table C-1. Guidelines for the Use of Soil as a Decontaminant

- Use any relatively dry soil as a decontaminant. Under adverse conditions, wet soil is better than nothing.
- Begin the decontamination procedure as soon as possible so that a high percentage of agents will be removed.
- Smear soil or mud on equipment prior to a chemical attack as a precautionary measure. This will provide preemptive sorption of liquid chemical agent. A soil or mud coating will also help protect against agent aerosols or vapor. A soil or mud patch could serve as a temporary barrier to seal small breaks or tears in protective coverings.
- Establish an order of priority when decontaminating unprotected surfaces so that items with porous surfaces are decontaminated first. For porous materials, the elapsed time between contamination and decontamination should be less than 15 minutes; for less porous materials, the elapsed time between contamination and decontamination should not exceed 1 hour. If these times are exceeded, decontamination with soil can still be performed; however, the effectiveness of the decontamination will be diminished.
- Rub soil over contaminated surfaces to hasten the agent absorption and facilitate the abrasive removal of the agent from equipment. Use caution when removing the agent from porous surfaces to avoid forcing the agent into the pores.
- Discard spent soil, and replace it with fresh soil between 30 seconds and 1 minute if additional decontamination is required. The absorptive capacity of soil used for decontamination will be exhausted.
- Use at least four times the minimum amount of soil required to remove the visible agent to complete decontamination.
- Identify or mark the used soil following decontamination so that it can be properly treated and avoided for as long as possible.
- Vacate any area where the soil was used as a decontaminant following decontamination because agent can slowly desorb as vapor from contaminated soil.

NOTE: If no better alternative exists, soil previously used for decontamination can be guardedly used again. Processes in the soil slowly deactivate agents, thus the longer the time lapse since the use of a soil, the safer it will be. Additionally, the agent will slowly desorb from the soil, which will further reduce soil contamination.

(c) STB Mixtures. STB may be mixed with water to form a wet mixture called "slurry", or it may be mixed with dry earth to form "dry mix."

- Slurry. There are two types of slurry: one for manual application and the other for application by a PDDA. For manual application with swabs, brushes, or brooms, the most effective slurry consists of approximately equal parts (by weight) of STB and water, prepared by mixing 50 pounds of STB with 6 gallons of water. The recommended load for a 500-gallon PDDA is 1,300 pounds (or approximately 26 fifty-pound cans) of STB and 225 gallons of water. Detailed information about the preparation of slurry for use in the M12A1 PDDA is in applicable equipment TOs and TMs. To prepare the slurry, mix 100 pounds of STB with 20 gallons of hot water.

- Dry Mix. This mixture consists of STB thoroughly mixed with dry earth. The proportion by weight is two parts (two shovelfuls) of STB to three parts (three shovels full) of earth or other dry material. Personnel may shuffle their boots in dry mix before and after completing decontamination operations in which their boots are likely exposed to agents. Dry mix may be placed under equipment to decontaminate any agent flushed from it. For small-area decontamination, use approximately 1 pound of STB per square yard for short, grassy areas and 3 to 5 pounds per square yard for bushy or wooded areas for the decontamination of liquid chemical agents.

(d) Use in Cold Weather. STB mixtures (dry mix and slurry) do not effectively decontaminate agents that have become solidified as a result of low temperatures.

(e) Procedures after Decontamination. STB can be left on many surfaces after use. However, it must be rinsed thoroughly from metal surfaces immediately following the 30 minute contact time. Metal surfaces must then be oiled or greased to prevent corrosion. On wood or other porous surfaces, several applications of STB may be necessary. When decontamination is complete, surfaces must be flushed with water to remove slurry.

(2) High-Test Bleach (HTB) or HTH. HTH is a bleach material in granular or tablet form, containing a minimum of 70 percent calcium hypochlorite. The compound contains a higher percentage of chlorine than STB and is, therefore, more corrosive. HTH can be used for the decontamination of individuals and personal protective material. HTH will not blister paint during a decontamination operation that includes a prerinse and postrinse; however, it can severely corrode metals. See Tables C-2 through C-4 for information on preparing HTH solutions.

Table C-2. Preparation of Decontamination Solution Using HTH (6-Ounce Bottles)

% HTH Solution	Amount of Bottles per 4 Gallons Water[1]	Amount of Bottles per 10 Gallons Water[2]	Amount of Bottles per 20 Gallons Water[3]
1%	1	2	4.5
2%	2	5	9.5
3%	3	7	14.0
5%	5	12	24.0
10%	9	22	44.0

[1]Add 3 ounces of detergent.
[2]Add 9 ounces of detergent.
[3]Add 13 ounces of detergent.

Table C-3. Preparation of Decontamination Solution Using HTH (Granular)

Water	Amount of HTH (Granular) to Give 5% Available Chlorine (50,000 ppm)	Amount of HTH (Granular) to Give 0.2% Available Chlorine (2,000 ppm)
40 gal	25 lb	1 lb
5 gal	3 lb	2 oz (5 tbls)
1 gal	10 oz (1 to ½ cups)	½ oz (1 tbls)
1 qt	2 ½ oz (6 tbls)	1/10 oz (1 tsp)

Table C-4. Preparation of 0.5 Percent Available Chlorine Solutions

Decontaminant	Directions
HTH (6-oz bottle)	Mix one bottle HTH with 5 gallons of water.
Household bleach	Add one part bleach to ten parts water.

(3) Reactive Sorbent Powder. This sorbent is a free-flowing, reactive, highly absorptive powder manufactured from aluminum oxide. The M100 SDS replaces the M11

and M13 decontamination apparatuses, portable (DAPs) that were employed in spray-down operations associated with immediate decontamination. Each M100 SDS consists of two 0.7-pound packs of reactive sorbent powder, two wash mitt type sorbent applicators, a case, straps, and detailed instructions. An optional chemical agent-resistant mounting bracket is also available. The M100 SDS uses a reactive sorbent powder to remove chemical agents from surfaces. The use of the M100 SDS decreases decontamination time and eliminates the need for water.

    c. Miscellaneous Decontaminants.

        (1) Soap provides a good cleansing medium for removing surface contamination, dirt, or grease. By this action, mustard is emulsified and carried off; it is not neutralized. Hot, soapy water is effective for decontaminating (neutralizing) G agents. V agents will be destroyed slowly by hot, soapy water. Although soapy water will remain effective as long as suds are maintained, a solution of 10 pounds of soap in 11 gallons of water is recommended for the decontamination of G agents. An important use of soap is in personnel decontamination and the removal of contamination from aircraft. Soap solution may be used in PDDAs, and in bucket-and-broom procedures for the decontamination of materials and surfaces. Soap is used in the decontamination of clothing by laundering.

        (2) Caustic Soda (Sodium Hydroxide or Lye). Caustic soda is a white solid that dissolves easily in water or alcohol. The chemical name for caustic soda is sodium hydroxide; it is commonly known as lye. Considerable amounts of heat are generated when caustic soda is dissolved; therefore, containers must not be handled with bare hands. A water solution of caustic soda will destroy G agents on contact. Caustic soda hastens the hydrolysis of lewisite. However, mustard is destroyed only after prolonged contact with caustic soda. An alcoholic solution of caustic soda will decontaminate BZ and VX agents.

        (a) Preparation and Use. Water solutions of caustic soda are effective in most concentrations, but normally the more concentrated the solution, the faster the decontamination. Hot solutions decontaminate faster than cold solutions. A 5 percent solution prepared by dissolving 5 pounds of caustic soda in 12 gallons of water is recommended. Alcoholic solutions of caustic soda may be prepared by dissolving 5 pounds of caustic soda in a mixture consisting of 6 gallons of water and 6 gallons of alcohol. However, both woolen and cotton clothing are greatly deteriorated by even a 5 percent solution. Solutions should not be prepared in aluminum, magnesium, tin, or zinc containers. Contact with these metals causes the formation of flammable hydrogen gas. Iron or steel containers are suitable. Glass or earthenware containers can be used in an emergency if the solution is stirred constantly to keep the temperature down.

        (b) Safety Precautions. Skin areas that come in contact with either the solid or solution form of caustic soda should be washed immediately with a copious amount of water. Affected clothing should be removed immediately. If the eyes are involved, they should be flushed at once with a copious amount of warm water and the individual should seek medical treatment. Personnel handling caustic solutions should wear rubber gloves and protective masks or other respiratory and eye protective devices. Caustic soda burns human tissue and eats away clothing on contact. Ingestion causes damage to the digestive tract. Inhalation or ingestion of its dust or concentrated mist causes damage to the respiratory system and digestive tract. Seek medical attention immediately. The use of a mask and gloves is mandatory when handling caustic soda.

(3) Washing Soda (Sodium Carbonate). Washing soda is a white powder having alkaline properties. Commercial grades may contain large amounts of sodium carbonate. Common names include soda ash and laundry soda. It does not destroy blister agents as readily as caustic soda or sodium hypochlorite. In addition, it does not destroy V agents as readily as sodium hypochlorite. A hot solution of washing soda is an effective means of decontaminating CN. The solution, hot or cold, is very effective for the decontamination of G agents and is recommended.

(4) Ammonia (NH_3) or Ammonium Hydroxide (NH_4OH). Ammonium hydroxide is a water solution of ammonia. Ammonia or its water solution is an effective decontaminant (as a weak hydroxide) for several chemical agents. Ammonia may be used to decontaminate the G agents; however, it is slower acting than caustic soda or caustic potash.

(5) Common Solvents. Common organic liquids such as deicing fluids, kerosene, and alcohol may be used as solvents for many chemical agents. Most organic solvents are fire hazards, and some are toxic. Use suitable safety precautions. Solvents decontaminate by removing agents from contaminated surface; they do not destroy the agent. The solvent action of the liquid varies with the nature of the contaminated surface and the contaminant.

(a) Use. Solvents must be used carefully to avoid spreading the contamination. Swabs saturated with solvent are used on small areas. A contaminated area is swabbed several times; swabs are changed as necessary. The number of times an area is swabbed is determined by the amount of contamination, the amount of grease on the surface, and whether the area will be treated with another decontaminant.

(b) Safety Precautions. After being used on a contaminated surface, the cloth end of the swab must not touch bare skin or clothing. The solvent used to wash off the agent becomes contaminated and must be disposed of as contaminated waste. If ground contaminated with waste solvent is to be utilized, it must be decontaminated.

(6) Degreasing Solvent. Degreasing solvents are noncorrosive, water-dispersible liquids that are commonly used to clean aircraft and automotive engines by absorbing grease and oily dirt. The solvent may be used in decontaminating procedures. It may be diluted with water or kerosene and is effective in removing chemical agents by solvent action through the removal of grease and oil holding the agent. After being applied to contaminated equipment, the solvent is allowed to remain 15 minutes or more, depending on the degree of contamination. Water, preferably under pressure, is used to remove the solvent and to flush the dirt, grease, oil, and chemical agents from the equipment. Contaminated waste must be disposed of properly.

(7) Absorbents. Absorbents are various materials used to remove, but not destroy, agents. Earth, charcoal, coal dust, clay, and sawdust may be used as absorbents. The absorbents are contaminated after use and must be handled as contaminated waste.

(8) Adsorbents. Adsorbent is a material used to adhere or become attached mechanically or chemically to a chemical agent, but which does not destroy the agent. The adsorbent is contaminated after use and must be handled as contaminated waste.

(9) Household Bleach. Household bleach is 2 to 6 percent sodium hypochlorite in water. For vehicle wash down, household bleach will corrode the metal parts of vehicles. When the lack of water is a concern and a 5 percent available chlorine solution is needed,

household bleach could be used for vehicle wash down. Bleach is useful to decontaminate all types of microorganisms and most chemical agents.

    d.   Developmental Decontaminants.

        (1)   DF 200. The DF 200 is an aqueous solution containing a peroxide activator and hydrogen peroxide. DF 200 can be used for the decontamination of material and for the following contamination on porous surfaces: G agents on concrete, asphalt, sand, and soil; H agents on concrete; and V agents on asphalt and concrete. However, the operational constraints in Table C-5 apply for the use of DF 200. At all times, operators working with DF 200 will be in MOPP gear and all runoff will be collected and treated as potential hazardous waste. Standard decontaminants should continue to be used for all other chemical contamination and all biological decontamination.

Table C-5. Operational Limitations of DF 200

- Use mops and brushes as DF 200 applicators.
- Do not use degraded DF 200 for chemical and biological decontamination operations if STB or HTH is available. Degraded DF 200 is defined as DF 200 with compromised packaging, DF 200 without a lot number, DF 200 with an unknown storage temperature history, and/or DF 200 with a storage temperature history known to exceed 85°F.

NOTE: Surface corrosion (rust) may degrade the ability of DF 200 to decontaminate chemical agents. DF 200 will produce surface corrosion of many unpainted/uncoated metallic and alloy surfaces.

- Use a hot, soapy water prewash and two applications (15-minute contact time) of DF 200 during thorough decontamination for VX and HD. Use a hot, soapy water prewash and one application (15-minute contact time) of DF 200 GD. Apply the DF 200 as a scrub.
- Do not use DF 200 on aircraft or optics. Limit DF 200 use on synthetic rubber or plastic materials (plastic windshields and seals) as much as possible under field conditions. Inspect nonmetallic material components for degradation after exposure to DF 200.
- Do not use DF 200 for any biological contamination, including porous surfaces.
- Maintain surface wetness with DF 200 for 30 minutes as DF 200 is active only when wet. Reapply and restart the 30-minute wet contact time if the DF 200 dries.
- Use DF 200 within 6 hours after mixing.
- Rinse nonpermeable clothing with water following exposure to DF 200. Do not expose semipermeable protective garments to liquid DF 200.
- Replace mask filters after each DF 200 decontamination mission. Replace mask filters after every 12 hours of DF 200 decontamination operations if decontamination operations are continuous.
- Use butyl gloves for up to 6 hours following exposure to DF 200. Use only 14- and 25-mil gloves for 24 hours after exposure to DF 200.
- Do not treat sumps containing DF 200 with STB or HTH. Use additional DF 200 for sump treatment.
- Rinse DF 200 from vehicles.
- Do not mix DF 200 and STB/HTH, and do not store them together.
- Use the M256A1 to verify decontamination following decontamination by DF 200.

NOTE: Detector responses to DF 200 are similar to other field decontaminants. DF 200 can interfere with the accurate functioning of the USMC version of the CAM as well as all ICAMs, ACADAs, M8 paper, and M9 paper.

        (2)   Decon Green. This decontaminant provides the decontamination of CW agents even at low temperatures (-31°C). The solution is noncorrosive to common surfaces of military interest and leaves no toxic residue. Besides chemical agents, this decontaminant also affords the destruction of anthrax spores to undetectable levels. Decon green consists of three components that are mixed together to provide the active decontaminant. Once mixed, the solution must be used within 2 hours. When the solution

is applied, it should be rinsed off 15 minutes after application. The decontaminant can be applied using a spray applicator. Personnel must use MOPP4 when mixing or applying this decontaminant.

(3) Reactive Skin Decontamination Lotion (RSDL). The FDA has approved RSDL for use by the US military. The lotion removes chemical agents or the T-2 toxin and also reacts with the chemical agents, rapidly neutralizing them so they are non-toxic. RSDL must be applied to exposed skin (intact) as soon as possible after exposure to a chemical agent. The lotion is impregnated in a sponge pad packaged as a single unit in a heat-sealed foil pouch.

3. Decontamination Solution Preparation

Several precautions must be followed when mixing STB or HTH. Use Tables C-2 through C-4 (page C-5) to mix the appropriate decontamination solutions.

a. Mixing STB Slurry. Add the STB to the water. Do not add detergent.

> **WARNING**
> DO NOT mix STB with anything except water.

b. Mixing HTH Solutions. HTH is most effective in a solution with detergent. The detergent brings the agent into solution and, thus, in contact with the hypochlorite, where the chemical reaction can take place. In preparing the HTH decontamination solution, always add HTH to the water, mix to dissolve, and then add the detergent and stir thoroughly.

> **WARNING**
>
> **Never add water to HTH or add HTH to water with which detergent has already been mixed. A dangerous reaction may result in either case.**

4. Storage and Shelf Life

The shelf life of HTH is 2 years. An expiration date is printed on each bottle. HTH is an oxidizer and should be kept isolated from fuels, oils, greases, paints, organic solvents, cellulose products, and any other material that is easily oxidized. These materials are incompatible and may cause a violent reaction or fire. HTH will react with rags, fabrics, detergent, antifreeze, and ammonia in addition to the materials listed previously. When heated, HTH decomposes to chlorine gas, phosgene, and other toxic and corrosive fumes. Do not use HTH near heat sources or open flames because toxic gases may be produced. Do not stow oxidizers near heat sources, in areas adjacent to ammunition storage, or in areas where the maximum temperature exceeds 100°F (37.8°C) under normal operating conditions. Contact with moisture causes formation of toxic chlorine gas. Accidental mixture with small amounts of water spray from firefighting may cause toxic-gas formation. Drenching with excess water can control this reaction. Stowage areas shall be kept cool, dry, and well-ventilated. Containers used for holding oxidizers should have a warning label indicating their reactivity and associated hazards.

5. Decontaminants

See Tables C-6 through C-8 (pages C-11 to C-21) for a representative listing of standard, miscellaneous, and natural decontaminants.

Table C-6. Standard Decontaminants Available in the Supply System

Decontaminant	Agent	Use	Cautions/Safety	Preparation
STB (NSN 6850-00-297-6653)	Chemical G agents V agents Lewisite Biological	Allow 30-minute contact time, and rinse with clear water. Not effective against mustard if it has solidified at low temperatures. Apply to porous surfaces several times.	Will produce a very strong exothermic reaction on contact with a liquid blister agent or DS2. Will give off toxic vapors on contact with G agents. Is not recommended for ship use. Store it on the top deck only. Do not inhale or allow it to touch the skin. Wear a protective mask or respiratory protective device when preparing slurry. Store in an unheated warehouse away from combustibles and metals subject to corrosion. Has the following corrosive effects: Very corrosive to metals. Slight effect on nonmetals. Moderate effect on sealants. Is corrosive to most metals and damaging to most fabrics (rinse thoroughly and oil metal surfaces).	Slurry paste: mix one 50-pound drum of STB with 6 gallons of water. Slurry paste consists of equal parts (by weight) of STB and water. Dry mix: mix two shovelfuls of STB to three shovelfuls of earth or inert material (ashes). Slurry mix, chemical: mix 40 parts of STB to 60 parts of water (by weight). For M12A1 PDDA: use 1,300 pounds of STB, 225 gallons of water, 12½ pounds of antiset, and 24 ounces of antifoam. Slurry mix, biological: mix 7 parts of STB to 93 parts of water (by weight). For M12A1 PDDA: use 150 pounds of STB, 225 gallons of water, 12½ pounds of antiset, and 24 ounces of antifoam. Camouflage: lampblack or dye mixes may be added for camouflage.
Calcium hypochlorite (HTH or HTB) (NSN 6810-00-255-0471 [6 ounces]) (NSN 6810-01-225-2682 [25 pounds]) (NSN 6810-00-225-0472 [100 pounds])	Chemical G agents V agents Lewisite Mustards Biological including bacterial spores	Reacts rapidly (within 5 minutes) with mustards and lewisite. Acts faster than STB. Allow 15-minute contact time for biological agents. Use as a dry mix or slurry.	Precautions are the same as for STB. Pure HTH will burn on contact with VX and HD. Toxic vapor and will burn skin. Protective mask and rubber gloves are the minimum protective equipment needed when handling. HTH should only be used if STB is not available. Has the following corrosive effects: More corrosive than STB. Will destroy clothing.	Chemical: mix 5 pounds of decontaminant to 6 gallons of water (10% solution). Biological: mix 1 pound of decontaminant to 6 gallons of water (2% solution). PDDE: mix slurry of 1 part decontaminant to 2 parts water (any heavier slurry will clog the decontamination apparatus).

Table C-6. Standard Decontaminants Available in the Supply System (Continued)

Decontaminant	Agent	Use	Cautions/Safety	Preparation
Mask sanitizing solution	Chemical Biological	Use on a previously cleaned mask with filter elements and canisters removed. Place the mask face up; attach the canteen to the mask at the drinking tube. Drain one canteen full of sanitizing solution through the mask. Rinse the mask with two canteens of clear water. Immerse the mask and outserts in the sanitizing solution. Agitate the mask for 5 minutes. Rinse it twice in clear water, agitating 2 to 3 minutes each time. Dry all parts of the mask and reassemble it. Use 1 gallon of solution for every ten masks.	None	Fill a standard plastic canteen to the shoulder with water. Add a 0.5-gram tube of calcium hypochlorite from the water purification kit (NSN 6810-00-266-6976). Cover the canteen, and shake it vigorously for 30 seconds. Mix bulk quantities as follows: add 2 grams of calcium hypochlorite from a 6-ounce jar (NSN 6810-00-255-0471) to 1 gallon of water. Use a ratio of about 1 pound of soap per gallon of water for smaller amounts of solution. Mix 2 pints of detergent to 450 gallons of water in the M12A1 PDDA.
Soap and detergents: detergent, GP, liquid (NSN 7930-00-282-9699)	All agents (physical removal only)	Scrub or wipe the contaminated surface with hot, soapy water, or immerse the item in the solution.	Casualty-producing levels of contamination may remain in the runoff water and must be considered contaminated.	Mix 75 pounds of powdered soap in 350 gallons of water. If powdered soap is not available, use bar laundry soap (75 pounds of soap cut into 1-inch pieces and dissolved in 350 gallons of hot water). Use a ratio of about 1 pound of soap per gallon of water for smaller amounts of soap solution. Mix 2 pints of detergent to 450 gallons of water in the M12A1 PDDA.

Table C-7. Miscellaneous (Nonstandard) Decontaminants

Decontaminant	Agent	Use	Cautions/Safety	Preparation
Sodium hypochlorite (household bleach)	Chemical V agents Blister agents G Agents* Biological Radiological	Will react rapidly (within 5 minutes) with blister and V agents. Allow a 10- to 15-minute contact time for biological agents. Should be applied undiluted with brooms, brushes, or swabs. Is the preferred decontaminant for ship use. A 5:1 concentration is recommended.	Is harmful to the skin and clothing if undiluted. Remove from the skin and clothing by flushing with water. Has a limited storage problem. Should be stored in a cool place. Has the following corrosive effects: Is corrosive to metals unless rinsed, dried, and lubricated after decontamination.	For chemical decontamination: no mixing is required. For biological decontamination: dilute by adding two parts bleach to ten parts water. For decontamination of cotton clothing and utensils: mix 2 cups of bleach with 1 gallon of water. For application: mix bleach half and half with water, and spray it from the PDDE.
Ethylene glycol	Chemical (physical removal only)	Scrub on contaminated surfaces, and rinse thoroughly. Mix equal amounts of solution and water.	Removes contamination only; does not neutralize it. Runoff residue must be considered contaminated.	Mix equal amounts of solution and water.
Solvents (gasoline, DP8, diesel fuel, kerosene, and similar solvents)	Chemical (physical removal only)	Scrub on contaminated surfaces, and rinse thoroughly.	Removes contamination only; does not neutralize it. Runoff residue must be considered contaminated.	None
Sodium carbonate (washing soda, soda ash, or laundry soda)	Chemical G agents CN	Reacts rapidly with G agents, normally within 5 minutes. Is the preferred decontaminant for ship use. Should be used with a hot solution to decontaminate CN effectively. 5% by weight is the recommended concentration. Mix 10 pounds of washing soda to 12 gallons of water (10% solution).	Not to be used against VX. It cannot detoxify VX and creates extremely toxic by-products. Does not dissolve or detoxify mustard agents. There are no storage limitations.	Mix 10 pounds of washing soda with 12 gallons of water (10% solution).
Ammonia or ammonium hydroxide (household ammonia)	Chemical G agents	Slower acting than sodium hydroxide or potassium hydroxide. Ammonium hydroxide is a water solution of ammonia.	May require the use of a SCBA or special-purpose mask.	None
Diethyl ether	Chemical	Good decontaminant for use in arctic regions. The freezing point is -241°F; the boiling point is 93°F.	Is extremely flammable. Does not neutralize agents.	None

* The reaction time between sodium hypochlorite and G agents will be slower than that for V or H agents.

Table C-7. Miscellaneous (Nonstandard) Decontaminants (Continued)

Decontaminant	Agent	Use	Cautions/Safety	Preparation
2-propanone (acetone)	Chemical (physical removal only)	Effective for dissolving and flushing agents. Good decontaminant for use in arctic regions. The freezing point is -203°F; the boiling point is 133°F (evaporates rapidly).	Is extremely flammable. Does not neutralize agents.	None
Hexachloramelamine	Chemical Mustard	Is not soluble in water, but is soluble in organic solvents such as gasoline, kerosene, and paint thinner.	May require the use of a protective mask and rubber gloves when used. Is corrosive to metal.	Is not soluble in water, but is soluble in organic solvents such as gasoline, kerosene, and paint thinner.
Dichlorimine B and Dichoramine T	Chemical Mustard	None	May require the use of a protective mask and rubber gloves when used. Is corrosive to metal.	Is not soluble in water, but is soluble in certain organic solvents (e.g., dichlorethane). Is normally mixed as a 10% solution in dichloroethane.
Perchloroethylene (tetrachloroethylene)	Chemical (physical removal only)	Is good for use in arctic climates. The freezing point is -8°F; the boiling point is 250°F. Dissolves H and V agents, but not G agents. Requires no mixing (practically insoluble in water).	Removes contamination only; does not neutralize it. Runoff residue must be considered contaminated. Nonflammable. Low toxicity.	None

Table C-7. Miscellaneous (Nonstandard) Decontaminants (Continued)

Decontaminant	Agent	Use	Cautions/Safety	Preparation
NaOH, sodium hydroxide (NSN 6810-00-174-6581 [100 pounds])	Chemical G agents Lewisite Biological, including bacterial spores	Will neutralize G agents on contact. Allow 15-minute contact time. Must flush with large amounts of clear water. For small amounts, mix 10 pounds of lye with 12 gallons of water (10% solution). Mix it in an iron or steel container. Add lye to the water to prevent boiling and splattering due to heat being emitted. Use while hot. Will cause a red color change upon contact with M8 detector paper. Effectiveness is directly proportional to the strength of the solution.	Will damage the skin, eyes, and clothes; and can cause upper respiratory or lung damage if inhaled. The affected area must be washed immediately with large amounts of water and flushed with diluted acetic acid or vinegar. Remove affected clothing. If eyes are involved, flush them at once with large amounts of warm water and seek medical attention. Full rubber protective clothing, gloves, boots, and a mask are required when using. Runoff is highly corrosive and toxic. Drain runoff into a sump, and bury it. Is not recommended for ship use. Store it on the top deck only. Is not recommended if less toxic caustic decontaminants are available. Can substitute with calcium hydroxide, potassium hydroxide, or trisodium phosphate. Is corrosive to most metals.	Small amount: Mix 10 pounds of lye with 12 gallons of water (10% solution). Mix it in an iron or steel container (never aluminum, zinc, or tin). Add lye to the water to prevent boiling and splattering due to heat being emitted. Do not handle the mixing container with bare hands. Large amount (PDDE use): Mix 227 grams (½ pound) of lye with each gallon of water. Pump 350 gallons of water into the tank unit. Connect the tank unit, pump unit, and heater together. Heat the water to 122°F. Disconnect the heater unit, and add 175 pounds of lye to the heated water. Circulate the solution with the pump unit until all the lye is dissolved. The temperature will increase noticeably. Use while hot. Simultaneous mixing and applying: Sprinkle dry lye on the contaminated area and then dissolve it with a spray of steam or hot water. Do not wash the lye off the surface while applying the steam or hot water. Paint removal: 1 pound of lye per 2½ gallons of water is capable of removing an average coat of paint from about 11 square yards of surface. This solution is effective in removing paint on which chemical contamination has absorbed.

Table C-7. Miscellaneous (Nonstandard) Decontaminants (Continued)

Decontaminant	Agent	Use	Cautions/Safety	Preparation
Potassium hydroxide (caustic potash)	Chemical G agents Lewisite Biological	Will neutralize G agents on contact. Allow 15-minute contact time. Must flush with large amounts of clear water. For small amounts, mix 10 pounds of lye with 12 gallons of water (10% solution). Mix it in an iron or steel container. Add lye to the water to prevent boiling and splattering due to heat being emitted. Use while hot. Will cause a red color change upon contact with M8 detector paper. Effectiveness is directly proportional to the strength of the solution.	Will damage the skin, eyes, and clothes; and can cause upper respiratory or lung damage if inhaled. The affected area must be washed immediately with large amounts of water and flushed with diluted acetic acid or vinegar. Remove affected clothing. If eyes are involved, flush them at once with large amounts of warm water and seek medical attention. Full rubber protective clothing, gloves, boots, and a mask are required when using. Runoff is highly corrosive and toxic. Drain runoff into a sump, and bury it. Is not recommended for ship use. Store it on the top deck only. Is not recommended if less toxic caustic decontaminants are available. Can substitute with calcium hydroxide, potassium hydroxide, or trisodium phosphate. Is corrosive to most metals.	Small amount: Mix 10 pounds of lye with 12 gallons of water (10% solution). Mix it in an iron or steel container (never aluminum, zinc, or tin). Add lye to the water to prevent boiling and splattering due to heat being emitted. Do not handle the mixing container with bare hands. Large amount (PDDE use): Mix 227 grams (½ pound) of lye with each gallon of water. Pump 350 gallons of water into the tank unit. Connect the tank unit, pump unit, and heater together. Heat the water to 122°F. Disconnect the heater unit, and add 175 pounds of lye to the heated water. Circulate the solution with the pump unit until all the lye is dissolved. The temperature will increase noticeably. Use while hot. Simultaneous mixing and applying: Sprinkle dry lye on the contaminated area and then dissolve it with a spray of steam or hot water. Do not wash the lye off the surface while applying the steam or hot water. Paint removal: 1 pound of lye per 2½ gallons of water is capable of removing an average coat of paint from about 11 square yards of surface. This solution is effective in removing paint on which chemical contamination has absorbed.
Detrochlorite	Biological	Thickened bleach useful on vertical surfaces. Allow 30-minute contact time, rinse with water. Apply by means of the PDDA. Coverage is 1 gallon per 8 square yards.	Mixing the wetting agent and calcium hypochlorite in a dry and undiluted state may cause an explosion. Agent is very corrosive.	Mix by weight 19.3% diatomaceous earth, 0.5% anionic wetting agent, 2.9% calcium hypochlorite (70% available chlorine), and 77.3% water. Mix the wetting agent and diatomaceous earth with water before adding the calcium hypochlorite.

Table C-7. Miscellaneous (Nonstandard) Decontaminants (Continued)

Decontaminant	Agent	Use	Cautions/Safety	Preparation
Iodine water purification tablets	Biological	Use when it is impractical to boil drinking water. Two iodine tablets per canteen are effective against most biological agents	None	None
Ethylene oxide	Biological, including bacterial spores	Should be applied in the strength of 30 pounds for every 1,000 cubic feet. Allow a 6-hour contact time (contact time must be doubled for each 20°F drop in temperature below 75°F). Should be used in an airtight enclosure.	Flammable and explosive. Not recommended for interior use.	None
Disinfectant chlorine (NSN 6840-00-270-8172)	Biological	Use to decontaminate utensils, mess gear, exteriors of sealed containers, and food products that can withstand soaking. Allow a 30-minute contact time (stir occasionally). Rinse thoroughly in potable water. Make fresh solutions for rinsing and disinfecting utensils for each 100 persons. Prepare an emergency solution by mixing one level MRE spoonful of calcium hypochlorite (water disinfecting powder) to each 10 gallons of water. If liquid chlorine bleach is available, use about 1/3-canteen cup of 5% chlorine bleach to each 10 gallons of water.	Dispose of any food or vegetables that are damaged and any outer leaves that are bruised or torn. Do not cut or peel fruits and vegetables before disinfecting. Use the solution only once.	Dissolve one package of disinfectant in 20 gallons of warm, potable water (100°F).
Hyamine (benzethonium chloride)	Biological	Allow a 5- to 30-minute contact time. Use a 0.1% to 1% solution (1 pound of hyamine for every 12 gallons of water yields a 1% solution).	Very toxic; the estimated fatal dose to man is 1 to 3 grams. Care should be taken when mixing to avoid the inhalation of powder. Agent is not to be used on aircraft or ships.	Mix 1 pound of hyamine to every 12 gallons of water (yields a 1% solution).

Table C-7. Miscellaneous (Nonstandard) Decontaminants (Continued)

Decontaminant	Agent	Use	Cautions/Safety	Preparation
Formalin (formaldehyde)	Biological, including bacterial spores	Used for interior decontamination of relatively close areas. Allow vapors to remain 16 hours in a closed structure; aerate until the odor is no longer objectionable. Optimum conditions for spraying formalin are 70°F to 80°F with an 85% relative humidity. The minimum effective relative humidity is 70%. Increase exposure time to 24 hours at 60°F. Agent is applied as a vapor from standard insecticide sprayers or is vaporized by heat or a bubbling steam from a pan.	Personnel entering an area containing formalin vapors should— • Wear a protective mask. • Wear washable outer clothing, fastened to prevent vapors from entering at wrists, ankles, or neck. • Remove outer clothing after emerging from vapors. • Shower and put on clean clothing as soon as possible. Vapors are very toxic. Vapors are not flammable; open flame should not be used for vaporizing when methanol has been added to the agent. When steam is used, the source of the steam should be outside the area being decontaminated. Corrosive. Formalin will curl and discolor paper. Leaves a white residue.	No mixing is required. However, less residue remains and less aeration is required if the mixture of five parts formalin and three parts methanol is used. Use this mixture at a rate of 4 to 5 quarts per 1,000 cubic feet of space.

Table C-7. Miscellaneous (Nonstandard) Decontaminants (Continued)

Decontaminant	Agent	Use	Cautions/Safety	Preparation
Peracetic acid (PAA)	Biological, including bacterial spores	Allow a 10-minute contact time. Wipe with a rag or swab (immerse small items). Remove excess acid and aerate for 10 to 15 minutes or until no objectionable odor remains. Available as a 40% solution. Mix 1 quart of PAA to 3½ gallons of water (add PAA to the water).	Protective mask and clothing are required. Fumes are highly irritating. Burns and blisters on the skin will occur. A violent explosion may result if heavy metal ions come in contact with the agent. A 40% solution has a low flash point (105°F); a 3% solution is nonflammable. Store in original containers under refrigeration to prevent decomposition. Corrosive. Prolonged exposure will damage most material. Prolonged exposure will corrode iron and deteriorate rubber, plastic, and leather.	Available as a 40% solution. Mix 1 quart of PAA to 3½ gallons of water (add PAA to the water).
Carbon dioxide and ethylene oxide mixture (>87% ethylene oxide)	Biological	Recommended for interior use. Use in an airtight enclosure. Allow a 12-hour contact time (doubled for each 20°F drop in temperature below 75°F). Apply 30 pounds for every 1,000 cubic feet. Aerate items next to the skin for 18 to 24 hours.	Nonflammable. Will blister the skin.	None
Oxidizing agents (nitric acid, aqua regia, sodium dichromate, and potassium permanganate)	Radiological	Effective in dissolving surfaces containing absorbed radioactive contamination. Apply to the surface, or dip the item. Rinse the surface thoroughly with water and detergent and then with clear water.	Use only under the supervision of a trained individual. Will require the use of a neoprene or rubber protective apron, gloves, boots, and safety glasses when handling. (Rubber offers only limited protection.) Extremely corrosive. Exposure must be limited due to the corrosive nature of the solution.	Aqua regia is prepared by mixing three parts of concentrated hydrochloric acid and one part of concentrated nitric acid. Other oxidizing agents do not require mixing.

Table C-7. Miscellaneous (Nonstandard) Decontaminants (Continued)

Decontaminant	Agent	Use	Cautions/Safety	Preparation
Complexing agents (versene, citric acid, sequesterene, sodium citrate, tartanic acid, sodium oxalate, sodium tartrategoxalic acid, othophosphoric acid, and similar agent)	Radiological (physical removal only)	Allow a 30-minute contact time, and then flush with water. Apply as a film over the surface using a PDDE, firefighting apparatus, or a tree or garden sprayer.	Does not neutralize contamination. Runoff will be contaminated.	Mix 3% to 5% of the agent (by weight) in water.
Acids (sulfuric acid, hydrochloric acid, oxalic acid, and similar acids)	Radiological	Effective solvents for rust and mineral deposits holding radioactive material on metal surfaces. Allow a 1-hour contact time. Must be flushed with water, scrubbed with a water-detergent solution, and flushed again with water.	Will require the use of respiratory protection when used in closed areas. May require the use of rubber boots, gloves, aprons, and goggles when used. Can produce boiling and splattering of the solution when mixed. Difficult to handle and is harmful to the body, especially the eyes. Flush the area immediately with water. Use a 5% solution of water and baking soda (sodium bicarbonate).	None

Table C-8. Natural Decontaminants

Decontaminant	Agent	Notes	Cautions/Safety
Water	(Physical removal only) Chemical Biological Radiological	Can be used to flush contamination from surfaces. Hot, soapy water is more effective in removing agents. Boiling for 15 minutes (30 minutes at high altitude) destroys biological agents.	Is effective in physically removing contamination, but does not neutralize it. Do not use water on lewisite.
Sea water	(Physical removal only)	None	None
Steam	Chemical Biological Radiological	None	Is effective in physically removing contamination, but does not neutralize it.
Absorbents (earth, sawdust, ashes, rags, and similar materials)	(Physical removal only) Chemical Biological Radiological	Used to physically remove gross contamination from surfaces.	The contamination is transferred from the surface to the absorbent. The absorbent becomes contaminated and must be disposed of accordingly. Sufficient contamination to produce casualties may remain on surfaces.
Sealants (concrete, asphalt, earth, paint, and similar materials	(Physical seal only) Chemical Biological Radiological	Sealants are used to physically seal in or shield contamination. Chemical - 4 inches of earth provides good protection. Biological - Burying items is an effective means of sealing off contamination. Radiological - 12 inches of earth provides good protection from fallout (3 inches will reduce the dose rate about one-half). Radiological - 1 inch of asphalt or concrete completely absorbs alpha and beta radiation. Radiological - ¼ inch of grout shields alpha and beta radiation.	A break in the surface of the sealant will expose the contamination. Contaminated areas covered with sealants must be marked with appropriate CBRN warning signs.
Weather/time	Chemical Biological Radiological	UV light kills most bioorganism agents, organisms, and radiation decay over time. Should be used when time and the mission permit.	None
Burning	Chemical Biological	N/A	Creates downwind hazards. Requires that sentries be posted to keep people out of the danger area.

THIS PAGE IS INTENTIONALLY LEFT BLANK.

Appendix D
DECONTAMINATION OF SPECIFIC SURFACES AND MATERIALS

This appendix should be used to determine how to decontaminate various surfaces. Table D-1 lists specific surfaces or materials and briefly explains the representative methods of how to conduct a CBRN decontamination. In turn, detection and identification equipment must be used to check the completeness of decontamination.

Table D-1. Decontamination Procedures for Specific Surfaces and Materials

Surface or Material	Types of Contamination and How to Decontaminate		
	Chemical	Biological	Radiological
Asphalt roads	Weather. Flush with water. Spray with an STB slurry from the PDDE. Cover with STB (pure form). When liquid contamination is visible and personnel are nearby, use STB dry mix. Cover small areas or paths across roads with 4 inches of earth.	Weather (remain masked). Wet with water (will help prevent secondary aerosols, but does not decontaminate). Pour, spray, or spread oil on the surface (suppresses dust and associated reaerosolization). For critical, but limited, areas: • Spray with an STB slurry from the PDDE. • Apply 2% household bleach solution.	Brush or sweep. Flush with water (this may drive some of the contamination into the surface; waste must be controlled). Clean with a vacuum.
Roofs	Weather. Flush with water. Spray with an STB slurry from the PDDE. Cover with STB (pure form). When liquid contamination is visible and personnel are nearby, use STB dry mix. Cover small areas or paths across roads with 4 inches of earth.	Weather (remain masked). Wet with water (will help prevent secondary aerosols, but does not decontaminate). Pour, spray, or spread oil on the surface (suppresses dust and associated reaerosolization). For critical, but limited, areas: • Spray with an STB slurry from the PDDE. • Apply 2% household bleach solution. • Apply detrochlorite. Leave it on at least 30 minutes, and then flush it with water.	Brush or sweep. Flush with water (this may drive some of the contamination into the surface; waste must be controlled). Clean with a vacuum.
Brick and stone roads	Weather. Wash with soapy water, preferably hot. Spray with an STB slurry from the PDDE or apply with brushes and brooms. Leave the slurry on for 24 hours, and then flush it with water. Cover small areas or paths across roads with 4 inches of earth.	Weather (remain masked). Wet with water (will help prevent secondary aerosols, but does not decontaminate). Pour, spray, or spread oil on the surface (suppresses dust and associated reaerosolization). For critical, but limited, areas: • Spray with an STB slurry from the PDDE. • Apply 2% household bleach solution.	Brush or sweep. Flush with water (this may drive some of the contamination into the surface; waste must be controlled). Clean with a vacuum. Use abrasion (sand blasting). This provides direct and complete removal of contaminated dust; however, sand and equipment being used becomes contaminated.

Table D-1. Decontamination Procedures for Specific Surfaces and Materials (Continued)

Surface or Material	Types of Contamination and How to Decontaminate		
	Chemical	**Biological**	**Radiological**
Brick and stone buildings, bunkers, gun emplacements, and tank obstacles	Weather. Wash with soapy water, preferably hot. Spray with an STB slurry from the PDDE or apply with brushes and brooms. Leave the slurry on for 24 hours, and then flush it with water. Use STB (pure form or dry mix) around buildings where wastewater runs.	Weather (remain masked). Wet with water (will help prevent secondary aerosols, but does not decontaminate). Pour, spray, or spread oil on the surface (suppresses dust and associated reaerosolization). For critical, but limited, areas: • Spray with an STB slurry from the PDDE. • Apply 2% household bleach solution. • Apply detrochlorite. Leave it on at least 30 minutes, and then flush it with water.	Brush or sweep. Flush with water (this may drive some of the contamination into the surface; waste must be controlled). Clean with a vacuum. Use abrasion (sand blasting). This provides direct and complete removal of contaminated dust; however, sand and equipment being used becomes contaminated.
Concrete roads	Weather. Spray with an STB slurry from the PDDE. Cover with an STB slurry or dry mix. Cover small areas or paths across roads with 4 inches of earth. Scrape the layer of contaminated earth to the side of the road.	Weather (remain masked). Wet with water (will help prevent secondary aerosols, but does not decontaminate). Pour, spray, or spread oil on the surface (suppresses dust and associated reaerosolization). For critical, but limited, areas: • Spray with an STB slurry from the PDDE. • Apply 2% household bleach solution.	Brush or sweep. Flush with water (this may drive some of the contamination into the surface; waste must be controlled). Clean with a vacuum. Use abrasion (sand blasting). This provides direct and complete removal of contaminated dust; however, sand and equipment being used becomes contaminated.
Earth: roads, gun emplacements, bivouac areas, pathways, and bomb craters	Weather. Spray with an STB slurry from the PDDE. Cover with STB (pure form). When liquid contamination is visible and personnel are nearby, use STB dry mix. Cover small areas or paths across roads with 4 inches of earth. Scrape the layer of contaminated earth to the side of the road.	Weather (remain masked). Wet with water (will help prevent secondary aerosols, but does not decontaminate). Pour, spray, or spread oil on the surface (suppresses dust and associated reaerosolization). For critical, but limited, areas: • Spray with an STB slurry from the PDDE. • Apply 2% household bleach solution. • Burn.	Earthmoving (removal): Try to control contaminated dust, as equipment may become contaminated. Consider waste disposal. Sealing (with earth): Equipment may become contaminated.

Table D-1. Decontamination Procedures for Specific Surfaces and Materials (Continued)

Surface or Material	Types of Contamination and How to Decontaminate		
	Chemical	**Biological**	**Radiological**
Grass: fields, low vegetation, and open terrain	Weather. Burn. Spray with an STB slurry from the PDDE. Cover with STB (pure form or dry mix). Explode drums of STB. Clear paths through the area using detonating cord or other detonating devices.	Weather. Burn. Weather (remain masked). Wet with water (will help prevent secondary aerosols, but does not decontaminate). Pour, spray, or spread oil on the surface (suppresses dust and associated reaerosolization). For critical, but limited, areas: <ul><li>Spray with an STB slurry from the PDDE.</li><li>Apply 2% household bleach solution.</li></ul>	Earthmoving (removal): Try to control contaminated dust, as equipment may become contaminated. Consider waste disposal. Sealing (with earth): Equipment may become contaminated.
Undergrowth: tall grass, meadows, jungles, and forests	Weather. Burn (may cause a downwind vapor hazard). Spray STB slurry with a PDDE. Explode drums of STB. Clear a path with detonating cord, bangalore torpedoes, or demolition snakes.	Weather (remain masked). Wet with water (will help prevent secondary aerosols, but does not decontaminate). Pour, spray, or spread oil on the surface (suppresses dust and associated reaerosolization). For critical, but limited, areas: <ul><li>Spray with an STB slurry from the PDDE.</li><li>Apply 2% household bleach solution.</li></ul>	Earthmoving (removal): Try to control contaminated dust, as equipment may become contaminated. Consider waste disposal. Sealing (with earth): Equipment may become contaminated.
Sand: beaches and deserts	Weather. Flush with water. Spread STB (pure form) or spray STB slurry over the surface. Cover paths with roofing paper. Scrape off 2 to 4 inches of the contaminated top layer.	Weather (remain masked). Wet with water (will help prevent secondary aerosols, but does not decontaminate). Pour, spray, or spread oil on the surface (suppresses dust and associated reaerosolization). For critical, but limited, areas: <ul><li>Spray with an STB slurry from the PDDE.</li><li>Apply 2% household bleach solution.</li></ul>	Earthmoving (removal): Try to control contaminated dust, as equipment may become contaminated. Consider waste disposal. Sealing (with earth): Equipment may become contaminated.

Table D-1. Decontamination Procedures for Specific Surfaces and Materials (Continued)

Surface or Material	Types of Contamination and How to Decontaminate		
	Chemical	**Biological**	**Radiological**
Fabrics: canvas, covers, tarpaulins, tentage, mask carriers, web gear, and clothing	Cotton: **NOTE: Do not use for MOPP gear.** Immerse in boiling, soapy water for 1 hour (1 pound of soap to 10 gallons of water) and stir. Use a 5% sodium carbonate solution for G agents. Immerse in boiling water for 1 hour. Launder by standard methods. Use STB slurry. Weather, except for V agents. Woolen: Immerse in warm, soapy water (100°F) for 1 hour or longer with light agitation. Dry items slowly because the fabric may shrink.	Cotton: Boil in water for 15 minutes. Immerse in a 2% household bleach solution for 30 minutes and rinse immediately. Launder (destroys or inactivates all but highly resistant spores). Woolen: Launder (fabric may shrink).	Brushing removes contamination dust, but it presents a dust hazard to personnel. Laundering is the most practical procedure; however, the fabric may shrink. Try to control waste.
Leather: boots, gloves, belts, and other nonsensitive items	Scrub with hot, soapy water and rinse. Immerse in warm, soapy water at 120°F for 4 hours and rinse. Use a 5% sodium carbonate solution for G agents. Aerate.	Immerse in a 2% household bleach solution for 30 minutes, followed by a water rinse and aeration. Equipment that should not be immersed can be wiped with hypochlorite or peracetic acid.	Brush. Flush with water or soapy water.
Glass windows and other glass surfaces (except lenses)	Use an IEDK. Wash with hot, soapy water. Rinse with clear water or an organic solvent. Blot off the surface. Air. Weather.	Use an IEDK. Clean with chlorine or peracetic acid solutions.	Use an IEDK. Wash with a detergent. Flush with water. Wipe with solvents.
Glass lenses	Wash with hot, soapy water. Rinse with clear water or an organic solvent. Blot off the surface. Air. Weather.	Wipe with alcohol or hypochlorite, and remove it quickly with soap and water.	Brush or wipe (be careful so as not to scratch the lens). Use compressed air to blow the contamination from the surface.
Metal (unpainted) ammunition	Wipe with soapy water. Wipe with organic solvent and dry. Aerate.	Wipe with a 2% household bleach solution. Aerate.	Brush or wipe.
Metal (unpainted) machinery	Wipe with soapy water. Wipe with organic solvent and dry. Aerate.	Weather. Clean with soapy water.	Brush or wipe. Wash with a detergent. Flush with water.

Table D-1. Decontamination Procedures for Specific Surfaces and Materials (Continued)

Surface or Material	Types of Contamination and How to Decontaminate		
	Chemical	**Biological**	**Radiological**
Metal (painted) vehicles, weapons, and equipment	Use IEDK to decontaminate individual gear. Weather. Wash with hot, soapy water and rinse. Spray with STB slurry from the PDDE, remove it in 1 hour, and oil the surface.	Weather. Wash with a detergent. Steam-clean using a detergent. Apply STB slurry.	Brush or wipe. Wash. Use organic solvents, caustic agents (not on aluminum or magnesium surfaces), complexing agents (of small value on weathered surfaces), or abrasives.
Wood: buildings, vehicle bodies, boxes, crates, and similar items	Apply STB slurry with the PDDE, brooms, or swabs. Let the slurry remain 12 to 24 hours then flush the surface with water. Repeat the application, and flush it again. Scrub with hot, soapy water and rinse. Weather.	Weather. Apply STB slurry. Apply detrochlorite to vertical surfaces; leave it on at least 30 minutes, and then flush it with water.	Wash the interior with large amounts of water (some contamination may soak into surfaces of unpainted wood). Wipe the contamination from the surface.
Plastics (opaque): insulation, telephones, and panel boards	Aerate. Wash with hot, soapy water and rinse. Weather.	Wipe with hypochlorite or peracetic acid.	Wipe or brush. Wash with a detergent. Flush with water.
Plastics (transparent): eyepieces and airplane canopies	Aerate. Wash with hot, soapy water and rinse. Weather.	Wipe with alcohol or hypochlorite, and remove it quickly with soap and water.	Wipe or brush. Wash with a detergent. Flush with water.
Unsealed electronic equipment	Use a mild, evaporative solvent such as alcohol. Use a mild detergent and water. Rinse with distilled water. Keep the solution out of adjustable switches, connectors, and relays. Use hot-air blowers.	Use a mild, evaporative solvent such as alcohol. Use a mild detergent and water. Rinse with distilled water. Keep the solution out of adjustable switches, connectors, and relays. Use hot-air blowers.	Wipe or brush. Use hot-air blowers.
Rubber (impermeable): aprons, suits, and other items	Immerse in soapy water (just below the boiling point) for 1 hour. Do not agitate. Rinse with clear water, and hang to dry. Use a 10% sodium carbonate solution for G agents, rinse, and air. Apply hot, soapy water with brushes and rinse. Spray with an STB slurry from the PDDE. Wash off with clear water after a few minutes.	Immerse in a 2% household bleach solution for 30 minutes, followed by a water rinse and aeration. Equipment that should not be immersed can be wiped with hypochlorite or peracetic acid.	Brush. Scrub or flush with water or soapy water.

Table D-1. Decontamination Procedures for Specific Surfaces and Materials (Continued)

Surface or Material	Types of Contamination and How to Decontaminate		
	Chemical	Biological	Radiological
Rubber (natural and synthetic): gloves and boots	Aerate. Spray with a 10% mixture of HTH and rinse. Immerse in STB slurry for 4 hours, rinse, and dry. Use an IEDK in emergencies.	Immerse in a 2% household bleach solution for 30 minutes, followed by a water rinse and aeration. Equipment that should not be immersed can be wiped with hypochlorite or peracetic acid.	Brush. Scrub or flush with water or soapy water.
Rubber: mask facepieces and other rubber articles coming in direct contact with the skin	Use an IEDK in emergencies. Wash with warm, soapy water.	Use an alcohol or peracetic acid wipe followed by aeration for 10 minutes.	Brush. Scrub or flush with water or soapy water.
Rubber: tires, hoses, mats, and insulation	Aerate. Spray with a 10% mixture of HTH and rinse. Apply an STB slurry. Allow the slurry to remain on the surface at least 30 minutes, and then flush with clear water (may be left on tires). Apply hot, soapy water. Weather.	Immerse in a 2% household bleach solution for 30 minutes, followed by a water rinse and aeration. Equipment that should not be immersed can be wiped with hypochlorite or peracetic acid.	Brush. Scrub or flush with water or soapy water.
Water	Use trained water purification personnel to decontaminate.	Boil small amounts for 15 minutes. (Boiling will not inactivate some toxins.) Treat with chlorine or iodine tablets. Pass water through a reverse osmosis system.	Flocculation (requires special chemicals to remove suspended matter). Ion exchange (removes radians from solution).
Mess gear, canned rations, and food (canned, bottled, or protected by impermeable container)	Immerse in boiling, soapy water for 30 minutes and rinse. Immerse in boiling water for 30 minutes. Wash in hot, soapy water; rinse; and air.	Wash in hot, soapy water, and rinse in chlorine solution. Boil in water for 15 minutes (does not kill toxins or anthrax spores). Immerse in peracetic acid solution, rinse, and aerate.	Wash with soap and water, and then rinse. Brush, and then wipe contamination from surfaces and containers.
Food (not canned or protected by impermeable container)	Do not consume food that is suspected of being contaminated with chemical agents until approved by veterinary personnel.	Boil in water for 15 minutes. Cook food thoroughly. Immerse in or spray with a 2% household bleach solution. (Packaged food or food that is peeled or pared can be immersed or sprayed with the solution.)	Wash or trim contamination from unpackaged food.

Table D-1. Decontamination Procedures for Specific Surfaces and Materials (Continued)

Surface or Material	Types of Contamination and How to Decontaminate		
	Chemical	Biological	Radiological
Paper currency	Destroy by burning. Do not decontaminate.	Destroy by burning. Do not decontaminate.	Destroy by burning. Do not decontaminate.
Coins	Wipe with soapy water. Wipe with an organic solvent.	Aerate. Expose to UV rays. Wash with soapy water. Wipe with a 2% household bleach solution.	Brush or wipe. Wash with a detergent. Flush with water.

THIS PAGE IS INTENTIONALLY LEFT BLANK.

Appendix E
SPECIAL DECONTAMINATION CONSIDERATIONS

1. Background

This appendix addresses decontamination considerations for sensitive equipment, munitions, CBRN munitions disposal, sample transfer and processing, DU, radioactive isotopes, and contaminated remains.

2. Vulnerable/Sensitive Equipment

Most military equipment has not been critically assessed for its ability to withstand decontamination without adverse effects. As more materiel testing is done, specific decontamination instructions will be included in the applicable TMs/TOs for all types of equipment. We know that some equipment is extremely vulnerable to damage when subjected to decontamination. The decontamination of equipment containing vulnerable components presents certain challenges. Electronics and optics are especially vulnerable to damage if not carefully decontaminated. Some materials, such as canvas and rubber, tend to absorb chemical agents. As a result, decontaminating absorbent surfaces is extremely difficult, if not impossible. Many decontaminants are highly corrosive and cannot be used on certain materials. They may also corrode and render ammunition unserviceable.

> **CAUTION**
> Do not subject vulnerable equipment to unnecessary decontamination.

   a. Electronics. Moisture, dust, and corrosive decontamination materials can damage unsealed electronic equipment circuitry. Most field electronic equipment is watertight for environmental protection. This also provides good protection against CBRN contamination. Contamination will probably not penetrate gasket-equipped protective covers and sealed components on electronic equipment; but if exposed, the contaminants may be present on the outside of cases containing the electronic equipment. Wipe down the outside portions of the equipment case with a designated decontaminant. After decontaminating the outside, wipe down the equipment with water or an approved solvent to remove traces of decontaminant solutions. If equipment seals appear damaged or the penetration of CBRN contamination into the inside of the equipment is suspected, then the unit should be treated as if it was unsealed. Under no circumstances should electronic equipment be immersed in a decontaminant solution or subjected to high-pressure application of decontaminant solutions. The following high-value electronic equipment presents examples of items that would be damaged by corrosives:

- Joint, Helmet-Mounted Cueing System.
- AN/PVS-4 night vision goggles.
- AN/TVS-5A night vision goggles.
- AN/PVS-7B night vision goggles.
- M12 range finder.

- Tow sight.
- M49 telescope.
- AN/TAS-5 Thermal Imagery System.
- AN/TAS-6 night vision sight, Thermal Imagery System.
- AN/GRC-160 radio set.
- AN/MRC-69 radio-telephone set.
- AN/PRC-119 radio set.
- AN/PRC-139 radio set.
- AN/TRC-68 radio set.
- AN/VRC-12 radio set.
- AN/VRC-87 radio set.
- AN/VRC-92 radio set.
- AN/VRC-87 Single-Channel, Ground and Airborne Radio System (SINCGARS).
- AN/VRC-92 SINGARS.

(1) For chemical contamination, use M100 sorbent on metal electronic cases. For biological agents, wipe the equipment exterior with a cloth and hot, soapy water or use a miscellaneous decontaminant (see Appendix C). If contamination is not extensive, use the M295 decontamination kit.

(2) Corrosive decontaminants should never be used on unsealed electronic equipment. This type of equipment is often found inside shelter assemblies and helicopters. Refer to the appropriate TMs or TOs for acceptable decontamination procedures for unsealed electronic equipment.

(3) For radiological contamination, brush, wipe, or vacuum contamination from equipment. The contamination is not destroyed, just moved from one place to another. So, control the runoff and treat it as a hazardous substance.

b. Optics. Optical systems are extremely vulnerable to decontamination materials that might scratch or adversely affect the lenses. Wipe optical systems with a soft, nonabrasive material such as a lens-cleaning tissue, cotton wadding, or a soft cloth dipped in hot, soapy water. Wipe the optical system with decontaminants. Do not immerse it.

(1) Hot, soapy water is the preferred decontaminant for chemical and biological contamination. The M291 SDK may be used if hot, soapy water is not available.

NOTE: Do not use the M295 IEDK. It contains an abrasive sorbent, which may damage the optics.

(2) Radiological contamination should be blown off with a stream of air or wiped off with hot, soapy water. Rinse the surface by wiping with a sponge dipped in clean water.

c. Ammunition. Decontaminate contaminated ammunition with cool, soapy water. Apply with a PDDE, brushes, mops, rags, or brooms. Cool, soapy water is the preferred decontaminant for all types of contamination on ammunition.

> **CAUTION**
>
> Do not use STB on ammunition. It removes critical markings from ammunition. It may also corrode and render ammunition unserviceable. Do not use nonstandard decontaminants that are corrosive. They also may remove critical markings from the ammunition.

  d. Supplies.

    (1) Canvas Items. Some materials, such as canvas, tend to absorb chemical agents and may not be decontaminated and reused. These items include LBE and web gear. Decontamination is difficult. It may be necessary to burn or bury them if they are heavily contaminated with a chemical agent. Either STB dry mix or slurry may be used. Slurry is more effective. In many cases, weathering may be the preferred decontamination technique because scrubbing canvas frequently imbeds the contamination further and worsens the situation. If the item must be decontaminated, boiling for 1 hour in soapy water is the preferred decontaminant for chemical and biological contamination. Radioactive contamination can be removed by brushing and then washing. It may also be vacuumed. Other options for disposing of contaminated canvas should be considered against METT-TC. CBRN protective covers protect vulnerable items, but these covers should be buried or destroyed after use.

    (2) Subsistence and Water.

      (a) Decontamination removes the contaminant and provides food that is safe for consumption. Food salvage operations require extensive efforts to assess, identify, and evaluate. These efforts are further compounded if food supplies are suspected of being comprised by CBRN contaminates. Decontamination efforts require even more elaborate procedures that impact labor, time, and supplies of operational forces. The use of appropriate decontamination must be emphasized to fit the situation and meet the mission. That is, decontaminate just enough to sustain operations and keep fighting, rather than creating a contamination-free environment. Normally, decontamination efforts will be limited to the scope and nature of the packaging and packing materials.

      (b) The first critical step is to take appropriate personal precautions before starting decontamination procedures and dividing suspected exposed food items into groups. Based on the division of food items, the time of exposure and the possible exposure agent may be identified. Listed below are the food groups by priority, based on the ease of decontamination and the ability to monitor the items in question:

- Group I. Canned or packaged items exposed only to a CW agent vapor.

- Group II. Canned or packaged items that are contaminated on the outside with a liquid CW agent, a BW agent, or radioactive fallout.

- Group III. Unpacked or poorly packaged items that have been exposed to any CBRN agent.

- Group IV. Food contaminated through the food chain.

(c) There are three levels of decontamination for subsistence. These are individual, unit, and support levels. See FM 4-02.7 for definitive information on subsistence decontamination.

- Individual decontamination of subsistence is performed by each service member on the subsistence items in his possession at the time of the attack. Decontamination procedures are conducted as outlined in the unit tactical standard operating procedure (TSOP) and in FM 4-02.7.

- Unit personnel under the supervision of CBRN-trained personnel organic to the unit perform this level of decontamination as soon as possible after a CBRN attack and in conjunction with area decontamination procedures. Decontamination is attempted only on subsistence items that are in original, intact containers that do not permit or have not allowed CBRN penetration. Special decontamination requirements and advisability of decontamination efforts are relayed to unit commanders through command or medical channels as required.

- Specially trained and equipped decontamination units and teams accomplish support levels of decontamination. This is accomplished at major subsistence storage facilities and areas, such as the general support (GS) Class I activities in the theater. Medical personnel advise on technical matters pertaining to the decontamination operations involving subsistence items and also monitor the decontamination results and recovery operations.

(d) Contaminated water must not be used until it has been treated by quartermaster water production and distribution units or other equally capable water purification units and approved for use by the medical authority. The treatment of contaminated water requires chemicals and equipment that are only available to specialized water purification units; individuals or units should not attempt to treat their water. The decontamination of water is only undertaken when uncontaminated sources are not available, and then only with the approval of the medical authority. See FM 10-52 for details.

(3) Painted Surfaces. Chemical agents will penetrate alkyd-painted vehicles and will desorb small quantities of agent for hours to days (depending on certain factors, such as temperature). However, most systems are CARC-painted. CARC-painted surfaces significantly reduce agent penetration and are decontaminated more effectively than alkyd-painted surfaces.

(4) Vegetation. Vegetation also affects the persistency of chemical contamination. When dispersed over vegetation, some of the chemical agent droplets cling to the vegetation. This increases the surface area of agent exposed to the elements and the rate of evaporation, but the contamination may be more dangerous because personnel may be more likely to come into contact with the contaminated plants. In shaded woods, despite the greater surface area covered by the agent, the reduced ambient temperature and winds increase the persistency of the chemical agent.

3. Chemical, Biological, Radiological, and Nuclear Munitions Disposal

CBRN enemy munitions or other improvised devices may be encountered. Captured enemy CBRN munitions or agents may have sustained damage or be leaking due to deterioration. Leaking munitions must be decontaminated, evacuated, and disposed of safely by specialized units, such as EOD, who have properly trained personnel to perform this task. All personnel must use the applicable IPE when there is a possibility of exposure. Notify an EOD unit for the disposal and decontamination of CBRN munitions.

4. Sample Transfer, Evacuation, and Processing

If the decontamination unit headquarters requires a sample of the agent for confirmation, it will be collected and packaged by the unit or activity obtaining the sample. The sample is properly labeled, bagged, and prepared for evacuation. The sample is evacuated according to the procedures outline in *Multiservice Tactics, Techniques, and Procedures for Biological Surveillance.*

5. Depleted-Uranium Decontamination

DU is an extremely dense metal used in munitions to penetrate heavy armor or as protective shielding (armor packages). DU is also used as equipment components. Unfired shells or intact DU armor does not exceed peacetime regulatory standards for personal exposure. Unfired or intact DU does not present a health risk.

a. DU exposure and incidents may occur anytime there is damage to the DU armor package, a vehicle is hit with DU munitions, DU munitions are damaged, or equipment components containing DU are damaged. The DU armor can be damaged during vehicle maneuvers, onboard fires, maintenance activities, or ballistic impacts. DU munition problems may occur during storage, transportation, combat, testing, or manufacturing. DU contamination may be present on the ground in areas where equipment was destroyed or damaged. The USAF primarily uses DU in aircraft counterbalances and in 30-millimeter (mm) armor-piercing and incendiary munitions.

(1) DU can present a number of hazards, depending on its physical (solid versus particulate) and chemical forms. These hazards can be grouped into three categories: radiological, toxicological, and pyrophoric.

(a) Radiological.

- DU presents a radiological hazard from external and internal radiation dose standpoints. Externally, DU and its decay products emit beta and gamma radiations that can serve as sources of external radiation for personnel. Contact gamma dose rates from bare DU can be 15 millirems per hour (mrem/hr), while skin contact dose rate due to beta radiation from bare DU is approximately 238 mrem/hr.

- Internally, insoluble DU oxide can be inhaled and deposited into the lungs, where irradiation by alpha particles is the primary concern. In general, aircraft counterbalances and DU penetrators used in munitions are typically covered to prevent corrosion (oxidation). The primary groups at risk for external exposure are munitions handlers and aircraft maintenance personnel. The primary groups at risk for internal exposure are personnel involved with DU contamination that can potentially become airborne and subsequently inhaled.

(b) Toxicological. Soluble forms of DU can present a significant toxicological hazard. Like any heavy metal, DU can be ingested or inhaled into the body and, subsequently, enter the blood stream. It may be toxic to the kidneys and other organs.

(c) Pyrophoric. The pyrophoric hazard presented by DU is normally associated with fine particulates of metallic DU generated during fabrication processes.

Particulate oxides of DU are generated as a result of normal corrosive processes on exposed DU, fires, and penetrator impact with armor, but are not pyrophoric.

(2) Military and civilian vehicles may become contaminated with DU either as a result of direct penetrator strikes, by traveling through a DU-contaminated environment, or as a result of an accident or fire. Penetrators striking an armored target essentially burn their way through the armor. As a result, DU oxide particles are formed and can be deposited in or on the vehicle or short distances downwind (typically less than 100 yards). The metal surrounding the DU penetration hole is generally the area of highest contamination. The amount of DU contamination resulting from a crash of an aircraft having DU counterbalances is dependent on its physical integrity.

(3) Environmental media (and water) can be a receptor of contamination from other sources (i.e., weathering of intact DU components, DU released from penetrator strikes or fire). The level of this contamination is minor in comparison to that encountered on vehicle surfaces, exposed counterbalance surfaces, etc. The one exception is hard-target range operations involving DU munitions that are left exposed to oxidize and further add to the soil contamination.

(4) Ingestion or inhalation of DU from any form of contaminated media is the primary hazard of concern. Taking the necessary precautions to minimize these risks requires appropriate PPE (i.e., clothing and detection equipment) and procedures. Required procedures and equipment will vary depending on the type of work to be accomplished. Some common sense rules to apply when dealing with radioactive material are—

(a) Evacuate or cordon off the area and avoid it when radioactive contamination is present. If you must work in a contaminated environment, wear protective equipment. Also, health monitoring or exposure control operations will be required.

(b) Ensure that your protective equipment is operational and appropriate for the task to be accomplished.

(c) Do not eat, drink, or smoke in a potentially contaminated area.

(d) Roll down your sleeves, wear gloves, and cover any exposed skin areas. This provides protection from alpha and beta radiation in the form of particles. Pay particular attention to protecting open cuts or wounds, and wear a protective mask. Depending on temperature, protective clothing availability, DU contamination levels, and tasks to be performed, wear your overgarment or coveralls or roll down your sleeves and blouse your trousers as directed by CBRN or medical personnel. Dust off your uniform after leaving a vehicle and before removing your protective mask. Always exercise standard field hygiene, including washing your hands and face.

(e) Limit external hazards by wiping or washing exposed areas as soon as possible.

(f) Minimize time, maximize distance, and maximize shielding to keep any doses received as low as possible.

(g) Assume a DU contamination zone at 50 meters around actively burning fires involving any armored combat vehicles or ammunition supply vehicles.

b. DU contamination may include DU oxides (dust), contaminated shrapnel, munitions components, or armor components. DU primarily emits alpha particles; however, beta, gamma, and X-ray ionizing radiation are also emitted. DU contamination can be inhaled, ingested, or injected. DU contamination does not pose an immediate health risk. Damaged or destroyed enemy or friendly armor vehicles may be DU-contaminated. Unless an individual has a valid reason to enter such vehicles, he should stay away from them. Consequently, contamination should be removed from personnel or vehicle surfaces when directed by the unit commander based on METT-TC considerations.

c. Visual signs that DU contamination is present include heavy, dull, black dust or small, round holes. DU contamination can only be verified with a radiac meter. An AN/VDR-2 (beta shield open) or AN/PDR-77 with an alpha or beta probe (flat-pancake surface) is used to detect and measure DU contamination. These probes are included in the radiological protection officer kit.

d. General decontamination procedures are as follows:

- Use a radiac meter to determine if DU contamination is present.

- Provide protection, including appropriate clothing, for workers as directed by the unit chemical or medical personnel.

- Identify what is to be decontaminated.

- Obtain necessary equipment and materials.

- Brush, wash, or wipe off contamination with a damp cloth. Use a HEPA filter vacuum cleaner if available.

- Work from the outside of the contaminated area to the inside.

- Cover fixed contamination with tape, paint, paper, plastic, or other disposable material.

- Use the standard double-bag-and-tag process for hazardous waste. The only contaminated waste generated by DU will be the vacuum cleaner bags after use on multiple vehicles.

6. Decontamination of Specific Radioisotopes

Radiological contamination may occur in the form of one element. In this section, the decontamination of six specific, commonly found radioactive elements is discussed. The discussion is applicable not only to these elements but also to other elements having similar chemical properties.

a. Cesium. The common radioisotope of cesium is cesium-137. It emits beta and gamma radiation, decaying to stable barium-137. Cesium-137 is widely used in gamma sources. It occurs in these sources as cesium chloride pellets. Cesium chloride is a soluble salt. The contamination from a sealed source leak absorbs water, becomes damp, and creeps. Contamination from a sealed cesium source is best decontaminated by wet procedures unless the contamination is on a porous surface, in which case, vacuuming should precede wet procedures. Cesium is known to adsorb from solution onto glass surfaces. The decontamination of a cesium liquid-contaminated surface is best accomplished by wetting the surface, absorbing the solution with a rag or other absorbent material, and rinsing the area several times with water. If the contamination persists, brushing and a detergent solution should be used. A cesium-contaminated solution which has been standing for some time is best decontaminated by absorbing any remaining liquid, treating the surface several times with water (allowing the water to stand on the surface about 1 minute each time), and then absorbing the liquid from the surface. If the contamination remains, further treatment depends on the surface. Metallic surfaces are treated with strong mineral or oxidizing acids. Waxed surfaces are removed. If contamination still persists, abrasion or other removal techniques are used.

    b.   Cobalt. The common radioisotope of cobalt is cobalt-60, a beta gamma emitter. Metallic cobalt-60 is commonly used in sealed gamma sources. Particles of cobalt dust adhering to small articles are readily removed by ultrasonic cleaners or by dipping in a dilute solution of nitric, hydrochloric, or sulfuric acid. Cobalt dust contamination that exists over a large area is best removed by vacuuming. Sealed cobalt sources may leak as a result of an electrolytic action between cobalt and the container. The result is often a soluble cobalt salt that creeps and spreads. This is best decontaminated with a detergent or ethylenediaminetetraacetic acid (EDTA) solution, followed by treatment with mineral acids. Contamination from solutions containing cobalt may be treated with water solutions.

    c.   Plutonium. The most common isotope in which plutonium may be present as a contaminant is plutonium-239, an alpha emitter. This isotope is present in the AN/UDM-6 calibration source. Plutonium contamination may be a result of a nuclear-weapon accident, in which case the plutonium will be scattered as metal or oxide in a dust form. Both forms of plutonium are insoluble. The aging of plutonium-239 contamination is impractical since it has a 24,000-year half-life. Plutonium contamination that covers a small area is best decontaminated by vacuuming. If contamination remains, the area should be washed with a detergent solution. Any contamination that remains can be sealed in a protective coating of paint, varnish, or plastic. Plutonium oxide or metal dust spread over a large area (e.g., a field) is best decontaminated by removing the top layer of soil and disposing of it as radioactive waste. Personnel should wear respiratory protection when decontaminating or moving the soil.

    d.   Strontium. The most common radioisotope of strontium is strontium-90, a beta emitter. The daughter particle of strontium-90 is yttrium-90, which is also a beta emitter. Strontium-90 and yttrium-90 are commonly used in sealed beta sources, such as the M6 source. Generally it is present as chlorine or carbonate. The chlorine is hygroscopic; it absorbs water and creeps out of the container. This contamination is best decontaminated by vacuuming, followed by treatment with water, complexing agent solution, and mineral acid in that order. Contamination resulting from a dilution containing strontium is best decontaminated by absorbing the solution and washing the area with a detergent solution. If strontium contamination persists, the top layer of the surface should be removed by abrasion or another removal procedure and a sealing coat should be placed over the surface.

    e.   Tritium. Tritium is the radioisotope of hydrogen and is a weak beta emitter. If it is released to an area as a gas, the best method of decontamination is to flush the area with air. Since inhalation of tritium can present an internal hazard, personnel entering an area containing tritium gas should wear an appropriate SCBA. Objects in an area exposed to tritium may absorb the gas and should be disposed of if possible. They may be degassed under a vacuum by flushing with helium or hydrogen. A cleaned surface may be contaminated again in a matter of hours by percolation of absorbed tritium to the surface. There is no practical way of removing tritium oxide from water due to its similarity to natural water.

f. Uranium. The most probable source of uranium contamination is a nuclear-weapon accident in which the fissionable uranium is spread as metal or oxide dust. The common isotopes of uranium contamination are uranium-235 and uranium-238. This metal or oxide is insoluble and is best removed from a contaminated surface by brushing or vacuuming, treating with mineral acids or oxidizing acids, and then sealing. Large-area uranium contamination is best decontaminated by removing the top layer of the surface or by sealing.

7. Contaminated-Remains Decontamination

Mortuary affairs personnel are responsible for coordinating the disposition of contaminated remains. This includes the decontamination of remains when required.

a. Introduction. Command responsibilities (i.e., service, combatant commander, subordinate unit) for mortuary affairs are outlined in Joint Publication (JP) 4-06. The TTP for processing contaminated remains are also outlined in JP 4-06.

(1) Command mortuary affairs support plans are prepared based on supporting the operational requirements of the command. Mortuary affairs support plans may differ in scope, detail, objectives, and available resources between commands.

(2) When planning the level of mortuary affairs support, consider multiple factors, to include the possibility of searching, recovering, evacuating, and decontaminating contaminated remains.

(3) When a CBRN event has occurred on the battlefield, there is a possibility that deceased personnel were exposed to contaminating agents. If the situation does not lend itself to the determination of a hazard on an individual basis, all remains within the affected area will be treated as if contaminated. If the theater surgeon or staff determines that biological agents have been employed, all remains will be treated as if contaminated.

b. Concept of the Operation. A mortuary affairs decontamination collection point (MADCP) may become operational whenever the threat of CBRN warfare exists. The Joint Mortuary Affairs Office (JMAO) acts as the theater central point of contact for coordination for this operation. The handling of contaminated remains is a process consisting of the following:

(1) The MADCP is deployed to the area concerned for the recovery of contaminated remains. The MADCP will set up operations just outside the contaminated area.

(2) Upon verification that the remains have been decontaminated, they are evacuated to the theater mortuary evacuation point or designated holding area.

(3) The final verification of decontamination completeness will be conducted within the theater.

c. Responsibilities.

(1) Geographic combatant commanders are responsible for searching, recovering, tentatively identifying, and evacuating remains from their areas of responsibility (AORs). They ensure that the proper planning, training, staffing, and equipment is furnished for mission requirements (e.g., ensuring proficiency of team personnel on CBRN protective measures and providing CBRN specialists for the MADCP).

(2) Service component commanders are responsible for providing or arranging

for mortuary affairs support for their personnel.

   (3) Subordinate commanders at all levels are responsible for the initial search, recovery, tentative identification, and evacuation of all deceased unit personnel within their area of operation (see FM 10-64 and JP 4-06). If the threat of CBRN is suspected or present, commanders will request MADCP support to perform recovery operations and the subsequent decontamination of remains.

  d. CBRN Search, Recovery, Tentative Identification, and Evacuation Operations.

   (1) CBRN search, recovery, tentative identification, and evacuation are the first steps in the care and handling of deceased personnel during MADCP operations. To ensure successful mission accomplishment, the leader of the MADCP conducting the search and recovery must gather all available information for the mission such as coordinating with intelligence, medical, and CBRN personnel on potential hazards. Personnel assigned to support MADCP must be thoroughly trained in CBRN defense and the use of personnel protective measures and personnel detection. During search operations, if a CBRN hazard is suspected or if an unknown hazard situation exists, the MADCP will assume the appropriate protective posture (e.g., MOPP4).

   (2) MADCP recovery personnel will be in CBRN IPE when conducting recovery missions. When remains are encountered, check them for unexploded ordnance, explosives, and booby traps. Ensure that all hazardous items are removed. Coordinate with a supporting CBRN or EOD specialist/team for assistance or guidance when CBR agents or hazardous items are suspected. Once contaminated remains are determined to be safe to handle, proceed with the recovery.

   (3) The remains are placed in a CB human remains pouch, if available, and care is taken to minimize the spread of contamination. When a CB pouch is not available, the Type II-A human remains pouch should be used.

NOTE: The human remains pouch does not retain all fluids, and off-gassing of vapor can occur through pouch membranes.

   (4) Recovery site operations outlined in FM 10-64 are followed, to include indicating (if known) whether the remains are contaminated and marked (i.e., annotating applicable forms and markers to indicate CBR contamination).

   (5) Personnel evacuating contaminated remains to a MADCP remain in IPE. The transport means used to evacuate contaminated remains is monitored and decontaminated as required.

  e. Mortuary Affairs Decontamination Collection Point.

   (1) Mortuary affairs personnel establish and operate the MADCP. MADCP operations adhere to the procedures outlined in JP 4-06.

   (2) Personnel support is required after completing the evacuation mission to the MADCP, such as thorough DTD. The conduct of DTD takes about 1 hour. The MADCP site will also receive support from a supporting decontamination unit for a complete DTD.

8. Animals

Throughout history, animals have played an important part in military operations. Today, military working dogs (MWDs) continue to provide support to the warfighter.

a. The decontamination of MWDs and other government-owned animals (GOAs) should be accomplished by MWD handlers and supporting veterinarian personnel in accordance with FM 4-02.18. Contaminated MWDs and other GOAs are decontaminated in a manner similar to that of service members. The initial decontamination of the animal should be completed with an M291 SDK. The initial decontamination of the handling equipment (leashes, collars, muzzles) should be completed with an M295 IEDK, a 5 percent hypochlorite solution, or a 5 percent sodium solution (G agents only).

NOTE: Each MWD handler should carry several extra M291s and an extra M295.

b. Definitive decontamination requires the removal and replacement of all contaminated handling equipment and the thorough washing of the animal with soap and water, followed by a thorough rinsing with water. If soap is not available, copious rinsing with water alone should provide adequate decontamination. Each handler should store extra handling equipment in a chemically protected container.

THIS PAGE IS INTENTIONALLY LEFT BLANK.

Appendix F
EFFECTS OF THE ENVIRONMENT ON DECONTAMINATION

1. Background

US forces may find themselves anywhere in the world and subjected to the conditions in that region. Weather and terrain conditions will influence the decontamination process used. The conditions in cold weather and arctic areas, hot weather and desert areas, urban areas, mountains, and jungles impact how decontamination operations are performed. If METT-TC allows, permitting the contamination to weather is generally a preferred option. However, marking, reporting, and periodically rechecking the contamination is required. The effects of the environment will also impact decontamination manpower requirements.

2. Cold Weather

Cold can kill, maim, and disable without any help from a human foe. Cold weather regions are characterized by extreme cold weather and deep snow during winter months. Whiteout, gray out, and ice fog are weather phenomena that have an impact on northern operations. In whiteout, a person seems to be surrounded by an unbroken white glow. Gray out is similar to a whiteout except that the horizon is distinguishable. Depth perception and orientation are lost in the absence of shadows, the horizon, and clouds. Ice fog forms when water vapor is produced by human activities and the air at low temperatures is unable to hold the moisture. Ice fog may appear over personnel, vehicles, bivouac areas, and permanent facilities, marking their location. Ice fog can obscure vision.

   a. Chemical Agents. Chemical agents also react differently at extremely low temperatures. For example, at 32°F (0°C), HD, CX and HT become solids. As the temperature drops to minus 15°F (minus 25°C), AC, CK, HN-3, and PD become solids. Munitions containing normally persistent agents become very persistent at low temperatures, and some normally nonpersistent chemicals become persistent. GB, a normally nonpersistent agent, could remain a transfer hazard for up to 30 days in arctic climates. Although frozen agents do not present a significant problem in solid state, they become hazards when they warm up. See Table F-1 (page F-2) for the freezing/melting points of selected chemical agents.

Table F-1. Freezing Points and Melting Points of Selected Chemical Agents

Agent	Symbol	FP	MP	Boiling Point
Nerve Agents				
Tabun	GA	-50°C	Data not available	248°C
Sarin	GB	-56°C	Data not available	150°C
Soman	GD	Data not available	-42°C	198°C
Cyclosarin	GF	-30°C to -50°C	-12°C	228°C
O-Ethyl-S-Methyl Phosphonothiolate	VX	Below -51°C	Data not available	292°C
V sub x	Vx	Data not available	Data not available	256°C
Blister Agents				
Mustard	HD	14.45°C	Data not available	218°C
Nitrogen Mustard	HN-1	Data not available	-34.2°C	192°C
Nitrogen Mustard	HN-2	-70°C		177°C
Nitrogen Mustard	HN-3	Data not available	-3.74°C	257°C
Distilled Mustard and T Mixture	HT	Data not available	1.3°C	No constant temperature
Lewisite	L	-44.7°C to -1.8°C	Data not available	196°C
Distilled Mustard and Lewisite Mixture	HL	Munitions: -42°C Pure: -25.4°C	Data not available	200°C
Phenyldichloroarsine	PD	-22.5°C	Data not available	233°C
Ethyldichloroarsine	ED	Data not available	Below -65°C	156°C
Methyldichloroarsine	MD	-54.8°C	Data not available	132.6°C
Phosgene Oxime	CX	Data not available	39°C	129°C
Blood Agents				
Hydrogen Cyanide	AC	Data not available	-13.3°C	25.5°C
Cyanogen Chloride	CK	-6.9°C	Data not available	12.8°C
Arsine	SA	Data not available	-116°C	-62.2°C
Choking Agents				
Phosgene	CG	Data not available	-128°C	7.8°C
Diphosgene	DP	Data not available	-57°C	127°C

b. **Decontaminants.** Decontamination is a problem because low temperatures also reduce the effect of decontaminants. When temperatures reach 32°F, water can no longer be used. In such situations, use STB or HTH as a dry mix (two parts of STB to three parts of unfrozen earth). If unfrozen dirt is not available, use snow (same proportion). Apply the dry mix by shoveling it on contaminated surfaces or by filling sandbags with the mix and dusting it on the surfaces. Remove the dry mix by brushing, scraping, or using uncontaminated earth or snow to "wash" it off. Other decontaminating methods using nonstandard solvents and fuels may be used, but observe fire safety, protect personnel from corrosives, and take precautions against supercooling effects. Because of their low freezing points, solvents such as aviation fuel (JP-8), diesel fuel, and kerosene may be used to physically remove contamination. These solvents only flush the agent from the surfaces. They generally do not neutralize agents nor do they eliminate agents that soak into surfaces. Nonstandard solvents generally are very flammable and must be handled with care.

c. Decontamination Operations.

(1) Decontamination apparatuses and water trucks may have to be deployed with empty tanks instead of full ones as in temperate climates. To prevent freezing, it may be necessary to preheat water when loading water trucks and the tanks of decontaminating apparatuses and keep it heated until it is used. These vehicles may have to be enclosed and warmed so that the engines will start. Decontaminate apparatuses and drain water trucks immediately after use to prevent damage from freezing.

(2) Vehicles and personnel covered with contaminated snow should be decontaminated before the snow has a chance to melt and freeze. Such snow forms layers of ice that make contamination difficult to remove. Radioactive fallout that is mixed with snowfall must be removed as soon as possible. Use tree branches (if available) to remove contaminated snow.

(3) Snow can be used to cover contamination; however, the snow can blow away or the contamination can resurface when tracked vehicles, personnel movement, or digging disturbs it. Snow cover provides some protection if left undisturbed, but this protection is too uncertain to rely on.

(4) Personnel supporting cold weather decontamination operations may use warming areas for rest and relief. However, if personnel get a frozen agent on their clothing, the agent will be hard to detect because low temperatures have slowed its evaporation.

(5) Moving vehicles through the decontamination site will be a challenge. Caution must be exercised. It will be hard for the vehicles to navigate and stop if there is ice present on the ground.

3. Hot Weather (Desert and Jungle)

Hot weather can considerably complicate decontamination operations.

a. Desert Areas. Extreme temperatures characterize desert regions with ranges varying between 30°F to 130°F over a 24-hour period. These regions have long drought periods, which are interrupted by sudden rains that bring flash floods. There are shortages of suitable groundwater. Large areas suitable for tracked-vehicle maneuvers may sometimes have impassable ravines; wet, spongy grounds; and sand areas.

(1) Water. The principal problem for decontamination in the desert is the lack of water. The use of STB slurry will burden the logistical system because of the water required for mixing and rinsing. Non-water-based decontaminants (natural solvents) may be required. Contamination avoidance becomes increasingly important in desert operations because of limited water sources.

(2) Heat Stress. Heat stress is a critical issue for personnel. Operating decontamination stations in daytime temperatures may require short periods of work followed by long periods of rest. See Chapter II for guidance on work/rest cycles.

(3) Weathering. Weathering is a viable decontamination option. High daytime temperatures can increase the evaporation of liquid contamination. For example, if a vehicle were contaminated with THD in a hot, desert environment, at least 99 percent of the contamination would have evaporated within 2 hours. Therefore, vehicle wash down may not be necessary. As a result, vapor concentrations will be high but should not last

long. If liquid contamination soaks into soft, porous soil (such as loose sand), evaporation is not as quick. Strong winds also increase the evaporation rate. Low temperatures during the night have a reverse effect and tend to increase the persistency of chemical and biological contamination. The sandblasting effect of sandstorms may remove contamination from surfaces facing the storm. Desert sunlight and high temperatures will destroy many CB agents without additional decontamination measures.

(4) Bearings and Other Critical Moving Parts. Bearings and other critical moving parts need extra lubrication in the desert. This complicates decontamination because lubricants tend to absorb chemical agents. After a sandstorm, maintenance must be conducted regardless of the last scheduled maintenance. Therefore, perform decontamination first and, if time is critical, decontaminate only those surfaces that will be touched during maintenance. This will not eliminate vapor hazards.

b. Jungle Areas. The characteristics of jungle climates vary with the location. Close to the equator, all seasons are nearly alike, with rains throughout the year. Farther from the equator, especially in India and Southeast Asia, jungles have distinct wet (monsoon) and dry seasons. Both zones have high temperatures averaging 78°F to 98°F, heavy rainfall (as much as 400 inches annually), and high humidity (90 percent) throughout the year.

(1) Temperature/Humidity. Many tasks in the jungle take more time than in other environments. When temperatures rise to the 85°F to 100°F range, personnel can only continue medium or heavy workloads by reducing their MOPP level. Since decontamination crews will be more susceptible to heat stress, leaders should plan for frequent crew rotations and provide enough decontamination personnel to conduct decontamination operations. Biological agents can persist in the heat, humidity, and shade, which are characteristics of the jungle. Therefore, weathering is not a practical means of biological decontamination. See Chapter II for information on work/rest cycles.

(2) Rain. Tropical rainstorms will flood decontamination sites unless the sites are adequately drained. Decontamination sites should be put on high ground during the rainy season. Ground that appears firm may become impassable. Rain can help the decontamination process by washing away contamination on exposed surfaces. Rain can also hydrolyze some agents. However, runoff may contaminate the soil.

(3) Terrain. Contamination will be retained temporarily in the jungle canopy, reducing the immediate hazard. Later, rains will wash these particles to the ground and concentrate them in low areas. These areas are likely to become contamination "hot spots." The thick vegetation can reduce sunlight and wind, increasing the persistency of some CB agents.

(4) Decontaminants. Solid decontaminants, such as STB powder, tend to cake and decompose at a faster rate than in temperate climates. Caking is no problem, but the decomposition eventually makes STB powder ineffective.

(5) Lubricants. Frequently oil exposed metal parts and grease wheel bearings to protect them from moisture. Since POL tends to absorb chemical agents, additional decontamination may be needed. Measures taken to protect electronic communications equipment from moisture may reduce the need for decontamination since these measures provide good CBRN protection.

4. Urban Areas

The need for decontamination operations in urban areas may also exist, and it may be easier to support. Water sources are generally available, and commercial chemicals may be used as decontaminants. Decontamination operations in urban areas will not differ significantly from similar operations in the field; however, keep the following considerations in mind:

   a. Structures. Wood and concrete tend to absorb liquid agents, and they may give off toxic vapors for days or weeks. Building decontamination is very difficult and requires large quantities of decontaminants. Covering the contamination with plastic sheets, STB slurry, sodium silicate, or other substances that cover or absorb the agent can reduce the hazard. Even though a particular part of a building is not intended for occupation, it may still need to be decontaminated to prevent the contamination from spreading.

   b. Streets and Sidewalks. Streets and sidewalks also absorb liquid agents and then give off toxic vapors when heated by the sun. These surfaces may need to be decontaminated several times to reduce hazards. Streets, sidewalks, or other porous surfaces are best decontaminated by weathering if the time and the situation permit.

   c. Sanitation Systems and Runoff. Urban areas may have sophisticated sanitation systems. When those systems are destroyed, sanitary conditions become far worse than those in areas where sanitation systems have never existed. Sanitation systems must be maintained to avoid overloading decontamination capabilities. Contaminated water and residue must be controlled so that it will not create a hazard. Support may be necessary to construct controlled runoff areas.

5. Mountains

Excluding extremely high, Alpine type mountains, most mountain systems are characterized by heavy woods or jungle, compartments and ridge systems, limited routes, and highly variable weather conditions. All these factors will affect decontamination operations.

   a. Mobility. The terrain and the disruption of existing routes may dictate that decontamination operations be decentralized. Additional water-carrying vehicles may be needed to support decontamination. Forces must be organized to be self-sufficient and may have decontamination elements attached to them initially. Decontamination elements must be equipped with greater hauling capabilities, especially for water.

   b. Weather. Although there is a general climatic correspondence between high latitudes and high altitudes, there are factors that act as additional local variables that may impact decontamination.

      (1) Wind. Mountains have changing weather and constant winds that promote weathering at a faster rate.

      (2) Temperature. Cool or cold temperatures have an adverse effect on decontamination operations. Air temperature drops about 6.5°C for each kilometer of rise in altitude. The drier the air, the more pronounced the drop in temperatures. At high altitudes, there may be differences of 40°F to 50°F between the temperature in the sun and that in the shade. Low temperatures that normally exist at extremely high altitudes may demand decontamination procedures and precautions similar to those used in cold-weather operations. Daytime operations can be scheduled to avoid some low-temperature problems.

(3) **Sunlight.** Increasing altitude results in increased sunlight because the air becomes clearer as altitude increases. At high altitudes, exposed surfaces are heated much more than they would be in the lowlands. The clearer air also results in a greater loss of heat by radiation at night. Sunlight destroys most biological agents.

c. **Altitude.** The body must adjust to the lower air pressure at high altitudes. These adjustments take time. As much as 70 percent of sea level work capacity may be attained after months in a high-altitude environment by acclimatized personnel. Practically all unacclimatized personnel can be expected to show some altitude effects above 2,100 meters.

Appendix G
DECONTAMINATION UNITS AND ASSETS

1. Background

This appendix contains basic information on service decontamination capabilities.

2. Army

This paragraph describes the organizational structure, mission, capabilities, limitations, C2, and basis of allocation of Army CBRN units that have a decontamination capability. The basis of allocation is determined by the number and type of units being supported, and capabilities are available at brigade and battalion level to provide C2 of subordinate unit decontamination assets.

    a. Chemical Brigade. The chemical brigade commander, with the advice of his staff and in conjunction with the theater/corps/JTF chemical section, evaluates and determines the chemical unit support requirement for the supported commander. The brigade commander advises his higher commander concerning the employment of CBRN decontamination units.

        (1) Mission. Provide C2 of two to six battalions and other assigned or attached separate companies.

        (2) Capabilities.

- Provide C2, and supervise the operation of the brigade and two to six subordinate chemical battalions or separate companies.
- Plan and coordinate for the combat, combat support, and CSS operations for all assigned and attached units.
- Allocate units and resources to conduct CBRN decontamination.
- Provide necessary logistical and administrative support to the brigade HQ.
- Provide organizational level maintenance to the brigade HQ.

        (3) C2 HQ. Normally supports a theater, corps, or JTF.

        (4) Basis of Allocation. One per corps and one per theater support command (TSC).

    b. Chemical Battalion. There are many different organizations that a chemical battalion can support. The nonenhanced chemical battalion may support a corps or larger sided AO. Smaller scale operations may require the chemical battalion to work directly for a JTF. In all situations, the chemical battalion commander, in conjunction with the supported unit chemical staff, will develop the CBRN decontamination plan according to METT-TC considerations. The functions and responsibilities of the chemical battalion are usually constant but will depend on the command and support relationship given it by the higher HQ.

        (1) Mission. Provide C2 of two to five chemical companies.

        (2) Capabilities.

- Provide C2 and supervision for the operation of the battalion and two to five subordinate units.

- Plan and coordinate the combat, combat support, and CSS operations for all assigned and attached units.

- Provide organizational maintenance and mess support, and establish and operate internal and external mobile subscriber equipment, radio, and wire communications nets.

(3) C2 HQ: Chemical brigade, chemical division, or JTF.

(4) Basis of Allocation. One per two to five chemical companies in a corps. One per two to seven chemical companies assigned to a theater Army and above.

c. Chemical Companies. Chemical companies are the basic unit of employment for the Army Chemical Corps in support of military operations. Companies are task-organized to support military elements operating within the AO based on capabilities and METT-TC considerations. The capabilities described below will only address unit decontamination capabilities.

(1) Chemical Company (Combat Support) (Table of Organization and Equipment [TO&E] 03496F000). This company provides CBRN reconnaissance and surveillance (R&S) and decontamination support for elements operating within a division AO. The unit has three decontamination platoons and is 100 percent mobile.

(a) Mission. Provides CBRN R&S and decontamination to support an assured access strategy.

(b) Capabilities.

- A platoon can C2 and support a single DED operation for thorough decontamination.

- A platoon can support up to three independent decontamination operations by operating as independent squads.

- A platoon can conduct fixed-site, area, and route decontamination.

(c) Limitations.

- The company has no organic water resupply capability for decontamination operations.

- The decontamination platoon cannot operate the DTD during thorough decontamination operations.

(d) C2 HQ. Chemical battalion (TO&E 03496F000).

(e) Basis of Allocation. Three per division or one per tactical brigade.

(2) Chemical Company (Corps) (TO&E 03498F100). This company provides CBRN R&S, biological surveillance, and decontamination support for elements operating within a corps forward AO. The company generally supports units in the corps forward AO, but may provide support to units in a corps rear AO, the communications zone (COMMZ), or forward within a division AO. The company may also provide specialized decontamination support, such as aircraft or terrain decontamination. The company has four decontamination platoons and is 100 percent mobile.

(a) Mission. Provides CBRN R&S, and decontamination support.

(b) Capabilities.

- A platoon can C2 and support a single DED operation for thorough decontamination.

- A platoon can support up to three independent decontamination operations by operating as independent squads.

- A platoon can conduct fixed-site, area, and route decontamination.

(c) Limitations.

- The company has no organic water resupply capability for decontamination operations.

- The decontamination platoon cannot operate the DTD during thorough decontamination operations.

(d) C2 HQ. Chemical battalion (TO&E 03496F000).

(e) Basis of Allocation: Three per corps.

(3) Chemical Company (Heavy)-TO&E 03498F200. This company provides CBRN R&S, biological surveillance, and decontamination support for elements operating within a corps rear AO and within the theater Army. The company generally supports units in the corps rear AO, but may provide support to the corps forward AO and the COMMZ. The company may also provide specialized decontamination support, such as aircraft or terrain decontamination. The company has four decontamination platoons and is 100 percent mobile.

(a) Mission. Provides CBRN R&S and decontamination to support an assured access strategy.

(b) Capabilities.

- A platoon can C2 and support a single DED operation for thorough decontamination.

- A platoon can support up to three independent decontamination operations by operating as independent squads.

- A platoon can conduct fixed-site, area, and route decontamination.

(c) Limitations.

- The company has no organic water resupply capability for decontamination operations.

- The decontamination platoon cannot operate the DTD during thorough decontamination operations.

(d) C2 HQ. Chemical battalion (TO&E 03496F000).

(e) Basis of Allocation: Two per corps and five per theater Army.

3. Marine Corps

The USMC NBC defense teams consist of personnel trained in NBC decontamination and NBC reconnaissance in support of USMC MAGTF operations. NBC decontamination teams are formed primarily at the company level from assigned personnel with oversight and supervision provided by NBC specialists (MOS 5711/5702) at the battalion level and higher. NBC defense teams at the company level may be reinforced by the attachment of other company teams as directed by the senior commander. Positioning NBC defense teams at the company, squadron, and battalion levels allows the USMC to task-organize its NBC decontamination and reconnaissance elements/assets across the MAGTF, depending on the situation and mission.

a. Decontamination Teams. Decontamination teams are the backbone of the MAGTF decontamination capability. Teams are trained and equipped in a manner that facilitates task organization and are tailored towards specific decontamination operations. These decontamination teams are capable of rapid employment through the use of organic vehicles that have been dedicated to the teams. Teams are force-multiplied to support sustained operations.

(1) Major Subordinate Command (MSC) Decontamination Teams. Each MSC has a decontamination team comprised of NBC defense specialists that is task-organized as required to support MAGTF operations. The team organization is based upon providing one decontamination section for each MSC civil engineer (CE), regiment, Marine aircraft group (MAG), and five for each force service support group (FSSG). Each section is staffed with one section leader and three section members. Teams are task-organized to perform their operational decontamination missions based on mission requirements and the commander's priorities. The nuclear, biological, and chemical center (NBCC) operations coordinator will direct the task organization and employment and will coordinate the support for the team. The actual common operating environment (COE) will be based upon the vulnerability analysis and adjusted as required to respond to the enemy's use of NBC agents. Each operational decontamination section is trained and equipped to support casualty decontamination, MOPP drop, MOPP gear exchange, and vehicle/aircraft wash down.

(2) Subordinate Command Decontamination Teams. All battalions and squadrons that function as an integral unit during combat operations are trained and equipped to support casualty decontamination, MOPP drop, MOPP gear exchange, and vehicle/aircraft wash down. Team members come from the unit command element. Teams task-organize to perform their operational decontamination missions based on mission requirements and the commander's priorities. Decontamination teams provide the commander with the ability to—

- Prepare contaminated casualties for transport to a casualty decontamination site by removing as much contamination from the casualty as possible.
- Conduct MOPP drop.
- Conduct MOPP exchange.
- Conduct vehicle/aircraft wash down.
- Provide site workers for thorough/clearance and casualty decontamination operations.

(3) USMC NBC Decontamination Teams. The USMC NBC decontamination teams may also be task-organized in support of the following decontamination operations:

(a) Patient (Casualty) Decontamination. Casualty decontamination is conducted in accordance with the procedures outlined in this manual and MCRP 4-11.1F. Each MSC maintains a capability set with sufficient supplies and materials to set up one casualty decontamination site (CDS) that is capable of decontaminating 100 casualties. The decontamination team/section will require additional personnel augmentation to set up and sustain operations at the CDS. This augmentation will consist of any available USMC (CDS workers) and medical personnel who are familiar with triage and the treatment of casualties with conventional and CBRN agent injuries. Personnel working on the CDS will be rotated in accordance with the work rates and work/rest cycles contained in *Multiservice Tactics, Techniques, and Procedures for Nuclear, Biological, and Chemical Protection*. Medical personnel required to support the CDS will be task-organized based on mission requirements and the commander's priorities. The shock trauma platoons located in the medical battalion are ideally suited for supporting the CDS. The MAGTF NBCC will direct the establishment of at least one CDS whenever the vulnerability analysis indicates the likelihood of encountering CBRN contamination. MSCs will establish additional CDSs in those instances when the single MAGTF site does not adequately support their decontamination needs. The personnel used to man the CDS will conduct MOPP drop to remove their CBRN IPE prior to crossing the contamination control line (hot line) or entering any clean area.

b. Thorough Decontamination. The MAGTF is prepared to conduct thorough decontamination of its vehicles, equipment, DED, aircraft, and DAD. Personnel decontamination will be accomplished primarily by using the MOPP drop and/or the MOPP gear exchange procedures identified in this publication.

(1) The MAGTF decontamination elements are structured and equipped in a manner that provides a flexible capability. Operational decontamination will be used to support the high OPTEMPO associated with FP. Thorough decontamination will be conducted in support of retrograde operations or as required to support unusual circumstances.

(2) The MAGTF CE CBRN operations coordinator will organize and coordinate thorough decontamination operations. The MSC and subordinate command operational decontamination teams, medical personnel, engineers, and other augmentees are task-organized as required to support the MAGTF thorough decontamination operations. The divisions and FSSGs will each maintain a capability set with sufficient supplies and materials to set up one DED that is capable of decontaminating 100 medium tactical vehicle replacements (MTVRs) (7-ton) each. The wings will maintain a capability set with sufficient supplies and materials to set up one DAD capable of decontaminating 100 aircraft (Marine attack squadron [VMA]/Marine light/attack helicopter squadron [HMLA]).

(3) All vehicles, equipment, and aircraft must be checked for contamination during retrograde operations. Contaminated vehicles, equipment and aircraft must go through thorough (clearance) decontamination operations.

c. MAGTF NBCC. The MAGTF NBCC will task-organize decontamination teams as required to support the following operations:

- Terrain decontamination.
- Fixed-site decontamination.
- Sensitive-equipment decontamination.
- DU decontamination
- Contaminated-remains decontamination.

d. USMC Chemical/Biological Incident Response Force (CBIRF). The CBIRF was established by the direction of the Commandant of the USMC as a result of Presidential Decision Directive 39 (PDD-39), which states that the United States shall give the highest priority to developing the capability to manage the consequences of NBC materials or weapons use by terrorists.

(1) Mission. When directed, the CBIRF forward-deploys domestically or overseas in order to provide FP and/or mitigation in the event of a WMD incident. CBIRF is prepared to respond to no-notice WMD incidents with a rapidly deployable initial-response force (IRF) and follow-on forces (FOF) if required. CBIRF also conducts FP training for Fleet Marine Force units.

(2) Organizational Structure. The CBIRF is composed of 350 to 375 USMC and USN personnel and consists of three elements. In garrison, the CBIRF is under the operational control (OPCON) and administrative control (ADCON) of the 4th Marine Expeditionary Brigade Antiterrorism (4th MEB/AT) who falls under the II Marine Expeditionary Force (II MEF) and USMC Forces, Atlantic (MARFORLANT). The CBIRF is an incident response force that executes CM operations in support of a combatant commander or lead federal agency. The CBIRF has limited organic equipment decontamination capability, but does not conduct DED or area decontamination operations. Further, the majority of CBIRF personnel are trained in Level A and B operations. TIC and TIM are potential threats to US forces, even OCONUS, since littoral areas include port and industrial complexes where the storage and manufacture of these materials are common. The CBIRF also has state-of-the-art monitoring and detection equipment used to identify, sample, and analyze NBC hazards, including TIC and TIM, as well as oxygen (O2) and lower-explosive levels (LEL).

(3) Command Element.

- Provides liaison teams to other agencies or commands.
- Interfaces with local and military commanders.
- Coordinates all on-site CBIRF operations.
- Establishes data/voice reach-back to scientific and medical advisors.
- Prepares CBR plume models.

(4) Reaction Force Company Capabilities.

- Agent detection and identification.
- Sampling and collection.

- Monitoring of concentration and exposure levels.
- Decontamination for unit personnel.
- Decontamination for first responders.
- Casualty decontamination on scene.
- Victim search in the area and confined spaces.
- Technical rescue and casualty extraction.
- EOD (FP).

(5) Medical Capabilities.
- Emergency medical care in contaminated areas.
- Casualty triage and stabilization.
- Transfer into the local emergency medical system.

(6) Helicopter-Born Package.
- Eighty personnel on 1-hour alert status.
- Decontamination of 35 to 50 ambulatory casualties per hour.
- Decontamination of 20 to 35 nonambulatory casualties per hour.

(7) Follow-On Force (Vehicle/Fixed-Wing Operations).
- Decontamination of 200 to 225 ambulatory casualties per hour.
- Decontamination of 65 to 75 nonambulatory casualties per hour.
- Mobile laboratory.

4. Air Force

This paragraph provides an overview of the USAF CBRN structure and decontamination response capabilities.

a. AB CBRN Defense Capabilities. USAF CBRN forces are structured to support AB survivability and operations. Each AB has one central focal point for CBRN defense, the CE readiness flight (office symbol CEX), which is contained in the CE squadron. Representative decontamination related functions include—

- Conducting CBRN defense training for all USAF personnel and training unit CBRN teams (contamination control, shelter management).
- Developing base CBRN defense plans and procedures.
- Advising the commander on all nonmedical aspects of CBRN defense.
- Establishing personnel CCAs.
- Advising contamination control teams (CCTs).
- Marking contaminated areas.

(1) CBRN defense actions require a force structure that includes both primary duty and base augmentation forces. Primary duty CBRN defense forces are located within the CE squadron readiness flight.

(2) In-place and deployed units provide augmentation manpower for CCTs and CCA teams. Deliberate planning guidelines for identifying specialist and augmentation support for NBCC defense are found in AFI 10-204. The installation, theater, or USAF planning agent determines the actual requirements after considering the threat and missions for each in-place and deployed location.

b. AB NBC Defense Structure. The AB NBC defense structure includes a defined C2 structure and CONOPS for wartime operations. The host wing commander sets alarm conditions, MOPP levels, and FP conditions for the entire base. The survival recovery center (SRC) is the (base) command post element that develops, recommends, implements (with wing approval), and tracks pre-, during-, and postattack passive-defense activities on the base. The SRC broadcasts alarm conditions and MOPP exchanges to all units on base, activates the base siren, tracks casualties and damage to installation resources, and directs recovery efforts. The SRC tracks the location of all known postattack hazards on the base.

c. Unit Control Center (UCC). The next level down in the command structure, below the SRC, is the UCC. It monitors the status of unit activities and maintains a log of unit actions. The UCC passes information to and from the SRC, and it directs and monitors the implementation of unit pre-, during-, and postattack actions. UCCs maintain a base map with all unit structures, shelters, bunkers, and primary operating areas color-coded or marked to enable quick identification. UCC checklists outline tasks and responsible unit functions under each alarm condition. Following attacks, the UCC directs (in coordination with the SRC) and reports postattack hazards to the SRC and coordinates recovery actions.

d. UCC Capabilities. UCCs track the location of all known postattack hazards that may affect their unit personnel or mission. This includes hazards such as contamination and unexploded ordnance (UXO). The UCC advises unit personnel of hazard locations and directs the movement of unit assets away from hazard areas. If the base uses the NBC sector or zone concept, the UCC tracks the alarm condition and MOPP for the sectors/zones and controls movement of unit resources into and out of the contaminated areas.

e. Deployable Teams. Within the USAF, deployable teams with a decontamination capability (see Table G-1) are organized under unit type codes (UTCs). UTCs prescribe specific team support for a given contingency. Within this concept, trained individuals are deployed for assignment to these teams when the need arises. The teams have multiple capabilities.

Table G-1. USAF UTCs

USAF UTCs		
4 F 9 D A	NBCC Threat Response Core Team	Provides limited NBCC defense supporting activities ranging from small-scale contingency operations to MTWs and response to major accidents and natural disasters for an AB with up to 1,200 personnel. Capabilities include preliminary risk/VAs and threat analysis; planning, detection, identification, warning, and reporting; decontamination; CCA; disaster response equipment; technical data; roll-on/roll-off capability, and 463L pallets. Personnel will deploy with IPE, clothing, weapons, and ammunition.

Table G-1. USAF UTCs (Continued)

USAF UTCs		
4F9DB	NBCC Threat Response Light Team	Provides minimal NBCC defense supporting activities ranging from small-scale contingency operations to MTWs and response to major accidents and natural disasters for AB with up to 600 personnel. Capabilities include preliminary risk/VAs and threat analysis; planning, detection, identification, warning, and reporting; decontamination; CCA; disaster response equipment; technical data; roll-on/roll-off capability; and 4,63L pallets. Personnel will deploy with IPE, clothing, weapons, and ammunition.
4F9DC	NBCC Threat Response Light Team	Provides additional technical expertise, support, and manpower to other UTCs in full-spectrum threat response to NBCC defense, major accidents, and disaster response operations. Personnel capabilities include detection, identification, warning, reporting, decontamination, and contamination control operations. Provides additional manpower supporting activities, ranging from smaller-scale contingency operations to MTWs. Personnel deploy with IPE, clothing, weapons, and ammunition.
4F9DE	NBCC Response CCT Equipment Set	Provides limited full-spectrum threat response and contamination control capabilities for sustained operations in an NBCC environment. Provides contamination avoidance resources, such as decontamination apparatuses and supplies, M295 decontamination kits, protective covers, decontaminants, and application devices. Requires manpower augmentation (10 personnel) from the supported unit for the setup, maintenance, and operation of contamination control equipment.
4F9DM	NBCC Threat Response Core Team	Provides NBCC defense capability to respond to attacks, major accidents, and natural disasters in support of small-scale contingency operations (without augmentation) or MTWs for an AB with up to 1,200 personnel (with augmentation by UTC 4F9DC). Capabilities include preliminary risk/VAs and threat analysis; planning, detection, identification, warning, and reporting; decontamination; CCA; disaster response equipment; technical data; roll-on/roll-off capability; and 463L pallets. Personnel will deploy with IPE, clothing, weapons, and ammunition.
4F9DQ	Wartime Medical Decontamination Team (UTC FFGLB)	Provides the capability to remove or neutralize NBC agents on casualties immediately prior to being admitted to the MTF. Standardized WMDs and equipment assemblages can be deployed, assigned, or pre-positioned to support and enable USAF MTFs to safely and effectively treat contaminated casualties without contaminating medical personnel, equipment, or facilities. Decontamination sites/facilities are constructed in the vicinity of the MTF. Personnel decontamination is accomplished by clothing removal and skin washing using soap or hypochlorite. The WMDT conducts the contamination control of medical personnel and assets as needed.
FFGLB	Expeditionary Medical Decontamination Team	Provides the capability to remove CBRN contamination from contaminated casualties prior to admission to an MTF.

   f.   Casualty Decontamination. The decontamination of casualties protects them from the detrimental effects of contamination and protects those who move and treat them. Units and individuals have the responsibility for immediate decontamination during the self-aid buddy care (SABC) process (i.e., use of M291 and M295 decontamination kits). This should be done as soon as contamination is found and prior to moving casualties to the medical facility; quick action saves lives. Upon completion of SABC efforts, units should move contaminated casualties into the medical treatment system as soon as possible, even if decontamination is not complete. The MTF will plan for and provide patient decontamination depending on the local threat conditions. The wartime patient decontamination team provides this capability and may be deployed, depending on the NBC threat. Medical units without a patient decontamination team may need to establish a decontamination capability using personnel and material of opportunity. Commanders at the employment location may need to provide manpower augmentation to the medical unit in the event of insufficient medical resources. Ambulatory personnel with no significant symptoms should process through unit or area CCAs for decontamination whenever practical. Patient decontamination resources are limited and are best-suited for personnel in need of medical care. See Table G-2 for a synopsis of CE and CBRN decontamination capabilities.

Table G-2. CE and Medical CBRN Decontamination Capabilities

CE UTCs	Medical UTCs
Provide alarm conditions and MOPP level recommendations based upon the threat.	Assist with NBC postattack risk assessments and management.
Conduct NBC reconnaissance to determine contamination footprint(s) and related operational protective measures.	Detect NBC agents at the MTF; report to the SRC and NBC cells.
Collect and consolidate postattack reports from NBCC teams, UCCs, and the SRC.	Dispatch to identified NBC footprints for the further identification and quantification of hazard concentrations and the collection of samples (surveillance for health protection).
Advise the incident commander on TTP to conduct sustained operations in a contaminated environment.	Sample food and water for NBC contamination.
Provide additional technical expertise, support, and manpower to NBCC defense.	Conduct surveillance activities in reduced MOPP level sectors.
Manage CCA operations and advise on entry and exit control point procedures.	Document individual exposure (PRD-5) requirements.
Advise the SRC commander on NBC operational aspects (persistency, contamination isolation, and control).	Identify groups of personnel in hazard areas (e.g., squadrons in contaminated sectors) and track exposure to NBC agents (PRD-5 requirements).
Provide MOPP level recommendations (operational), to include split MOPP/reduced MOPP operations.	Advise the SRC commander on the health effects and health risks of NBC agents
Coordinate the collection, storage, and disposal of contaminated waste.	Advise the SRC on the health/medical aspects in support of reduced MOPP levels.
	Perform patient decontamination.
	Perform the appropriate level of decontamination for medical vehicles, shelters, and equipment

5. Navy

This paragraph provides an overview of USN decontamination CBRD capabilities and organization.

   a. Afloat. CBRD is coordinated aboard each ship according to the specific CBRD bill for that ship. The responsibility for the CBRD normally rests with the damage control officer, who organizes the CBRD team. Personnel are assigned to operate decontamination stations as designated by the damage control officer.

   b. Ashore. Disaster preparedness teams are established by the naval shore activity commanding officer. CBRD decontamination teams consist of the following assets:

      (1) CBR Survey Team. Surveys the assigned areas to determine CBR contamination locations and levels and marks hazardous areas.

      (2) Personnel Decontamination Team. Conducts chemical and radiological decontamination of personnel who are not seriously injured.

(3) Facilities and Area Decontamination Team. Is responsible for performing CBR decontamination of essential facilities and areas.

(4) Radiation Monitor Team. Provides radiation monitoring capability and equipment to personnel performing rescue, first aid, and firefighting.

(5) Dosimetry Team. Determines the radiation dosage of personnel by reading dosimeters and recording readings.

(6) Clothing Decontamination Team. Retrieves contaminated clothing from personnel decontamination stations and determines its reusability. Delivers clothing to decontamination stations and returns it to the clothing supply team.

(7) Nuclear Accident Team. Provides assistance to the on-scene commander and performs emergency actions that may be necessary to minimize the initial results of a nuclear accident/incident.

(8) Shelter Management Team. Provides the orderly administration of all activities related to the comfort and welfare of all inhabitants of an assigned shelter.

6. Other Units

Selected units, such as USA reserve component CBRN units, are equipped with additional resources to support casualty decontamination requirements. The mission of these units is to provide a domestic response capability for casualty decontamination in support of CM operations.

a. These units are equipped with a platoon set of domestic response style equipment (see Table G-3, page G-12) to decontaminate both ambulatory and nonambulatory casualties. The set includes a quickly erectable tent with runoff containment included for the actual decontamination, two other tents for sun protection for the workers and victims, showers for washing and rinsing, and rollers for decontaminating nonambulatory victims.

Table G-3. USA Reserve Component Platoon Equipment for Casualty Decontamination

Line	Description	Remarks	Identification Number
1	Reeves Decontamination System	1 per platoon 3 per company	DCJ-10
2	Western Shelter System	2 per platoon 6 per company	N/A
3	DRCD kit accessories	1 per company	N/A
4	ICAM	3 per platoon 9 per company	6665-01-657-8502
5	CAMSIM	1 per platoon 3 per company	6665-99-001-9985
6	Radiac meter, AN/PDR-77	1 per platoon 3 per company	6665-01-347-6100
7	Radiac meter, AN/UDR-13	5 per platoon 15 per company	6665-01-407-1237
8	Radiac meter, AN/VDR-2	1 per platoon 3 per company	6665-01-222-1425

Table G-3. USA Reserve Component Platoon Equipment for Casualty Decontamination (Continued)

Line	Description	Remarks	Identification Number
9	ACADA, M22	2 per platoon 5 per company	6665-01-438-6963
10	Carrier, litter, wheeled	2 per platoon 6 per company	6530-01-220-7186
11	PA system, portable with rechargeable battery, remote operation	2 per company	9925-01-450-0074
12	Level B suit (TYCHEM 9400, hooded)	140 per company	N/A
13	Filter canister, C2A1	140 per company	4240-01-361-1319
14	Gloves, CP, rubber, 15 mil	140 per company	8415-01-033-3519
15	Skin, hood, M40	140 per company	4240-01-413-1543
16	Hood, M40	140 per company	4240-01-376-3152
17	EMT shears, red	50 per company	N/A
18	EMT shears, black	50 per company	N/A
19	Radio, handheld	15 per company	5820-01-Z68-0002
20	Battery, rechargeable, ICAM	10 per company	N/A
21	Charger, battery, rechargeable, ICAM	2 per company	N/A
22	ACAA, simulator	Request in sets; 1 per DRCD kit	N/A
23	Chemical-agent patient decontamination, medical equipment set	1 set per 60 patients	N/A
24	Chemical-agent patient treatment, medical equipment supplies	1 set per 30 patients	N/A
25	STB (50 pounds)	See CTA	N/A
26	Cover, chemical protective wrap	See CTA	N/A

b. USA reserve units, while designed for overseas deployment, have the capability to provide domestic-response casualty decontamination (DRCD) in support of CM. These units are not designed or intended to replace functions carried out under the ICS or functions normally performed by the emergency first-responder community. Instead, these units provide additional capability as needed to support CM. They are not designed for a rapid response, but can be mobilized and deployed within days. The basic functions performed by these units include the following:

- Receive the mission, activate the mobilization plan, and initiate unit movement.
- Conduct mission assessment to develop a force packet.
- Coordinate unit movement and deployment.
- Conduct liaison operations.
- Conduct staging operations.
- Conduct incident integration operations.
- Conduct decontamination site selection, parameters, and setup.

- Receive and process casualties from a WMD event.
- Establish a triage site, and triage casualties from a WMD event.
- Provide critical medical intervention for casualties suffering from the effects of a CBRN event.
- Provide FP for individuals working within the decontamination line.
- Establish log-in site procedures.
- Establish the domestic decontamination site.
- Conduct ambulatory casualty gross decontamination.
- Conduct ambulatory casualty clothing removal and contaminant neutralization.
- Conduct ambulatory casualty rinse procedures.
- Determine the level of decontamination effectiveness on an ambulatory casualty.
- Conduct nonambulatory casualty gross decontamination.
- Conduct nonambulatory casualty clothing removal and contaminant neutralization.
- Conduct nonambulatory casualty rinse procedures.
- Determine the level of decontamination effectiveness on a nonambulatory casualty.
- Receive personal property and equipment for decontamination.
- Establish a personal property and equipment line, and perform decontamination procedures.
- Determine the level of decontamination effectiveness on personal items and equipment.
- Establish and maintain a hazardous waste site in support of casualty decontamination.
- Establish and maintain a contaminated water collection site in support of casualty decontamination.
- Conduct hazardous wastewater sampling to determine neutralization effectiveness.
- Control runoff of contaminated water in support of casualty decontamination.
- Conduct rehabilitation procedures.
- Sustain operations during inclement weather or limited visibility.
- Conduct the unit recovery mission.
- Conduct the postincident debriefing.

THIS PAGE IS INTENTIONALLY LEFT BLANK.

Appendix H

DECONTAMINATION KITS, APPARATUSES, AND EQUIPMENT

1. Background

Table H-1 lists the decontamination equipment and materials, and Table H-2 (page H-2) lists detection equipment and materials. Various materials and equipment are used in decontamination operations. Some are simple to use and are readily available to personnel. Others are very complex to use and are available only to specially trained teams.

Table H-1. Decontamination Equipment and Materials

Item and Description	Use	Limitations
Individual		
Decontaminating kit, skin, M291 SDK (20 kits per box)	To decontaminate your skin completely, through physical removal, absorption, and neutralization of toxic agents without long-term effects. NOTE: Use this kit for both actual combat and training purposes.	The M291 is for external use only. **WARNING** Keep decontamination powder out of eyes, cuts, or wounds. It could slightly irritate the skin or eyes.
Decontaminating kit, individual equipment, M295, IEDK	To decontaminate your chemical protective gloves, mask, hood, overboots, LCE, and weapon.	**WARNING** Do not use for skin decontamination. Keep off the skin and out of wounds, eyes, and mouth.
Battalion Decontamination Crew and Chemical Company		
SDS, M100. Each M100 consists of two 0.7-lb packs of reactive sorbent powder, two applicators, a carrying case, and two straps	To perform immediate decontamination of equipment, vehicles, and crew-served weapons. NOTE: Use this kit for both actual combat and training purposes.	Do not use on sensitive items. The operating temperature is -25°F to 120°F. **WARNING** Do not use for skin decontamination. Keep off the skin and out of wounds, eyes, and mouth.
Decontaminating apparatus, power-driven, skid-mounted, multipurpose, integral, 500-gallon, M12A1 PDDA. The apparatus includes a pump unit, tank unit, and M2 water heater (all mounted on skids).	To spray decontaminating agents, STB slurries and solutions, and hot, soapy water rinses during field decontamination operations. To pump water or foam to fight fires, deice items, wash vehicles, and pump various fluids.	Do not use with defoliants, herbicides, or insecticides.

Table H-1. Decontamination Equipment and Materials (Continued)

Item and Description	Use	Limitations
Battalion Decontamination Crew and Chemical Company (Continued)		
Decontaminating system, lightweight, M17 LDS, NSN 4230-01-251-8702. The M17 is a portable pump and water-heating unit for producing hot water and steam. The system incorporates a 1,580- to 3,000-gallon collapsible water tank, two wand assemblies, and connecting hoses.	To perform operational and thorough decontamination of vehicles and equipment. To provide troop showers, as necessary.	None
MPDS. The system includes one high-pressure hose, two high-temperature hoses, a lance-and-gun assembly, and a 3,000-gallon collapsible water tank.	To perform operational and thorough decontamination of vehicles and equipment.	None
FSDS. This system includes a pump unit and a bulk decontaminant tank. The system includes a spray bar for terrain decontamination, a deck gun for fixed-site equipment, and a spray hose.	To perform fixed-site and terrain decontamination. To perform operational and thorough decontamination of vehicles and equipment.	None

Table H-2. Detection Equipment and Materials

Item and Description	Use	Limitations
Paper, chemical agent, detector, M8. The paper is issued in a book of 25 sheets, perforated for easy removal. A color comparison bar chart is printed on the inside front cover.	To detect the presence of liquid V, G, and H chemical agents.	It cannot be used to detect vapors or chemical agents in water or petroleum products. It may give false readings.
Paper, chemical agent, detector, M9. The paper is issued in a 7-ounce dispenser box that contains one 30-foot roll of 2-inch-wide detector paper and plastic storage bags. The paper has an adhesive back for attaching to equipment and clothing.	To detect the presence of liquid V, G, and H chemical agents.	It cannot be used to detect vapors or chemical agents in water. It will not stick to dirty, oily, or greasy surfaces. Contamination indications cannot be read under a red light or by a color-blind soldier. The following can cause false readings: • Temperatures above 125°F. • Brake fluid. • Aircraft cleaning compound. • DS2. • Petroleum products. • Insect repellent.

Table H-2. Detection Equipment and Materials (Continued)

Item and Description	Use	Limitations
ACAA, M22	To detect chemical nerve agents in the air.	**WARNING** Radiation hazard—contains beta emitters.
ACAA, M8A1. It can be vehicle-mounted, backpacked, or ground-emplaced.	To detect chemical nerve agents in the air.	**WARNING** Radiation hazard—contains Americium (AM241).
ICAM	To detect nerve- and blister-agent vapors. To search out areas; to search and locate contamination on personnel, equipment, ship's structure, aircraft, land vehicles, buildings, and terrain; and to monitor for the effectiveness of decontamination. Can also be used for monitoring collective protection.	It is a point monitor only. It cannot give an assessment of the vapor hazard over an area from one position. It can only report conditions at the front of the inlet probe. **WARNING** Beta radiation hazard.
Detector kit, chemical agent, M256A1. It contains M8 detector paper for liquid agents and samplers/detectors for vapors.	To detect liquid G, V, and H chemical agents using M8 detector paper and to detect and determine the type of vapor (G, V, H, and AC) using samplers and detectors.	None
Radiac set, AN/VDR-2. The instrument consists of a radiac meter with an internal sensor for obtaining dose rates during both mounted and dismounted operations. It has a second sensor housed in a probe and attached to the radiac meter with a cable and input connector. The radiac set uses a pre-settable, an audible, and a visual warning device integral to the radiac meter. The system is air-transportable and organic to all units.	To measure gamma radiation dose rates from 0.01 µGy/hr to 100 Gy/hr. To detect and display the level of beta particle dose rates from 0.1 µGy/hr to 5 cGy/hr. To measure, store, and display accumulated dose rates from 0.01 µGy to 9.99 Gy. To monitor personnel, supplies, and equipment.	None
Computer indicator, radiac, CP696/PDR-75; detector, radiac/ DT236/PDR-75; radiac set, AN/PDR-75	To measure the accumulated neutron and gamma radiation dose recorded by the DT236. A person who may become exposed to radiation from tactical nuclear weapons wears the DT236 on his wrist.	None

Table H-2. Detection Equipment and Materials (Continued)

Item and Description	Use	Limitations
Radiac set, AN/UDR-13	Measures gamma radiation only and provides total dose or dose rate. It will replace the IM-93/UD dosimeter.	None
DOD biological sampling kit	Provides presumptive identification for a limited number of biological agents.	Not to be used as single means of identification. The sampling kit should never be used for diagnostic purposes.
ADM-300	Detects, measures, and digitally displays dose and dose rate levels of beta and gamma radiation.	None
Water testing kit, M272	Detects and identifies CW agents in raw or treated water sources.	None

2. Decontamination Devices for Personnel

Decontamination devices for personnel are the warfighter's first defense against contamination on the skin. They are an integral part of immediate decontamination.

    a.   M291 SDK.

        (1)   Users: All services and components.

        (2)   Description. The M291 kit (Figure H-1) consists of six identical packets that contain a mixture of activated resins. This resin mixture adsorbs and neutralizes liquid chemical agents present on an individual's skin and neutralizes agents. The mixture consists of an adsorbent resin, a resin containing sulfonic acid, and a hydroxylamine-containing resin. The black powder residue will provide a visual confirmation of the thoroughness of application and will not cause any skin irritation even after prolonged contact with skin. However, normal precautions must be observed so that the powder does not enter open wounds, the mouth, or the eyes. This kit will also be used for training; no training aid will be produced. The issue is 20 M291 SDKs per box.

        (3)   Mission. The M291 is used to decontaminate the skin, mask hood, and protective gloves. After masking, the individual opens a packet from the kit, removes the applicator pad, and applies an even coating of resin powder while scrubbing the entire skin area suspected to be contaminated.

        (4)   Capabilities. One applicator pad will decontaminate both hands and the face if necessary. If the face must be decontaminated, the neck (including the throat area) and the ears must also be decontaminated using a second applicator pad. The black powder resin will provide a visual confirmation of the thoroughness of application and will not cause any skin irritation even after prolonged contact with skin.

Figure H-1. M291 Skin Decontamination Kit

b. RSDL.

(1) Users. All services and components.

(2) Description. RSDL is a broad-spectrum liquid CW agent decontaminant that will remove and destroy military chemical agents on contact. After CW agent destruction, RSDL leaves a nontoxic residue that may be washed off with water. It does not need to be removed immediately. RSDL is safe for use on all intact skin surfaces and for limited duration use in the eyes. RSDL reacts rapidly, providing the full removal and destruction of CW agents within 2 minutes, enabling efficient decontamination of casualties. The RSDL kit is fielded with three kits per package.

(3) Mission. The RSDL is used to decontaminate intact skin only. It is impregnated in a sponge pad and packaged as a single unit in a heat-sealed foil pouch. When exposed to CW agents, the user wipes the exposed skin with the lotion.

(4) Capabilities. RSDL acts within seconds of being applied to the skin, neutralizing the toxicity of chemical agents by breaking down their molecules. Apply the lotion within 1 minute of contamination. The lotion is effective against cutaneous nerve and blister agents, such as mustard, GB, and VX.

3. Decontamination Devices for Equipment

Decontamination devices are used for all levels of equipment decontamination (e.g., immediate, operational, and thorough).

a. M295 IEDK.

(1) Users. All services and components.

(2) Description. The M295 kit (see Figure H-2, page H-6) provides a means to decontaminate individual equipment through physical removal and absorption of chemical agents, with no long-term harmful side effects. The M295 consists of four individual wipe-down mitts—each enclosed in a protective packet. Each wipe-down mitt consists of a decontaminating powder contained within a pad material. When used, the sorbent powder from the mitt flows freely through the pad material. The M295 allows for the decontamination of individual equipment, such as gloves, footwear, weapon, helmet, and LBE through physical removal and sorption of chemical agents. The residue of the powder

shows where the powder has been used or, more importantly, what areas have not been decontaminated.

Figure H-2. M295 IEDK

(3) Mission. The M295 kit is used to decontaminate the individual's personal equipment (i.e. protective gloves, mask, hood, NBC overboots, helmet, LBE, and weapon). Each packet consists of a decontamination mitt filled with 22 grams of the decontaminant compound, 20 M295 kits are packed in a fiberboard-shipping container.

b. M100 SDS.

(1) Users: All services and components.

(2) Description. The M100 SDS (Figure H-3) uses a reactive sorbent powder to remove and neutralize chemical agents from surfaces. The use of the M100 SDS decreases decontamination time and eliminates the need for water. Each M100 SDS consists of two 0.7-pound packs of reactive sorbent powder, two wash mitt type sorbent applicators, a case, straps, and detailed instructions. An optional chemical-resistant mounting bracket is also available. The sorbent decontamination system provides a simple, rapid, and efficient system to decontaminate small and individual issue items. The sorbent is used during the operator's wipe-down portion of immediate decontamination on surfaces that personnel must touch or contact to operate the equipment, such as door handles, crew-served weapons, etc. The sorbent powder is applied to the mitt or flat surfaces prior to decontaminating. The M100 SDS is not classified as a hazardous material and, therefore, can be shipped through normal transport processes.

(3) Mission. The M100 replaces the M11/M13 DAP and associated decontamination solution number 2 (DS2) used in operator wipe down (immediate decontamination) with a reactive, neutralizing sorbent powder.

Figure H-3. M100 SDS

4. Power-Driven Decontamination Systems

Power-driven decontamination systems provide a myriad of decontamination capabilities to the warfighter. The most significant capability of these systems is their ability to dispense high-pressure water for the physical removal of contamination.

    a.   M17 LDS.

        (1)   Users. USA, USMC, and USAF.

        (2)   Description. The M17 is a portable decontamination system. It consists of a 7.3-horsepower engine (Figure H-4, page H-8), a self-priming pump for drawing and pressurizing water, a fan assembly to deliver combustion air to the heater, a water heater with a coil of tubing 90 feet (27.45 meters) long, a self-priming pump for the heater fuel system, and a small generator to supply electricity for ignition and safety control functions. The M17 LDS includes diesel and gas fuel-powered systems.

        (3)   Mission. The M17 dispenses high-volume, low-pressure, hot or cold water for the removal of gross contamination. It is used to support operational decontamination missions.

        (4)   Capabilities. The M17—

        (a)   Is transportable by a 3/4-ton trailer, 5/4-ton cargo trucks, cargo aircraft, and helicopters (sling load).

        (b)   Provides pressurized water at temperatures up to 248°F (119.88°C) at a rate of up to 9 gallons (34.06 liters) per minute.

        (c)   Draws water from a natural source up to 30 feet (9.15 meters) away and 9 feet (2.75 meters) below pump level. There is an additional 3,000-gallon (113.55 hectoliter) water storage tank in the event a natural source of water is not available.

Figure H-4. M17 LDS

 b. Multipurpose Decontamination System.

  (1) Users. USA.

  (2) Description. The MPDS (Figure H-5) is a lightweight, modular decontamination system.

  (3) Mission. The MPDS decontaminates material with aqueous solutions in support of operational or thorough decontamination operations.

  (4) Capabilities. The MPDS provides—

   (a) Material decontamination with aqueous solutions or hot-foam treatment.

   (b) Equipment decontamination with dry steam.

   (c) Personnel decontamination by supplying warm water to shower systems.

   (d) Multiple operating modes: cold water, hot water, steam, and dry steam.

   (e) Engine winter start capability to -30°C (-22°F).

   (f) Self-priming, high-pressure pump for water intake from all water sources, including seawater.

   (g) Water flow and pressure that are infinitely adjustable.

   (h) Automatic protection against calcification.

   (i) Single fuel system.

Figure H-5. MPDS

c. M12A1 Power-Driven Decontamination Apparatus.

(1) Users. USA.

(2) Description. The M12A1 consists of a 500-gallon tank, a pumper unit, and an M2 water heater. Each unit is mounted on a skid base. Power for operating the equipment is supplied by the pump unit, which uses a 20-horsepower military standard gasoline or diesel engine to drive a centrifugal pump and a 28-volt direct current generator. The M2 water heater is electrically connected through a main power cable to a generator in the pump unit. A personnel shower assembly stowed on the tank unit in disassembled form can be readily assembled in varying configurations to shower up to 24 personnel at one time.

(3) Mission. The M12A1 is used to support thorough, operational, and terrain decontamination missions.

(4) Capabilities. The M12A1—

(a) Is used to spray water, STB slurry, and other decontaminants.

(b) May be used for firefighting and spraying water.

d. Fixed-Site Decontamination System (FSDS).

(1) Users. USA.

(2) Description.

(a) The FSDS (Figure H-6, page H-10) is a compressed-air, foam-generating system, consisting of a pump and bulk decontaminant tank that can be mounted on a commercial vehicle or trailer. The system may be used in three different modes: a spray bar is mounted at the rear of the trailer for terrain decontamination, a deck gun is mounted in the truck bed for fixed-site equipment and facility decontamination, and a foam dispensing nozzle with a 100-foot spray hose is mounted on the trailer for direct decontaminant application and to supplement deck gun operations.

NOTE: Decontaminant in "foam" form is not authorized for use at this time. DF 200 is currently approved for CENTCOM use only.

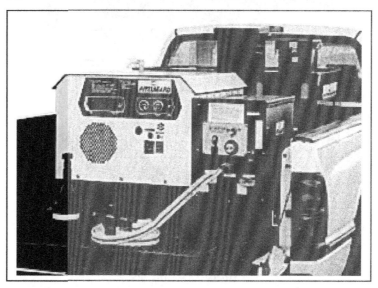

Figure H-6. FSDS Placed in a Civilian Vehicle

(b) The systems primary decontaminant is DF 200.

(3) Mission. The primary function of the FSDS is to provide a decontamination capability for APODs and SPODs. The system also provides the capability to perform decontamination on main supply routes (MSRs), vehicles, equipment, and aircraft. Inherent in the mission to decontaminate APODs and SPODs is the requirement to decontaminate staging areas, runways, roads, buildings, and container expresses (CONEXs). Each of these areas requires different approaches, configurations, and planning factors. (See paragraph 5 for the TTP to support FSDS operations.)

(4) Capabilities. The FSDS provides—

- Mobile terrain decontamination.
- Fixed-site and facility decontamination.
- Equipment decontamination.

5. Fixed-Site Decontamination System Tactics, Techniques, and Procedures

Three individuals (supervisor, driver, and spray cannon/wand operator) man the system. The system has three modes of operation: spray bar at the rear of the trailer, deck gun on the truck bed, and 100-foot spray hose on the trailer. Only one mode of operation is possible at one time. To decontaminate horizontal surfaces (staging areas, docks, and roads) the rear spray bar is the primary mode of operation. To decontaminate buildings, structures, and containers, the deck gun is the primary mode. The spray hose will be used to augment the deck gun and also will be available for smaller areas, vehicles, and aircraft and to perform self-decontamination of the system.

The primary decontaminant is DF 200. DF 200 is supplied as a three-part solution: Part A, Part B and Part C activator. The system is configured with a trailer that contains three separate storage tanks for the solution. There are two 500-gallon tanks, one each for Parts A and B, and a 30-gallon tank for Part C. Tank C pours directly into Tank B so activation occurs prior to mixing of Parts A and B. Tank C should be released prior to movement in order for Parts B and C to get mixed well. The system mixes the solutions as it operates and, therefore, premixing of the solutions is not required. The system can be filled and standing ready without the need to perform the loading after the mission is received. This allows for a quick response when a mission must be performed.

a. Mission Receipt.

(1) The planner determines the surface composition of the contaminated area in order to determine the effects on the mission (i.e., absorption and desorption rate, reaction of surface with decontaminant, concerns of contaminant transfer due to uncontrolled runoff).

(2) The planner determines the extent of the contamination in order to identify the quantity of required decontamination applicators. Table H-3 identifies the capability of one system with a 1,000-gallon load of DF 200. The planner also determines the extent of the contamination, which will determine the resupply quantities required.

Table H-3. Typical Mission Parameters (1,000 gallons of DF 200)

Contaminated Areas	Time	Speed	Coverage
Roads, runways, and staging areas	18 minutes	2–3 mph	25,000 square feet

(3) The planner identifies any additional requirements (i.e., additional pumps, detectors, and nonstandard equipment).

(4) The planner assesses the weather conditions (temperature, precipitation, and winds) and determines how they may affect the mission. The assessment will also evaluate whether the mission must be adjusted based on the conditions. For example, extreme heat may cause the contaminant to dissipate faster than a thorough decontamination operation can be completed, so a limited area may be decontaminated to maintain operations until weathering effects are complete.

(5) The planner determines the entry and exit routes. The locations of the routes depend on factors such as the locations of the contamination and the threat. Additionally, multiple start points may be used because two FSDSs can be used at the same time.

(6) The planner determines support requirements (e.g., engineer, logistical, security, and other assets) needed to safely complete the mission.

b. Mission Preparation.

(1) Dispatch resupply vehicles, and coordinate the supply linkup location.

(2) Determine IPE requirements, and request resupply quantities of all IPE and other expendable items and equipment.

c. Precombat Checks.

(1) Individual Equipment. Inspect IPE, to include M40 protective mask and filter, BDO or JSLIST, overboots, gloves, wet-weather gear, and TAP aprons.

(2) FSDS. Conduct preventive-maintenance checks and services (PMCS), and fill fuel and decontaminant tanks. Load Tank A with Solution A, or load Tank B with Solution B, and fill Tank C with the fortifier. Ensure that the washer fluid reservoir is topped off, and load extra wiper fluid and wiper blades. Also ensure that wet wipes are on board for the gunner to use to wipe DF 200 residue off his protective mask eye lenses.

(3) Weapons. Ensure that all individual and crew-served weapons are serviceable and that ammunition has been issued to all personnel.

(4) Communications System of the FSDS. Ensure that PMCS has been performed on all communications systems. Obtain call signs and frequencies, and load communications security into all systems. If nonsecure communication devices are used (handheld, etc.), make communications checks with all personnel. Radios must have earpieces and microphones that can operate under the mask hood. The primary communications contact in a vehicle must be the driver; the vehicle commander, once dismounted, will not have access to interior communications systems.

(5) Convoy Route. Brief all personnel on the convoy route and the type of road march to be conducted.

(6) Support Requirements. Ensure that any external support elements are integrated into the mission (e.g., security).

(7) Coordination. Although the FSDS has the ability to decontaminate itself, decontamination support may have to be coordinated to ensure that the FSDSs are decontaminated thoroughly upon completion of the assigned mission in preparation for subsequent missions.

d. Mission Execution.

(1) As the systems depart the starting point, the fortifier in Tank C will be released into Tank B. During the convoy, the fortifier will be thoroughly mixed with Solution B. When the squad reaches the RP, the DF 200 will be ready for decontamination operations.

(2) Upon arrival at the identified site, the FSDS supervisor will direct the driver to stop prior to entering the contaminated area and will start the FSDS in the trailer. Once the supervisor and the spray operator exit the vehicle and the mission starts, they will not reenter the vehicle until the unit has been decontaminated. They should don either TAP aprons or wet-weather gear prior to entering the contaminated area.

(3) The FSDS will proceed down the road/MSR at approximately 2 to 3 miles per hour while the spray bar dispenses DF 200. The driver will place the vehicle in four-wheel drive, low and allow the vehicle to move while idling.

(4) Any obstacles encountered while conducting spray operations (vehicles, debris, etc.) will also be sprayed with decontamination solution so that they may be safely removed after the contamination has been neutralized. The operator at the system controls may have to stop the vehicle, turn off the spray bar, and spray this equipment with the

hose or deck gun. If two systems are available, one may be used to spray the equipment and obstacles while the second is used to spray surfaces.

(5) The contamination will be approached from the upwind direction, and the area will be decontaminated in 10-feet-wide slices. Multiple systems may work in tandem, each covering a 10-foot swath, ensuring that the swaths overlap and result in full coverage. Since the system operates at a slow speed (2 to 3 mph), the driver must maintain close attention to the trailer. If the spray pattern does not overlap, the contamination will remain. The slow speed increases the time it takes to return to the correct pattern. For example, Figure H-7 indicates two systems conducting terrain decontamination.

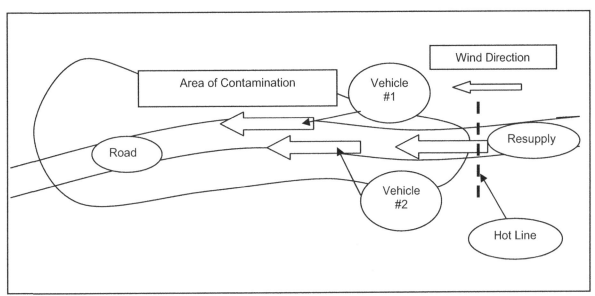

Figure H-7. Two FSDSs Conducting Terrain Decontamination

(a) When operating in tandem, the drivers must ensure that spray patterns overlap. Driving the low speed required can cause the vehicle to drift, and if full overlap is not obtained, the area not covered must be resprayed. The vehicle supervisor or gunner should walk alongside the vehicle as it proceeds and ensure that overlap occurs by communicating the progress to the driver. Figure H-8 (page H-14) shows FSDS operations conducting terrain decontamination operations that overlap.

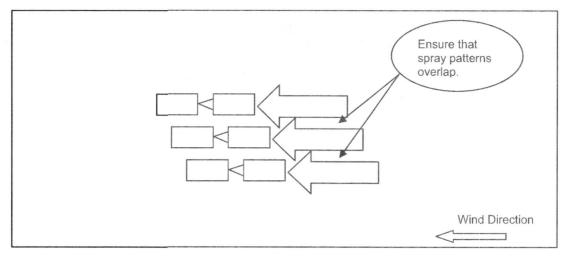

Figure H-8. FSDS Overlap Operation

(b) The CBRN decontamination unit must establish an overwatch position and control decontamination operations. The decontamination control point (DCP) (Figure H-9) is the primary location to observe progress and control resupply operations. Since all contaminated situations are different, the leadership can determine if planned resupply operations will be sufficient to complete the mission.

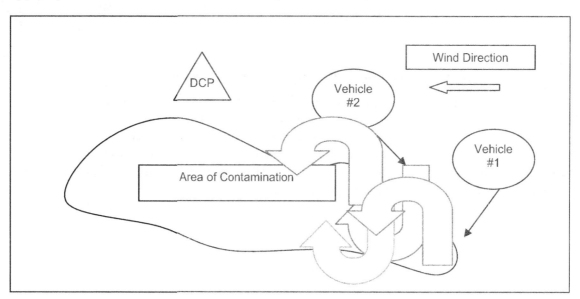

Figure H-9. Decontamination Control Point

(c) Obstacles or objects (such as vehicles, equipment, debris, or buildings) will be sprayed with the deck gun or spray hose as they are reached. If several systems are used, one can be identified as a deck gun/spray hose applicator while the other concentrates on horizontal surfaces.

(d) If multiple systems are used, they can work in relays; as one is spraying, the second can be conducting resupply. Application will progress through the contamination as vehicles resupply and continue where the last application finished. In this case, multiple vehicles will reduce the time it takes to complete decontamination. Resupply vehicles should remain upwind of the contaminated area. Figure H-10 demonstrates how resupply vehicles will approach the hazard area and not cross into that area.

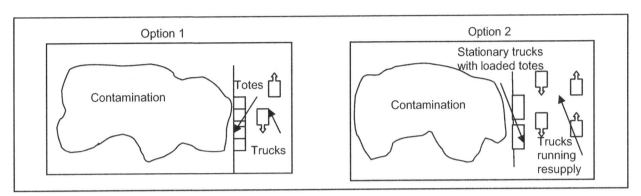

Figure H-10. Resupply COAs (Options 1 and 2)

 e. Resupply COAs.

  (1) Option 1. Five-ton or larger trucks drop totes (i.e., supplies) at a hot line near the contaminated area. This method should be used primarily if a good estimate of the amount of decontaminant needed can be determined.

  (2) Option 2. A 5-ton truck with a forklift conducts a tank exchange at a hot line. Another forklift would be needed at the supply issue point. This method can be used if unit leadership feels that there may be a need for resupply during the mission. Resupply for the system should be conducted in such a manner that the supply vehicles remain clean. The supply vehicles move to the resupply point located upwind of the contaminated area. A hot line will be established, and supply vehicles will not move downwind from that line. Totes will be dropped based on the estimated requirements determined during a recon of the contaminated area. Once the mission is completed, resupply trucks, hoses, and totes will be contaminated and will need to be decontaminated. If accurate estimates of DF 200 requirements can be made, the DF 200 can be pre-positioned and the resupply trucks should not need decontamination.

 f. Large-Area Missions. Large-area missions (such as airfields, staging areas, assembly areas, APODs, and SPODs) will be treated in a similar manner as MSR and runways. Decontamination personnel will recon the area and develop a plan to cover the contaminated surfaces with decontamination solution as depicted in Figure H-11 (page H-16).

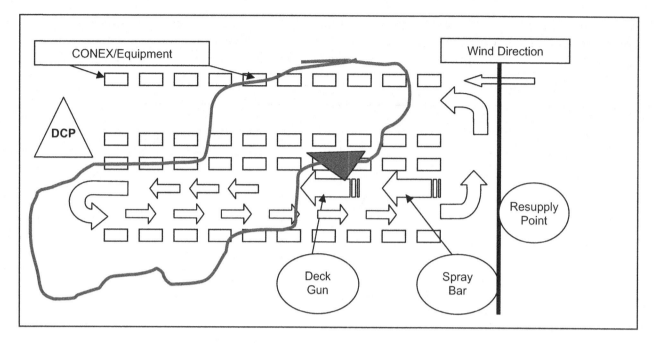

Figure H-11. Large-Area Missions

g. **Building and Vertical Surfaces.** Ascertain the wind direction to determine the start point for decontamination operations (start upwind). Determine areas where runoff from decontamination will occur, and apply additional decontamination solution in these areas to reduce agent concentrations. The order of application will be from the top down and from left to right. Attention must be made to entry or exit points and any areas where contamination could collect, such as around ventilation equipment and heating and cooling equipment. When operating the hose reel, ensure that two personnel are available to reel in the hose (see Figure H-12).

h. Safety and Coordination.

(1) When operating the spray cannon or spray wand, the operator must keep a supply of wipes available to continuously clear the mask eye lenses. The vehicle commander should also keep wipes available to assist the driver by cleaning the vehicle windows if necessary.

(2) When operating the spray wand, careful coordination must be made between the tank commander (TC), system controls operator, and the spray operator. When pressure is introduced to the hose, the operator must be aware that the pressure can be very powerful and could cause injury.

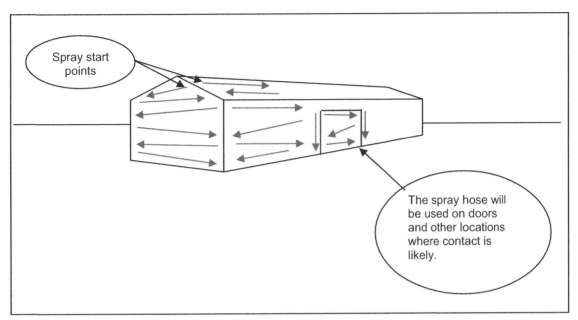

Figure H-12. Hose Reel Operation (Two-Person)

i. Postmission Actions.

(1) Interior decontamination of the vehicle should begin immediately upon completion of the mission. Interior seat covers and other interior covers must be removed and bagged as contaminated waste. If a crew member exits the vehicle, he should not reenter the interior until the mission is complete. This prevents the spread of contamination. If the crew member must reenter the vehicle, the SDS kit should be used to decontaminate gloves, boots, and contact areas.

(2) When all contaminated areas have been decontaminated, the FSDS will move toward the hot line at the upwind location of the contamination and commence standard equipment and troop decontamination operations. A thorough equipment decontamination and DTD site will be established, and all equipment and soldiers will process through the site.

NOTE: It has not been determined if a complete decontamination of the truck is possible.

(3) Security personnel must ensure that all access to the contaminated area is denied until sufficient contact time between the decontaminant and contaminant is achieved to guarantee the neutralization of the agent. Security personnel will remain upwind of the contamination and restrict entry until the area is determined to be uncontaminated. Following a mission, the FSDS hoses should be purged and all tanks drained.

(4) The unit should prepare an NBC4 report and send it to higher HQ and adjacent units.

THIS PAGE IS INTENTIONALLY LEFT BLANK.

Appendix I
TERRAIN DECONTAMINATION

1. Background

a. Most terrain surfaces (excluding unpainted metal and glass) absorb agents. Thus, an agent may be transferred to clothing or skin by physical contact. The agent may also be transferred through vaporization and subsequent inhalation or diffusion into eyes and clothing. The decontamination of terrain allows personnel to increase stay time in an area and provides passage through an area. Large-scale terrain decontamination requires extensive amounts of equipment, material, and time. Thus, terrain decontamination is limited to areas of critical importance. Contaminated areas that can be avoided need no decontamination other than weathering. If they must be used, decontamination may be necessary. Wear PPE or IPE when decontamination is not practical.

b. Terrain decontamination may be accomplished using several methods. The most effective techniques for terrain decontamination are the natural methods (weathering or aging). Using standard decontaminants should be a last resort. It will quickly exhaust your resources. Usually, the most practical method is to scrape contaminated surfaces. Fire is an acceptable method; however, consideration must be given to the potential downwind vapor hazard. If possible, a contaminated area should be evacuated until time and weather remove the contaminant. STB slurry can be used for vital areas.

c. Terrain decontamination provides more long-term than short-term benefit. Generally, terrain cannot be decontaminated well enough to allow a reduction of MOPP level right away. At best, the decontamination process may help speed the weathering process. Terrain decontamination can be so expensive and so ineffective that the commander may consider not doing it.

d. If the commander decides to conduct terrain decontamination, a limited amount will probably be conducted. Planning may result in building a causeway or breaching a path through the contamination for entry or exit into a major facility. Movement restriction will apply to those personnel who must work. Remain in MOPP. If possible, the contaminated area should be evacuated.

2. Terrain Decontamination Methods

There are various methods for terrain decontamination. The type of contamination present will determine the decontamination method used. These methods are listed in the order of decreasing effectiveness. Although terrain decontamination can reduce the contact hazard, terrain decontamination will probably not prevent hazardous vapors desorbing from chemically contaminated surfaces. Therefore, appropriate protective measures must still be taken.

a. **Weathering.** Weathering is the simplest and easiest form of decontamination.

(1) CB Contamination. Warm, windy weather can significantly reduce terrain contamination. In some cases, this occurs in a few hours, but it may take a few days. Many variables affect the persistency of CB hazards, so it is impossible to accurately predict how long it takes CB contamination to weather. Sunlight is especially effective against most biological agents.

(2) Radiological Contamination. Although the term "weathering" is used to describe the decontamination process, weather has little effect on radiological hazards. Heavy rain and wind may remove some contamination, but only time will reduce the radiation emanating from the contamination.

b. Removing or Covering. Removing or covering contamination does not destroy it, but it does keep the hazards away temporarily.

(1) CB Contamination. Contamination can be removed from paths and unpaved roadways by scraping off a layer of earth with heavy earthmoving equipment (bulldozers and road graders). Contaminated paths and paved surfaces can be covered with a 4-inch layer of earth, roofing paper, plastic sheets, or wood mats. This is a temporary measure because the agents may penetrate the covering. When the contamination penetrates the covering or when the covering is removed, the hazards will reappear. The coverings may also extend the life of the contamination hazard by reducing its exposure to air and sunlight.

(2) Radiological Contamination. Radiological contamination must be covered by thick layers of dense material (e.g., earth). Three inches of earth will decrease radiation dose rates by half because of the shielding provided by the soil; however, 12 inches is more effective. The job will be easier with earthmoving equipment, but the equipment and operators must undergo decontamination.

c. Neutralizing. The STB dry mix or STB slurry may be used effectively against CB contamination, but not against radiological contamination. Trained personnel and equipment are required when using the STB slurry, which is costly in time and material.

(1) CB Contamination. The STB dry mix is spread on solid surfaces and raked into soft surfaces like sand or earth. The STB slurry is applied to terrain by using a spray hose that is attached to an M12A1 PDDA. Operators wear TAP aprons over their MOPP gear and sit on the front fenders of a vehicle to spray the STB slurry. The speed of the vehicle should be adjusted according to the terrain; this is normally 2 to 4 miles per hour. The operators spray a fan pattern 3 to 5 feet ahead of the vehicle. The pattern overlaps on the center and extends past both sides of the vehicle. The STB slurry forms a seal over the surface and must be renewed periodically due to deterioration from traffic or weathering. One load of STB slurry will decontaminate a concrete surface about 328 by 33 feet. Other surfaces may require more decontaminants. It takes about an hour to load and mix one load of STB slurry.

(2) Radiological Contamination. The STB dry mix and STB slurry have no effect on radiological contamination or its hazards.

d. Burning. Burning works well against CB-contaminated vegetation, but it is of no value against radiological contamination.

(1) CB Contamination. Fuel may be used to burn grass or short undergrowth. Burning also works on dirt surfaces. Soak the area with diesel fuel, kerosene, or fuel oil and ignite remotely. Do not use gasoline; it burns too quickly. Burning will cause vapor hazards downwind, and protective measures will have to be used by downwind units. Area commanders must warn these units of the vapor hazards.

(2) Radiological Contamination. Radiological-contaminated surfaces should not be burned. Burning will not destroy radiological contamination or its hazards. It may

spread contamination if radioactive particles become suspended in smoke spread by the wind.

 e. Exploding. Explosives can be used to blow up areas that have CB contamination; however, they are of no value against radiological contamination.

  (1) CB Contamination. Detonating cord, bangalore torpedoes, or mine-clearing charges may be used with the STB dry mix to clear small paths through a contaminated area. The two methods are used as follows:

   (a) First Method. Remove the holding band, and loosen the lid of the bleach drum. Set the drum with the lid in place upside down over about 3 feet of looped detonation cord. Remove the drum, and leave the bleach piled on the lid as shown in Figure I-1, A. Lids may be fired in a series with a single strand of detonation cord connecting the loops.

   (b) Second Method. Remove the holding band, and loosen the lid of the bleach drum. Set the drum in a shallow hole as shown in Figure I-1, B. Make sure the lid is loose. Use 5 feet of looped detonating cord (7 feet in soft ground) for each drum. The drums may be fired individually or in a series. For gross contamination, additional firings may be necessary.

   (c) For either emplacement method, the suggested spacing for charges is 33 feet apart for a 100-foot front contaminated area. The charges should be placed along the upwind edge of the contaminated area (see Figure I-1, C). Drums may be fired individually or in a series.

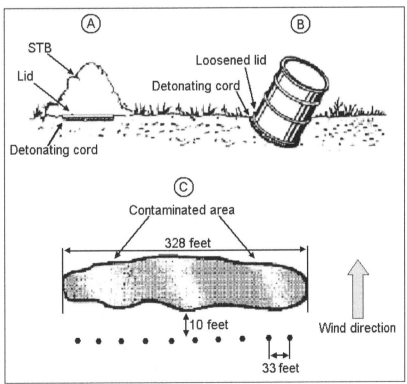

Figure I-1. Decontamination by Exploding

  (2) Radiological Contamination. Explosives will not destroy radiological contamination or its hazards.

f. Flushing. Flushing with large quantities of water removes contamination. A pressurized stream of hot, soapy water delivered by the M12A1 PDDA, M17 LDS, or fire trucks can remove significant amounts of an agent. Scrubbing removes even more agent.

(1) CB Contamination. Flushing is not very effective against some kinds of agents, especially thickened agents. However, flushing may speed up the weathering process.

(2) Radiological Contamination. Flushing is very effective for removing loose radioactive contamination such as fallout. Rainout, however, can coat surfaces with a film that resists flushing. Such films must not be scrubbed. Any contamination removed by flushing and scrubbing will remain radioactive, so control the runoff.

NOTE: Use the lid of an STB drum as a plunger to push STB into the air. Use a 1-meter length of detonation cord and form a loop smaller than the drum lid. Place the loop on the ground. Loosen the lid of an STB drum. Hold the lid in place while turning the drum upside down, and set it over the loop. Remove the drum (the decontaminant will be piled on top of the lid). Use the decontaminant drum as a makeshift mortar. The top end of the drum must be pointed in the direction you wish to propel the decontaminant. Position the drum by digging a shallow hole to hold and point the drum. Place a 1½-meter loop of detonation cord in the bottom of the hole (2 meters in soft soil). Loosen the holding band on the drum, loosen the lid, and set the drum upside down in the shallow hole.

g. Clearing. To clear passageways, remove the contaminated layers covering the terrain.

(1) CB Contamination. Most liquid chemical agents will not penetrate the soil more than 2 inches, and biological agents penetrate even less. Earthmoving equipment or hand tools can be used to scrap aside contamination. By scraping off 2 to 4 inches of earth, a passageway can be created that is free of transfer hazards. However, contamination on either side of the passageway will continue to present a vapor hazard.

(2) Radiological Contamination. Fallout does not penetrate the top layer of soil unless it is followed by rain. It can be scraped aside. Move contaminated soil as far away as possible; the piles tend to concentrate radiation. Immediately below a nuclear blast area, the soil may be radioactive to a depth of 5 feet. In most cases, the decontamination of this much earth is not practical.

3. Types of Surfaces

The type of surface will influence the type of decontamination method selected. Sample decontamination methods are described for the following representative surfaces:

a. Beaches.

(1) Removing. Use earthmoving equipment or hand tools to scrape off a 5- to 10-centimeter (2- to 4-inch) layer of earth. Most liquid chemical agents will not penetrate more than 5 centimeters (2 inches) beneath the surface. Immediately below a nuclear blast area, the soil may be radioactive to a depth of 1½ meters. In such cases, decontamination is not practical.

(2) Covering. Use roofing paper, wood mats, or other covering material to furnish a protective mat for the passage of personnel.

(3) Flushing. A pump and hose may be used. The agent exposed to the surf is decontaminated by wave action. The extent of decontamination depends on the number of washings by the tide, the type of beach, the type of contamination, and the weather.

(3) Neutralizing. Spread STB over the surface, using caution on liquid agents.

b. Hard Surfaces.

(1) Flushing. If the surface is well-drained and sufficient water is available, flush the surface thoroughly with water.

(2) Neutralizing. Spray the surface with slurry from a PDDA.

c. Dirt Roads.

(1) Removing. Scrape the contamination to the side with road graders.

(2) Covering. Cover paths across the road with at least 10 centimeters (4 inches) of earth.

(3) Neutralizing. Spray the surface with STB slurry.

d. Grass and Low Vegetation.

(1) Burning. Burning is the quickest and most efficient method of decontaminating CB agents when the area is covered with grass or short undergrowth. Dry grass and dry wood burn readily; gasoline, kerosene, fuel oil, or fire bombs may be used to burn green or wet vegetation. Normally, burning a contaminated area does not completely destroy the agent and protective equipment (protective clothing and mask) must still be worn. Spreading dry mix after the vegetation has been removed by burning will reduce the hazard further. If the contamination is radiological, do not burn it. Burning will spread contamination if radioactive particles become suspended in the smoke.

(2) Exploding. Clear paths through low vegetation with detonating cord, bangalore torpedoes, or mine-clearing line charges.

THIS PAGE IS INTENTIONALLY LEFT BLANK.

Appendix J
THOROUGH DECONTAMINATION STATION CHARTS FOR SUPERVISORS AND ATTENDANTS

This appendix provides sample charts for the support of the thorough decontamination process (Figures J-1 to J-10, pages J-2 to J-11). They can be laminated and posted at each station. The charts provide the station number and instructions for the station supervisor and attendant. They are not meant to be all-inclusive and do not include setup procedures or equipment requirements, just an informative guide for station supervisors and attendants.

STATION 1
Individual Gear Decontamination

Task: Remove contamination to a negligible risk from individual gear (LCE, mask carrier, helmet, and weapon).

NOTE: Individuals wearing the JSLIST chemical protective overgarment will execute Station 1 procedures in the same manner as prescribed for the BDO.

- **Individual**
  - ___ Decontaminates his own gear by washing or scrubbing it for 6 minutes with hot, soapy water or an STB slurry.
  - ___ Decontaminates his hose and canister (M42 mask) with either hot, soapy water and a sponge or an STB slurry mix.
  - ___ Dips his gear into the clean water, rinses it for 4 minutes, hands it to the attendant, and proceeds to the next station.
- **Attendant**
  - ___ Takes the gear to the equipment checkpoint and places it on the "dirty" side of the contamination control line (engineer tape).
  - ___ Checks the gear using the appropriate detection device and procedures associated with that device.
  - ___ Recycles the gear for decontamination if residual contamination exceeds negligible risks.
  - ___ Places the gear on the clean side of the contamination control line if it passes the check.
  - ___ Carries the gear to the reissue point.

NOTE: Change the slurry mix after 20 personnel have decontaminated their gear, and change the rinse water after 10 personnel or when it appears dirty (place the waste in the sump).

Figure J-1. Sample Station 1 Checklist

STATION 2 (BDO)
Overboot and Hood Decontamination

Task: Neutralize gross contamination on overboots, lower trouser legs, the protective mask, and the hood.

- **Individual**
  - The individual walks into the shuffle pit and spreads his legs apart (double-shoulder width), bends at the waist, and uses his hands to thoroughly rub the STB dry mix or the STB slurry on his overboots and lower trouser legs.
  - Buddy 1 cuts the shoulder straps and draw cord on Buddy 2's hood if a replacement hood is available. He pulls Buddy 2's hood inside out over the front of the mask, being careful not to touch the exposed neck or head. Buddy 1 gathers Buddy 2's hood in one hand and uses a cutting tool to cut away the hood as close as possible to the eye lens outsert, voicemitter, and inlet valve cover. Make sure that nothing is left dangling below the bottom of the mask.
  - Buddy 1 decontaminates and rolls Buddy 2's hood in the same manner as for a MOPP gear exchange if a replacement hood is not available.
  - Buddy 1 and Buddy 2 reverse roles.
- **Attendant**
  - Instructs Buddy 1 on how to roll Buddy 2's hood to ensure that it is accomplished to standard.
  - Monitors the shuffle pit and adds more STB after 10 personnel have processed through it.

Figure J-2. Sample Station 2 (BDO) Checklist

> **STATION 2 (JSLIST)**
> **Overboot and Hood Decontamination**
>
> Task: Neutralize gross contamination on overboots, lower trouser legs, the protective mask, and the hood.
>
> - **Individual**
> __ The individual walks into the shuffle pit and spreads his legs apart (double-shoulder width), bends at the waist, and uses his hands to thoroughly rub the STB dry mix or the STB slurry on his overboots and lower trouser legs.
> __ Buddy 1 decontaminates his own gloves. He loosens Buddy 2's overgarment hood by unfastening the barrel lock. He then loosens the draw cord around the edge of the hood and unfastens the hook-and-pile fastener tape at the chin. Buddy 1 takes care to avoid touching Buddy 2's skin and throat area.
> __ Buddy 1 removes Buddy 2's overgarment hood by opening the front closure flap and pulling the slide fastener from the chin down to the chest. Buddy 1 instructs Buddy 2 to turn around. Buddy 1 grasps the back of Buddy 2's hood, folds the hood inside out (being careful not to contaminate the inner garment), and pulls the hood off.
> __ Buddy 1 and Buddy 2 reverse roles.
> - **Attendant**
> __ Instructs Buddy 1 on how to roll Buddy 2's hood to ensure that it is accomplished to standard.
> __ Monitors the shuffle pit and adds more STB after 10 personnel have processed through it.

Figure J-3. Sample Station 2 (JSLIST) Checklist

STATION 3 (BDO)
Overgarment Removal

Task: Remove the contaminated overgarment before the agent penetrates the material and touches the undergarments or the skin.

NOTE: Avoid touching the individual's skin or inner clothing. If contact is made, decontaminate immediately and then proceed with the overgarment removal.

Attendant
- ___ Assists the individual in removing his overgarment jacket.
- ___ Cuts and removes the M9 detector paper from around the individual's wrist.
- ___ Unfastens the hook-and-pile fastener over the jacket zipper, waist cord, and wrist.
- ___ Unfastens the back snaps and instructs the individual to make a fist.
- ___ Pulls the individual's jacket down and away from him.
- ___ Assists the individual in removing his overgarment trousers.
- ___ Cuts and removes the M9 detector paper from the individual's trousers.
- ___ Unfastens the hook-and-pile fastener straps and unzips the zipper on the cuffs of the individual's trousers.
- ___ Unfastens the front waist snaps and unzips the front zipper.
- ___ Has the individual lift one leg, point that foot down, and bend slightly at the knees for stability.
- ___ Grasps the cuff of the elevated boot, with a hand on each side, and pulls the cuff in an alternating, jerking motion until the individual can step out of the trouser leg.
- ___ Repeats the last two steps on the other leg.

NOTE: Ensure that the individual steps wide enough so that he does not rub his clean leg against the contaminated boot or overgarment.

Figure J-4. Sample Station 3 (BDO) Checklist

STATION 3 (JSLIST)
Overgarment Removal

Task: Remove the contaminated overgarment before the agent penetrates material and touches the undergarments or the skin.

NOTE: Avoid touching the individual's skin or inner clothing. If contact is made, decontaminate immediately and then proceed with the overgarment removal.

Attendant

__ Assists the individual in removing his overgarment.

__ Cuts and removes the M9 detector paper from around the individual's wrist.

__ Releases the hook-and-pile fastener tapes at the wrists and at the bottom of the trousers. Unties the bow in the coat retention cord if necessary. Unfastens the webbing-strip snaps at the bottom of the jacket and releases the coat retention cord.

__ Touching only the outside surfaces of the jacket, the attendant loosens the bottom of the jacket by pulling the material at the bottom away from the individual's body. The individual locates his trouser suspender snap couplers by feeling for them on the outside of his jacket and releases them. Unfastens the front closure flap on the front of the jacket and pulls the slide fastener from the top of the chest down to the bottom of the jacket.

__ Instructs the individual to turn around, extend his arms in front of him, and make a fist to prevent the removal of his chemical protective gloves. The attendant grasps the jacket near the shoulders and removes it by pulling it down and away from the individual's body.

NOTE: If there is difficulty removing the jacket in this manner, pull one arm out at a time.

__ Instructs the individual to turn back around. Cuts and removes the M9 paper from the individual's trousers.

__ Unfastens the hook-and-pile fastener tapes at the waistband of the trousers, unfastens the front closure snaps, and opens the fly slide fastener. Grasps the individual's trousers at the hips and pulls the trousers down to the individual's knees.

__ Has the individual lift one leg, point that foot down, and bend slightly at the knee for stability.

__ Grasps the trouser leg of the elevated foot, with a hand on each side, and pulls the trouser leg in an alternating motion until the individual can step out of it. Repeat the last two steps on the other leg.

NOTE: Ensure that the individual steps wide enough so that he does not rub his clean leg against the contaminated boot or overgarment.

Figure J-5. Sample Station 3 (JSLIST) Checklist

STATION 4
Overboot and Glove Removal

Task: Remove the contaminated overboots and gloves to limit the spread of contamination (the overboots and gloves may also be decontaminated for reissue, if serviceable).

NOTE: Individuals wearing the JSLIST chemical protective overgarment will execute Station 1 procedures in the same manner as prescribed for the BDO Station 2.

Attendant

- Use engineer tape to mark the liquid contamination control line.
- Unfastens or cut the elastic closures on the individual's overboots.
- Have the individual stand next to and face the liquid contamination control line and then step back about 12 inches from the control line.
- Step on the back of the individual's overboot and instruct him to lift his heel, work his foot out of the overboot, and step across the liquid contamination control line. Repeat the process on the other foot.
- Cut off the overboot and discard it into the designated container if it cannot be removed by this process.
- Have the attendant from Station 6 carry the individual's filter canister until the mask is removed if the individual is wearing an M42 protective mask.
- Have the individual hold the fingertips of his gloves and partially slide his hands out.
- Remove the individual's gloves.

NOTE: Check all items for holes, tears, and punctures; and discard any defective items. Do not decontaminate items that are unserviceable.

NOTE: The attendant performs his duty from the "dirty" side of the liquid contamination control line.

___ Submerge the gloves and overboots in the container of hot, soapy water, ensuring that no water remains inside when removed from the container.
___ Submerge the gloves and overboots in the STB/HTH solution and thoroughly scrub them. , Submerge each item once more after scrubbing.
___ Rinses the scrubbed items thoroughly, making sure that they are rinsed inside and out.
___ Place the usable items on a poncho or a plastic tarp to air dry.
___ Place the air-dried usable items into plastic trash bags along with an M256A1 detector kit. If the kit shows contamination remaining, recycle the items or discard them. However, if the kit shows no contamination, reuse them.

Figure J-6. Sample Station 4 Checklist

STATION 5
Monitor

Task: Identify contamination on personnel (spot decontamination capability and medical aid are provided, as required).

- **Monitor**
__ Checks the individuals for contamination using an ICAM. Liquid contamination can be detected with M8 detector paper.
__ Remonitors individuals if decontaminated.
- **Medic**
__ Checks the individuals for any chemical-agent symptoms and treats them as necessary.
- **Individual**
__ Reports any damage to their MOPP gear that was identified at Stations 2, 3, and 4.
- **Attendant**
__ Uses an SDK to decontaminate any areas identified as contaminated.

NOTE: If all the liquid contamination is absorbed into the clothing, the M8 detector paper will be negative even though there is a hazard.

NOTE: If time is not available, the NBC NCO will have replacement chemical suits, overboots, and gloves at this station for reissue. If time is available, personnel will receive this equipment at the postdecontamination AA.

Figure J-7. Sample Station 5 Checklist

STATION 6
Mask Removal

Task: Remove the mask without contaminating the individual.

- Pull the hood over the front of the mask, grab the mask by the voicemitter cover, and pull the mask off the individual while he holds his breath.
- Hold the mask open so that the individual can remove the inserts without touching the outside of the mask.
- Have the individual walk upwind approximately 5 meters, cross the vapor contamination control line, and then resume breathing.
- Bring the mask to Station 7.

NOTE: If the wind direction remains constant, no vapor hazard is expected beyond the vapor contamination control line.

- The CBRN defense unit positions the M8A1 or M22 ACAA upwind of the site.
- The individual moves straight ahead while his mask, which may still be emitting vapors, is held on the "dirty" side of the vapor contamination control line and taken to the next station.

Figure J-8. Sample Station 6 Checklist

STATION 7
Mask Decontamination Point

Task: Remove all contamination from the protective mask.

- **Attendant**
  ___ Removes the eye lens outserts and the hoods if the hoods were not cut off at Station 2.
  ___ Removes the filters or canisters and disposes of them in the properly marked containers.
  ___ Washes the masks, hoods, eye lens outserts, and hoses on the M42 and M43 masks in hot, soapy water.
  ___ Rinses these items in clean water.
  ___ Dips them in the sanitizing solution and agitates them for 5 minutes.
  ___ Rinses them in clean water again.
  ___ Adds one tube of mask-sanitizing solution (calcium hypochlorite) to each quart of water.
  ___ Wipes the masks with rags dipped in solution until the masks are almost dry.
  ___ Discards each gallon of mask-sanitizing solution into a sump after every 10 masks.
  ___ Checks the masks for contamination with an ICAM.
  ___ Recycles the masks if they are still contaminated
  ___ Decontaminates the gloves.
  ___ Takes the unassembled masks to the reissue point if they are not contaminated.

Figure J-9. Sample Station 7 Checklist

STATION 8
Reissue Point

Task: The mask with its components is provided to the individual for reassembly.

___ The unit CBRN NCO reissues the masks with their components to the individuals.
___ The individuals reassemble the masks in the AA.
___ The unit CBRN NCO affixes canisters to the cleaned M42 and M43 hoses.
___ The individuals pick up individual gear and move to the postdecontamination AA.

Figure J-10. Sample Station 8 Checklist

THIS PAGE IS INTENTIONALLY LEFT BLANK.

Appendix K
CONTAMINATED-WASTE COLLECTION AND DISPOSAL

1. Background

This appendix provides planners, commanders, and unit personnel with operational guidance and procedures on the collection and disposal of contaminated waste. The use of contamination avoidance material may increase the amount of contaminated waste that must be properly collected and disposed of after an attack. Contaminated items may include IPE, field gear, M8/M9 paper, components of M291 and M295 kits, pallet covers, bulk plastic, tarps, and other contamination avoidance covers and decontamination solutions. Waste must be collected and disposed of properly to limit hazards. Depending on the type and quantity of contaminated material, waste accumulation areas could increase local hazards and require increased protective measures. Advance planning is the key to the successful handling and disposal of contaminated waste.

2. Responsibility

It is the responsibility of all personnel to ensure safe operations.

a. Unit commanders ensure that waste collection sites are established, properly marked, reported, and maintained.

b. All personnel apply contamination avoidance techniques and procedures, establish and maintain waste collection points, and segregate wastes for localized collection. Deployed personnel are responsible for limiting, to the greatest extent possible, cross contamination, postconflict cleanup, and restoration actions.

c. The CBRN control center (CC) provides technical guidance and oversight for establishing unit contaminated waste disposal areas and marks and plots accumulation points and disposal areas on local area and grid maps.

d. Medical authorities provide technical oversight and guidance for personal safety and health-related issues.

3. Contaminated-Waste Holding Areas

It is probable that multiple sites may be required with one large centralized accumulation point.

4. Unit Waste Accumulation Points

Units must effectively plan for the disposition of waste during decontamination operations.

a. Planners should consider site selection based on a number of factors, such as terrain and prevailing seasonal winds. The area must be located downwind of work areas and rest and relief locations.

b. Accumulation points should be downwind from the rear or entrance to areas such as bunkers, fighting positions, or CCAs.

c. All unit accumulation points should be identified and reported to the CBRN CC. The CBRN CC has the responsibility to mark and plot each accumulation point on local, grid, or area maps.

d. When feasible, waste accumulation points should be located on concrete, asphalt, or other paved surfaces. Avoid positioning the accumulation point on grass or vegetated areas. Position waste accumulation points so that personnel can transverse a straight line from their shelter, bunker, or facility to the area without having to cross wet, muddy, or vegetated areas.

e. Waste should be separated by type (solid versus liquid and combustible versus noncombustible). No sharp objects that could puncture the plastic liner are to be placed directly into the waste container. Sharp objects should be packaged in a rigid waste container. Collecting sharp objects or material in a cardboard box overwrapped with a 6-mil plastic bag should prevent objects from penetrating or perforating the protective cover.

f. Proper marking prevents unintentional contact and alerts personnel of the hazard.

g. Containers holding contaminated waste must be in good condition and compatible with the waste being stored.

(1) The container must always be closed during storage, except when it is necessary to add or remove waste.

(2) Large trash receptacles, 55-gallon barrels, or similar containers are ideal vessels for collecting contaminated solid waste. These should be lined with a double layer of 6-mil plastic bags.

(3) Liquid waste can be stored in 5-gallon or larger containers. A small containment berm should be placed around any liquid-holding area to control potential runoff or spills. The use of sandbags or other suitable material should be used to construct a small containment berm.

h. If sufficient equipment exists, place automatic vapor alarms around or just upwind of the area.

(1) CBRN reconnaissance personnel should also periodically monitor just outside the area with handheld vapor detection devices such as the CAM or the M256.

(2) To indicate contamination from an attack or cross contamination, M8 or M9 paper should be positioned around the accumulation point.

5. Equipment and Material

The following items or a suitable substitute should be available for establishing and maintaining the waste accumulation point. Quantities of this material will vary based on the number of individuals and area supported.

a. Containers for solid-waste and liquid-waste streams (e.g., waste receptacle [44-gallon] National Stock Number [NSN]: 7240-00-151-6630; 5-gallon Jerri can, water, NSN: 7240-00-089-3827).

b. Marking material: NBC marking kit (sign kit, contamination, M274, NSN: 9905-01-346-4716; chemiluminescent lights, white, 8-hour, NSN: 6260-01-247-0367; surveyor's tape, red, NSN: 9905-01-458-1192; paper and grease pencils or permanent markers).

c. Plastic sheeting, 0.006 thick, clear, NSN: 8135-00-579-6489.

d. Plastic bags, 60 by 30 inches, 0.006 thick, NSN: 8150-01-221-3239.

e. Pressure-sensitive tape (multiple NSNs available).

f. Personal decontamination materials: M291 kit, NSN: 6850-01-276-1905; M295 kit, NSN: 6850-01-357-8456; 5 percent bleach; water; and bucket or catch basin.

g. CBRN detection equipment.

h. Funnel for pouring liquid waste into collection containers.

i. Sandbags, NSN: 8105-00-285-4744.

6. Procedures for the Collection of Contaminated Waste

The potential for personnel to be cross-contaminated is at its highest during the collection of contaminated material for disposal. The following activities are examples to minimize the time and effort to perform them:

a. The collection of contaminated waste should be accomplished in the least amount of time by at least two trained personnel.

b. Supervisors assign personnel trained to perform the duties to detect contamination and remove contaminated coverings in and around their area.

(1) A systematic search of the area for contamination should be planned and communicated to unit personnel.

(2) The priority for removing protective covers from unit assets must be established. Priority should be given to immediate-use items and high-value and/or limited-quantity items that directly effect mission accomplishment.

c. Prior to starting the operation, personnel must check to ensure that IPE is properly worn, using the buddy system.

d. Unit personnel must check for contamination in assigned areas.

(1) Starting with the priority items, remove and replace contaminated M8 and M9 paper and contamination avoidance material.

(2) Contaminated material collected should be placed in a 6-mil plastic bag (preferably clear plastic). When collection bags are approximately three-quarters full, personnel must seal the top of the bag closed.

(3) Place the first bag into a clean 6-mil bag. To reduce the potential of contaminating the outside of the clean bag, the assistance of a second person may be required.

(4) Perform immediate glove decontamination, utilizing M291 or M295 kits or 5 percent bleach solution (see Figure K-1, page K-4).

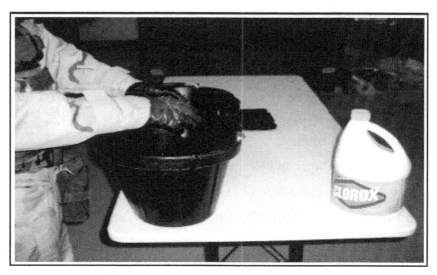

Figure K-1. Glove Decontamination

(5) Repeat the bag-sealing process for the outer (clean) bag.

(6) Perform immediate glove decontamination utilizing M291/M295 kits or 5 percent bleach solution.

(7) Prepare the material for transport to the waste accumulation point.

(8) Place contaminated markings on the outer bag. The bags must be clearly marked with the contents, type of contaminant or agent, date, time, and location (see Figure K-2).

Figure K-2. Markings

NOTE: Supervisors will contact the controlling unit for waste pickup. Waste that is not properly labeled and packaged will not be picked up until the problem is corrected.

e. Material (such as pallet covers and bulk plastic) that will not fit into standard 6-mil trash bags require a different procedure or process as follows:

(1) Starting from the long end of the material, with arms extended, grasp the bottom and roll the material onto itself. Properly done, this will contain any contamination

inside the cover or plastic, away from the individual, while reducing air pockets and the bulkiness of the material.

(2) After the material is rolled, fold the two outer ends toward the center and secure the material with tape or string so that it will not unfold or unroll.

(3) Secure and seal the material in an outer wrapping.

- If ground contamination is/was suspected, place a drop cloth on the ground to reduce the potential for cross contamination of the outer wrapper.

- Avoid kneeling on the ground.

- Place the material on a section of clean 6-mil plastic sheet, large enough to fully wrap the material.

- Perform immediate glove decontamination utilizing M291 or M295 kits or 5 percent bleach solution.

- Fold the ends of the outer wrapper toward the center, overlap the material, and secure the seams with pressure-sensitive tape.

(4) Perform immediate glove decontamination utilizing M291 or M295 kits or 5 percent bleach solution.

(5) Prepare the material for transport to the unit waste accumulation point.

(6) Place contaminated markings on the outer wrapping. The outer wrapping must be clearly marked with the contents, type of contaminant or agent, date, and time.

NOTE: Leaders will contact the unit operation center for waste pickup and transportation to the contaminated-waste site.

7. Transportation Procedures

The transportation of contaminated waste should be coordinated and controlled through the CBRN CC. This is accomplished to effectively control and account for the contaminated waste, reduce the contamination of multiple vehicles, and eliminate unnecessary risk to personnel.

a. Transporters will wear appropriate protective clothing and have personal decontamination kits immediately available.

b. Prior to starting the transportation and collection process from unit accumulation sites to a centralized disposal site, the vehicle driver will—

- Ensure that the vehicle is properly marked as contaminated.

- Position contamination marking signs on the vehicle.

- Allow no one to ride in the open back of a vehicle or trailer.

(1) A layer of 6-mil plastic may be positioned in the bed of the vehicle to minimize the spread of contamination.

(2) As waste material is collected, checks are conducted to verify that contaminated bags or containers are properly marked.

8. Waste Collection Point

Establishing waste collection points must be a well-thought-out process to ensure the safety of all personnel in the area.

a. Planners must coordinate with joint and HN forces for proper siting of the CBRN waste accumulation site. To avoid multiple large accumulation points, consideration must be given for the consolidation of contaminated waste from nearby friendly forces or sister services. Site selection should be based on prevailing seasonal winds and be away from any living, working, and rest or relief areas, terrain, and security. The location and size will vary based on the amount of waste generated. Preferred locations are downwind of the friendly forces, on flat, unvegetated terrain, in a secure but remote area, and away from areas that are populated by friendly forces or civilians.

b. Any contaminated waste must be disposed of in accordance with applicable local guidance.

c. Waste should be separated by type (solid versus liquid and combustible versus noncombustible).

d. The disposal site and waste are clearly identified. Contaminated marking signs are also prepared in advance to mark containers after use. Proper marking prevents unintentional contact and alerts personnel of the hazard. The collection containers must be marked with their contents, along with the type of contamination or agent, date, and time. Additionally, personnel should establish a cordon around the immediate area and put up signs to control unauthorized access.

e. If sufficient equipment exists, automatic vapor alarms are placed around or just upwind of the area. CBRN reconnaissance personnel should also periodically monitor just outside the area with handheld vapor detection devices, such as the ICAM or the M256.

f. When contaminated material or waste material require disposal, different methods can be used to dispose of the material.

(1) For example, burning produces a vapor hazard and the CBRN CC must submit an NBC5 report if material is burned in order to warn downwind units.

(2) Burial is another method that is effective for all types of contamination. The area must also be marked to help ensure that the area is avoided. The unit that closes the decontamination site must also notify the CBRN CC. The CBRN CC must submit an NBC5 report outlining the contaminated-waste burial site.

9. Disposal Procedures

The proper disposal of contaminated waste is paramount to safely conducting decontamination operations.

a. The three primary ways of handling the problem of waste disposal are open storage, burying, and burning.

b. All personnel directly or indirectly engaged in disposal operations must be properly trained in the operational procedures, hazards, and safety precautions.

c. Disposal procedures must be coordinated with the CBRN CC.

10. Open Storage

The HN or command guidance may prohibit the burning or burial of waste. Garbage, rubbish, and other such material may have to be stored pending transportation to a waste disposal facility. Wastewater poses significant challenges.

   a. The laundering of potentially contaminated items (i.e., suits) will generate a considerable amount of wastewater that must be controlled and analyzed for contamination.

   b. The use of water or 5 percent hypochlorite solution for decontamination will generate a considerable amount of liquid that requires disposal. To reduce volume, planners should consider the use of evaporation tanks/lagoons.

   c. Planners should consider the use of large containers, such as sea and land shipping containers, during open storage for storing or consolidating the waste.

      (1) For open storage of contaminated waste, the use of large containers offers advantages, such as ample storage space, protection from the environment, limited access to the contaminated material, the ease of loading, availability at most deployed locations, and low cost.

      (2) The primary disadvantage and hazard is that the size of the containers makes them difficult to move, and sealed containers will contain off-gassing vapors.

11. Burying

Burying contaminated items should be well-thought-out, planned and recorded.

   a. When closed, the burial pit should have a mound of dirt placed over the top. Marking signs must be placed to indicate the type of pit, pits contents, date closed, and unit designation. Maintaining accurate records on the type and quantity of material buried is critical for postconflict cleanup actions

   b. Other guidance includes—

   - Marking contaminated material that is placed in the burial pit.
   - Recording all items placed in the burial pit.
   - Using containers for placement in the burial pit.

12. Open Burning

Open burning is the burning of any material wherein air contaminants resulting from combustion are emitted directly into the air, without passing through a stack or chimney from an enclosed chamber.

   a. Site selection. Planners must consider prevailing winds along with the potential for release of toxic vapors and hazardous ash during the selection of the site.

      (1) Contaminated waste should be disposed of in an open space where there are no woods or heavy brush that might trap fumes close to the operation, especially in the downwind direction.

      (2) The area should be cleared of all combustible material, out to a 250-foot radius if possible. No burning shall occur within 250 feet of a power line or within 500 feet

of a frequently traveled road, fuel storage area, or pipeline. The disposal site should be constructed on a flat, compacted surface that is free of vegetation and combustible material.

    b.   The emission of toxic fumes released during burning may result in the release of heavy metals and toxic chemicals such as dioxin.

    c.   Disposal shall not be undertaken without prior approval of the CBRN CC. Local procedures will dictate how far in advance disposal operations must be coordinated, but for most operations, a minimum 24-hour notice is required. This will allow the CBRN CC to up-channel required reports to notify friendly forces of a potential toxic cloud in the downwind area.

    d.   Prior to conducting burning operations, the following agencies should be notified:

- CBRN CC.
- Medical facility.
- Security forces.
- Higher HQ.
- Bioenvironmental engineering (BEE).
- Sister services and HN personnel, as appropriate.

    e.   Weather precautions. No burning shall be conducted during unfavorable meteorological conditions (see Table K-1) such as:

- During an electrical storm or when such a storm is approaching.
- During high winds (wind velocity exceeding 20 mph).
- During an unsatisfactory temperature gradient.

Table K-1. Weather Conditions

Factor	Condition			Unsatisfactory
	Excellent	Fair	Fair (Winter)	
Temperature	75°F (24°C) and above	55°F–75°F	Under 55°F	Under 55°F
Sky	Clear	Partly cloudy	Clear	Cloudy
Wind	4–15 mph (6.5–24 kph)	5–20 mph (8–32 kph)	7–15 mph (11–24 kph	Under 3 mph (4.8 kph) or over 20 mph (32 kph)
Time of Day	1000–1600	1000–1600	1000–1600	1600–0959

    f.   Burning should be conducted during daylight hours only.

    g.   Fire prevention is an integral part of any disposal operation. Firefighting equipment must be available on site or immediately available for response.

- No open flames are allowed in or near the disposal site.
- Fires must be attended at all times. Attendants must remain upwind and outside the area until all smoke and fumes dissipate.

h. Records will be kept of all burning operations. These records shall include, at a minimum, the type and quantity of all material destroyed and the disposition of any residue.

   i. The burn pit should be a minimum of 1.22 meters (4 feet) deep with sides sloping enough to prevent cave in. The length and width of the trench will be determined by the quantity of material anticipated for disposal.

   (1) Place combustible material, such as scrap wooden pallets or dunnage, in the bottom of the pit at least 0.31 meter (1 foot deep).

   (2) Place contaminated waste on the combustible material, ensuring that the combustible material extends beyond the layer of waste. Continue adding waste to the pit until the top of the waste is within 0.31 meter (1 foot) from the top of the pit or trench. To ensure a through burn, do not compact layers of waste material into the pit.

   (3) Ensure that the area is clear of all unnecessary personnel and vehicles.

   (4) Pour a refined petroleum product (diesel fuel or kerosene) over the entire pile. Contaminated fuel can be used. Do not use gasoline or any volatile, flammable liquid.

   (5) Remotely ignite the pit or trench. The fire department or EOD can provide detailed training or assistance on how to accomplish this.

   (6) Do not reuse the pit for 24 hours after all burning has ceased.

   j. The burn furnace method includes the following:

   (1) Fire box burners provide more control, and they are safer to operate.

   (2) An air curtain incinerator is a portable or stationary combustion device that directs a plane of high-velocity, forced-draft air through a manifold head into a pit with vertical walls in such a manner as to maintain a curtain of air over the surface of the pit and a recirculating motion of air under the curtain.

   (3) Personnel must follow the manufacturers' recommended procedures for the operation of the incinerator and blower unit.

      (a) Material should be added to the incinerator remotely (i.e., with a front-end loader).

      (b) Operators must remain upwind and away from any smoke and fumes when adding material to the incinerator.

13. Marking Requirements

The marking of unit waste accumulation points is essential for ensuring the safe return to operations and for future remediation efforts of potentially contaminated areas.

   a. A critical component of the unit waste accumulation point is the proper marking and isolation of the contaminated waste. The waste accumulation point is clearly identified, and all containers containing contaminated waste are labeled. Proper marking prevents unintentional contact and alerts personnel of the hazard. The collection containers must be marked with the type of contamination or agent, date, time, and location of origin. Additionally, the immediate area should be cordoned off and signs posted to control unauthorized access.

b.   Signs and markers should be placed so that they are visible from all potential approach directions. Include dual language, if required, to warn HN personnel of the hazard. Area signs and markers should be placed around—

- All disposal areas.
- Boundary of zones and TFAs.
- Entry control points and holding areas.
- Contaminated waste.
- Aeration areas.
- Monitoring stations and equipment.
- Transportation routes.

REFERENCES

Department of Defense

DOD 4000.25-1-M, *Military Standard Requisitioning and Issue Procedure (MILSTRIP) Desk Guide*, 28 April 2004.

DODD 3025.1, *Military Support to Civil Authorities (MSCA)*, 15 January 1993.

Joint

Joint Publication 1-02, *Department of Defense Dictionary of Military and Associated Terms*, 12 April 2001 as amended through 31 August 2005.

Joint Publication 3-11, *Joint Doctrine for Operations in Nuclear, Biological, and Chemical (NBC) Environments*, 11 July 2000.

Joint Publication 4-06, *JTTP for Mortuary Affairs in Joint Operations*, 28 August 1996.

Multiservice

FM 3-3-1/FMFM 11-18, *Nuclear Contamination Avoidance*, 9 September 1994.

FM 3-11 (FM 3-100)/MCWP 3-37.1/NWP 3-11/AFTTP (I) 3-2.42, *Multiservice Tactics, Techniques, and Procedures or Nuclear, Biological, and Chemical Defense Operations*, 10 March 2003.

FM 3-11.4/MCWP 3-37.2/NTTP 3-11.27/AFTTP(I) 3-2.46, *Multiservice Tactics, Techniques, and Procedures for Nuclear, Biological, and Chemical (NBC) Protection*, 2 June 2003.

FM 3-11.9/MCRP 3-37.1B/NTRP 3-11.32/AFTTP (I) 3-2.55, *Potential Military Chemical/Biological Agents and Compounds*, 10 January 2005.

FM 3-11.14/MCRP 3-37.1A/NTTP 3-11.28 AFTTP 3-2.54, *Multiservice Tactics, Techniques, and Procedures for Nuclear, Biological, and Chemical Vulnerability Assessment*, 28 January 2004

FM 3-11.19/MCWP 3-37.4/NTTP 3-11.29/AFTTP(I) 3-2.44, *Multiservice Tactics, Techniques, and Procedures for Nuclear, Biological, and Chemical Reconnaissance*, 30 July 2004.

FM 3-11.21/MCRP 3-37.2C/NTTP 3-11.24/AFTTP (I) 3-2.37, *Multiservice Tactics, Techniques, and Procedures for Nuclear, Biological, and Chemical Aspects Of Consequence Management*, 12 December 2001.

FM 3-11.34/MCWP 3-37.5/NTTP 3-11.23/AFTTP (I) 3-2.33, *Multiservice Procedures for Nuclear, Biological, and Chemical (NBC) Defense of Theater Fixed Sites, Ports, and Airfields*, 29 September 2000.

FM 3-11.86/MCWP 3-37.1C/NTTP 3-11.31/AFTTP (I) 3-2.52, *Multiservice Tactics, Techniques, and Procedures for Biological Surveillance*, 4 October 2004.

MCWP 3-37.6/NTTP 3-02.1.1 *Tactics, Techniques, and Procedures for Recovery Operations in a Chemical, Biological, Radiological, and Nuclear (CBRN) Environment*, to be published within 6 months.

NAVAIR-01-1A-509/TO 1-1-691/TM 1-1500-344-23, *Aircraft Weapons Systems Cleaning and Corrosion Control,* 1 May 1996.

NAVAIR-16-1-540/TO 1-1-689/TM-1-1500-343-23), *Organizational/Unit and Intermediate Maintenance for Avionic Cleaning and Corrosion Prevention/Control,* 1 September 2000.

NWP 3-02.1/MCWP 3-31.5, *Ship-To-Shore Movement,* August 1993.

Army

BG Russ Zajtchuk, et al. (eds), *Textbook of Military Medicine: Medical Aspects of Chemical and Biological Warfare,* Office of the Surgeon General, 1997.

DA, Deputy Undersecretary of the Army for Operations Research (SAUS-OR), Memorandum, Subject: *Decontamination Formula 200 (DF 200) Military Utility Assessment in (MUA) in Support of CENTCOM Urgent Operational Need Statement,* 20 February 2003.

FM 3-7, *NBC Field Handbook,* 29 September 1994.

FM 3-11.22, *Chemical, Biological, Radiological, and Nuclear Response in Support of Incident Management,* to be published within 6 months.

FM 4-02.7, *Health Service Support in a Nuclear, Biological, and Chemical Environment Tactics, Techniques, and Procedures,* 1 October 2002.

FM 4-02.18, *Veterinary Services, Tactics, Techniques and Procedures,* 30 December 2004.

FM 4-02.33, *Control of Communicable Diseases Manual,* 1 June 2005.

FM 8-10-6, *Medical Evacuation in a Theater of Operations, Tactics, Techniques, and Procedures,* 14 April 2000.

FM 10-64, *Mortuary Affairs Operations,* 16 February 1999.

FM 10-52, *Water Supply in Theaters of Operations,* 11 July 1990.

Air Force

AFI 10-404, *Base Support and Expeditionary Site Planning,* 9 March 2004.

AFI 10-2501, *Full Spectrum Threat Response (FSTR) Planning and Operations,* 3 August 2005.

AFMAN 10-2602, *Nuclear, Biological, Chemical, and Conventional (NBCC) Defense Operations and Standards,* 29 May 2003.

AF 1800, *Operator's Inspection Guide and Trouble Report (General Purpose Vehicles),* 1 April 1987.

AFMAN 32-4005, *Personnel Protection and Attack Actions,* 30 October 2001.

AFMAN 32-4017, *Civil Engineer Readiness Technician's Manual for Nuclear, Biological, and Chemical Defense,* 29 May 2003.

AF TO 11C15-1-3 *Chemical Warfare Decontamination, Detection, and Disposal of Decontaminating Agents* June 1997

HQ AMC CB CONOPS, *Air Mobility Operations in a Chemical and Biological Environment*

Navy

COMNAVSURFORINST 3541.1, *Condition II Damage Control,* 13 August 2003; Change Transmittal 1, 27 January 2004.

NAVAIR 00-80T-121, *Chemical and Biological Defense, NATOPS Manual,* 1 October 2004.

NSTM 070, *Nuclear Defense at Sea and Radiological Recovery of Ships After Nuclear Weapons Explosion,* 30 July 1998.

NSTM 470, *Shipboard BW/CW Defense and Countermeasures,* 6 August 1998.

NSTM 670, *Stowage Handling and Disposal of Hazardous Use Consumables,* 30 May 2002.

NTTP 3-20.31, *Surface Ship Survivability,* January 2000.

NWP 3-20.31 (REV. A), *Surface Ship Survivability,* January 2002

Marine Corps

MCRP 4-11.1F, *MTTP for Health Service Support in a Nuclear, Biological, and Chemical Environment,* 23 April 2003.

Other Sources

North American Emergency Response Guide, 2000.

AMEDD, Information Paper, "SUBJECT: Information on Skin Exposure Reduction Paste Against Chemical Warfare Agents (SERPACWA)," 13 February 2003.

Andrew C. Parker, et. al., *Counter Proliferation-Biological Decontamination,* DPG/JCP-098-002, June 1998 (554561).

STANAG 2103, *Reporting Nuclear Detonations, Biological and Chemical Attacks, and Predicting the Warning of Associated Hazards and Hazard Areas (Allied Tactical Publication (ATP)45(B),* 1 July 2001.

Cecil O. Eckard, C.K. Ramachandran, *Technical Report: Effects of Weathering on Reduction of Chemical Agent Contamination From Deposition Surfaces,* DPG/TA-89/017, March 1989, (547480).

C.K. Ramachandran and Lloyd D. Larsen, *Decontamination of Bio-Agents Using the M17 SANATOR: Field Test with Bacillus subtilis var. nlaer (BG) on Vehicles,* DPG/JCPD-93/005, March 1993 (548555).

C.K. Ramachandran, *Weathering After Hasty Decontamination: Field Tests Using Methyl Salicylate on Vehicles and Aircraft Wings,* DPG/JOD-92/031, September 1992 (549067).

Daniel J. Peddicord, *Technical Report: Decontamination of Electronic Equipment,* DPG/JOD-92/016, June 1992 (548938).

DASG-HCF, Information Paper, "SUBJECT: Skin Exposure Reduction Paste Against Chemical Warfare Agents (SERPACWA)," 20 February 2003.

David C. Stark, et. al., *Chemical/Biological (CB) Technical Data Source Book: Decontamination of Chemical Warfare Agent,* DPG/JCP-098-004, June 1998 (554570).

EAI Corporation, *Technical Report: Commercial and Field Expedient Chemical Warfare Agent Decontaminants,* DPG/TA-88/23, February 1988 (546913).

EPA, Office of Pesticide Programs, *Chlorine Dioxide*, 27 December 2001, 19 November 2003.

EPA, Pesticides: Topical & Chemical Fact Sheets, Ethylene Oxide, 19 May 2003, http://www.epa.gov/pesticides/factsheets/chemicals/etofactsheet.htm, 19 November 2003.

EPA, Radionuclide Table: Radionuclide Carcinogenicity – Slope Factors (Federal Guidance Report No. 13 Morbidity Risk Coefficients, in Units of Picocuries), http://www.epa.gov/radiation/heast/, 3 December 2002.

Eugene J. Mezey, et. al., *Technical Report: Effects of Water Temperature and Soap on Decontamination*, DPG/TA-89/011, March 1989 (547379).

FDA News, *FDA Clears Skin Lotion for Military to Protect Against Chemical Burns*, 28 March 2003.

G.W. Wagner, et. al., *DECON Green*, ECBC poster presented at 23rd Army Science Conference 2–5 December 2002.

Jerry R. Montgomery, Technical Report: Decontaminative Effects of Soil, DPG/TA-89/024, December 1989 (547725).

Joint C/B Technical Data Source Book, *Volume V: Blister, Blood, and Choking Agents, Part 4, Agents HN, Q, T, L, and HL*, October 1993 (549944).

John F. Weimaster, SBCCOM, "Interim DS2 Replacement Risk Analysis" John Kerch, *SBCCOM/CMSL Quarterly Decon Review: Decontaminating Solution 2*, 18 March 2002 (FOUO).

Joseph Kohlbeck, *Technical Report: Effects of Chemical Warfare Agents and Decontaminants on Selected Weapons Systems and Metal Alloys*, DPG/JOD-92/002, February 1992 (548550).

Kenneth S.K. Chinn, *Battledress Overgarment Decontamination with Resin-Based Decontamination Kits*, DPG/JCP-94/006, April 1994 (550296).

Kenneth S.K. Chinn, *Decontamination of Individual Protective Clothing and Equipment*, DPG/JCP-95/021, September 1995 (551738).

Kenneth S.K. Chinn, *Dusty Agents and Simulants: Desorption at Various Environmental Conditions and Effects of Sweat on Dusty Agent*, DPG/JCP-94/003, December 1993 (549890).

Kenneth S.K. Chinn, *Effectiveness of Water, Soapy Water, and Steam for Hasty Decontamination*, DPG/JOD-92/038, November 1992 (549048).

Kenneth S.K. Chinn, *Effectiveness of Swimming for Clothing Decontamination*, DPG/JCP-95/005, January 1995 (551164).

Kenneth S.K. Chinn, et. al., *Decontamination Effectiveness of Seawater on Naval Landing Craft Materials*, DPG/JCP-95/015, March 1995 (551168).

Kenneth S.K. Chinn, *Technical Report: Reduction of Water Requirement for Decontamination*, DPG/JCP-96/005, April 1996 (552449).

Kenneth S.K. Chinn, *Technical Report: Theoretical Consideration and Practical Approach to Chemical Decontamination*, DPG/TA-87-02, October 1986 (551078).

Kenneth S.K. Chinn, *Wound Decontamination*, DPG/TA-KG/87-01, July 1987 (551073).

Lloyd D. Larsen and C.K. Ramachandran, *Use of M291 Kit for Decontamination of Skin After Exposure to Bacterial or Viral Aerosol*, DPG/JCP-094/011, November 1994 (550836).

McGraw-Hill Dictionary of Scientific and Technical Terms, 6th ed., 2003.

Patrice L. Abercrombie, *Physical Property Data Review of Selected Chemical Agents and Related Compounds: Updating Field Manual 3-9 (FM 3-9)*, September 2003, ECBC-TR-294.

Paula P. Nicholson, *M17 Sanator Hasty Decontamination: Chemical Field Trials*, DPG/JOD-93/004, March 1993 (549306).

PDD-39, *Presidential Decision Directive on Terrorism*, 21 June 1995.

Robert L. Stearman, *Technical Report: Problems of Chemical Defense Operations in Extreme Cold*, DPG-S-TA-85-08, June 1995 (546024).

Robert L. Stearman, *Technical Report: Effect of Decontamination and Protective Coatings on Air Defense Radars, Communication Equipment, and Repair Parts*, DPG-S-84-502, October 1983 (545236).

Sharon Reutter, et. al., *Review and Recommendations for Human Toxicity Estimates for FM 3-11.9*, September 2003, ECBC-TR-349.

The Merck Index, An Encyclopedia of Chemicals, Drugs, and Biologicals, 12th ed., Merck Research Laboratories, Whitehouse Station, NJ, 1996.

THIS PAGE IS INTENTIONALLY LEFT BLANK.

GLOSSARY

PART I—ABBREVIATIONS AND ACRONYMS

A

AA	assembly area
AAV	amphibious assault vehicle
AB	airbase
AC	hydrogen cyanide
ACAA	automatic chemical-agent alarm
ACCA	aircrew contamination control area
ACDE	aircrew chemical defense equipment
ACE	air combat element
AD	air defense
ADCON	administrative control
AF	Air Force
AFB	Air Force base
AFFF	aqueous film-forming foam
AFI	Air Force instruction
AFMAN	Air Force Manual
AFRRI	Armed Forces Radiobiology Research Institute
AFSC	United States Air Force specialty code
AFTTP (I)	Air Force tactics, techniques, and procedures (interservice)
AL	Alabama
ALSS	advanced logistics support site
AO	area of operation
AOR	area of responsibility
APC	armored personnel carrier
APOD	aerial port of debarkation
APOE	aerial port of embarkation
ATP	Allied Tactical Publication
ATTN	attention

B

BB	bare base
BDO	battle dress overgarment
BDU	battle dress uniform
BEE	bioenvironmental engineering
BFV	Bradley fighting vehicle
bio	biological
BN	battalion
BP	boiling point
BW	biological warfare
BZ	3-Quinuclidinyl benzilate (an incapacitating agent)

C

C	Celsius
C2	command and control
CAM	chemical-agent monitor
CAMSIM	chemical-agent monitor simulator
CARC	chemical agent-resistant coating
CAW	carrier air wings
CB	chemical-biological
CBIRF	chemical/biological incident response force
CBR	chemical, biological, and radiological
CBRD	chemical, biological, and radiological defense
CBRN	chemical, biological, radiological, and nuclear
CBRN CC	chemical, biological, radiological, and nuclear control center
CC	control center
CCA	contamination control area
CCS	contamination control station
CCT	contamination control team
CDS	casualty decontamination site
CE	civil engineering
CENTCOM	Central Command
CFR	Code of Federal Regulations
CG	commanding general; phosgene
cGy	centigray
cGy/hr	centigray per hour
CHA	contact hazard area
chem	chemical
CK	cyanogen chloride
CM	consequence management
CMO	chief medical officer
CMWDS	countermeasure wash down system
CN	chloroacetophenone (tear gas or mace)
COA	course of action
COB	colocated operating base
COE	common operating environment
COMMZ	communications zone
CONEX	container express
CONOPS	concept of operations
CONUS	continental United States
CP	collection point
CPDEMED	chemically protected, deployable medical system
CPO	chemical protective overgarment
CPS	collective protective shelter
CPU	chemical protective undergarment
CR	dibenz (b,f)-1:4-oxazepine
CRAF	Civil Reserve Air Fleet
CRRC	combat rubber raiding craft

CS	civil support, o-chlorobenzylidene malononitrile (a tear agent)
CSG	carrier strike group
CSS	combat service support
CTA	common table of allowance
CVCUS	combat vehicle crewman uniform system
CW	chemical warfare
CX	phosgene oxime

D

DA	diphenylchloroarsine (a vomiting agent); Department of the Army
DAD	detailed aircraft decontamination
DAP	decontaminating apparatus, portable
DC	diphenylcyanoarsine (a vomiting agent); District of Columbia
DCA	damage control assistant
DCC	damage control center
DCO	defense coordinating officer
DCP	decontamination control point
decon	decontamination
DED	detailed equipment decontamination
DF	methylphosphonic difluoride
DHHS	Department of Health and Human Services
DISCOM	division support command (Army)
DM	diphenylaminochloroarsine (Adamsite) (a vomiting agent)
DOD	Department of Defense
DODD	Department of Defense directive
DOL	Department of Labor
DP	diphosgene
DRCD	domestic-response casualty decontamination
DS2	decontamination solution 2
DTG	date-time group
DTD	detailed troop decontamination
DTRA	Defense Threat Reduction Agency
DU	depleted uranium

E

ECBC	Edgewood Chemical and Biological Center
ECS	environmental control system
EDTA	ethylenediaminetetraacetic acid
EMDT	expeditionary medical decontamination team
EMT	emergency medical treatment
ENCU	environmental control unit
EOC	emergency operations center
EOD	explosive ordnance disposal
EPA	Environmental Protection Agency
ERG	Emergency Response Guidebook
ESF	emergency support functions

ESG	expeditionary strike group

F

F	Fahrenheit
FARP	forward arming and refueling point
FBI	Federal Bureau of Investigation
FEMA	Federal Emergency Management Agency
FHP	force health protection
FL	Florida
FLOT	forward line of own troops
FM	field manual (Army)
FOD	foreign object damage
FOF	follow-on forces
Force RECON	force reconnaissance
FP	force protection
FRAGORD	fragmentary order
FRP	Federal Response Plan
FSB	fire support battery
FSDS	Fixed-Site Decontamination System
FSSG	force service support group
FSTR	full-spectrum threat response

G

G-4	Army or Marine Corps component logistics staff officer
GA	tabun (a nerve agent)
G agent	a nerve agent
GB	sarin (a nerve agent)
GCE	ground chemical ensemble
GD	soman (a nerve agent)
GI	government issue
GOA	government-owned animals
GP	general purpose
GPM	gallon(s) per minute
GPU	ground power unit
GS	general support
GZ	ground zero

H

H agent	a blister agent
HAS	hardened aircraft shelter
HAZMAT	hazardous materials
HD	distilled mustard (a blister agent)
HEMTT	heavy, expanded-mobility, tactical truck
HEPA	high-efficiency particulate air
HHA	handheld assay

HHD	headquarters and headquarters detachment
HL	mustard-lewisite mixture
HLD	homeland defense
HLS	homeland security
HMLA	Marine light/attack helicopter squadron
HMMWV	high-mobility, multipurpose, wheeled vehicle
HN	host nation; nitrogen mustard (HN-1, HN-2, HN-3)
HNS	host nation support
HQ	headquarters
hr	hour(s)
HSS	health service support
HT	distilled mustard and T mixture
HTB	high-test bleach
HTH	high-test hypochlorite

I

ICAM	improved chemical-agent monitor
ICS	incident command system
IEDK	individual equipment decontamination kit
IPB	intelligence preparation of the battlespace
IPE	individual protective equipment
IPPDC	in-place patient decontamination capability
IRF	initial-response force

J

JFC	joint force commander
JMAO	Joint Mortuary Affairs Office
JP	joint publication
JRA	joint rear area
JSLIST	joint-service, lightweight, integrated suit technology
JTF	joint task force
JTTP	joint tactics, techniques, and procedures

K

km	kilometer(s)

L

L	lewisite
lb	pound(s)
LBE	load-bearing equipment
LCAC	landing craft air cushion
LCE	load-carrying equipment

LCM	landing craft, mechanized
LCU	landing craft, utility
LDS	lightweight decontaminating system
LEL	lower-explosive level
LLR	low-level radiation
LOC	line of communication
LPD-4	amphibious transport dock
LSD	landing ship dock

M

m	meter(s)
MADCP	mortuary affairs decontamination collection point
MAG	Marine aircraft group
MAGTF	Marine air-ground task force
MARCORSYSCOM	Marine Corps Systems Command
MARFORLANT	Marine Corps Forces, Atlantic
max	maximum
MCCDC	Marine Corps Combat Development Command
MCE	mission-critical equipment
MCRP	Marine Corps reference publication
MCWP	Marine Corps warfighting publication
MD	Maryland
MEB/AT	Marine Expeditionary Brigade Antiterrorism
MEDEVAC	medical evacuation
MEDSURV	medical surveillance
MEF	Marine Expeditionary Force
METT-T	mission, enemy, terrain, troops, and time available
METT-TC	mission, enemy, terrain and weather, time available, troops and civilian
MGX	MOPP gear exchange
MILSTRIP	military standard requisitioning and issue procedure
min	minimum
MLG	main landing gear
MO	Missouri
MOA	memorandum of agreement
MOB	main operating base
MOPP	mission-oriented protective posture
MOS	military occupational specialty
MOU	memorandum of understanding
MP	military police
MPDS	multipurpose decontamination system
mph	mile(s) per hour
mrem/hr	millirem(s) per hour
MSC	major subordinate command
MSCA	military support to civil authorities
MSR	main supply route

MTF	medical treatment facility
MTP	mission tasking plan
MTTP	multiservice tactics, techniques, and procedures
MTVR	medium tactical vehicle replacement
MTW	major theater war
MWD	military working dog

N

N/A	not applicable
NATO	North Atlantic Treaty Organization
NATOPS	Naval air training and operating procedures standardization
NAVAIR	Naval air
NBC	nuclear, biological, and chemical
NBCC	nuclear, biological, and chemical center
NBCWRS	Nuclear, Biological, and Chemical Warning and Reporting System
NBG	Naval beach group
NCO	noncommissioned officer
NCOIC	noncommissioned officer in charge
NEC	Navy enlisted classification
NGO	nongovernmental organization
NIOSH	National Institute for Occupational Safety and Health
NLG	nose landing gear
No.	number
NRC	National Response Center
NRP	National Response Plan
NSN	national stock number
NSTM	Naval ships technical manual
NTRP	Naval technical reference publication
NTTP	Navy tactics, techniques, and procedures
NWDC	Navy Warfare Development Command
NWP	Naval warfare publication

O

O2	oxygen
OCONUS	outside the continental United States
OEG	operational exposure guide
OPCON	operational control
OPLAN	operation plan
OPORD	operation order
OPR	office of primary responsibility
OPTEMPO	operating tempo
OS	operator's spray down
OSHA	Occupational Safety and Health Administration
OW	operator's wipe down
oz	ounce(s)

P

PA	public address
PASGT	personnel armor system, ground troops
PD	phenyl-dichlorarsine
PDD	Presidential decision directive
PDDA	power-driven decontamination apparatus
PDDE	power-driven decontamination equipment
PDS	patient decontamination station
PL	platoon
PLL	prescribed load list
PMCS	preventive-maintenance checks and services
POC	point of contact
POL	petroleum, oils, and lubricants
POMCUS	pre-positioning of materiel configured to unit sets
PPE	personal protective equipment
PPW	patient protective wrap
PRD	personal radiation device
PSG	platoon sergeant
psi	pound(s) per square inch
PT	point
PVNTMED	preventive medicine
PW	personal wipe down

Q

qt	quart(s)

R

R&S	reconnaissance and surveillance
RD	round
RDD	radiological dispersal device
RDIC	resuscitation device, individual, chemical
RFA	request for assistance
RFI	request for information
RI	Rhode Island
RM	risk management
RP	release point
RSDL	reactive skin decontamination lotion

S

SA	situational awareness; arsine
SABC	self-aid buddy care
SCALP	suit, contamination avoidance, liquid protection
SCBA	self-contained breathing apparatus
SD	skin decontamination

SDK	skin decontamination kit
SDS	Sorbent Decontamination System
SecDef	Secretary of Defense
SINCGARS	Single-Channel, Ground and Airborne Radio System
SITREP	situation report
SME	subject matter expert
SMT	shelter management team
SOI	signal operating instructions
SOP	standard operating procedure
SPOD	seaport of debarkation
S/RTF	search and recovery task force
SRC	survival recovery center
SSPDS	Small Shelter, Personnel Decontamination System
STB	super tropical bleach

T

TADS	Tactical Air Defense System
TAP	toxicological agent-protective
TC	Transportation Corps (Army)
tech	technical
TFA	toxic-free area
TGD	thickened soman
THD	thickened distilled mustard (a blister agent)
TIC	toxic industrial chemicals
TIM	toxic industrial material
TL	team leader
TM	technical manual
TO	technical order
TO&E	table of organization and equipment
TPU	tank pump unit
TRADOC	United States Army Training and Doctrine Command
TSC	theater support command
TSOP	tactical standard operating procedure
TSP	training support package
TTP	tactics, techniques, and procedures
TX	Texas

U

UCC	unit control center
US	United States
USA	United States Army
USAF	United States Air Force
USACMLS	United States Army Chemical School
USAMRICD	United States Army Medical Research Institute of Chemical Defense
USAMRIID	United States Army Medical Research Institute of Infectious Diseases

USCG	United States Coast Guard
USG	United States Government
USMC	United States Marine Corps
USN	United States Navy
UTC	unit type code
UV	ultraviolet
UXO	unexploded ordnance

V

VA	vulnerability assessment; Virginia
VHA	vapor hazard area
VMA	Marine attack squadron
VW	vehicle wash down
VX	nerve agent (O-ethyl-diisopropylaminomethyl methylphosphonothiolate)

W

WARNORD	warning order
WBGT	wet bulb globe temperature
WMD	weapons of mass destruction
WMDT	weapons of mass destruction team

PART II – TERMS AND DEFINITIONS

absorption. A process in which one substance becomes incorporated within another substance; also used to describe interactions between electromagnetic radiation and matter. (Fundamentals of Analytical Chemistry)

adsorption. A process in which a substance becomes attached to the surface of another substance. (Fundamentals of Analytical Chemistry)

activity. 1. A unit, organization, or installation performing a function or mission, e.g., reception center, redistribution center, naval station, naval shipyard. 2. A function, mission, action, or collection of actions. (JP 1-02)

aerosol. A liquid or solid composed of finely divided particles suspended in a gaseous medium. Examples of common aerosols are mist, fog, and smoke. (JP 1-02)

airburst. An explosion of a bomb or projectile above the surface as distinguished from an explosion on contact with the surface or after penetration. (JP 1-02)

air defense. All defensive measures designed to destroy attacking enemy aircraft or missiles in the Earth's envelope of atmosphere, or to nullify or reduce the effectiveness of such attack. (JP 1-02)

area of operations. An operational area defined by the joint force commander for land and naval forces. Areas of operation do not typically encompass the entire operational area of the joint force commander, but should be large enough for component commanders to accomplish their missions and protect their forces. Also called **AO**. (JP 1-02)

area of responsibility. The geographical area associated with a combatant command within which a combatant commander has authority to plan and conduct operations. Also called **AOR**. (JP 1-02)

assessment. 1. Analysis of the security, effectiveness, and potential of an existing or planned intelligence activity. 2. Judgment of the motives, qualifications, and characteristics of present or prospective employees or "agents." (JP 1-02)

avoidance. Individual and/or unit measures taken to avoid or minimize nuclear, biological, and chemical (NBC) attacks and reduce the effects of NBC hazards. (JP 1-02)

battlespace. The environment, factors, and conditions that must be understood to successfully apply combat power, protect the force, or complete the mission. This includes the air, land, sea, space, and the included enemy and friendly forces; facilities; weather; terrain; the electromagnetic spectrum; and the information environment within the operational areas and areas of interest. (JP 1-02)

biological agent. A microorganism that causes disease in personnel, plants, or animals or causes the deterioration of materiel. (JP 1-02)

biological defense. The methods, plans, and procedures involved in establishing and executing defensive measures against attacks using biological agents. (JP 1-02)

biological environment. Conditions found in an area resulting from direct or persisting effects of biological weapons. (JP 1-02)

biological threat. A threat that consists of biological material planned to be deployed to produce casualties in personnel or animals or damage plants. (JP 1-02)

biological weapon. An item of materiel which projects, disperses, or disseminates a biological agent including arthropod vectors. (JP 1-02)

blister agent. A chemical agent which injures the eyes and lungs and burns or blisters the skin. Also called vesicant agent. (JP 1-02)

blood agent. A chemical compound, including the cyanide group, that affects the bodily function by preventing the normal utilization of oxygen by body tissues. (JP 1-02)

casualty. Any person who is lost to the organization by having been declared dead, duty status – whereabouts unknown, missing, ill, or injured. (JP 1-02)

chemical agent. Any toxic chemical intended for use in military operations. (JP 1-02)

chemical ammunition. A type of ammunition, the filler of which is primarily a chemical agent. (JP 1-02)

chemical defense. The methods, plans, and procedures involved in establishing and executing defensive measures against attack utilizing chemical agents. (JP 1-02)

chemical dose. The amount of chemical agent, expressed in milligrams, that is taken or absorbed by the body. (JP 1-02)

chemical environment. Conditions found in an area resulting from direct or persisting effects of chemical weapons. (JP 1-02)

chemical, biological, radiological, and nuclear hazards. Those toxic chemical, biological, radiological or nuclear (CBRN) hazards that are released in the presence of US forces or civilians, not necessarily in quantities that could cause mass casualties. CBRN hazards include those created from a release other than attack, toxic industrial chemicals (specifically toxic inhalation hazards), biological agents of operational significance and radioactive matter. Also included are any hazards resulting from the deliberate employment of nuclear, biological, and chemical weapons during military operations. (JRO draft Terms of Reference)

chemical weapon. Together or separately, (a) a toxic chemical and its precursors, except when intended for a purpose not prohibited under the Chemical Weapons Convention; (b) a munition or device, specifically designed to cause death or other harm through toxic properties of those chemicals specified in (a), above, which would be released as a result of the employment of such munition or device; (c) any equipment specifically designed for use directly in connection with the employment of munitions or devices specified in (b), above. Also called **CW**. (JP 1-02)

civil affairs. Designated Active and Reserve component forces and units organized, trained, and equipped specifically to conduct civil affairs activities and to support civil-military operations. Also called **CA**. (JP 1-02)

collective nuclear, biological, and chemical protection. Protection provided to a group of individuals in a nuclear, biological, and chemical environment which permits relaxation of individual nuclear, biological, and chemical protection. (JP 1-02)

combatant command. A unified or specified command with a broad continuing mission under a single commander established and so designated by the President, through the Secretary of Defense and with the advice and assistance of the Chairman of the Joint Chiefs of Staff. Combatant commands typically have geographic or functional responsibilities. (JP 1-02)

contamination. (1) The deposit, absorption, or adsorption of radioactive material, or of biological or chemical agents on or by structures, areas, personnel, or objects. (2) Food and/or water made unfit for consumption by humans or animals because of the presence of environmental chemicals, radioactive elements, bacteria or organisms, the byproduct of the growth of bacteria or organisms, the decomposing material (to include food substance itself), or waste in the food or water. (JP 1-02)

contamination control. Procedures to avoid, reduce, remove, or render harmless, (temporarily or permanently) nuclear, biological, and chemical contamination for the purpose of maintaining or enhancing the efficient conduct of military operations. (JP 1-02)

decontamination. The process of making any person, object, or area safe by absorbing, destroying, neutralizing, making harmless, or removing chemical or biological agents, or by removing radioactive material clinging to or around it. (JP 1-02)

desorption. The process of removing a sorbed substance by the reverse of adsorption or absorption. (McGraw-Hill Dictionary of Scientific and Technical Terms)

detection. In nuclear, biological, and chemical (NBC) environments, the act of locating NBC hazards by use of NBC detectors or monitoring and/or survey teams. (JP 1-02)

host nation support. Civil and/or military assistance rendered by a nation to foreign forces within its territory during peacetime, crises, or emergencies, or war based on agreements mutually concluded between nations. Also called **HNS**. (JP 1-02)

hydrolysis. 1. Decompostion or alteration of a chemical substance by water. 2. In aqueous solution of electrolytes, the reactions of cations with water to produce a weak base or of anions to produce a weak acid. (McGraw-Hill Dictionary of Scientific and Technical Terms)

identification. 1. The process of determining the friendly or hostile character of an unknown detected contact. 2. In arms control, the process of determining which nation is responsible for the detected violations of any arms control measure. 3. In ground combat operations, discrimination between recognizable objects as being friendly or enemy, or the name that belongs to the object as a member of a class. Also called **ID**. (JP 1-02)

individual protection. Actions taken by individuals to survive and continue the mission under nuclear, biological, and chemical conditions. (JP 1-02)

individual protective equipment. In nuclear, biological, and chemical warfare, the personal clothing and equipment required to protect an individual from biological and chemical hazards and some nuclear effects. (JP 1-02)

immediate decontamination. Decontamination carried out by individuals immediately upon becoming contaminated. It is performed in an effort to minimize casualties, save lives, and limit the spread of contamination. Also called emergency decontamination (JP 1-02).

mission-oriented protective posture. A flexible system of protection against nuclear, biological, and chemical contamination. This posture requires personnel to wear only that protective clothing and equipment (mission-oriented protective posture gear) appropriate to the threat level, work rate imposed by the mission, temperature, and humidity. Also called **MOPP**. (JP 1-02)

mission-oriented protective posture gear. Military term for individual protective equipment including suit, boots, gloves, mask with hood, first aid treatments, and decontamination kits issued to soldiers. Also called MOPP gear. (JP 1-02)

nerve agent. A potentially lethal and chemical agent which interferes with the transmission of nerve impulse. (JP 1-02)

nonpersistent agent. A chemical agent that when released dissipates and/or loses its ability to cause casualties after a passage of 10 to 15 minutes. (JP 1-02)

nuclear, biological, and chemical-capable nation. A nation that has the capability to produce and employ one or more types of nuclear, biological, and chemical weapons across the full range of military operations and at any level of war in order to achieve political and military objectives. (JP 1-02)

nuclear, biological, and chemical defense. Defensive measures that enable friendly forces to survive, fight, and win against enemy use of nuclear, biological, or chemical (NBC) weapons and agents. US forces apply NBC defensive measures before and during integrated warfare. In integrated warfare, opposing forces employ nonconventional weapons along with conventional weapons (NBC weapons are nonconventional). (JP 1-02)

nuclear, biological, and chemical environment. Environments in which there is deliberate or accidental employment, or threat of employment, of nuclear, biological, or chemical weapons; deliberate or accidental attacks or contamination with toxic industrial materials, including toxic industrial chemicals; or deliberate or accidental attacks or contamination with radiological (radioactive) materials. (JP 1-02)

nuclear defense. The methods, plans, and procedures involved in establishing and exercising defensive measures against the effects of an attack by nuclear weapons or radiological warfare agents. It encompasses both the training for, and the implementation of, these methods, plans, and procedures. (JP 1-02)

operational decontamination. Decontamination carried out by an individual and/or a unit, restricted to specific parts of operationally essential equipment, materiel and/or working areas, in order to minimize contact and transfer hazards and to sustain operations. This may include decontamination of the individual beyond the scope of immediate decontamination, as well as decontamination of mission-essential spares and limited terrain decontamination. (JP 1-02)

persistency. In biological or chemical warfare, the characteristic of an agent which pertains to the duration of its effectiveness under determined conditions after its dispersal. (JP 1-02)

protection. Measures that are taken to keep nuclear, biological, and chemical hazards from having an adverse effect on personnel, equipment, or critical assets and facilities. Protection consists of five groups of activities: hardening of positions, protecting personnel, assuming mission-oriented protective posture, using physical defense measures, and reacting to attack. (JP 1-02)

protective mask. A protective ensemble designed protect the wearer's face and eyes and prevent the breathing of air contaminated with chemical and/or biological agents. (JP 1-02)

residual contamination. Contamination which remains after steps have been taken to remove it. These steps may consist of nothing more than allowing the contamination to decay normally. (JP 1-02)

survey. The directed effort to determine the location and the nature of a chemical, biological and radiological hazard in an area. (JP 1-02)

thorough decontamination. Decontamination carried out by a unit, with or without external support, to reduce contamination on personnel, equipment, materiel, and/or working areas equal to natural background or to the lowest possible levels, to permit the partial or total removal of individual protective equipment and to maintain operations with minimum degradation. This may include terrain decontamination beyond the scope of operational decontamination. (JP 1-02)

toxic chemical. Any chemical which, through its chemical action on life processes, can cause death, temporary incapacitation, or permanent harm to humans or animals. This includes all such chemicals, regardless of their origin or of their method of production, and regardless of whether they are produced in facilities, in munitions or elsewhere. (JP 1-02)

toxic industrial biological. Biological material found in medical research or pharmaceutical manufacturing that are toxic to humans and animals or damages plants. (FM 4-02.7)

toxic industrial chemical. Chemical materials or compounds that are used for multiple purposes such as fuels or solvents, or in manufacturing that are toxic to humans and animals or damages plants. (FM 4-02.7)

toxic industrial materials. Toxic industrial biological, toxic industrial chemical and toxic industrial radiological materials. (FM 4-02.7)

toxic industrial radiological. Radiation materials used in research, power generation, and medical treatment that are harmful to humans and animals if released outside their controlled environments. (FM 4-02.7)

weapons of mass destruction. Weapons that are capable of a high order of destruction and/or of being used in such a manner as to destroy large numbers of people. Weapons of mass destruction can be high explosives or nuclear, chemical, biological, and radiological weapons, but exclude the means of transporting or propelling the weapon where such means is a separable and divisible part of the weapon. Also called WMD. (JP 1-02)

THIS PAGE IS INTENTIONALLY LEFT BLANK.

INDEX

A

air cargo decontamination 8-1

Air Force I-7, IV-4, X-7, G-7

aircraft decontamination I-6, VIII-1, VIII-3, VIII-9, VIII-10, VIII-11, VIII-13, VIII-14, IX-13, XII-7

aircraft munitions, VIII-1, VIII-21

aircrew decontamination VIII-1, VIII-3

airfield II-3, III-3, IV-1, V-1, V-3, VII-1, VIII-1, VIII-2, VIII-6, H-15

animal E-11

Army patient decontamination X-5, X-6

Aviation IV-1, IV-28, IV-29, IV-30, IV-31, V-1, V-2, VIII-5, IX-1, IX-11, IX-13, F-2

B

battledress overgarment See BDO

BDO IV-14, IV-16, IV-17, IV-18, IV-36, IV-37, IV-38, V-9, V-14, VII-11, IX-10, IX-12, J-2, J-3, J-5, J-7

biological decontamination B-5, C-8, C-13, F-4

biological warfare See BW

biological weapons

building decontamination

burning

BW I-3, III-1, IV-1, V-1, VI-4, IX-1, IX-4, B-3, B-6, B-7, C-2, E-3

C

CARC I-4, I-6, V-21, V-23, VIII-20, B-9, E-4

cargo decontamination VIII-1, VIII-24, VIII-25, VIII-26

cargo movement VIII-3, VIII-23, VIII-24, VIII-26, VIII-27

CBIRF G-6,

CBRD IX-1, G-19,

CCA VII-3 VIII-4, VIII-5, VIII-6, VIII-7, VIII-8, VIII-9, VIII-10, VIII-11, VIII-12, VIII-13, IX-3, IX-8, IX-9, IX-10, IX-12, IX-14, IX-16, G-7, G-9, G-10, K-1

CCS VII-13, VII-14, VII-15,

chemical agent resistant coating See CARC

chemical decontamination V-30, V-13

chemical protective overgarment See CPO

chemical, biological, and radiological defense See CBRD

chemical/biological incident response force See CBIRF

civil reserve aircraft decontamination See CRAF

civil support See CS

clearance decontamination I-2, I-4, I-6, I-7, I-9, V-21, VI-1, VI-2, VI-3, VI-4, VI-5, VIII-9, IX-2, G-5

CM II-3, II-6, XI-1, XI-2, G-6, G-11, G-12, G-13,

CMWDS IX-1, IX-2, IX-3, IX-15, IX-16,

cold weather C-1, C-2, C-5, F-1, F-3, F-6

combat effectiveness I-7

combat operations I-3, I-6, I-8, I-10, II-4, V-1, VI-3, VI-4, VIII-13, G-4,

combat service support See CSS

concept of operations See CONOPS

CONOPS II-1, VII-11, G-8

consequence management See CM

consumption rates II-11, XII-1

contact time III-1, III-2, V-21, V-24, V-26, V-27, V-28, V-29, VIII-15, VIII-19, XI-6, C-5, C-8, C-11, C-13, C-15, C-16, C-18, C-19, H-17

containment VI-1, VI-3, VI-5, VII-8, VIII-11, VIII-14, IX-8, IX-9, IX-13, G-11, K-2

contaminated remains E-1, E-9, E-10, E-11, G-6

contaminated waste collection VIII-3, K-1

contaminated waste disposal V-7, VII-4, VII-5, VII-11, VIII-28, K-1

contaminated waste holding area K-1

contamination control area See CCA

contamination control station VII-13

contamination level I-4, I-5, V-2, V-11, V-22, VIII-1, VIII-3, VIII-15, VIII-23, IX-2, XI-2, E-6

contract I-9, VIII-1, VIII-21, IX-6, IX-18

conversion A-1, A-2

countermeasure washdown system See CMWDS

CPO IV-16, IV-27, IV-38, V-9, V-14, J-2, J-7,

CRAF VIII-21,

CS I-1, I-9, II-6,

CSS V-1, V-20, XII-2,

D

DAD I-4, I-6, V-1, VIII-13, VIII-14, VIII-15, VIII-16, VIII-17, G-5,

damage control assistant See DCA

damage control center See DCC

DCA IX-1, IX-4, IX-5, IX-14,

DCC IX-1, IX-5, IX-4, IX-14, XI-6,

decontaminants I-4, II-7, III-2, V-30, VIII-4, VIII-5, VIII-6, VIII-7, VIII-22, XII-1, XII-2, C-1, C-2, C-4, C-6, C-7, C-8, C-10, C-11, C-12, C-13, C-14, C-15, C-16, C-17, C-19, C-20, E-1, E-2, E-3, F-2, F-3, F-4, F-5, G-9, H-4, H-9, I-1, I-2

decontamination apparatus IV-4, V-20, VIII-19, XII-3, C-5, C-11, F-3, G-9, H-9, I-2

decontamination area IV-4, V-4, V-7, V-30, VII-7, VIII-9, VIII-10, VIII-11, VIII-20, IX-3, IX-10, X-5, X-6

decontamination assets II-2, II-3, II-4, II-6, IV-4, V-2, VIII-3, X-8, G-1

decontamination equipment II-5, II-7, II-9, II-10, IV-4, VII-2, X-5, X-6, X-7, X-8, XII-3, H-1, H-2, K-5,

decontamination kits I-6, I-9, III-1, VII-5, VII-12, VIII-3, VIII-21, VIII-22, G-9, H-1, H-5,

decontamination procedures I-2, II-7, IV-1, V-1, VI-3, VI-4, VII-3, VIII-2, VIII-3, VIII-13, IX-3, IX-4, IX-5, IX-6, IX-7, IX-8, IX-9, IX-11, IX-14, IX-16, IX-17, IX-18, X-3, X-4, X-5, X-6, X-7, X-8, XI-12, XI-4, XI-8, C-1, D-1, D-2, D-3, D-4, D-5, D-6, E-2, E-3, E-4, E-7, F-5, G-13

decontamination techniques III-1, IV-2, V-3, VII-2, VIII-1, IX-1, XII-4, XII-5, XII-6

decontamination training I-10, II-2

decontamination units II-12, V-1, V-19, V-20, V-24, V-26, VI-2, X-6, XII-8, E-4, G-1

DED I-4, I-6, I-8, II-10, II-11, II-12, V-1, V-2, V-3, V-5, V-7, V-7, V-19, V-20, V-24, V-25, V-26, V-27, V-28, V-29, V-30, V-31, VIII-13, XII-2, XII-3, XII-4, XII-5, XII-6, G-2, G-3, G-5, G-6

depleted uranium See DU

desert I-2, D-3, F-1, F-3, F-4

detailed aviation decontamination See DAD

detailed equipment decontamination See DED

detailed troop decontamination See DTD

detection equipment I-8, III-2, V-10, V-29, V-30, B-11, E-6, G-8, H-1, H-2, H-3, H-4, K-3

DF 200 C-7, C-8, H-10, H-12

domestic XI-1, G-6, G-11, G-12, G-13,

DTD I-4, I-8, II-10, II-11, II-12, V-1, V-5, V-7, V-8, V-9, V-19, V-22, V-28, V-30, V-31, XII-2, XII-3, XII-4, XII-5, XII-6, E-11, G-2, G-3, H-17

DU I-8, E-1, E-5, E-6, E-7, G-6

E

EOD VII-12, IX-1, E-5, E-10, G-7, K-9

equipment decontamination I-5, III-1, V-1, V-7, VIII-13, IX-2, IX-3, IX-17, X-3, XII-2, XII-6, XII-8, G-6, H-8, H-10

evacuation X-1, X-2, X-3, X-4, B-10, E-5, E-9, E-10, E-11,

exercises I-8, I-10, II-4

exploding I-3, I-6

explosive ordnance disposal See EOD

F

FARP VIII-1, VIII-4,

FHP I-6, I-7, I-8, VI-1, VI-5,

field expedient IV-32, IV-36, IV-39, VIII-10, IX-14, X-3, XI-3, C-2,

fixed site decontamination VII-1, VII-2, G-6, H-9, H-10,

flash point C-18, F-2

force health protection See FHP

force protection See FP

forward arming and refueling point See FARP

FP II-4, VI-1, VI-3, VII-5, G-6, G-7, G-8, G-13,

freezing point C-13, C-14, F-2

FSDS H-2, H-9, H-10, H-12, H-13, H-14, H-17

G

GCE VII-4, VII-5,

ground crew ensemble See GCE

H

half-life B-4, E-8

health service support See HSS

helicopter VII-2, VIII-3, VIII-9, VIII-10, IX-10, IX-12, IX-13, X-2, B-8, E-2, G-7, H-7

high test hypochlorite See HTH

HLD I-8, I-9, II-6, VI-1, X-8, XII-7,

HLS I-8, I-9, I-10, II-6, VI-1, XI-1, XI-2, XII-7

homeland defense See HLD

homeland security See HLS

hot weather F-1, F-3

HSS II-3, II-4, II-9, V-31, VI-4, IX-10, X-1, X-2, X-3, X-6, X-7, X-8, E-4

HTH III-3, V-9, V-14, V-15, V-16, V-19, V-22, VIII-19, IX-9, IX-17, X-6, C-5, C-8, C-9, C-10, C-11, D-5, D-6, F-2, J-7,

I

IEDK III-1, IV-7, IV-8, IV-11, IV-13, IV-17, IV-19, IV-20, IV-23, IV-25, IV-27, IV-28, IV-29, IV-31, IV-32, IV-34, IV-36, IV-36, IV-38, IV-39, IV-41, V-8, V-III, VIII-5, VIII-20, VIII-24, VIII-25, XII-1, XII-3, XII-4, D-4, D-5, E-2, E-11, H-1, H-5, H-6 immediate decontamination I-2, I-5, I-7, I-9, II-3, III-1, V-3, VIII-2, VIII-3, VIII-21, VIII-22, VIII-26, VIII-27, X-1, X-2, X-3, XI-3, B-3, C-5, G-9, H-1, H-6

individual equipment decontamination kit See IEDK

individual protective equipment See IPE

intelligence preparation of the battlespace See IPB

IPB VI-1, VI-5,

IPE I-6, II-6, IV-1, VIII-1, VIII-2, VIII-9, VIII-12, VIII-13, VIII-26, VIII-27, IX-3, IX-6, IX-9, IX-11, IX-12, IX-14, XI-5, B-3, E-5, E-10, E-11, G-5, G-9, H-12, K-1, K-3,

L

Layout V-1, V-8, V-15, V-22, V-24, V-25, V-26, V-27, V-28, VII-7, VII-8, VII-9, VII-10, VIII-10, VIII-17, X-8

LDS V-3, V-20, V-22, V-26, V-27, V-28, VIII-19, XII-2, XII-3, H-2, H-7, H-8, I-4

lightweight decontamination system See LDS

line source B-6,

LLR G-12,

Logistics II-2, II-3, II-4, II-5, II-6, II-7, II-11, IV-1, V-20, VI-3, VI-4, VII-12, VIII-14, XI-4, XII-1, XII-3

low level radiation See LLR

M

M100 SDS I-5, III-2, XII-1, C-5, H-6, H-7

M11 C-5, H-6

M12 IV-5, V-21, VIII-10, E-2

M13 C-5, H-6

M17 LDS V-3, V-22, V-26, V-27, V-28, VIII-19, XII-2, XII-3, H-2, H-7, H-8, I-4

M291 SDK III-1, X-3, XII-4, E-2, E-11, H-1, H-4

M291 skin decontamination kit See M291 SDK

M295 IEDK III-1, XII-4, E-2, E-11, H-1, H-5, H-6

M295 individual equipment decontamination kit See M295 IEDK

maintenance considerations XII-7

Marine Corps patient decontamination X-6

maritime decontamination IX-1

mass casualty II-4, IX-10, XII-7

mass decontamination II-6, XI-2, XI-3,

MCE VII-12

Measurements A-1,

medical treatment facility See MTF

METT-TC I-4, I-7, I-8, II-2, II-5, IV-1, IV-2, IV-5, IV-7, V-1, V-25, E-3, E-7, F-1, G-1, G-2

mission critical equipment See MCE

mission, enemy, terrain and weather, troops available and civilian Considerations See METT-TC

mission-essential operating areas VII-2

mission-oriented protective posture See MOPP

MOPP gear exchange I-4, I-6, II-10, II-12, III-1, IV-1, IV-2, IV-3, IV-4, IV-5, IV-6, IV-7, IV-8, IV-9, IV-10, IV-11, IV-12, IV-13, IV-14, IV-16 to IV-41, V-12, V-13, V-15, V-30, XII-1, XII-6, G-4, G-5, J-3

Mountain F-1, F-5,

MPDS IV-5, V-20, V-22, V-26, V-27, V-28, XII-2, XII-3, H-2, H-9,

MTF I-5, II-9, V-31, VII-2, VII-6, VII-7, VII-13, VII-15, X-2, X-3, X-4, X-5, X-6, X-7, X-8, G-9, G-10

multinational forces II-6, VI-1, VI-4,

multipurpose decontamination system See MPDS

munitions decontamination VIII-1, VIII-21

munitions disposal E-1, E-5

N

natural decontaminant C-1, C-10, C-20

Navy patient decontamination X-7

neutralization I-2, I-3, V-21, VIII-19, IX-3, IX-7, XI-3, XI-9, G-13, G-14, H-1, H-17, I-5

neutralizing C-6, C-9, H-5, H-6, I-2,

night V-30, B-7, C-1, E-1, E-2, F-4, F-6

nonstandard III-2, VIII-6, VIII-13, B-10, C-13, C-14, C-15, C-16, C-17, C-18, C-19, E-3, F-2, F-3, H-11

nuclear weapon decontamination

O

operational decontamination I-2, I-4, I-5, I-7, II-8, II-10, IV-1 to IV-42, V-3, V-9, VIII-4, VIII-6, VIII-9, VIII-10, VIII-11, VIII-13, VIII-14, VIII-21, IX-11, IX-13, IX-17, X-3, X-4, XII-1, XII-2, XII-3, B-3, G-2, G-3, G-4, G-5, H-7,

operator wipedown I-4, I-5, III-2, XII-1, H-6

P

patient decontamination I-9, II-4, II-9, V-4, V-31, VII-6, VII-7, VII-13, IX-10, X-2, X-3, X-4, X-5, X-6, X-7, X-8, XII-3, XII-7, G-9, G-10, G-12

patient evacuation X-1,

PDDE II-9, V-24, V-25, V-26, VIII-16, VIII-19, XII-1, XII-3, C-11, C-13, C-15, C-19, D-1, D-2, D-3, D-4, D-5,

personal wipedown I-4, I-5, III-1, VIII-3, XII-1

personnel processing VII-1, VII-3, VII-6, VII-13, VII-14

petroleum, oils, and lubricants See POL

physical removal I-1, IX-3, IX-7, C-12, C-13, C-14, C-19, C-20, H-1, H-5

planning considerations II-3, II-6, V-1, V-25, VIII-1, XI-1, XI-3

planning decontamination II-1, II-4

point source B-6

POL VII-1, VIII-4, VIII-5, VIII-14, F-4

post decontamination II-10, II-11, V-7, J-8, J-11

power driven decontamination apparatus See PDDA

power driven decontamination equipment See PDDE

power driven decontamination system See PDDS

pre-decontamination II-10, IV-4, V-4, V-5, V-6, V-7, VI-5, VIII-2, XII-3

R

radioisotope E-7, E-8,

radiological decontamination IX-1, G-10

radiological dispersal device See RDD

radiological weapons B-1

rain III-2, VII-6, VII-13, C-2, F-4, I-2, I-5

RDD I-3, B-1,

Reach back B-10, B-11, G-6

record keeping VI-5

recovery I-8, I-9, II-1, II-3, II-8, II-11, IV-1, V-1, V-4, VI-1, VI-3, VIII-6, IX-1, IX-3, IX-4, IX-5, IX-6, IX-11, IX-13, IX-14, IX-15, IX-16, XII-2, B-1, B-7, E-4, E-9, E-10, G-8, G-14

recycle criteria V-23, VIII-20

replenishment XII-1

residual hazards VI-1, VI-3, VI-5

restoration I-8, I-9, II-11, VI-3, IX-3, K-1

retrograde VI-1, VI-4, VI-5, VIII-1, IX-10, G-5,

RSDL C-9, H-5,

S

SA II-3, II-7, II-9,

sample VII-2, VIII-17, VIII-24, E-1, E-5, G-6, G-10, H-3, I-5, J-1,

SCBA XI-4, XI-8

SDS I-5, III-2, XII-2, C-5, H-1, H-6, H-7, H-17,

self-contained breathing apparatus See SCBA

sensitive equipment IX-2, E-1, G-6

service decontamination XI-1, G-1

shelf life C-10,

shipboard I-9, IV-1, V-1, IX-1 to IX-18, X-6, X-7, XII-7

site clearance IV-2, IV-3, IV-7, V-5

situational awareness See SA

skin decontamination I-4, I-5, III-1, VIII-3, X-5, XII-1, XII-6, C-9, H-1, H-5,

sorbent decontamination system See SDS

special decontamination VII-3, IX-10, E-1, E-4, G-6

staging area II-10, V-5, V-6, V-7, VII-3, IX-10, X-3, H-10, H-11, H-15

standard decontaminant III-2, C-2, C-8, C-11, C-12, I-1

STB dry III-2, IV-7, IV-11, IV-19, IV-23, IV-28, V-11, V-21, V-29, D-1, D-2, E-3, I-2, I-3, J-3, J-4

STB slurry V-8, V-9, V-10, V-11, C-9, D-1, D-2, D-3, D-4, D-5, D-6, F-3, F-5, H-9, I-1, I-2, J-2, J-3, J-4

storage VII-5, VII-12, VIII-11, VIII-21, VIII-22, VIII-23, IX-14, IX-15, X-5, X-6, B-10, C-4, C-8, C-10, C-13, E-4, E-5, G-6, G-10, H-2, H-7, H-11, K-2, K-6, K-7,

surface types C-1

T

technical reachback B-10, B-11

terrain decontamination I-5, VII-3, G-3, G-6, H-2, H-9, H-10, H-13, I-1 TO I-6

TFA VII-3, VII-4, VII-5, VII-6, VII-7, VII-11, VII-12, VII-13

thorough decontamination I-2, I-4, I-6, I-8, II-2, II-8, II-10, II-12, IV-1, V-1 to V-32, VI-4, VI-5, VIII-1, VIII-2, VIII-3, VIII-6, VIII-13, VII-14, VIII-15, VIII-20, IX-2, IX-11, IX-14, IX-15, IX-16, IX-17, X-3, X-4, X-6, X-7, X-8, XII-3, C-8, G-2, G-3, G-5, H-2, H-8, H-11

thorough decontamination station charts J-1 to J-12

TIM I-1 to I-4, II-1, II-2, II-4, II-6, VI-2, VI-4, VI-5, X-3, XI-5, B-1, B-9, B-10, G-6

toxic free area See TFA

toxic industrial material See TIM

training I-8, I-10, II-1 to II-4, II-6, VI-4, VIII-21, IX-11, XI-2, XI-6, E-10, G-6, G-7, H-1, H-4, K-9

two lane washdown IV-4

U

UCC G-8,

unit control centers See UCC

unit waste K-1, K-5, K-9

unusual conditions V-30

urban area F-1, F-5,

V

VA II-1, II-7, VII-3,

vapor hazard area See VHA

vapor pressure B-8, B-9, C-1

vehicle washdown I-4, I-6, II-10, II-12, IV-1, IV-3, IV-4, IV-5, XII-1, XII-6, C-7, F-3

VHA VII-5, VII-11, VII-12

vulnerable equipment E-1

vulnerability assessment See VA

W

waste accumulation points K-1, K-2

water consumption XII-2, XII-3,

weathering I-2 to I-4, I-6, I-8, IV1, V-7, V-22, V-23, VI-3 to VI-5, VII-2, VII-11, VIII-2, VIII-6, VIII-9, VIII-15, VIII-25, IX-2, IX-3, IX-4, IX-6, IX-8, IX-11, IX-18, B-9, C-1, C-2, E-3, E-6, F-3, F-4, F-5, H-11, I-1, I-2, I-4

work/rest II-5, V-7, V-25, V-27, V-29, X-6, F-3, F-4

Y

FM 3-11.5
MCWP 3-37.3
NTTP 3-11.26
AFTTP(I) 3-2.60
4 April 2006

By Order of the Secretary of the Army:

PETER J. SCHOOMAKER
General, United States Army
Chief of Staff

Official:

JOYCE E. MORROW
Administrative Assistant to the
Secretary of the Army
0607401

DISTRIBUTION:
Active Army, Army National Guard, and U.S. Army Reserve: To be distributed in accordance with the initial distribution number 110737, requirements for FM 3-11.5.

By Order of the Secretary of the Air Force:

BENTLEY B. RAYBURN
Major General, USAF
Commander
Headquarters Air Force Doctrine Center

Air Force Distribution: F

Marine Corps PCN: 14300000600

Reprinted By:

PrepperSurvivalGuides.com

Military / Survival Manual Series

Army Special Operations
Camouflage and Concealment
Cold Weather Manual
Combat Training with Pistols
Combatives Hand-to-Hand
Counter-Insurgency Tactics
CounterIntelligence
Desert Operations
Explosive Ordinance Disposal
Explosives and Demolition
Field Hygiene
First Aid
Human Intelligence Collection
Improvised Explosive Device Defense
Improvised Munitions Handbook
Intelligence
Jungle Operations
Law of Land Warfare
Long Range Surveillance
Map Reading and Land Navigation
Military Working Dogs
Mine / Countermine
Mountain Operations
Mountaineering
Multiservice Escape and Evasion
Multiservice NBC Decontamination
NBC Field Handbook
Pathfinder Operations
Physical Fitness
Psychological Operations
Ranger Handbook
Ranger Medic Handbook
Reconnaissance Surveillance
Rifle Marksmanship M16/M4
Sniper Training
Soldier Combat Skills
Special Forces Handbook
Special Forces Medic Handbook
Special Forces Sniper Training
Survival
Unexploded Ordinance Procedures
Urban Operations

PLUS MANY MORE

One More Thing...

When you turn the page, Kindle will give you the opportunity to rate this book and share your thoughts on Facebook and Twitter. If you believe the book is worth sharing, please would you take a few seconds to let your friends know about it and leave a positive review? If it turns out to make a difference in their lives, they'll be forever grateful to you, as will I.